ON POLITICS

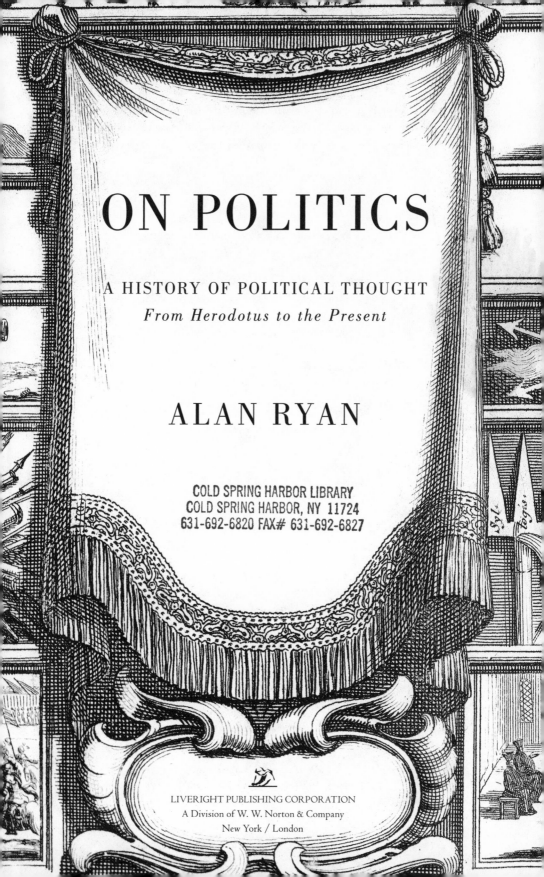

ON POLITICS

A HISTORY OF POLITICAL THOUGHT

From Herodotus to the Present

ALAN RYAN

LIVERIGHT PUBLISHING CORPORATION
A Division of W. W. Norton & Company
New York / London

Adapted from the frontispiece of *Leviathan, or, The Matter, Forme & Power of A Common-Wealth Ecclesiaticall and Civil. 1651.* Engraving by Abraham Bosse. Courtesy of the Rare Books Division, New York Public Library, Astor, Lenox and Tilden Foundations.

For information about permission to reproduce selections from this book, write to Permissions, Liveright Publishing Corporation, a division of W. W. Norton & Company, Inc., 500 Fifth Avenue, New York, NY 10110

For information about special discounts for bulk purchases, please contact W. W. Norton Special Sales at specialsales@wwnorton.com or 800-233-4830

Manufacturing by RR Donnelley, Harrisonburg
Book design by Ellen Cipriano
Production manager: Anna Oler

Library of Congress Cataloging-in-Publication Data

Ryan, Alan, 1940–
On politics : a history of political thought from Herodotus
to the present / Alan Ryan. — 1st ed.
v. cm.
Includes bibliographical references and index.
ISBN 978-0-87140-465-7 (hardcover)
1. Political science—Philosophy—History.
2. Political scientists—History. I. Title.
JA71.R93 2012
320.01—dc23

2012012351

Liveright Publishing Corporation
500 Fifth Avenue, New York, N.Y. 10110
www.wwnorton.com

W. W. Norton & Company Ltd.
Castle House, 75/76 Wells Street, London W1T 3QT

2 3 4 5 6 7 8 9 0

BOOK ONE

HERODOTUS TO MACHIAVELLI

FOR YURI RYAN SIMONOVICH

CONTENTS

BOOK TWO: Hobbes to the Present

Introduction: Thinking about Politics

T HIS IS A LONG BOOK, and a long time in the making. At first, I
was reluctant to embark on it at all, knowing how long such projects
take. In 1892 the brothers R. W. and A. J. Carlyle began to write an
account of medieval political theory. The six volumes appeared between
1903 and 1936; by the time the final volume of *A History of Mediaeval
Political Theory in the West* appeared, Sir Robert Carlyle had been dead two
years; he did not die young, but at the age of seventy-five in retirement
from a long career in the India Office. It remains an indispensable source
for students of the subject, but today it would be the work of a team
of authors and research assistants. When a publishing friend suggested
thirty-five years ago that I might write a successor to George Sabine's
History of Political Theory, I thought of the Carlyles and demurred. It was
not merely that I had no brothers to help me—Robert Carlyle was fully
employed in managing the affairs of India; most of the work fell to his
brother, a historian at Oxford. More importantly, I was not sure what
would give a long book its intellectual unity. If history is, as Henry
Ford inelegantly put it, one damn' thing after another, was the history
of thinking about politics merely one damn' thinker or one damn' idea
after another? Was it even, as Macbeth more elegantly but more despair-

ingly might have feared, a tale full of sound and fury signifying nothing, a chronicle of verbal fisticuffs at the end of which we were no wiser
than at the beginning? But a flood of interesting work then appeared on
particular writers and particular historical periods—Quentin Skinner's
Foundations of Modern Political Thought, for instance, or John Pocock's work
on the history of republican thought, *The Machiavellian Moment*. The plot
formulated itself behind my back.

I start with Herodotus because the question turned out to be whether
the Persians had defeated the Greeks, and we could do nothing about it.
Perhaps the modern world, modern politics, and the modern state were
the delayed revenge of the Persian Empire on the victors of Marathon
and Salamis. The Greeks, and particularly the Athenians, fought to protect a distinctive and distinctively political way of life. In their view, the
subjects of the great king of Persia were to all intents and purposes slaves
even when not literally of a servile status. As Hegel later said, under an
oriental despotism, one man alone was free. Yet Persia was an effective
state, gathering taxes, administering justice, fielding armies; its subjects
were more prosperous than the Greeks. It is not too fanciful to see Persia
as the prototype of the modern nation-state, and not only because the
U.S. Post Office is so deeply attached to Herodotus's description of the
great king's messengers of whom he wrote, "Neither rain, nor snow, nor
heat nor gloom of night stays these couriers from the swift completion
of their appointed rounds." The essence of a modern state is centralized
authority, bureaucratic management, the efficient delivery of the public services that only a state can provide; Persia provided fewer services
than a modern state and "outsourced" much of the work to officials in
semiautonomous political dependencies, but the principle was there. As
to the early modern states to which our own political systems are the
heirs, Louis XIV may have said, "L'état, c'est moi," but he knew what
a state was: a legal person rather than a physical one. It was the state's
all-encompassing authority that he embodied in his own majestic person. It was on the state's behalf that he was obsessed with the need to
know whatever could be known about the resources of his kingdom and
the lives of his subjects so that he could better manage their lives and
resources for their own welfare.

The contrast between the Persian state—and by the same token the late Imperial Roman, Bismarckian, or modern European state—and the Greek polis is far from the only theme that dominates this story. A familiar contrast is between Athenian and Roman notions of freedom and citizenship. The Athenians practiced a form of unfiltered direct democracy that the Romans thought a recipe for chaos; the Romans gave ordinary free and male persons a role in politics, but a carefully structured and controlled one. Roman freedom was most basically a matter of not being a slave; secondarily, it was the possession of a legal status, being able to secure one's rights in court; thirdly, it carried political rights and duties, carefully graded accorded to one's financial status. It was also a status that exposed any free individual to taxation and military service, again according to financial capacity. As Rome grew, citizenship was extended to conquered cities, initially without extending the voting rights that the Romans had; the *civis sine suffragio*—a citizen without a vote—was nonetheless a free man. He could say, *civis Romanus sum*—"I am a Roman citizen"—and it meant something real, particularly if he was facing a court, or afraid that an official might be about to have him scourged, or detained without the prospect of a fair trial. The Athenian obsession with the right to speak and vote in the Assembly ruled out the thought that a *civis sine suffragio* was fully a free man; it ruled out also the thought that a citizen who was entitled to vote but not to hold any sort of judicial position was fully a free man. The Athenians associated freedom with unvarnished political equality, *isegoria*, or equal rights in the Assembly, and they would have regarded the Roman restrictions on access to judicial and political office as oligarchical. Variations on the argument between Athens and Rome have dominated European and American political thought since the English Civil War of the 1640s. How far we can, indeed how far we should be tempted to try to, follow the Athenians in securing the political equality of all citizens in the face of differences in wealth, education, civic-mindedness, competence, or public spirit is an unanswered question.

Much of the time, the question goes unasked in prosperous liberal democracies like Britain or the United States, because most of us see political equality as exhausted by "one person, one vote" and dig no deeper; we know that one person, one vote coexists with the better-off and better-organized buying influence through lobbying, campaign contributions, and use of the mass media, but we find ourselves puzzled to balance a belief that everyone has the right to use his or her resources to influence government—which is certainly one form of political equality—with our sense that excessive inequality of political resources undermines democracy. We must not sentimentalize the distant past when we wonder whether the better-off have too much political power. Although they often turned on them and dismissed them at a moment's notice, the Athenians were led by men of "good family." Nor should we think that the only source of political inequality in the modern world is the ability of the well-off to convert money into influence by buying politicians' loyalty. If the economically less well-off organize themselves, perhaps by piggybacking on trade union membership, or ethnic or religious identity, they may be equally formidable. The discrepancy in political effectiveness in modern industrial societies is between the unorganized and the organized; money is the life blood of organization, but not money alone. Can democracies protect the public at large—unorganized individuals—against well-organized special interests? The question plagues all modern democracies. Neither intellectually nor institutionally have we advanced very far beyond Rousseau's identification of the problem two and a half centuries ago in the *Social Contract*.

Although the Romans disavowed Athenian democracy, there are many "Roman" arguments for involving the citizenry in political life as deeply as possible. Machiavelli had no taste for Athenian democracy, but preferred citizen armies to mercenary troops, and like Roman writers before him and innumerable writers after him thought that, given the right arrangements, the uncorrupted ordinary people could check the tendency of the rich to subvert republican institutions. That was a commonplace of antiaristocratic republican thinking in eighteenth- and nineteenth-century Europe; it is a standing theme of American populism. Many writers on the left have taken a simpler view of the need for popular participation. It is an old thought that unless the less well-off use their numerical strength to offset the advantages of the better-off, they will lose out in the distribution of the economic benefits that a modern industrial society can provide. It is the most obvious of the instrumental arguments for universal suffrage; unless the worse-off have an adequate say in the rules that regulate the economy in which they earn their living, they will find themselves exploited. The history of trade union legislation in Britain and the United States is a textbook example of that simple point. Not all arguments for widespread participation are instrumental, however. Many writers, across the whole political spectrum, have thought that it is morally better to be an active citizen than a mere consumer of whatever benefits accrue in virtue of being an ordinary, economically productive member of one's society. All republicans, whether Athenian or Roman, agreed on that, even when they had grave doubts about just who could be an active citizen: certainly not women, but ordinary workingmen?

The modern anxiety about popular participation in political life has a long history, but has taken a distinctive form. Greek city-states were plagued by civil war between oligarchs and democrats; the last hundred years of the Roman Republic were marked by conflicts between *populares* and *optimates*, the (proclaimed) defenders of the interests of the people and the upper classes. For the past two centuries, the argument has focused on the political roles of elites and masses. "The masses" is a relatively modern term, whether applied optimistically, in looking to the awakened proletarian masses to make the revolution that ushers in the socialist millennium, contemptuously in belittling the low tastes of the uncultivated masses, good-naturedly when we welcome the huddled masses yearning to be free, or merely descriptively, as meaning simply a lot of people. The term emerged during the industrial revolution at a time of rapid population growth and rapid urbanization; but the contrast between the elite and the rank and file is ancient. The thought that astute practitioners of the political arts can do almost anything they like with the masses is as old as the critics of Athenian democracy, and so is its relatively benign counterpart, the Platonic vision of the statesman as a shepherd, no more expecting to be second-guessed by the ordinary man than the shepherd expects to be second-guessed by his sheep.

From Machiavelli to the present, thinkers have distinguished between the adept elite and the incompetent many. We may think that anyone who draws such a distinction and in such terms can be no friend to democracy; that is not true. If we are persuaded that in all societies only a small number of people will actually play a role in governing the society, it makes all the difference just *how* the elite secures and retains the allegiance of the many. A totalitarian elite employs the secret police; a democratic elite employs pollsters and advertising agencies. Totalitarian elites, military juntas, and the like intend to hold power for life; democratic elites allow themselves to be thrown out by the electorate. They may do their very best to cajole, persuade, or even bamboozle the voter, but they do not corrupt the courts, politicize the army, or send the secret police to the polling booth. Unillusioned commentators on modern democracies describe democracy as rule by *competing* elites. The competition produces better government than elite rule without competition and better government than rule by mass meeting, or whatever direct democracy might involve. We are destined to be ruled by elites, but "the circulation of elites" will ensure that incompetent elites are replaced by more-competent elites. The people may only get to choose between one elite and another, but open competition and free elections produce good government. Nonetheless, just who gets to be a member of the political elite, or elites, and how that person gets there remains a contentious issue; even in Western liberal democracies there might be a fierce competition between politicians, but a restrictive system of recruitment to the ranks of the competitors. The American system of primary elections was established to counter just that problem; its success has been only partial.

So-called elite democracy, or government by competing elites who gain power through the ballot box, is also often described as "rule by professional politicians." We should not be too quick to disparage professional politicians; there are many worse political systems than contemporary liberal democracies. The fact that professional politicians are in interesting ways not very like the population they represent is not in itself a source of anxiety; physicians are not very like the majority of the patients they care for, either. If politicians do a poor job of promoting the best interests of the people they represent, this may be less a matter of simple incompetence than of the conflicting pressures upon them, on the one hand, and the near-impossibility of the tasks they are asked to perform, on the other. All the same, those who hanker after something more Athenian than rule by professional politicians may wonder whether the role of the professional politician could be diminished and the ordinary citizen given more work to do. That is a question that runs through what follows.

Another way of framing the question was provided by the French political thinker Benjamin Constant early in the nineteenth century. His lecture on the difference between classical and modern conceptions of freedom is a liberal sacred text. Freedom for the citizens of ancient republics like Sparta or Athens was a matter of having a share of the sovereign authority; it was essentially public and political. It came at a high price; not only did such societies depend on the existence of slaves in order to free the citizens to do their citizen duties, but they were societies of mutual surveillance, in which everyone was under the scrutiny of everyone else. Modern freedom in contrast was essentially private; it was the ability to pursue our private economic, literary, or religious concerns without having to answer to anyone else. It was freedom *from* the political sphere rather than freedom *in* the political sphere. The subject of a modern liberal democracy benefits from its liberal aspect by having a full measure of modern freedom: occupational, educational, religious. Indeed, when most people talk of democracy today, they have these liberties much more clearly in their minds than any particular system of voting rights; that is hardly surprising when barely half of them exercise their right to vote in important national elections, and far fewer in local elections. Skeptics about participation will insist that what matters is accountability rather than mass participation; voting for any particular party or candidate matters less than the ability to vote against them. That is the democratic aspect of "liberal democracy," and it is impossible to achieve in the absence of the liberal freedoms. In what used to be called "people's democracies"—otherwise one-party communist states—or "guided democracies"—otherwise dictatorships—there was a very high level of participation, along with frequent opportunities to register enthusiasm for the ruling party and its policies. What there was not was the opportunity to canvass alternatives, to press for different policies or a different political leadership without risking imprisonment, torture, or death. Imperfect as liberal democracy is, it yields a measure of accountability to the public that the experience of the past hundred years suggests is indispensable to decent government and the rule of law.

Turning our gaze away from politics momentarily, we should also reflect that when we talk of democracy we very often mean something social rather than political, what Alexis de Tocqueville called equality of condition. I do not in what follows say very much in celebration of the modern Western world's commitment to forms of inclusiveness that would have astonished our ancestors, not least because they are so obviously worthy of celebration that adding my voice to the chorus seems otiose. Societies that think of themselves as unusually "democratic" do so because they pride themselves on an absence of snobbery, or because women occupy large numbers of senior positions in business or government, or because they have been successful in integrating large numbers of immigrants, or in diminishing race-based economic and other forms of inequality. They are democratic in the sense that they have removed many, if not all, previously acceptable grounds for claiming advantage: race, birth, gender in particular. To call this "social democracy" invites confusion, because the Marxist and post-Marxist socialist parties of western Europe called, and still call, themselves Social Democrats, and democracy in the sense described in this paragraph is very much at home with capitalism and free markets: if the claims of race, birth, and gender are rejected, what is left are the claims based on the contribution we make to the welfare of other individuals or society at large. Those contributions may range very widely, from simple manual labor to whatever it is that celebrities add to our lives, and the obvious way to discover what our contributions are worth is to see how they fare in the marketplace. Of course, all actual societies realize such values only very imperfectly, and markets are notoriously imperfect, too. Nonetheless, the thought that the core values of modern liberal democracies are social rather than political is far from foolish.

A presupposition of what follows is that the project of entering into the thoughts of the long dead and rethinking them for our own purposes is both possible and useful. That raises the question whether I am committed to the view that there is nothing new under the sun, or more guardedly to the view of Thucydides and Machiavelli, among many others, that since human nature is the same at all times and in all places, we can draw morals about what is likely to happen to us from what our predecessors have thought and done. The answer is "not exactly." The last fifth of this book takes very seriously the thought that over the past two and a half centuries several revolutions dramatically changed the world that politics tries to master. In no particular order, and without assigning priority to one aspect of an interconnected process, the industrial revolution, the demographic revolution, the literacy and communications revolution, and the political revolutions of the late eighteenth century and more recently have created a world that is in innumerable ways quite unlike the ancient, medieval, and early modern worlds. The most important of these ways reflect our greatly enhanced technological capacities. To put it brutally, we can keep vastly more people alive than ever before, and we can kill vastly more people than ever before.

Advances in agriculture allow us to feed ourselves healthily and reliably, the availability of clean water and efficient sewerage means we suffer fewer infections, medical advances allow us to treat previously untreatable diseases and injuries; and during the twentieth century two world wars showed how effective we were at killing millions of one another. To put it less brutally, our ability to produce so much more than our predecessors means that along with the useful things we produce, we produce much we wish we did not, pollution of all kinds with all its destructive impacts on our environment. Because all this happens on a global scale, the tasks that modern governments must grapple with not only are more numerous and more complex than our predecessors could have imagined but threaten evils on a larger scale than they could have imagined. So I end with some anxious reflections on the politics of an interconnected and increasingly crowded planet. Demography may not be destiny, but managing the problems of a planet of more than seven billion people is a very different enterprise from ensuring that a city-state of two or three hundred thousand could feed itself, protect itself from its enemies, and cultivate the rich civic life that even now we contemplate with envy.

Thinking about Politics

There are many people who, like me, have spent a working lifetime teaching and writing about what is commonly called "political thought" or "political theory." Yet there is surprisingly little agreement on what "political thought" is. It is not exactly history, although it engages with the ideas of long-dead thinkers; it is not exactly philosophy, although it engages with the arguments of thinkers both living and dead. It is not exactly sociology, although it is a valid complaint against anyone writing about politics that he is sociologically naïve. A colleague once described political theorists as people who were obsessed with two dozen books; after half a century of grappling with Mill's essay *On Liberty*, or Hobbes's *Leviathan*, I have sometimes thought two dozen might be a little on the high side. Even if they are hard put to it to explain themselves to one another, political theorists have no doubt that they are engaged in productive, if sometimes frustrating, conversations across the centuries with their long-dead predecessors, as well as their contemporaries. They want anyone who might be interested to overhear these conversations and join in. We are eavesdropping in the Elysian Fields, hoping to catch the cynical Machiavelli taunting Socrates for his otherworldliness, or hear Jefferson admit that Alexander Hamilton foresaw the American future more accurately than he.

There is no way to do this without running the risk of foisting our own views on the unresisting dead. It is the obvious danger of attempting to have a conversation with great, but absent, thinkers who cannot tell us we are talking nonsense. I am a great admirer of Isaiah Berlin, whose essays in the history of ideas provide one model for what I do here; nonetheless, there are moments in his work that make the reader wonder whether it is Montesquieu speaking or Berlin, or whether Machiavelli would have recognized the causes for which Berlin recruited him. The early twentieth-century philosopher and historian R. G. Collingwood claimed that historical explanation was a matter of rethinking past thoughts, and that thought was reflected in Berlin's work as it is in what follows. As to not foisting my ideas on the unresisting dead, I can only say that I have tried to keep the critical voices of my colleagues in my head as I wrote. One further element that gives Berlin's writings their extraordinary vividness is an almost uncanny ability to engage with the temperament of the thinkers he wrote about. The difficulties that beset the attempt to know just what someone thought equally beset the attempt to know just what it would have been like to meet him or her in the flesh, perhaps even more so. Nonetheless, if we are to see our predecessors in the round we must take the risk.

Like many contemporary commentators who bemoan the decline of the "public intellectual," I am uncomfortable with the thought that serious thinkers about politics may retire into the ivory tower and write difficult—if often very interesting—essays and books for their colleagues alone, leaving debates over the prospects of modern political life to the punditry of contributors to the op-ed pages, or the shouting matches that pass for political debate on some television channels. I am not particularly gloomy; the fact that a book such as Allan Bloom's lugubrious essay called *The Closing of the American Mind* could become a best seller suggests that the American mind was much less closed than he thought, and although I did not greatly admire Francis Fukuyama's book *The End of History and the Last Man*, its success demonstrated that there were public intellectuals in the marketplace, and a substantial audience for their ideas. History and biography have always had a wide popular appeal, and we are all richer for the work of Simon Schama or Gordon Wood, to name just two. But some accounts of the history of philosophy have secured an enviably wide audience. Bertrand Russell's *History of Western Philosophy*, which I read avidly at the age of fifteen, was one. Together with Mill's *On Liberty*, it changed my life, but reading it again years later was a salutary experience; questions of inaccuracy aside, it was spectacularly prejudiced—though very funny. I have taken Russell's lucidity as a benchmark, though the ability to write so transparently and easily, which rightly earned him a Nobel Prize in Literature, is a gift I can only envy. As to his prejudices, I share some of them, but have done my best to leave them out. One respect in which he is not a model is that he was too often dismissive, even contemptuous, of thinkers with whom he disagreed. Here I am sometimes sharp with thinkers whose greatness is indisputable: Plato and Marx, to take two obvious examples. I am neither contemptuous nor dismissive of them. My sharpness is addressed only to their arguments about how we may best govern ourselves; Plato's metaphysical speculation is deep, rich, inexhaustibly interesting, but his remedy for political chaos is not. Marx's thoughts about economic analysis and his historical sociology are endlessly fascinating, but his evasiveness about just how one might manage a socialist economy is unforgivable. Mockery of either is unthinkable; criticism is not.

As that suggests, I am a political enthusiast; I am fascinated by politics in all its forms, and avidly devour newspapers and current affairs programs. I am also a skeptic: like most people, a skeptic about the motives, intelligence, and competence of politicians; but unlike most people, skeptical about the way we talk about politics. Many ideas that governments, politicians, commentators, and ordinary citizens appeal to when they talk about politics have little substance; others made sense long ago, but not in the modern world. Notoriously, almost every modern government calls itself a democracy; but self-described democracies do not much resemble one another, and none resemble the political system for which Athenians fought and died two and a half thousand years ago. Are modern democracies really democracies, or something else? (The answer is "strictly speaking, something else," as we shall see.) We may wonder why we give them a misleading name, and whether it matters. It may not; many people share my surname, but we are rarely confused with each other.

On the other hand, it may be a mistake to operate new institutions under old labels, arousing impossible expectations and causing needless disappointment. It may have worse effects, perhaps enabling a plutocracy to exploit a political system for its own benefit, with "bread and circuses" pacifying the worse-off, who are flattered and cajoled but exploited nonetheless. We may be less deceived than self-deceived, knowing in our hearts that we are subjects, not citizens, that the world is divided between the givers of orders and the takers of orders, and that we are among the latter, but pretending to ourselves that we might make it all the way from the log cabin to the White House. The coins and armors of imperial Rome carried the legend "Senatus Populusque Romanus"; but "the Senate and people of Rome" lived under a military and bureaucratic dictatorship.

Raising such questions is not to condemn modern politics—life is vastly safer in most modern societies than in the ancient world; the politics of modern "democracies" are usually more rational than the politics of Athens, and less brutal than the politics of Rome; they are much less chaotic and less dangerous than the politics of Renaissance Italy and Reformation Germany. In the modern Western world, individuals have a host of rights—to free speech, to worship as they choose, to occupational freedom, to live where they like—that earlier ages never dreamed of conferring on ordinary people; the poor have votes, and women play a role in politics that would once have been thought impossible, dangerous, wicked, or unnatural, if not all four at once. But we should at least wonder *what* we are praising when we praise democracy; and when we pledge our commitment to liberty and justice for all, we should wonder whether these are the liberty and justice of the American founders, let alone the liberty and justice that Cicero or Marsilius said we could achieve only when the common good was pursued by selfless rulers. The best way to explore such questions is by contrasting our ideas and allegiances with those of thinkers from other places and other ages. Rome and Athens held very different views about freedom from one another and ourselves; yet we have acquired our vocabulary and its buried assumptions from both, while many of our institutions come from other sources entirely. It is perhaps surprising that we are not more confused than we are about democracy, freedom, justice, and citizenship.

This is a book about the answers that historians, philosophers, theologians, practicing politicians, and would-be revolutionaries have given to one question. How can human beings best govern themselves? That question raises innumerable others: can we manage our own affairs at all? Many writers have thought we are not the masters of our destinies, but the playthings of a malicious fate, or the unwitting agents of divine providence. Perhaps prayer rather than politics is the answer to the human condition. If we can control some of what happens, there is little agreement on how much and what. Many writers have thought that only some people were morally entitled or intellectually able to control their fates, for example, men but not women, Greeks but not Persians, property owners but not the laboring poor, Christian Europeans but not pagan Amerindians, free Americans but not slaves. Answers to our question over two and a half millennia form the subject of this book: they include "give yourselves over to the unfettered discretion of the wisest," "try to make sure that neither the rich nor the poor can dominate decision making," "find a godly ruler and give him absolute authority," and "do not ask; accept the powers that be and think of your immortal soul." Such answers are both ancient and contemporary. They raise more questions in turn: religious, philosophical, historical, biological, and sociological—what kind of justice the state should seek, whether there is a pattern to history, whether we are doomed by our biology to fight endless wars; ultimately, what the point may be of human existence. Different convictions may lead us to think the goal of politics is physical survival, the good life, glory, liberty, salvation in the afterlife, the liberation of human nature by the revolutionary overthrow of capitalism. All these answers have influenced political thinking and practice.

I follow the deeper questions only as far as they illuminate ideas about how we should govern ourselves. With philosophers such as Plato or Hobbes, this is a long way; with a skeptic like Machiavelli, only to explain why he eschewed deep questions. This is a book about politics, and only secondarily about philosophy, religion, biology, or sociology. It is also a book about books: what our forebears wrote. They wrote historical narratives, marshaled philosophical arguments, compiled handbooks of political advice, and often all these at once, but always trying to persuade their readers to follow one political path or another. Their readers took much for granted that we do not, and recognized the local implications of what they read as we cannot do without assistance, and sometimes not at all.

I hope what follows will inspire a taste for what they wrote and make comprehensible what might otherwise be hard going; but although there is a good deal of plot summary here, this book is no substitute for reading the originals. My hope is that readers will be moved to wrestle with these authors and their work for themselves. I have footnoted only sparsely, to give readers the chance to check up on my accuracy, but not to engage in battles with other interpretations; for that reason, I have also suggested further readings for each chapter, so that anyone interested can dig deeper than space permits here. Although this is a book about texts as well as their authors, it is not a textbook so much as a context book and a pretext book, concerned with settings and motives as well as the works themselves. Its success will be measured by the readers who pick up Plato's *Republic*, Hobbes's *Leviathan*, Hegel's *Phenomenology of Spirit*, and find themselves engrossed rather than baffled—and even when they are baffled, are happy to go on reading, interrogating, and arguing with their authors for themselves.

BOOK ONE

HERODOTUS TO MACHIAVELLI

PART I

THE CLASSICAL CONCEPTION

CHAPTER 1

Why Herodotus?

Talking Greek (and Latin) about Politics

WE HAVE INHERITED FROM the Greeks of twenty-five hundred years ago the words they used to talk about their political arrangements: "politics," "democracy," "aristocracy," and "tyranny" are all direct borrowings. We share many of their political ideals: most importantly, a passion for freedom, independence, and self-government. They were acutely aware that the Greek polis, the city-state of Greek antiquity, was an unusual political form, whose survival was always at risk from civil war, or from conquest by powerful foreign states, or neighboring city-states. The origins of the polis are obscure, but it flourished from around 600 BCE until the conquest of the Greek world in the middle of the fourth century by Philip of Macedon and his son Alexander the Great. Even after the failure of the Athenians' final attempt to recover their independence after Alexander's death in 322 BCE, the polis did not disappear. Greek cities practiced limited self-government under the Hellenistic monarchies until the middle of the second century BCE, and thereafter under the umbrella of the Roman Republic and Empire. It was a sadly diminished self-rule; they had lost what they most valued, the freedom of action in military and interstate affairs that they had suc-

cessfully defended against the Persian Empire in the first two decades of
the fifth century BCE.

We are very attached to describing ourselves as the Greeks described
themselves; try persuading a friend that the United States is not really
a democracy. But it is not clear that their ideals, and ambitions, and the
assumptions embodied in that vocabulary, or the views on the best way
to govern ourselves of those who created that vocabulary, make much
sense in a world as different as ours. Think, first, of the demographic differences: democratic Athens at the beginning of the Peloponnesian War
(431 BCE) contained perhaps 50,000 adult male citizens, 200,000 free
native inhabitants, and perhaps 300,000 inhabitants in all, including
slaves and foreigners. Athens and the countryside of Attica covered seven
hundred square miles, about half the area of Rhode Island. A quarter
of the population lived in the city, the rest in the countryside, and many
city dwellers were farmers who walked to their nearby farms. Athens was
much larger than other Greek city-states. We think about modern states
with up to a billion inhabitants in terms bequeathed to us by people who
lived in very different conditions. If this is not as surprising as it seems at
first sight, it should make for caution when reading newspaper editorials
or listening to politicians and commentators demanding "democracy"
and meaning many very different things.

The tradition this book explores began when Greek thinkers saw
that they governed themselves in a way their Asiatic neighbors did not,
and concluded that they practiced *political* government while the Persians
did not. *Politics*, they thought, could exist only in self-governing city-
states—in a polis or republic, and under the rule of law.[1] There was no
politics in Persia because the great king was the master of slaves, not the
ruler of citizens. The point is beautifully made by Herodotus, the father
of history and our own starting point. The exiled Spartan king, Demaratus, had taken refuge at the court of the great king of Persia, Darius I,
in 491 BCE. Darius made him the ruler of Pergamum and some other
cities. In 480 Darius's son and successor, Xerxes, took him to see the
enormous army he had assembled to avenge his father's humiliation by
the Athenians in an earlier attempt to conquer Greece. "Surely," he said
to Demaratus, "the Greeks will not fight against such odds." He was dis-

pleased when Demaratus assured him that they certainly would. "How is it possible that a thousand men—or ten thousand, or fifty thousand, should stand up to an army as big as mine, especially if they were not under a single master but all perfectly free to do as they pleased?" He could understand that they might feign courage if they were whipped into battle as his Persian troops would be, but it was absurd to suppose that they would fight against such odds. Not a bit of it, said Demaratus. They would fight and die to preserve their freedom. He added, "They are free—yes—but they are not wholly free; for they have a master, and that master is Law, which they fear much more than your subjects fear you. Whatever this master commands they do; and his command never varies: it is never to retreat in battle, however great the odds, but always to remain in formation and to conquer or die."[2] They were citizens, not subjects, and free men, not slaves; they were disciplined but self-disciplined. Free men were not whipped into battle. A "republic" could be ruled by kings or aristocrats or democratic assemblies; but its independence was of the essence. So was the idea that its active members were citizens. Democracy—the idea that "the many" should rule—was far from a defining feature of politics. The Spartans lived under a system admired for millennia, and an influence on the American founding, which mixed monarchical, aristocratic, and democratic elements; but the Spartans were socially repressive, obsessively religious, and dependent on the manual labor of the so-called helots, neighboring peoples they had enslaved. Even under a democracy "the many" did not mean all. In Athens, only a proportion of the resident population was politically active; foreigners and slaves could not participate, and women were wholly excluded from public life. Still, the Athenians discovered that once citizenship is extended to the lower classes, the genie is out of the bottle, and nobody can govern without the consent of the citizens.

Political thought as we understand it began in Athens because the Athenians were a trading people who looked at their contemporaries and saw how differently they organized themselves. If they had not lived where they did and organized their economic lives as they did, they could not have seen the contrast. Given the opportunity, they might not have paid attention to it. The Israelites of the Old Testament narrative were very conscious of their neighbors, Egyptian, Babylonian, and other, not least because they were often reduced to slavery or near-slavery by them. That narrative makes nothing of the fact that Egypt was a bureaucratic theocracy; it emphasizes that the Egyptians did not worship Yahweh. The history of Old Testament politics is the history of a people who did their best to have *no* politics. They saw themselves as under the direct government of God, with little room to decide their own fate except by obeying or disobeying God's commandments. Only when God took them at their word and allowed them to choose a king did they become a political society, with familiar problems of competition for office and issues of succession. For the Jews, politics was a fall from grace. For the Greeks, it was an achievement. Many besides Plato thought it a flawed achievement; when historians and philosophers began to articulate its flaws, the history of political thought began among the argumentative Athenians.

The Birth of the Polis

The Athenians of the fifth century had a very fragmentary knowledge of the history of their own institutions and were not attentive to the modern line between "real" *history* and "mere" *myth*. Because the origins of the polis were obscure to them, they are obscure to us. Aristotle in the middle of the fourth century BCE set his students to compile an account of 158 Greek constitutions, of which only that of Athens has come down to us. It is unreliable on arrangements much earlier than the date of its compilation. There were two views of how a polis was formed. The first was military: a scattered group of people came to live in one city behind a set of protective walls. The other was political: a group of people agreed to live under one authority, with or without the protection of a walled city. *Synoikismos*, or "living together," embraces both. Any political entity implies a population that recognizes a common authority, but the first "city-states" were not always based on a city. Sparta makes the point. We think of Sparta as a *city*, but the Spartans were proud of the fact that they lived in villages without protective walls: their army was their wall and "every man a brick." Nonetheless, they belonged to one political entity.

There was no uniform pattern of political organization. In most cases, power and even citizenship were initially confined to a small group of aristocrats; some are described as having "kings."

The division of society into rich and poor was unquestioned, and in every society, including democratic Athens, the leading families, the *eupatridae*, or "wellborn," supplied political leaders. Nonetheless, class warfare was a constant threat. The poor feared they would be reduced to slavery by their betters; and the rich feared they would have their land and wealth seized by the poor. In many cities, tyrants were able to seize power by offering to protect the poorer citizens against the rich or vice versa. "Tyrant" is a word with an unlovely ring to it, but did not inevitably imply that a ruler was brutal or self-seeking, only that he had acquired power unconstitutionally, and governed as a sole ruler. Some tyrants governed moderately and rationally. The Peisistratids, father and sons, who ruled Athens in the late sixth century BCE, were such. Athens had been a democracy in the early sixth century, but even after the reforms of Solon, conflict between rich and poor, and between leading families, was uncontrollable. The tyranny of the Peisistratids averted civil war and was largely unbrutal. Still, although Athens prospered, they were not loved—aristocratic families thought it was their birthright to rule, and the poor wanted a guaranteed voice in public affairs. In 510 the tyranny was overthrown by a domestic insurrection assisted by Sparta.

Athenian Democracy

The replacement of the tyranny by an increasingly radical democracy was a Spartan achievement and wholly unintended. Sparta's policy was to install friendly oligarchies in other Greek city-states. In Athens they were disappointed. The radical Athenian democracy endured with interruptions for almost two centuries as the constitution of an independent state; for more than two millennia it stood as an inspiration to radicals and the poor, a warning to conservatives and the rich, and as a landmark in the history of political inventiveness, alongside the Roman

Republic and the United States. An aristocrat started the process. From 508 onward, Athenian politics were dominated by Cleisthenes, whose reforms aimed at military preparedness and at keeping social peace by opening political life to the poorer citizens. These things were connected; the lowest enfranchised class, the *thetes*, supplied the rowers of the Athenian fleet.

"The poorer citizen" was not just anyone dwelling within the boundaries of Athens. Athenian society rested on slavery, and its political morality rested on two sharp contrasts: between free and servile, and Athenian and alien. The boundary between free and servile was sacrosanct; no marriage between a free Athenian and a slave was countenanced, and the children of such an illicit union were slaves. There was no naturalization process; foreigners could not become citizens by long residence, and only with great difficulty and at great expense by specific legislation. It was a weakness of Greek cities that they were so ethnically exclusive, and it was one way in which the Athenians were less politically astute than the Romans, who made new Romans of the peoples they conquered. Athenian citizenship was by descent; a citizen had to be born to citizen parents. These fiercely binary oppositions extended to the contrast between male and female. In the fifth century Athens combined inventiveness in politics, trade, and warfare with a restrictive attitude to women that was not universal in Greece. This was not sexual puritanism; Athenian men were unabashed about frequenting prostitutes, and same-sex relationships between men and boys were commonplace. Nonetheless, high-status Athenian women were veiled in public and, apart from those who played a part in the religious life of the city, were expected to stay at home and to retire to the women's quarters if a male visitor arrived at the house. Working women were less restricted. As Athens became the dominant trading state in the eastern Mediterranean, it became a cosmopolitan city with a large foreign population. Plato's *Republic* grumbles about it. Athens developed a mercantile economy and systems of banking and insurance; Plato and Aristotle both complain about moneymaking. But rich foreigners remained foreigners; and women were citizens only in the sense that they were the daughters, sisters, mothers, and wives of citizens. They had no political role.

The key to Athenian democracy was the Assembly, or *ecclesia*. It was in modern terms legislature, judiciary, and executive, and there was no appeal against its decisions except to a later meeting of itself, or a court that was part of itself. Although its potential membership was 40,000, it operated through many smaller bodies, through courts of 500 members, and in particular through the 500 members of the governing council, or boule, whose members formed the Athenian administration for a year, and the *prytany*, the 30-strong body whose members formed the managing committee of the boule for a month at a time. Both bodies were chosen by lottery, after a careful scrutiny of the eligibility of those whose names went into the lottery. The next two centuries saw experiments with new committees and new courts, whose effect was to take power out of the hands of old aristocratic institutions and give it to the Assembly. To a modern eye, the fact that the Assembly was a court as much as a legislature seems strange, but it was an important aspect of the Athenians' suspicion of power. Anyone could be accused of misusing public office and be dismissed by the Assembly. There were no public prosecutors; all cases were brought by individuals, and very complicated rules governed the right to prosecute. Since the prosecutor was entitled to a share of whatever fines were imposed, it is unsurprising that the Athenians had a reputation for litigiousness. The system was wide open to abuse and nonetheless mostly remarkably effective.

Cleisthenes rationalized citizenship and membership of the Assembly and put the finances of the fleet and army onto a regular basis. The cost fell heavily on the better-off, because most of the population lived barely above subsistence level, but the expense was inescapable, and Athens was fortunate to have substantial silver mines and slaves to work them. Greek city-states existed on a permanent war footing; when not at war they soon might be, and when not actually fighting they were often in a state of armed truce. Cleisthenes solved the worst problems of internal conflict by organizing the citizens into ten "tribes"; these were geographical groupings, not class or kin groups, and they determined the political rights of their members no matter where they might live. The geographical units were the demes, or villages, of Attica. An Athenian would always identify himself as *so and so, from such and such a deme.* Each tribe supplied fifty members of the boule. The work of the boule was crucial because it prepared legislation for the Assembly and supervised the conduct of officials. Nobody could serve on it for longer than a year at a time, and eventually the rules were tightened so that nobody could serve more than twice in a lifetime. Given the small number of citizens and the large number of posts to be filled, ordinary Athenians had a good chance of being the equivalent of president of Athens for at least one day in a lifetime, and a member of the "cabinet" for a month. This reflected the Athenian passion for equalizing the political influence of every citizen; what we moderns would have to do if we shared that passion with the same intensity is an intriguing question, but it is doubtful we could keep many of our present political arrangements.

The ten tribes also supplied the ten *strategoi*, or generals. These positions were elective and could be held repeatedly. Some ceremonial offices were held for life, but they were either inherited or gained by lot, not election, and there was a permanent administration, inevitable in a city that sustained a substantial naval force and spent vast sums on beautifying the city. Military leadership was where Cleisthenes and his successors drew the line where democratic equality stopped, although even then a *strategos* could be dismissed on the spot by the Assembly. It is a crucial difference between the Athenians and ourselves that we rely on elected representatives whereas they took a random sample of the citizenry. It was a lottery only among the eligible; but as Athenian democracy grew more confident, restrictions on eligibility based on birth and wealth were removed. In the case of the *strategoi*, and other administrative positions, democratic principle was sacrificed to experience, expertise, and reliability. The most famous *strategos*, Pericles, who led Athens before the Peloponnesian War and during its early stages, was repeatedly reelected and exercised the authority of a modern president. Commenting on his career, Thucydides observed that "what was in name a democracy, became in actuality rule by the first man."[3] From the conservative aristocrat Thucydides this was praise. Modern commentators have noted that most leaders came from upper-class families and have suggested that Athens resembled modern democracies in being a de facto oligarchy; but Thucydides was not complaining. When he called Pericles "the first man," he meant he was the wisest and most honorable of the Athenians.

Pericles's hold over the Assembly was that of a demagogue, a leader of the demos, or common people. Those who thought ill of him, including Plato, did not hesitate to call him a demagogue, in the modern, abusive sense, meaning someone who cajoled the foolish many into doing whatever he wanted. Cleisthenes's creation was unlike a modern democracy not only in being a direct not a representative democracy. It was not a *liberal* democracy; there were no constitutional restrictions on what the Assembly could do, no boundaries between public and private life it could not transgress. The Athenians treated choice by lot as self-evidently the most egalitarian way of distributing power, where we use random selection for little beyond jury service. Athenian equality was narrowly political; the *eupatridae*, or wellborn families, had no doubt of their social superiority; men had no doubt of their superiority over women, nor did Athenians doubt their superiority to foreigners; a slave was at the bottom of the heap. Nonetheless, the Assembly's power was very real. It did not hesitate to dismiss Pericles, or other generals, and sometimes did so in a fit of ill temper and regardless of merit. Its sovereignty was absolute, and its members knew it. The consequences were predictable; unless the Assembly was on its best behavior, it could be seduced by flatterers, bamboozled by crooks, and led by the nose by the glib and quick-witted. If it lost its temper, it could behave atrociously.

The Glories and Failures of Democracy

It was astonishing that Cleisthenes's democracy survived its first three decades. Almost at once, Athens was fighting for its life. The fifth century was dominated by two great wars, the first a collective Greek triumph, the second an Athenian disaster. The Persian Wars lasted with interludes from 500 to 479 and at a lower level of intensity for twenty years more; the Peloponnesian War, between Athens and its allies on one side and Sparta, Corinth, and their allies on the other, broke out in 431 and ended in 404 with the utter defeat of Athens. After 479 Athens was the chief maritime power of Greece and the center of a maritime empire that embraced the Aegean and the western shore of Asia Minor. Fear of its growing power, especially in Corinth and Sparta, provoked the alliance that fought Athens in the Peloponnesian War. Even after its crushing defeat, Athens revived during its final three-quarters of a century as an independent state, and twice tried to re-create its Aegean empire. Only the decisive defeat of the allied Greek forces by Philip of Macedon at Chaeronea in 338 and a final defeat of the Athenian fleet by the forces of Macedon in the sea battle of Amorgos in 322 put an end to democratic Athens as an independent state.

The Persian and Peloponnesian wars called out the talents of two of the ancient world's greatest historians. Both were acute political commentators. Herodotus, the chronicler of the Persian Wars, was called both "the father of history" and "the father of lies." He has a reputation for swallowing tall stories, though later research suggests that where he had a chance of being right he usually was, and that many of his conjectures about what had happened centuries earlier were well founded. Thucydides, the chronicler of the Peloponnesian War, has never been accused of credulity and is one of the greatest political analysts of all time. Their histories are not evenhanded. Thucydides and Herodotus had aristocratic sympathies and thought democracies were vulnerable to dissension, inconstancy, and the wiles of ambitious scoundrels. Herodotus was sufficiently impressed by the effectiveness of the Persian monarchy to attract the accusation of being a *philobarbarian*. Herodotus leaves the reader surprised that Athenian democracy found the coherence to defeat the Persians, while Thucydides leaves the reader unsurprised that the Athenian Assembly could be self-destructive. Thucydides's history ends in 411, seven years before the defeat of Athens, but its inevitability stalks the narrative.

Herodotus wrote his *Histories* to explain why Greeks and Persians were doomed to fight one another; he never gave a definite answer, though one can be inferred. The wars began with the revolt of Miletus and other Greek cities on the western shores of Asia Minor in 500. They had succumbed to Persian invasion earlier in the sixth century and were subjects of the Persian monarchy for half a century before they revolted. The reason for the revolt is obscure. Their lives had not been much affected by subjection: they had to pay tribute, and intercity relations were controlled by the Persians, but internal government, religious ritual, and economic activity were their own affair, the pattern subsequently under the Hellenistic monarchies and the Roman Empire. Persian suzerainty had not become more oppressive at the end of the century, and the cities that revolted were prosperous. It may indeed have been a revolt of the prosperous and confident, not a lashing out by the downtrodden and wretched.

Asked for help, Athens sent twenty triremes. Its motives for putting itself in danger's way are obscure. The Athenians cited ties to former colonies, and "Ionian" loyalties, but such ties were usually treated lightly. Herodotus thought the conflict between despotic Persia and democratic Athens inevitable. Many writers after World War II followed Herodotus in thinking that autocracies and democracies cannot live quietly side by side; the visible presence of democratic governments inspires subjugated peoples to think of freedom, and oppressive regimes are tempted to expand their frontiers to prevent their democratic neighbors from subverting their subjects. In reality, tensions were never so great. Persians allied with Greeks and vice versa for their own ends, as the Peloponnesian War proved.

The revolt in Asia Minor was snuffed out in 494, and the Athenians realized that they had acquired a dangerous enemy. Darius I's first attempt at invasion in 492 was abortive: a huge storm wrecked his fleet. In 491 the Persians demanded "earth and water"—signs of submission—from the Aegean islands and mainland cities. Many submitted. Athens and Sparta not only stood firm but murdered the Persian ambassadors. The Athenians put them on trial and killed both the ambassadors and their translator for offenses against the Greek language; the Spartans simply threw them down a well. Darius invaded in 490, but his campaign ended on the seashore at Marathon, when an Athenian hoplite army routed a much larger Persian force. It was a wholly unexpected victory; the Athenians had no reputation as fighters on land, and the Spartans had failed to answer their pleas for assistance against the "barbarians" because they were engaged in a religious festival. Plataea unexpectedly sent its entire army of a thousand hoplites, which may well have been decisive. Marathon showed the Persians what they had to reckon with; and the fact that the Athenians and their allies achieved the victory without Sparta showed the Spartans—who arrived on the scene after the battle had been won—that their military supremacy was no longer unchallengeable. The Athenians began to aspire to become an imperial power in the Aegean. Hubris threatened.

Marathon did not mark the end of the Persian threat. Under Darius's son and successor, Xerxes, the Persians returned a decade later in greater strength; in the summer of 480 the Persian navy was checked but not defeated by an allied Greek fleet off Euboea, and the Persian army met the Greeks on land at the pass of Thermopylae. The narrowness of the space between the mountains and the sea gave a defending army the advantage over much larger forces, and without the treachery of Ephialtes, who showed the Persians a mountain path that ran behind the Greek positions, the seven thousand Greeks might have held their ground long enough to dissuade the Persians from going farther. Once their position was turned, the Spartan king Leonidas sent all but a small rearguard away, and three hundred Spartans made up for their hesitation ten years earlier by holding the pass long enough to let the main Greek force escape to more favorable positions; they died to the last man, together with seven hundred Thespians and several hundred Thebans and others. Their epitaph is legendary: "Go tell the Spartans, passerby, that here, obedient to their laws, we lie."[4] Demaratus was there with Xerxes's army.

Thermopylae was a triumph for Spartan values, but a military defeat; the Persian army could now march through Boeotia to Athens. The Athenian leader Themistocles persuaded the Athenians to abandon the city, sent a message to the Persian fleet suggesting he might be willing to change sides, and in September 480 lured the Persian fleet into the straits of Salamis, where it was comprehensively destroyed. After the Battle of Salamis, Xerxes returned to Persia, leaving his army under his general Mardonius to finish off the Greeks in the next campaigning season. Things went equally badly for the Persians in 479. A defeat on land at Plataea in which Mardonius was killed—this time the Greek forces were led by the Spartans—persuaded the Persians to abandon the attempt to conquer mainland Greece. It was not the end of conflict; there were battles in the eastern Aegean for many years. It was the end of a serious threat of invasion.

The next seventy-five years saw the rise and fall of radical Athenian democracy. Political writers for two thousand years and more saw in this history an object lesson in, variously, the dangers of hubris—overweening self-confidence—the folly of allowing the lower classes to dominate politics, the corrupting effects of power, and much else. The dominant lesson drawn thereafter was the impossibility of combining democratic politics and ordinary prudence. The problem was in essence simple; Athens turned itself into an empire and overreached. At the end of the Persian Wars, Athens was the dominant maritime power, and established an alliance of Aegean island states, whose purpose was to take advantage of Persian weakness to deplete Persian naval power and to loot Persian possessions by way of compensation for the war. This was the Delian League; it was based on the island of Delos, where its treasury was established. It swiftly turned into an Athenian empire. The members of the league became tributary states of Athens, and their taxes went to beautify the city and subsidize the political life of the Athenian lower classes; to run their form of democracy, the Athenians had to pay a subsidy to allow their lower-class citizens to take time off from earning a living, and they were not scrupulous about where the money came from. The Athenians did not moralize about this. They took it for granted that states tried to maximize their power; the more powerful would exploit the less powerful, even if they might keep exploitation within limits, in the hope of more willing assistance in the event of war.

The check on Athenian conduct was self-interest. If Sparta had kept its military and political leadership after the Second Persian War, the Athenians would have been more cautious; resistance from their island allies might have persuaded them that tribute seeking was not worth the candle. Neither obstacle stood in their way; Sparta was indecisive, and the tributary states were weak. Athens embarked on an extension of its democratic institutions. Ceremonial offices alone were reserved for the better-born. As power gravitated to the boule and the Assembly, no provisions were put in place to ensure the good behavior of the Assembly or the council; neither the modern idea of the separation of powers nor the modern view that a constitution should provide a check on the exercise of power made any headway. Both ideas are prefigured in Aristotle's *Politics* a century and a half later, and after the Peloponnesian War the constitution was modified in that direction, but mid-fifth-century Athenian practice was not. Athens was a radical democracy; the constitution placed absolute power in the hands of "the people," and on the good sense of the people the safety of the individual and the wise management of affairs depended.

The practice of ostracism illustrates the Athenian readiness to empower the common people. Ostracism allowed the citizens to expel whomever they wished, especially the eminent, for any reason or none. (The term "ostracism" was taken from the pieces of pottery on which citizens could scratch the name of the person they wished to expel.) A famous story was told about the ostracism of Aristides, a leading statesman and a hero of the Battle of Salamis. He was approached by an illiterate citizen who asked him to write the name of Aristides on his potsherd; inquiring whether the man had ever met Aristides, he was told no, but the man was fed up with hearing Aristides constantly described as "the just." Aristides wrote his name. The penalty was mild: it was notionally exile for ten years, but with no loss of property and with the right to return without question. Many victims left rather briefly. Aristides was exiled in 482 and recalled two years later, and this was common. Lesser mortals might be expelled because they were immoral, unneighborly, or excessively disagreeable.

Thucydides and His History

Athenian expansionism brought intermittent, low-level conflict with other Greek states over many years; but in 431 a war broke out that set Athens and its maritime allies against an alliance led by Corinth and Sparta. The alliance should have been swiftly victorious, given its overwhelming military superiority. Even without that disparity, Athens might without disgrace have sued for peace in the face of the plague that struck the city in the following year, or immediately afterward on the death of Pericles, the one man who could preserve unity in the face of disaster.

In fact, the war lasted twenty-seven years. Athens's ability to hold off the Peloponnesian League for so long reflected extraordinary ingenuity and energy, as well as an ability to raise money, equip fleets and armies, and appoint competent generals who remained loyal to the city in spite of the Assembly's habit of suddenly turning against them. Two and a half thousand years later, commentators still fall into the trap of thinking that we must choose between democratic politics and effective administration; Athens showed that this is a false dilemma. On the other hand, aspects of Athens's conduct of the war reflect quite badly enough, either on democracy, on the Athenians, or more generally on human nature itself.

The Peloponnesian War is better known than any before Caesar's campaigns because it was chronicled by Thucydides. Thucydides is much admired by political theorists who draw from the war the morals that he imposed on his account without always remembering that his history is a wonderful commentary on the shortcomings of democracy, because Thucydides wrote it as such. He was an aristocrat and a general who was dismissed and exiled by the Assembly in 424 when he failed to reach Amphipolis, in northern Greece, in time to stop the city from surrendering to the Spartans. Exile had its uses to the historian; he could see the war from the Peloponnesian side as easily as from the Athenian, but exile did not endear Athens to him. Three passages from his history stick in every reader's mind. The first is the funeral oration at the end of the first year of the war, in which Pericles praised the Athenian dead, celebrated Athens as "the teacher of Hellas," and defended the democratic way of life in terms that resonate today. Pericles's defense of Athenian courage, versatility, and intelligence forms a counterpoint to the debates between the Corinthians and their reluctant Spartan allies earlier in Thucydides's account. The Corinthians urge the Spartans to make war on Athens; the Spartans are not sure they can win. Both fear that Athens will wrongfoot them by sheer cleverness; their anxiety was a deeply sincere tribute.

The second episode is the Athenian massacre and enslavement of the inhabitants of the island of Melos; and the last, the disastrous expedition against Syracuse. Today we think a government is not "democratic" if it violates human rights. Contemplating the unabashed wickedness of the Athenian treatment of Melos should give us pause; Athens was unequivocally democratic and frequently wicked. We do not know what future generations will think of the way the democratic powers fought the Second World War, but firebombing civilian populations and the use of nuclear weapons against Japan may give our successors pause. We have also become convinced that democracies do not go to war against one another; during the twentieth century, the liberal democracies of North America, Europe, and the British Commonwealth were invariably allies. Democratic Athens made war on democratic Syracuse during the Peloponnesian War. Thucydides thought the Athenian democracy was addicted to war. The reason, equally true of the Romans later, was that ancient war could be profitable; looting paid better than agriculture, and the poor, who lived at the level of a bare subsistence, stood to benefit, if not on the scale of the rich. Thucydides thought that the aggressiveness of democracies was a universal trait. He told his readers that he had written his history "for ever"; human nature was the same at all times and places, and the political passions and ambitions of mankind were ineradicable, so any persons concerned with the politics of their own time could read Thucydides's account of the Peloponnesian War and derive instruction. A historically minded Plains Indian of the nineteenth century might have shared Thucydides's view of the aggressive and expansive habits of democracies. Certainly, international relations scholars in the twenty-first century read Thucydides for pleasure and instruction.

Pericles's Funeral Oration

Thucydides describes his literary technique beguilingly. *The Peloponnesian War* proceeds by a series of set-piece speeches that carry the action forward and reveal the characters of the participants in these great events. To the obvious question whether this is really what was said, Thucydides replies that where he knows what a man said, he quotes it; where he does not, he puts in his mouth what he ought to have said, given the occasion and its demands. Pericles's Funeral Oration is longer than Lincoln's Gettysburg Address and is two and a half millennia older, but they are widely regarded as the two greatest defenses ever written, not only of democratic government but of the ethos of a democratic society. Whether Lincoln modeled his address on Pericles's is unknown, but they feature a common rhetoric: the speaker insists that his words can do nothing to enhance the glory of the fallen, because their deeds speak for themselves; they praise their country's founders as well as the dead; and they praise the society and polity for which they died; grief at the loss of the dead must not undermine the determination that a unique polity and its way of life should survive. It does not diminish either speech that it was politically important to remind the audience what they were fighting for. Lincoln's Union was war weary. Pericles's Athenians were suffering far worse than they had expected. He had persuaded them to abandon the countryside and move into the city, knowing that the Athenian army could not prevent the Spartans and their allies from ravaging the countryside of Attica, and relying on the Athenian navy to secure food and supplies. It was an intelligent strategy, but it bore hard on everyone; the better-off faced the destruction of their houses and estates, and no farmer could bear the destruction wreaked by the Spartans and their allies. Military stalemate and plague disillusioned the Athenians; soon after, Pericles was fined and dismissed, then recalled, only to die of plague at the end of 429.

Athenian state funerals were an old tradition; the dead were commemorated and their remains interred in the Keramaikos cemetery. Pericles's speech, whether the words were his, Thucydides's, or a combination, represented a break with the usual pattern. He starts by saying that there should be no such speeches; the glory of the dead should not be imperiled by the clumsiness of commemorative speeches. He turns to honor the ancestors. These moves were probably conventional. Then he less conventionally turns to praise the city for which they died. "[Our form of government] is called a democracy on account of being administered in the interest not of the few but the many; yet even though there are equal rights for all in private disputes in accordance with the laws, wherever each man has earned recognition he is singled out for public service in accordance with the claims of distinction, not by rotation but by merit, nor when it comes to poverty, if a man has real ability to benefit the city, is he prevented by obscure renown."[5]

Pericles did not stop at extolling the virtues of appointment on merit and of holding rulers to account in a lawful way. He emphasized the liveliness of a free and open society. "In public life we conduct ourselves with freedom and also, regarding that suspicion of others because of their everyday habits, without getting angry at a neighbor if he does something so as to suit himself, and without wearing expressions of vexation, that inflict no punishment yet cause distress."[6] Still, it was a politically charged society of which he was speaking. "We do not say that a man who takes no notice of politics is a man who minds his own business; we say that he has no business here at all." This picture of a participatory democracy and a society in which political commitment was all but universal is one to which the twentieth century turned to measure its own success and failure in instituting democracy. Reformers in the late twentieth century disagreed about how far we can re-create the vivid, participatory world of ancient Athens in a modern industrial society, but few turned their back on the ideal.

Two moments in Pericles's oration give a modern reader pause. His peroration on the virtues of the Athenian dead includes the well-known line, "The whole earth is the tomb of famous men." He was praising the Athenians for valor in war; they can boast courage in war, steadfastness in defeat, and unwavering loyalty to their fellow soldiers and sailors. Their fame was bound up with the military expansion that had provoked the conflict in which they had died. Some readers may think Athens would have been better-off with a more peaceful idea of fame; Thucydides thought they should at least have been more moderate. The moment that makes the modern reader's heart sink comes when Pericles turns to the women in his audience. He tells them that they should mourn their dead heroes, but that is the limit of their public role. "Your renown is great through keeping to the standard of your basic nature, and if your reputation has the least circulation among men, whether for virtue or in blame."[7] This is not the modern democratic ideal.

The "Melian Dialogue"

Thucydides wrote his history around the speeches that participants in events either made or "were called for in the situation." This makes a long book strikingly lively. The most famous of these set-piece debates is between the Athenians and the Melians; in 416 Athens demanded that the Melians surrender their city and pay tribute to aid the Athenian war effort. The Melians claimed the right to remain neutral and would not yield. Athens meticulously carried out its threat to kill every man of arms-bearing age and to sell all the women and children into slavery. This act is famous as the worst atrocity committed by a usually decent society, but even more as the occasion of one of the most famous assertions in history of the rights of unbridled power. The Athenian insistence that "justice is what is decided when equal forces are opposed, while possibilities are what superiors impose and the weak acquiesce to"[8] has been discussed, both by practical people and by philosophers, ever since. Not everyone has rejected the Athenian case.

Thucydides's account of events implies that Melos wished only to continue to be neutral. This was not true. Melos was a Spartan colony; neutral in theory, Melos provided help to Sparta from early in the war. Moreover, the Melians knew what to expect. Athens had come close to slaughtering an entire city before. Mytilene, on the island of Lesbos, revolted at the beginning of the war and held out until 427 with the aid of Spartan hoplites and some naval assistance. When the city surrendered, the Athenians decided to kill the adult men and enslave the women and children. The ships sent to announce their distasteful task to the soldiers on Lesbos were in no hurry to get there, and soon after they left, the Assembly changed its mind and sent another fleet to countermand their murderous instructions. Happily for Mytilene, the second fleet overtook the first. Ten years later, with the war dragging on, the Athenians did not have second thoughts. They had Spartan precedents. When Sparta subdued the city of Plataea in 426, the Spartans had not hesitated. Thucydides says that it was at the instigation of the inhabitants of Thebes that the Spartans acted, and it was certainly the Thebans who completed the physical destruction of the city some years later. Still, it was the Spartans who carried out the massacre. Every Plataean male of fighting age was asked what he had done to assist Sparta; since Plataea was an obdurate foe, none had done anything to help their enemies, and all were executed. The women and children were sold into slavery, and Plataea ceased to exist. At the end of the Peloponnesian War, the Spartans seriously considered treating the Athenians in the same fashion.

The debate is artfully constructed. The Melians admit that their weakness leads them to search for whatever arguments may fend off the Athenians, but they stick tightly to the two most relevant points. One is Athenian self-interest, and the other the Athenians' sense of justice. They tell the Athenians that they will create opposition to their empire among the independent neutral states, but the Athenians shrug off the danger; the Melians tell the Athenians that the Spartans will surely come to their aid, but the Athenians know that Sparta will not hazard its forces at a distance, and shrug off that danger. The crux is thus the patent injustice of the Athenian attempt on the independence of a small and helpless power. The Athenian view has been described: it is the law of nature that the strong do what they can and that the weak do what they must. The Melians refused to give in, the Athenians invested the island, and after a long siege and spirited resistance, the inevitable occurred. The Melians were starved into surrender, their men of military age were killed, and their women and children were sold into slavery. Five hundred Athenian colonists replaced them. It was an event that should give pause to anyone who supposes that democracies are by their nature peace-loving, humane, and just. Their capacity for mass murder should not be underestimated.

After fifteen years of war, neither Athens nor Sparta had gained the upper hand. This amounted to an Athenian victory; Sparta's aim was the destruction of Athens and its empire, while Athens aimed only to hold what it had. At least, this had been the aim of Pericles. Although many Greek cities chafed under Athenian domination, Sparta was an unlikely friend of liberty and self-determination. Nobody needed to be reminded of the Spartan treatment of the helots. For all their self-discipline in battle, the Spartans invariably succumbed to corruption once they were away from Sparta itself, and because Spartan policy was based even more crudely on simple self-interest than that of Athens, Sparta was an unreliable ally. If the Athenians had been content with avoiding defeat, the Peloponnesian League would have had to settle for the frustration of its aims. It would have been a remarkable achievement and would have shown how formidable Athenian democratic institutions, economic resources, and military imagination really were.

Alcibiades and the Sicilian Disaster

Athens defeated itself. The downfall of Athens was caused by personal rivalries, internal dissension, and a fatal overestimation of its capacity. The disastrous expedition to Sicily sprang from the ambition of Alcibiades, one of the most brilliant, self-destructive, and wayward political entrepreneurs of all times. The ward of Pericles, and the favorite pupil of Socrates—who was enchanted both by Alcibiades's physical charms and his philosophical talent—Alcibiades grew up with a passion for fame and no inhibitions about attaining it. He betrayed Athens to Sparta after 415, then betrayed Sparta to Athens, and in middle age was dangerous enough for the Spartans to persuade the Persians to murder him in 404. He was astonishingly brave, a brilliant general, and an inspiring leader. He was by turn the hero of the rowers in the Athenian navy, and the strategist who showed the Persians how to help Sparta to defeat Athens by assisting the oligarchical party at Athens to undermine the democracy. He came to symbolize the way a clever, glamorous, and unscrupulous demagogue could play on the susceptibilities of gullible ordinary folk, with disastrous consequences all around.

After the death of Pericles, Athenian politics became unstable, with a handful of demagogues competing for the support of the *ecclesia*, while the war degenerated into an inconclusive stalemate. In 421 the Peace of Nicias, named after the Athenian statesman who negotiated it, provided for a five-year truce, although it was taken for granted that the two protagonists would spend the interlude reinforcing their positions for a resumption of hostilities. The Sicilian expedition of 415 to 413 was an

Athenian effort in this direction. Athens had no interest in the western Mediterranean; its empire was in the Aegean; but it had an interest in weakening the ability of Greek colonies in Sicily and southern Italy to assist Corinth and Sparta. Hence the expedition to Sicily. It was led by Lamachus, Alcibiades, and Nicias. Lamachus was an experienced and aggressive general; if his proposal to launch an immediate and all-out assault on Syracuse had been accepted, the expedition might well have succeeded. His two colleagues had long been enemies, however. Alcibiades mocked Nicias's peace treaty, which gave all sides five years' breathing space and advocated more aggressive policies against Sparta. They had united to defeat the demagogue Hyperbolos in 416–415; but they were ill assorted, Nicias being as cautious and elderly as Alcibiades was the reverse.

Thucydides says that the Athenians were uninformed about the size of Sicily and the resources of Syracuse, and recklessly committed themselves to a second war on the scale of the Peloponnesian War. This is unfair. An unwinnable war crept up on them. The Sicilian cities that Alcibiades hoped to recruit as allies feared that Athens meant to turn them into subject states, and formed an alliance to resist Athens. Athens devoted immense resources to the expedition; this was on the urging of Nicias, either because he feared defeat with fewer resources or because he hoped that when the Assembly saw the cost of the enterprise it would call it off. During the campaign, Alcibiades was recalled to answer a charge of blasphemy; on the night of the fleet's departure, the herms—phallic sculptures set up around the city—had been mutilated, and in his absence Alcibiades's enemies had accused him of orchestrating this blasphemous misbehavior. When he discovered that he had been sentenced to death in his absence, he deserted to the Spartans. Then Lamachus was killed in a skirmish, and the Athenian forces were left to the wavering leadership of Nicias. They failed to establish a siege of Syracuse, suffered a catastrophic naval defeat in the great harbor at Syracuse, were cut off from supplies, and faced a choice between surrender and starvation. They surrendered and were worked to death as slaves in the Syracusan quarries.

Astonishingly, this was not the end of the Athenian war effort. A crash shipbuilding program restored the fleet, although nothing could be done to prevent the further devastation of Attica by the Spartan army, which profited until 411 from the skill and advice of Alcibiades. The Sicilian disaster reinforced upper-class hatred of popular government and its burdens. In 411 there was a short-lived oligarchical coup, which aimed to abolish the voting rights of the *thetes*—the lowest of the citizen classes and the source of the rowers in the fleet—and restore what the supporters of the oligarchy claimed was the constitution of Solon and Cleisthenes. There was no uniformity of purpose among the oligarchs, and the reduction in the rights of the lower classes was watered down under threat from the rowers. Democracy was restored, and Alcibiades briefly recalled, although he had been instrumental in fomenting the coup in Athens by promising Persian assistance if an oligarchy could be installed. Two blunders led to the final defeat. The first was the refusal of a Spartan offer of peace after Alcibiades had secured an Athenian sea victory at Cyzicus. Small-scale victories in Asia Minor misled the war party as to Athenian strength. The second blunder was the refusal of a second Spartan offer of peace after the final Athenian naval victory, at Arginusae in 406. That victory was marked by a piece of self-destructive wickedness. After the battle, the victorious fleet failed to rescue some wounded survivors; the Assembly put the generals on trial—illegally, since capital trials were reserved to the council of the Areopagus; ten were sentenced to death and executed soon after. As a way of alienating the leaders of Athens from the ordinary people, it could hardly have done more damage if the Spartans had contrived it. It was the end; the Spartans and the Persians finally established an alliance; Persian money and the skill of the Spartan general Lysander enabled the Spartans to defeat the Athenian fleet at Aegospotami and install an unbreakable siege of the city. Capitulation in 404 saw the destruction of Athens's famous Long Walls, the reduction of the fleet to twelve ships, and the installation of a savage oligarchy, the Thirty Tyrants.

The importance of the Peloponnesian War for our purposes is obvious. First, it—on Thucydides's account of it—exemplifies the strengths and weaknesses of democracy in ways that every succeeding age has seized on. On the one side, the resourcefulness, patriotism, energy, and determination of Athens were astonishing; on the other, the fickleness, cruelty, and proneness to dissension were equally astonishing. Ever after, the friends of democracy could say that the common man was capable of courage and initiative in the highest degree, and that the institutions of democracy were capable of selecting talented generals, gifted organizers, and public-spirited politicians, while the enemies of democracy retorted that, without extraordinary good luck, democracy led to factionalism, chaos, and military disaster.

Second, it reveals one major reason for the ultimate failure of the Greek states to survive the rise of the Macedonian and Roman empires. Greek city-states were conscious both of being Greek and of their own narrower ethnicity: Athenian, Theban, Spartan. To us, it is obvious that the Greek states should have set aside their differences over borders and styles of politics and united against Macedon and Rome as they had united against Persia. Yet the ease with which Sparta allied with Persia to defeat Athens shows how readily enmity toward fellow Greeks overcame the fear of non-Greek powers. This was not a peculiarity of Sparta; in the fourth century an alliance of Persia and Athens destroyed Sparta's military hegemony. Nor is it true that the Greeks did not discern the solution to the problem of reconciling their intense localism with their need for a broader political and military unity. It was they who discovered the modern world's most successful political invention: the federal state. The founders of the American Republic cited the long-lived Lykian League—a grouping of city-states in the eastern Aegean—in defense of their new creation.[9] Nor is that the only comparison we might draw. The United States barely survived the bloody Civil War of the 1860s, so it is no surprise that the Greeks of the fourth century BCE failed to subordinate sectional interests to the greater interest of the Greek people.

The Trial of Socrates

At the end of the war in 404, a short-lived but violent oligarchy was installed, led by Critias and Theramenes. Theramenes was a moderate, who had been prominent in the oligarchy of 411 and done much to ensure a bloodless return to democracy. Critias was an extremist. The Thirty Tyrants, as they were later known, deprived all but some five hundred citizens of any say in Athenian politics, allowed only the wealthiest five thousand citizens the right to be tried before a jury, and murdered numerous opponents without the formality of a trial. Indeed, they turned on Theramenes and executed him along with their democratic opponents; to ensure his death, they stripped him of his citizenship so that he, too, could be executed without a trial. They lasted barely a year before being overthrown by Thrasybulus, a long-standing democrat and a distinguished general. Athenian democracy was restored in 403, on a more moderate basis than before: the franchise was restricted, and the powers of the Assembly were reduced. Thrasybulus was deservedly awarded an olive crown for refusing to execute the defeated oligarchs and allowing them to choose whether to stay in the city or leave unmolested. The regime he established flourished until the triumph of Philip of Macedon. But one of its earliest acts was to put Socrates on trial for impiety; the judicial murder of Socrates has always ranked alongside the destruction of Melos in indictments of Athenian democracy, even though some commentators—Hegel and Nietzsche among them—have admired Socrates while thinking that Athens was right to silence him.

With the trial of Socrates, the history of Western political thinking begins. Socrates's death sparked off Plato's astonishing philosophical career. Only five of Plato's dialogues are centrally concerned with politics, though many bear on the practice of Athenian democracy. Even if Plato had never been born, Socrates's death would have raised hard questions about the limits of state authority and the citizen's duty to obey the legally constituted authorities. He was condemned to death in 399 on a charge of impiety; the essence of the charge was that he had denied that the gods existed and had corrupted the young. Socrates was in fact strikingly, but unconventionally, pious. Since he wrote nothing, and disapproved of writing, we have only his memorialists' accounts to go on, however. He appears to have claimed that the gods could not be as human beings depicted them; the gods were all-wise and all-knowing, but the poets depicted them as adulterous, murderous, quick to anger and slow to forgive, vain, sentimental, and foolish. Homer's *Iliad* is the obvious target of this criticism; it is an epic, and a modern reader might read it as an adventure story. To the Greeks, it had a semisacred status, and mocking its depiction of gods and heroes was dangerous. More importantly, the Athenians were both urbane and superstitious; during the Peloponnesian War, the Assembly had passed new laws against blasphemy, thinking, as most ancient peoples did, that making light of the gods invited their displeasure. These were the laws under which Alcibiades had been sentenced to death, and under which Socrates was tried and sentenced.

Politics may also have lain behind the trial. Socrates's friendship with the opponents of the democracy, both in the recent past and earlier in the case of Alcibiades, had alienated his fellow citizens. They did not mean him to die. At his trial, he was offered the chance to stop teaching, but would not take it.[10] He had the chance to propose a lesser penalty than death in his speech in his own defense, but provoked the jury by asking for a reward for helping them to live virtuously. His view, as he explained, was that the only harm the jury could do a good man was to make him less virtuous, and merely dying would not diminish his virtue. In any event he was an old man, and dying sooner rather than later was, if anything, a blessing. It is unsurprising that he was convicted of blasphemy by a narrow majority of the 500-man jury, but sentenced to death by a much larger margin.

Even after he had been sentenced to death, he was encouraged to leave the city and go into exile. Socrates's response has been a source of astonishment ever since. He insisted that he was an Athenian, a citizen, a law-abiding member of society. It was worse for him to break the laws by which he had been sheltered all his life than to drink hemlock and die. He duly drank the hemlock and died.[11] He left behind questions that have puzzled mankind ever since, and a pupil of genius who pursued a vendetta against Athenian democracy and perhaps against all possible politics. That was Plato.

CHAPTER 2

Plato and Antipolitics

The Paradoxical Plato

ALMOST ALL ACCOUNTS OF the history of political thinking begin with Plato. This is a paradox, because Plato's political thought is *anti*political. Readers of his *Republic* see that in the polis of Plato's imagination, there is no politics, and are puzzled; but throughout European history there has been a current of thought that seeks the resolution of the conflicts that "ordinary politics" resolves in the creation of a such a degree of social harmony that the conflicts which everyday politics resolves have simply disappeared, and politics with them. The apolitical utopia was not first imagined in 1513 when Thomas More's *Utopia* was published. We may safely assume there will be no politics in the heavenly kingdom of the Judeo-Christian God, though the family feuds of Olympus and Valhalla are another matter. Utopian thinkers hope to maintain social order and meet the needs of the population without economic or political competition, and without rulers' having to justify their decisions to their peers or to the common people. The founder of European political thought is the founder of antipolitical thinking. One might think that the chaos of the Peloponnesian War makes explanation of Plato's antipathy to politics unnecessary; anyone might have despaired of Athenian politics. That is true, but not everyone disenchanted with

Athenian democracy provided an elaborate philosophical justification for giving up on politics as such; many wanted oligarchy, others a version of the Spartan constitution, others the moderate government described some decades later in Aristotle's *Politics*.

The treatment of Plato's political ideas here is brief and selective, and concentrates on two fascinating dialogues, *Gorgias* and *Republic*. The treatment is critical, but not dismissive. Plato was accused by some of his twentieth-century critics of racism, totalitarianism, fascism, and other political crimes with a very contemporary flavor. These accusations are too anachronistic to be taken seriously; whatever explains Hitler and Mussolini, it is not the dialogues of Plato. The more plausible complaint is that Plato does not take seriously the inescapability of politics in some form. Plato's metaphysics is fascinating; so is his conviction that the just man does better than the unjust man, *no matter what earthly fate befalls him*. His political thinking often amounts to an injunction to abolish the conflicts that politics exists to resolve and fantasies about how it might be done.[1] He is not the only writer against whom the charge can be leveled. More than two millennia later, Karl Marx refused to say anything in detail about the politics of a communist society, because he thought the abolition of capitalism would abolish economic conflict and with it the need for government and politics. Like their French predecessor Henri de Saint-Simon, Marx and Engels believed that coercive government would be replaced by technical management.[2] Their refusal to prescribe for an unknowable future was admirable; but their unwillingness to say more about how a communist society might operate, beyond saying that the first step was to establish the dictatorship of the proletariat, turned out to be disastrous.

Knowing why Plato took the short way he did is important, because philosophers, political theorists, and many rulers have been tempted to follow him; but, as Aristotle complained, Plato does not so much purify politics as purify it to death. There is, said Aristotle, a degree of unity in a state beyond which it is not a state at all.[3] Plato's impact on European political thought is not easy to describe. Plato's metaphysics was influential on Christian thinking almost from the beginning, especially by way of his *Timaeus*; but when the cultural renaissance of the twelfth century reinvigorated classical scholarship in western Europe, it was Aristotle's *Politics* rather than Plato's *Republic* that scholars turned to for political illumination. The revival of interest in Plato during the Renaissance was a revival of interest in his metaphysics; although *Republic* was translated into Latin, and could now be read in Greek by a substantial number of scholars, it was the metaphysical dialogues that were important. Quite when *Republic* acquired its present dominant status is hard to say; in part, it seems to have been an artifact of the Victorian obsession with educating young men for public life. Ever since, many commentators have thought of *Republic* as a treatise on education; its political message is the need to enlighten us so that we may become fit to live in *kallipolis*, the ideal city.

It is tempting to compare Plato with Marx; indeed, I have done so. Like Plato, Marx looked forward to a future in which the state, law, coercion, and competition for power had vanished and politics been replaced by rational organization. But we must not press the comparison. Marx looked to radical political action in the present to abolish the need for politics in future: a proletarian revolution requires political organization to bring it about. Marx's utopia is egalitarian: everyone can freely agree to the demands of rational organization; and Marx's utopia demands material abundance: communism is possible only in an affluent society where hard labor is unnecessary. Plato abolished politics by philosophical fiat; only philosophers rule, because only they have the wisdom freely to assent to what reason requires. As for affluence, Plato's ideal society is more Spartan than the historical Sparta, and although Plato scarcely discusses work in *Republic*—as distinct from *Laws*—the existence of slaves and common laborers is presupposed. As the myth of the three metals explains, the cosmos is hierarchical, and only a few have the golden souls of rulers.

To say that Plato has only one concern in his political writings is unfair to the dogged and detailed emphasis of *Laws* on how to organize a second-best state if the utopia of *Republic* cannot be achieved. *Laws* is rich in institutional detail; some of it reappears in Aristotle's work, although he was as critical of *Laws* as he was of *Republic*.[4] He complains that neither work says enough about the *constitution* of the state, and that is a reminder that the title *Republic* is misleading. The Greek is *politeia*. *Politeia* means "constitution," which for Aristotle was the theory of finding the proper balance between all the various legitimate forces that operated on a state. Plato does not tackle that subject; his subject is the ignorance of politicians. The thought that nothing will go well until kings are philosophers or philosophers are kings is the thought of a man who believed that knowledge was the root of salvation and ignorance the root of perdition. The obvious question is *knowledge of what*. What should politicians know that they do not; what do philosophers know that entitles them to rule? We may also wonder why Plato was convinced that lack of *knowledge* was the issue rather than greed, anger, or the other dangerous emotions to which we are prey. Alcibiades's ambition rather than his ignorance seems the more obvious place to start; he was an excellent student of philosophy but a political menace.

Plato's relationship to Socrates holds the answer. Of the historical Socrates we know as little as we know of Plato; he is mocked in Aristophanes's hilarious comedy *Clouds*, represented as a figure of superhuman wisdom in Plato's dialogues, and described admiringly but less hyperbolically by Xenophon.[5] Socrates believed he had been called to bring enlightenment to Athens; the Gods had told him to walk the streets and debate with young men their views on important matters. It is easy to see why he was unsettling. The uncertainty in which dialogues such as *Gorgias* end seems to reflect what discussions with Socrates were really like. He was famous for claiming to know nothing; when the oracle at Delphi called him the wisest man in Athens, he was puzzled, but came to think that the oracle was right because other men thought they knew a great deal, while he at any rate understood that he knew nothing.

He held at least some of the doctrines attributed to him and defended by Plato: that nobody does evil willingly; that wickedness is error; that it is better to suffer wrong than to do it; that the virtues are one as well as many. He did not share Plato's passion for mathematics. He was a moralist and a mystic. Nor was he interested in scientific speculation: one tradition held that he thought the natural world was too difficult to think about; more importantly, its workings were morally irrelevant. Socrates was uninterested in having his thoughts written down for posterity, and is said to have thought that the invention of writing had enfeebled the intellect. He has thus frustrated the attempts of later commentators to discover what he really thought, as distinct from what Plato puts in his mouth. This has not stopped them from trying, but it has prevented them from reaching a consensus.

The ideas that modern readers find least plausible in *Gorgias* and *Republic* are those with the clearest origin in Socrates's known doctrines, particularly the equation of virtue with knowledge and the doctrine that no one does evil willingly. Nobody knows how far Socrates shared the antidemocratic ideas of *Republic*. It is possible that he, like Plato, thought that democracy is the second-worst of all forms of government, one step better than tyranny, and often its precursor. His friends were aristocrats who felt threatened by democracy, and he may have been executed by the revived democracy at least partly because he was friendly with members of the oligarchy of the Thirty Tyrants. Absurdly enough, he had come close to being killed by those very oligarchs. He was ordered to help seize an innocent man whom the oligarchy wanted to murder, but he refused.[6] The point of sending him on an illegal mission was to implicate him in the oligarchy's misdeeds; his refusal was opposition they could hardly have tolerated. He seems to have been saved by the fall of the oligarchy, only to be executed by the regime that had saved him.

Plato's Life

As with Shakespeare's, the immensity of Plato's influence is matched by the paucity of reliable information about his life. He was born about 428 and died some eighty years later. He came from an upper-class Athenian family, and his relatives were members of the oligarchy that briefly replaced the Athenian democracy at the end of the Peloponnesian War. His mother's cousin Critias and her brother Charmides were two of the most extreme and violent leaders of the oligarchy of 404–403; both were killed during the overthrow of the regime. Plato says in the *Seventh Letter* that he was asked to join the regime, but was repelled by its violence. Subsequently he took no part in Athenian politics. He was an aristocrat who disliked democracy, but disliked murderous oligarchies more. He initially welcomed the restoration of democracy as the restoration of the rule of law, but was disillusioned by the judicial murder of Socrates.

The trial and execution of Socrates in 399 was a key moment in European thought; more immediately, it was a crisis in the lives of his students and disciples. Many of Socrates's followers went into voluntary exile elsewhere in Greece, Sicily, and Italy, Plato among them; he returned to Athens several years later, and founded the Academy in 387. He taught there for the rest of his life. The Academy has given its name to innumerable later centers for research and teaching, but itself took its name from a wooded grove in Athens. The Academy's motto "Let nobody approach who does not know geometry" suggests Plato's obsession with what could be *known* and not just *believed*, as well as his conviction that it was only in the abstract fields of geometry and mathematics that knowledge had been reached, and that other forms of knowledge must model themselves on them. The Academy was a novelty, but once founded, it continued its work, with interruptions caused by war, until it was suppressed 916 years later, in 529 CE, on the orders of the emperor Justinian as part of a general purge of non-Christian ideas. Its aim was to teach good ethical and intellectual habits to aristocratic young men. In Plato's philosophy, training the mind and training the character were one and the same. The assumption was that such young men would occupy important public positions.

There were competing schools, and others sprang up later, but there was an earlier tradition of individual teachers of rhetoric and philosophy giving instruction to ambitious young men who hoped to make a name in politics. They were the Sophists, who receive hostile treatment throughout Plato's *Dialogues*. Socrates himself was a Sophist of sorts; the term means only "a wise man," and the oracle said he was the wisest man in Athens. Prompted by the Gods, he offered to debate with any Athenian the issues on which they could receive instruction from a Sophist. There was one crucial difference: the Sophists took their clients' desire for worldly success as the starting point, and taught them what they needed for success in the lawcourts and in debate in the assembly, while Socrates subverted their worldly ambitions and taught them to think of the welfare of their immortal souls instead. They also charged for their services; he did not. Plato aimed to continue and regularize Socrates's work.

Plato's practical interventions in politics were limited, and they nearly cost him his life. During his exile, he was befriended by Dionysius I, the tyrant of Syracuse, who then became irritated with him, and may—if the story is true—have decided to sell him into slavery. He was grudgingly allowed to leave Sicily for Athens in 387 when he founded the Academy. In 366—again, if the *Seventh Letter* describing these visits is genuine—he was asked to teach his captor's son and successor, Dionysius II, how to be a philosopher-king. Things again went badly, and he escaped with difficulty. Some years later, he was cajoled into a third attempt to turn a tyrant into a philosopher-king, and again escaped with some difficulty after he fell out with Dionysius. A very long time afterward, the existentialist philosopher Martin Heidegger, who acquired an unhappy notoriety for defending the Nazis in the early 1930s, took the post of rector of the University of Marburg in the hope that he could teach Hitler how to be a philosopher-king. After ten months, he gave up and was met by a colleague with an apt greeting, "Hello, Martin, back from Syracuse?" These adventures aside, Plato spent his time teaching and conducting the affairs of his family. No propertied man would have been without practical anxieties in the litigious society of Athens; but Plato ignored Athenian political life as completely as he advised the philosopher to do in *Republic*. What he has left us is his dialogues. Attempts to date them precisely have been inconclusive; even the usual grouping of "early," "middle," and "late" is contentious. Although they are located at particular times and places, which is one element in their charm, Plato introduces characters who had in historical fact died before the apparent date of the discussion, or who are of quite the wrong age. They are works of art, not seminar reports. They are also inexhaustibly interesting.

Plato was an extraordinarily talented writer. His obsession with keeping the arts under political control and his proposal to expel the poets from the utopia of *Republic* suggest a belief in the impact of art that no untalented writer would have. Nonetheless, the literary pleasures of his dialogues are variable. Those in which Socrates is a vivid participant, in the thick of controversy and fighting for his philosophical life, are livelier than those where Socrates is only a mouthpiece for Plato's mature doctrines. This is not an invariable rule: the *Symposium* is late and full of drama. Of the distinctively "political" dialogues, however, *Gorgias* and *Protagoras* are more genuinely dialogical than *Republic* after book I, while *Republic* in turn is livelier than *Laws* and *Statesman*. Here I focus on *Gorgias* and *Republic* for reasons now to be explained.

Gorgias

There can be no thumbnail account of "what Plato thought." The attraction of the dialogue as a literary device is that it lets an author consider ideas in them from a variety of different angles without wholly committing himself, and in the most "Socratic" of the dialogues, Plato takes full advantage of this. Focusing on *Gorgias* and *Republic* is justified by Plato's own obsession: what our rulers should know; the nature of the justice that they should seek for themselves and for the polis that they govern; the training they must they have if they are to govern wisely; what happens when wise men are not in command.

Gorgias was probably written around 380, although it may have been written earlier, and takes its title from a noted orator, Gorgias, a Sicilian teaching in Athens. It divides into three parts: first, Socrates interrogates Gorgias about what he teaches young men when he teaches them rhetoric; there follows a long confrontation with Polus, a student of Gorgias, in which Socrates defends the proposition that the seemingly powerful are in fact powerless, because they do not achieve what they "really" want, which is to live a righteous life; this leads to the claim that doing justice is always better for us than committing injustice, the claim he makes good in a wonderfully rambunctious—and on Socrates's own admission entirely inconclusive—argument with Callicles. "Rhetoric" had few pejorative connotations at the time. We tend to characterize rhetoric as "mere rhetoric," as did Socrates, but this was a minority view in Socrates's Athens. There was no implication that it was a bag of tricks to fool the gullible; it was simply the art of instructive and persuasive speech. Teaching rhetoric in the Greek and Roman world was an important and honorable occupation. Before his conversion to Christianity, Saint Augustine briefly became a professor of rhetoric as a step to a career as an imperial administrator. The political arrangements of Athens and Rome were very different, but in both the ability to make a convincing case in public was vital to political success. The assemblies of classical antiquity were lawcourts as well as deliberative and legislative bodies. The modern distinction of legislature, judiciary, and executive was foreign to them. They were used to being addressed in the way in which a modern jury would be addressed by an advocate in an important case. A man's property, social standing, and his very life might hang on his own or his agent's rhetorical skills. Three hundred years later, Cicero followed Plato on many philosophical issues, but not on the value of rhetoric. Cicero thought that the great orator was greater than either the statesman or the philosopher, since he had to master the skills of both. He was biased by his own vanity, but he caught the sense of the ancient world, and not of the ancient world only.

Socrates began the contrary tradition of belittling rhetoric, and *Gorgias* undoubtedly represents his views. His contempt was on full display when he was tried by the Athenian Assembly on the charge of corrupting the morals of the young; he snubbed both the jurors and the rhetorical conventions of Athenian public life. He was expected to agree not to go into the streets and talk about dangerous subjects with impressionable young men; but he announced that if he was acquitted, discussing dangerous topics was exactly what he would go on doing, because it was his divinely imposed duty. The reader can infer the way speakers in the Assembly ingratiated themselves with their hearers, not only from Plato's complaints about the way demagogues flattered the Assembly while despising its members but also from Socrates's ironic treatment of the conventions.[7]

The most significant victims of Socrates's questioning in *Gorgias* are Polus and Callicles, especially the latter; he, too, was a student of Gorgias, and as with Polus, that is all that is known of him. Plato directs against them the arguments that he deploys against Thrasymachus in *Republic* some thirty years later—notably the argument that it is better to suffer injustice than to do it, and that the unjust man is unhappy, no

matter how much worldly success he may attain. Nonetheless, the dialogue rightly begins with the unraveling of Gorgias's claims as a teacher,
and the denunciation of rhetoric. Plato had to evict the rhetoricians from
the terrain of the philosopher, just as he had to evict the poets from the
polis he was constructing, where philosophers were to be kings and the
educational system required strict censorship. What young men must
learn was the nature of justice; only those who *knew* what justice was
could teach it; only philosophers knew what justice was. Everything else
was ancillary.

The upbringing of aristocratic young men mattered immensely to
the ancient world—even more than the upbringing of privileged young
people matters to ours. It was a commonplace that the sons of eminent
men often turned out a disappointment, and that talented young men
might be corrupted by fame and destroy themselves and their city. Alcibiades, the young man on whom Socrates doted, offers a leading example; his father was a good man, and Alcibiades was Pericles's ward, but
he was a menace. Pericles's biological sons were nonentities; they did not
inherit their father's wisdom or courage. If good fathers can have wicked
or merely useless sons, either the virtuous man knows something that
he cannot teach, or he acts well without knowing what he is doing. The
son of the virtuous father who becomes corrupt and dissolute must have
been ill trained; things would have gone better if he had been properly
educated. What must someone know before offering to teach young men
who will grow up to be statesmen; what must we be taught if we are to
behave justly and lead a good life?

Gorgias presents himself as a teacher who teaches upper-class
young men to be successful. Socrates pricks up his ears and wonders
what extraordinary skill Gorgias has for sale. He swiftly forces Gorgias to admit that he cannot teach any of the particular arts and crafts
on which we depend for everyday health and comfort, as it might be
shoemaking or husbandry. That remains to this day the first question
about the nature of philosophy and rhetoric. Philosophy seems to be
about nothing in particular—not like plumbing or car maintenance, for
instance—but it seems vitally important to its practitioners. Gorgias is
a teacher of rhetoric rather than philosophy, but he is vulnerable to the

same question: if he is not teaching a skill such as medicine or carpentry, nor a science such as astronomy, he needs to explain just *what* rhetoric is the knowledge of. The subtext to the question is that what it *should* be is the art of ensuring that justice is done.

Under cross-examination, rhetoric turns out to be the art of presenting a case to an audience so that it appears to them as you want it to appear, no matter its intrinsic merits or lack of them. In Aristophanes's comedy *The Clouds*, that is the accusation leveled against Socrates, who is not in the play distinguished from Sophists generally; the young man Pheidippides has run up enormous gambling debts, so his father, the elderly farmer Strepsiades, enrolls him in the *phrontisterion*—the "thinkery"—to learn from Socrates the art of bamboozling an Athenian jury by making the better look worse and the worse look better.[8] One can see that the historical Socrates might have wanted to put the record straight; his pupil Plato held that rhetoric was exactly the reverse of philosophy. The aim of philosophy is to understand things as they really are, no matter how they may appear; it is the deceptiveness of appearances that makes philosophy necessary. Philosophy is the art of seeing through appearances to discern the hidden reality. At the end of the discussion with Gorgias, Socrates says that rhetoric is not a skill at all; it serves no useful purpose and achieves nothing that assists human existence. Changing tack somewhat, he adds that if it is a skill, it belongs with the skills of the marketplace, among those that are bad for our health, such as the art of the pastrycooks, and what Socrates dismisses generically as "pandering." The truth about Gorgias's trade shows what is wrong with democratic politics and the democratic politician; the politics of flattery and deceit drives out the politics of truth.[9]

Socrates does not say that Gorgias's students are unsuccessful in the lawcourts and the Assembly, any more than he says that pastrycooks fail to make a living. He says that the successes Gorgias's students achieve are bad for them and for their city. Their badness is always the same, which is that they are based on making the worse appear better; Gorgias's skills promote injustice. Socrates's treatment of Gorgias seems to a modern reader thoroughly insulting, but the criticism is not personal. Gorgias does not prostitute his talents because he is wicked; but in a democracy everything is based on show and appearance and not on truth. Gorgias does not sin against the light, but in ignorance. Ignorance is not incurable, but it is unlikely to be cured in a democracy, where ignorance pays off and knowledge does not.

The underlying target of Socrates's attack is the commonplace Greek view that the unbridled pursuit of self-interest constitutes success. Gorgias says that he has the same power as a tyrant, or perhaps even more, because he can persuade people to do what the tyrant must force them to do; Socrates insists that this, too, is an illusion. What appears to be the successful pursuit of self-interest is nothing of the sort. The only thing worth having is a just soul. To bring about the death of your enemies and the confiscation of their property by unjust means is not success, but inner death. A man who had behaved like that and knew his real interests would wish to be punished for his crimes, not to get away with them. Unsurprisingly, this meets with entire disbelief from Gorgias's student Polus, who laughs at Socrates and points out that he will not find anyone to agree with him. Socrates points out that neither mockery nor majority opinion are good guides to the truth, and he asks Polus to show him the error of his ways by argument.

Socrates then defends against Polus the extreme version of the view that the unjust man is always worse-off than the just man, no matter what happens to them by way of earthly success. As the pupil of Gorgias, Polus proceeds, one might say, rhetorically. He mocks Socrates for believing what nobody else believes; Socrates is unmoved. Polus adduces examples of successful villainy, citing Archelaus, the king of Macedonia who gained his throne by murdering his uncle, cousin, and young brother; surely nobody could think that someone who possessed absolute power, who could do just what he wanted, could kill his enemies, seize their property, take their wives and daughters, was unhappy. The idea was absurd. There are two issues here, both of them central to Plato's distaste for conventional politics. The simpler is what motives impel people to seek political power. Polus takes it for granted that these are selfish motives, and he appeals to what he, like most of us, takes to be a universal truth: we much prefer to boss others about than to be bossed about ourselves. Like most of us, he assumes that if we had absolute power, we would be unrestrained in gratifying our urges, whether sexual, financial, or a taste for celebrity. One might think that unless Polus was broadly right, we would not take so much care to create constitutional systems to keep our rulers in check. Lord Acton's dictum that power corrupts and absolute power corrupts absolutely expresses just that anxiety. The oddity for a modern reader is the extent to which Polus's sympathies are unabashedly with the holder of absolute power.

The second, deeper issue is philosophical. Socrates disputes Polus's understanding of power. To put it paradoxically, having power is being able to achieve what you want, but getting what you want in the sense in which Polus understands it is not getting what you want and therefore not an exercise of power. One can sympathize with the exasperation of Socrates's critics. Happily, there is a simple translation. Socrates is drawing the familiar distinction between doing what you want and doing what is in your best interests. "You don't really want to eat that worm," we say to a child who has it in mind to do just that. What we mean is "Eating that worm will make you ill." Socrates thought that the ambitions that drove most political leaders were a form of madness or a sickness of the soul. Gorgias and Polus lack power over themselves; because they cannot pursue the good life that they do not understand, they cannot have power over others either.

Beneath the attack on Gorgias and Polus lies the argument that underpins both *Gorgias* and *Republic*. Socrates claims that we must try to teach justice; justice is not based on appearance; knowing what justice is is essential for a successful life; most importantly, justice benefits its possessor and is not socially useful only. Justice is good for its possessor *no matter what* may happen to him or her. Everyone reading Plato has wanted to defend some elements of this doctrine even though, or perhaps even because, the task seems so obviously impossible in the extreme form in which Plato states it. Weaker versions of the claim are easy to defend; stronger versions are defensible up to a point; the extreme case set out in *Gorgias* and *Republic* is another matter. But it was the extreme case that Socrates died for. One prefatory note is needed; all translations of Plato observe that the Greek term *dike* is not very happily translated as "justice." Its range is wider than the English term, and in this context, at least, is best thought of as "all-in rightness." The English term "righteousness" has too many biblical connotations to be quite satisfactory, but an *adikos* is certainly an unrighteous man, and English translations of the Bible as often speak of the just as they do of the righteous.

With Gorgias routed, and Polus leaving the debate, Callicles takes up the argument. One of the pleasures of the dialogues that seem truest to the historical Socrates is that Plato gives a no-holds-barred philosophical brawler the arguments that Socrates has the hardest time refuting. In *Gorgias* it is Callicles and in *Republic* Thrasymachus; but they argue the same case, equally noisily. Both begin by telling Socrates that he is a driveling and mewling infant who should not be let out without his nurse. Socrates claims that it is better to suffer evil than to do it—and in both *Gorgias* and *Republic* goes on to say that a wicked man is better off if he is punished than if he escapes punishment. Being treated justly is best for us, and acting justly is always the best thing to do, *no matter the consequences.* Callicles defends the commonsense view put forward by Polus, that a good man who suffers misfortune is worse-off than a wicked man who gets away with his crimes; he also defends what seems to modern readers a much less commonsense view, but one that was popular among Homeric heroes and attractive to Homer's readers, namely, that the good life consists of gratifying our impulses whatever they may be, with no regard for the interests of anyone else. The gods of the *Iliad* do it, and everyone would like to live like a god. That view itself has two different interpretations; one is that the good life for the individual is an immoral, or at least an amoral and *non*-just, life, the other the counterintuitive view that *justice according to nature* is *whatever one can get away with.* That was what the Athenians told the Melians. Plato was committed to the doctrine that nature is on the side of justice as we ordinarily understand it; indeed, that the cosmos is itself made orderly by justice. It is, of course, possible to think that both Plato and the Athenians were wrong; in *Republic* Glaucon produces an explanation of the nature of justice that rests on that assumption.

Callicles makes a shrewd observation that Socrates readily accepts. Philosophers are terrible politicians. An everyday politician will run rings around the most astute philosopher when it comes to winning a

debate or a case in court. Socrates agrees. In *Gorgias* Plato does not use
the analogy he appeals to in *Republic*, where he says that the philosopher
has been so dazzled by the sun of Truth that he can hardly see where
he is going in the world of mere appearances; here he depicts Socrates as
simply agreeing that, by the worldly-wise standards of the political practitioner, the philosopher cuts a sorry figure. So much for the worldly-
wise. Indeed, here as elsewhere, Socrates claims to be one of a very small
handful of true statesmen to be found in Athens. But a true statesman
can do nothing useful in a corrupt environment.

Callicles is wrong. Wickedness is bad for you. Socrates's argument
is similar in *Gorgias* and *Republic*. Both discussions raise the question of
how far Socrates's argument can get without an appeal to the existence of
an afterlife with a system of postmortem punishments and rewards; but
in both discussions Socrates leaves consequences, whether in this life or
in a future life, out of account until the end of the argument. It is *being
just for its own sake* in the here and now that the wise man is committed
to; he would be made unhappier by being unjust than by any earthly
pains. Nonetheless, in both discussions, Plato also imagines an afterlife
in which our souls will be inspected and our eternal happiness and misery
proportioned to the quality of our souls. He speculates that not many of
the world's rulers will have an agreeable time in the hereafter—Aristides
"the Just" is one of the few whom Socrates expects to be at ease on the day
of judgment. But the claim that postmortem punishments will outweigh
the this-worldly benefits of wickedness is very different from the claim
that even in the absence of such punishments the unjust man does worse
than the just man here and now. It is that claim which Socrates defends.

Socrates shows that Callicles is mistaken about the nature of good
and evil by teasing him with questions about what *counts* as being stronger or better or wiser, and showing that paradoxical results flow from
what looks at first sight simple: "My belief is," says Callicles, "that natural right consists in the better and wiser man ruling over his inferiors and
having the lion's share."[10] The better and wiser man rules over his inferiors in his *own* interests, not theirs. Socrates asks whether the better and
wiser man is to rule himself as well as others, and receives the scornful
answer that he certainly is not. Being ruled is shameful, even if it is being

ruled by oneself; controlling our desires is just feeble. This is a fatal slip; Callicles should have agreed that self-control is required for success in even wicked projects. Callicles returns to the claim that the man of large and immoderate appetite who is good at getting his own way is the man to admire. He is then lured into agreeing that satisfaction is good and dissatisfaction bad. Socrates springs the trap: the more insatiable our appetites, the greater our dissatisfaction. It is, says Socrates, like trying to fill an infinite number of leaky barrels.

Socrates does not stop at arguing that a person of moderate appetites is going to be less dissatisfied than the person of uncontrolled appetite. This is vulnerable to Callicles's retort that if the avoidance of dissatisfaction is the point of existence, sticks and stones do pretty well. Socrates takes Callicles through a series of questions which reveal that, like everyone else, Callicles distinguishes between good and bad pleasures. Callicles needs a test for being a good person because only the good person's pleasures are good; after all, Callicles thinks that the pleasures of the quiet and contemplative man are not worth having, because they are the pleasures of the wrong sort of person. This would not force a less impetuous philosopher than Callicles to renounce the doctrine that the right sort of person is the successful self-aggrandizer. But it would force him to agree that the self-aggrandizer needs some of the qualities of more conventionally good men.

In *Gorgias* Plato does not further explore the nature of the virtues, as he does in *Republic*. Instead, and what lends plausibility to the thought that the dialogue was written before 380 and perhaps not long after the execution of Socrates, Socrates embarks on a long excursus about the relationship between the statesman and the public. This returns the dialogue to the political realm where it began with the interrogation of Gorgias. Socrates insists that he—alone—has studied the true art of statesmanship and is the only true statesman in Athens. Given Socrates's aloofness from Athenian politics, this is richly paradoxical, but it leads to the final discussion not only of the relationship between philosophy and rhetoric but also of what the statesman and the public owe each other. So far from being entitled to "the lion's share," the true statesman serves for nothing. But the true statesman does not expect to persuade an

Athenian jury that reducing young men to baffled incomprehension is a public service. In which case, says Socrates, he will content himself with the thought that an innocent man who is persecuted by villains dies with cleaner hands than theirs.

Republic

Gorgias leaves readers struggling not only with the arguments but with the shape of the discussion. We want conclusions, but we are left with riddles. As an aid to teaching, nothing could be better, but in the absence of the teacher, we cannot guess what Plato's students and readers made of it. *Republic* is different. The first book is a self-contained discussion of the question whether we always do better to practice justice rather than injustice, written in the open-ended fashion of *Gorgias*, with several interlocutors given equal time. It leaves the subject so much up in the air that the search for a definition of justice has to begin all over again. From book 2 on, there are only three speakers, save for a brief reappearance by Thrasymachus and Polemarchus halfway through, as a rather lame literary device to make Socrates restart the discussion of the nature of the best state and tackle it in more depth. For long stretches, Socrates takes over the discussion, with occasional interjections from Glaucon and Adeimantus. The exposition of Plato's theory of justice and its political implications is far from straightforward, with the argument twisting and turning, and being held up for long periods by extended digressions into metaphysics and epistemology, but it is unequivocally an answer to the question how we should govern ourselves. It not only says that we must be governed by philosophers but says much about the education and way of life of the ruling elite; and it does what *Gorgias* does not, which is to provide an account of what justice *is* as well as a defense of the doctrine that the righteous man is happy no matter what.

The natures of a just society and a just political order are still central concerns of political theorists, who are as far as ever from being of one mind about the nature of justice or the institutions that a just society requires. It goes without saying that Plato did not provide a conclusive

argument for government by philosopher-kings; it is perhaps less obvious that Plato had a different conception of justice from the understanding of justice current in twenty-first-century liberal democracies, even
making allowances for the different nuances of the Greek *dike* and our
"justice." Outside the realm of "criminal justice," we think of justice
primarily in economic terms and think that a state committed to social
justice is aiming to achieve some form of economic fairness; Plato was
looking for the rule of the righteous, who can ensure that the polity as a
whole practices justice and displays in its organization and behavior the
qualities that the soul of the just individual displays. Nonetheless, much
of what Plato says in criticism of the politics of Athenian democracy
would be, and has been, echoed by critics of contemporary democracies,
as would much of what he says of the psychological chaos that rules the
souls of democratic citizens.

The subject of *Republic* is ostensibly the subject of the second half of
Gorgias, whether it is always better to suffer evil than to do it. Plato says
yes, but *Republic* is primarily a search for the just polis, it being assumed
that justice in the individual and justice in the state are one and the same.
To understand the just individual, we must consider the just society.
Plato presents that argument as the claim that it is easier to see what
justice is in the large rather than the small, so we should look for it in
the polis before we seek it in the individual.[11] It is a bad argument, but a
nice rhetorical device. To establish what justice in the polis really is, he
takes a roundabout route, setting up *kallipolis*, the beautiful city or utopia,
focusing on the education that the leaders of a perfectly just society must
receive, and on the social and economic arrangements of a society that
will be utterly unlike the febrile, inconstant, and thoroughly this-worldly
Athenian democracy. Plato's emphasis on order and stability raises the
question whether a state ruled by philosopher-kings will be wholly
invulnerable to change. One might think the answer is yes, but Plato says
not and provides an account of the cyclical historical process in which
states move between their best and their worst conditions. He ends this
account as he ends *Gorgias*, with a description of the wretched state of the
tyrant's soul, before rehearsing once more the conflict between poetry
and philosophy and the fate of us all in the hereafter.

Republic opens with Socrates meeting several friends in the street; there is some byplay as his friends insist that he should stay with them for the night so that they can go and see a newly established festival to a moon goddess. Athens was known as the city of festivals; the Athenians celebrated around 120 each year. His friends tempt him with the promise of a horseback relay race by moonlight, and the chance to talk with numerous young men. Socrates agrees, and the party goes into a nearby house to talk while waiting for the festival to start. There is piquancy both in the cast and in the location; the two characters who carry on the conversation for the bulk of the book are Plato's real-life brothers, Glaucon and Adeimantus. Polemarchus, in whose house the conversation takes place, is the son of Cephalus, a rich, elderly, and genuinely good man who represents both the possibility of unreflective traditional virtue and its incapacity to explain itself. In real life, Polemarchus was one of the victims of the Thirty Tyrants, and he is here entertaining the cousins and nephews of the men who were to kill him. The festival takes place at the temple of Bendis, which was the site of the battle in which the Thirty Tyrants were overthrown and Critias killed. One can only speculate about Plato's intentions in choosing the location and the cast. The wild man of the party, who plays the role Callicles played in *Gorgias*, is Thrasymachus of Chalcedon, a Sophist of whom little is known.

The discussion starts with Socrates asking Cephalus what he thinks of old age. Cephalus recalls Sophocles's remark that being liberated from sexual passion was like being liberated from a savage slave master, and says the tranquillity of age has much to be said for it. Socrates teases him by saying that other people might think that he is tranquil only because he is rich. Cephalus will have none of it: extreme poverty would be hard to bear, but a miserable person is miserable however rich. A good character is our most important possession, rich or poor. Socrates agrees, of course, but asks Cephalus what the value of wealth really is. This produces the first of many definitions of justice. All except the definition that Socrates arrives at much later are defective as *definitions*, but each illuminates just behavior under particular conditions—with the exception of Thrasymachus's view that justice consists in the rule of the stronger in his own interest. That is always wrong. Cephalus says that his wealth means he need never cheat or steal, and he can die knowing he told the truth and paid his debts. Those are two of the elements in the classical view of justice: "harm nobody, live honestly, give everyone his due."

Socrates asks the first seemingly foolish question. Cephalus defines justice as telling the truth and repaying our debts, but is it always good to return what we have borrowed? What if we have borrowed a knife and the owner has gone mad in the meantime and is likely to do himself harm? As to truth, should we tell our mad friend that he has gone mad? Cephalus hands the argument to his son, who offers a classical definition of justice: *to give every man his due.* Socrates's account of justice will eventually embrace that, but at this stage he asks another question. "Give each his due" is a *formal* principle; we need to know *what* is due to everyone, and Socrates wants Polemarchus to tell him. Polemarchus produces a traditionally Greek answer; justice means doing good to our friends and harm to our enemies. Benefits are due to friends and injuries are due to enemies. Riches and power are good because they allow us to benefit our friends and injure our enemies. When the Athenians were asked to account for their conduct during the Peloponnesian War, they were unabashed about saying that their power enabled them to help their friends and harm their enemies. Good is due to friends and harm to enemies; the principle holds for both states and individuals.

Socrates denies this. It is never right to injure anyone, which means, as he understands it, that it can never be right to make someone *worse than he is.* He reaches this conclusion by a detour that puzzles modern readers, whereas in *Gorgias* he had made the point directly that punishment does not injure the person who is justly punished. Here Socrates asks who will be good at practicing justice defined as benefiting friends and harming enemies. The question strikes us as odd because we do not think of "doing justice" as having much in common with, say, mending a car or plowing a field; we do not think of it as a *skill.* Plato does. The kind of skill matters because everyone should be just, and living justly must be something that everyone can do. Yet every practical activity seems to be the province of a particular skill, at which some people are better than others. That raises unanswerable questions about what skill the just man practices if all the various practical skills are allocated elsewhere. Sailors sail boats, surgeons perform operations, and so on; every activity has its own practitioners and its own expertise. What expertise does justice imply?

If every action is guided by its own *techné*, or "art" (which is to say a technique or practical skill), what room is left for morality? The answer, which Aristotle makes clearer than Plato, must be that morality controls the way we use the other "arts" or skills. Faced with the claim that justice requires us to do good to our friends and harm to our enemies, Socrates asks who will be best able to do this. Curing our friends and poisoning our enemies is best done by a doctor; if we are at sea, saving our friends and drowning our enemies is best done by a sailor. Where there is a task, there is an art devoted to it, such as medicine or seafaring. It is therefore obscure what justice is supposed to be concerned with; as Socrates jokingly says, it seems that justice is no use at all. It does not achieve anything, while all the various arts bring about particular useful results.

Plato would not say what a modern writer might, that "being just" or "doing justice" is not a skill at all. Justice does something to the souls of those who act justly and of those who are treated justly. His own view is left obscure until the definition of justice as "sticking to one's last" is eventually reached. One might wonder even then whether "sticking to one's last" is a skill of any kind, but the thought that putting our souls in their proper, harmonious order involves a sort of skill is less unpersuasive. His immediate aim is to undermine the claim that justice means doing good to friends and harm to enemies. Harming someone means making him worse, says Socrates, and the point of justice cannot be to make someone worse. Punishment may be disliked by the people who suffer it, but if it is justly imposed it does not harm them, because it does not make them worse. It makes them better, which is why it is their due. Socrates's hostility to the traditional Greek view that justice means doing good to one's friends and harm to one's enemies was a real breach with a moral position that Thucydides, for instance, thought the Athenians took for granted, but Socrates's view was not absolutely novel. There are premonitions of it in Sophocles. There are none in Homer.

By now, Thrasymachus is coming to the boil. Like Callicles in *Gorgias*, Thrasymachus enters the dialogue by accusing Socrates of talking drivel and ignoring how people behave. It is hard not to feel sorry for

Thrasymachus; Plato deals him a worse hand, philosophically speaking, than he dealt Callicles. He is first made to say that there are no moral standards at all and then made to defend a distinctive morality. It is a counterintuitive morality, but a morality nonetheless. Since the combination is incoherent, he is a sitting target. Thus Thrasymachus begins by claiming that when people make moral judgments, they are talking nonsense, and the intelligent man sees through the charade. The intelligent man acts to suit himself; if he feels kindly and generous, he will behave in a kindly and generous fashion; if not, not. What he will not do is clutter his mind with talk of morality, even if he decides to make concessions to the nonsense other people talk. That is the position of the philosophical amoralist. It is coherent and not difficult to defend, and was one of the views that Nietzsche popularized two millennia later.

Plato also imposes on Thrasymachus the much harder task of defending a very unusual morality. He is made to argue that we are *required* to engage in self-aggrandizing behavior. There were elements of this in Callicles's case. As soon as either argues that we are *wrong* in failing to act in accordance with nature and 'wrong to observe conventional moral standards, he is arguing for an alternative morality—even if one predicated on the thought that successful conduct consists in doing down everyone else and behaving as "badly" as we can. Once again, it is not impossible to argue for a variation on this: that *some* individuals, at least, great-souled, heroic, self-assertive figures such as Achilles, *ought* to live by a code that the rest of us could not and should not try to live by. The case requires some moral ruggedness: when those of us who are less great-souled than Achilles ask what is to happen to *us*, we learn that the heroic morality is not interested in us. We may provide the raw material for heroic projects, but what is interesting and important is the heroic project, not us. As Nietzsche observed, lambs dislike eagles, but so what?[12] It is not a view that appeals to humanitarians or the naturally timid; nonetheless, it is not incoherent.

Thrasymachus is made to tie himself in knots. Justice, he says firmly, is whatever is in the interest of the stronger. This may be understood as the claim that whoever gets the upper hand *defines* right and wrong to suit himself—the rich define it as preserving property; the poor define it as generosity to the hard up—or as the claim that justice is *really* what is *really* in the interest of the stronger. The first is amoralism and the second an unorthodox morality. Thrasymachus's premises suggest the first, but the argument thereafter makes sense only on the basis of the second. He begins by pointing out that once we know the form of government of a Greek city, we can work out in whose interest legislation will be framed—it will favor the poor in a democracy and the tyrant in a tyranny, and so on. That is the claim that people define justice to suit themselves. He is then tripped up by a patently unfair argument. Socrates gets him to agree first that subjects are obliged to obey their rulers, which is to say that they behave justly in doing so; he next gets him to agree that rulers sometimes make mistakes about their interests. Putting the two premises together yields the conclusion that it is sometimes just for subjects to do what is not in the interests of the stronger. In other words, it is just not to be just, which is simply incoherent.

As in *Gorgias*, Socrates takes the argument on a detour through the skills that minister to everyday life. The question is whose interests these skills promote. Medicine is about the interests of the patient, not the doctor; the captain of the ship superintends the sailors for the benefit of the whole crew and their passengers. If justice is a quality in rulers, they should be concerned with the welfare of their subjects rather than themselves; justice promotes the interest of the weaker, not the stronger. Like Callicles, Thrasymachus responds by suggesting that Socrates ought not to be let out without his nurse. Rulers may be shepherds, but shepherds tend their flocks so that the sheep can be fattened for the slaughter. Thrasymachus has made the fatal slip of accepting the ordinary notion of justice and abandoning his own. From now on, justice is understood as the familiar (if still undefined) value that leads men to keep promises, tell the truth, do their duty, and obey the laws. Thrasymachus has abandoned the project of redefining justice in novel ways. He must now stick to a simpler argument: doing justice (as ordinarily understood) is strictly for idiots. Nonetheless, the new argument continues to be couched in a way the modern reader will find odd, for Thrasymachus does not give up the attack on justice. If practicing justice is bad for us, justice is not a virtue.

So he plays his second card. Justice is for idiots. The unjust man will always get the better of the just man, and the just man will come to a bad end when he gets in the way of the ruthless and the clever. Thrasymachus still hankers after his earlier claim that justice is what is in the interests of the stronger, and he cannot resist observing that people who commit crimes on a sufficiently grand scale not only get away with them but end up being admired. The sneak thief is despised, but the looters of temples are glorified; behaving badly on a large enough scale is admirable. Some years later, a pirate brought before Alexander the Great made himself famous by telling Alexander that the difference between them lay in the scale of the crimes they committed. His small-scale theft was piracy; Alexander's large-scale looting of empires was glorious. The usual modern view is that Thrasymachus's best hope would be to accept the conventional notion of justice, and then say that because we have no selfish reason to be just, justice is for the softhearted and softheaded. We know that Thrasymachus disagrees with the conventional view, since he refuses Socrates's offer to "argue the matter along conventional lines." He holds that if injustice pays off, it is a virtue, and if justice does not pay, it is not. This is not the skeptical position that there is no such thing as justice, nor the conventional view that justice is a virtue, but at odds with self-interest. It is the view that if justice is at odds with self-interest it is not a virtue. Injustice is a virtue, and justice a vice. This would not have struck Plato's readers as oddly as it strikes us. The Greek conception of ethics was not ours; the "good life" must benefit the individual who leads it, which is why Socrates has to argue that the good man is happy no matter what.

Socrates repeats his response to Callicles in *Gorgias*. No matter his earthly fate, the soul of the just man is in a good state, and to have one's soul in a good state is what it is to be happy. This is the literal meaning of *eudaemonia*. Socrates also makes the more conventional observation that whatever the fate of the individual, justice is essential if a group is to achieve its goals. Thieves who rob one another do worse than thieves who practice justice among themselves in order to be more effective in robbing others. We now have Socrates's case in its full vulnerability. Justice must be in the interest of both individuals and the community.

Showing that the usual rules of justice enable individuals to cooperate, and that this means they will do better on average and on the whole, is not difficult. A community where everyone respects everyone else's rights will be more prosperous than one where everyone tries to cheat and steal. The difficulty is that from the point of view of any single individual, what *looks* like the option that is most in his interest as a single individual is to live in a community where everyone else takes justice seriously, and he gets away with behaving badly. There is an enormous modern literature on what is known as the "free-rider problem," which is to say the problem posed by the person who thinks along these lines, and wishes to "free-ride" on the back of everyone else's good behavior. (The term "free rider" comes from the homely example of a person who wants to use the train or bus without paying his fare. As long as others pay their fares, there will be a bus or train service, and he will get its benefits without paying his share of the cost.) Five minutes' reflection suggests that if we suspect one another of harboring such sentiments, mutual distrust will undermine all cooperation between us; it also suggests that we should police one another to ensure that anyone who does harbor such thoughts is deterred from acting on them.

Further reflection raises the specter of how to police those who do the policing: *quis custodet ipsos custodes?* We have good reason to hope that we can all be committed to acting justly for its own sake. Nonetheless, we also have good reason to fear that there will be many occasions when our best interests will be served by violating the precepts of justice. The problem is especially acute in the context of economic relationships, where everyone is assumed to be acting in a self-interested fashion; why should we assume that they will not cheat on their bargains? Anyone who wants to analyze politics on the assumption that we are rational actors who are out to maximize our own payoffs faces the problem in its most acute form. If we think that people interacting in the marketplace can be policed by the state, and *made* to do what justice demands, we must next explain how the agents of the state can be policed and kept honest. On the face of it, they have every incentive to rob the rest of us. The issue surfaced in the debate between Thrasymachus and Socrates; it cannot be said to have been resolved even now.

The Argument after Thrasymachus

Socrates takes up the task of showing that the conflict between justice and self-interest is only apparent. The creation of the most influential utopia in history is a surprising part of the undertaking. The opening discussion ends when Thrasymachus grumpily abandons the argument, and Socrates admits that although he has routed Thrasymachus, he does not think he has made much headway in defining justice. Glaucon restarts the discussion and poses the crucial question: *is* it always in the interests of the individual to be just? If we could get away with behaving badly, would we not have good reason to do it? If we possessed the "ring of Gyges" that could make us invisible, would we not use it to sleep with other men's wives, and to assassinate kings and rule in their stead? (In the myth, the ancestor of the Lycian king Gyges was a shepherd who found a magic ring and used it for just that purpose.) Glaucon sets Socrates the impossible task of showing that the just man is better-off than the unjust man, even if the unjust man is believed to be virtuous, and lives and dies prosperous and admired, while the just man is believed to be wicked, and dies a painful and despised death.

Plato's answer takes us through the creation of the perfect polis, and what it requires by way of the education of its leading members. First, Glaucon offers a commonsensical view about the origins of justice. Glaucon's view has been taken seriously by political thinkers ever since Thomas Hobbes's *Leviathan* in 1651. In *Republic* it falls flat. It is not entirely obvious why, since it was hardly news to a Greek audience that much of mankind was selfish, and a commercial people like the Athenians were well acquainted with contracts. Glaucon says that we are selfish creatures who prefer our own welfare to that of others. We would behave badly when it suited us if we could get away with it; but we are more eager to avoid suffering at the hands of others than we are to exploit them, and agree to restrain ourselves in order to secure the same forbearance from others. Morality, or moral conduct, is a form of insurance. Justice springs from an agreement "neither to do nor to suffer harm." Glaucon is philosophically deft. He agrees that this is not an actual agreement, but the agreement that we *would* have made. It embodies a negative Golden Rule; we "don't do as we would not be done by." Explaining justice in terms of a hypothetical contract has been a favored move among political theorists for several centuries and is popular today. Glaucon failed to start a tradition of such thinking; his views are ignored by Socrates and were lost in later natural law theories, which explained the rules of justice as dictates of nature.

It follows from Glaucon's view that *if* we were entirely immune to the threat of punishment, we would do well by behaving badly. This thought is less alarming than it seems; we do not possess Gyges's ring and are not immune; we are born as dependent infants who need to ingratiate ourselves with our parents, and other adults, and in the process get educated out of unrestrained selfishness. We acquire a conscience and are thereafter kept in check by it. This way of thinking about morality does not close the gap between *physis* and *nomos*, between nature and morality; it does not show that if we follow nature we shall be just. It therefore does not achieve what Plato seeks. On Glaucon's view, morality is artificial, and a human invention; it may well be the most important of all inventions, because it underpins other great inventions on which our safety and happiness depend—the institutions of politics, government, and law. Plato held that morality was inscribed in the natural order; he despised the Sophist view that nature was amoral, that men were selfish by nature, and that law—*nomos*—was a matter of convention. How far this view was common to the Sophists is unclear; it would be surprising if no Sophist had anticipated Aristotle's middle way by arguing that man was a creature whose nature was to live by conventions. The difficulty of resting justice on convention is evidently that we need some explanation of how it is that we are disposed to abide by conventions to which we have agreed. Modern writers[13] suggest that we have had a sense of fairness programmed into us by evolution, and point to the fact that most primates appear to react to "unfairness" much as we do. Evolutionary theory was two and a half millennia in the future when Plato wrote *Republic*. He tackles the Sophists head-on.

Socrates persuades Glaucon and Adeimantus that the nature of justice will be easier to see *en gros* if we look at justice in a polis, and they set out to describe a well-made polis. Society rests on the division of labor—an idea that Plato shares with Marx and many others, but that is at odds with the Stoic view that society springs from natural sociability and that we unite for the sake of one another's company. Plato's picture is more utilitarian, though it resonates with contemporary evolutionary theory. It also embodies his view of justice as "sticking to one's last." In the simplest society, each does what he is best at. We unite to get the benefits of specialization; if I am a good farmer and a terrible shoemaker, I shall walk more comfortably if I trade my wheat for the talented shoemaker's shoes. This suggests a more "consumerist" world than Plato is really looking for. He wants only minimal specialization, and his spartan, or Spartan, proclivities swiftly emerge; self-sufficiency is easier to attain if our tastes are frugal. Glaucon protests that the society that Socrates describes lives like pigs; Socrates retorts by arguing that societies inevitably move swiftly from the search for modest comfort to the greed and self-aggrandizement that brings endless wars for the acquisition of territory and wealth. Leaving this thought to do its work, Socrates switches the argument to the centerpiece of *Republic*. If prosperity means warfare and we must be ready to fight in self-defense, we need soldiers; if we need soldiers, we need good, well-trained soldiers. We need soldiers who protect their own people and attack only their enemies, and do not set up exploitative regimes at home. We need soldiers who *know* whom to protect and whom to attack. Good guard dogs know how to do that, says Socrates. Good guard dogs are therefore philosophers; their human equivalent must be philosophers. We are at the point where *Republic* becomes a treatise on education.

Guardians and Their Education

In two pages, Socrates launches the most famous of all defenses of meritocracy and the best-known discussion of political education: a well-ordered polis requires a division of labor that yields a ruling elite that provides military defense when its members are young and social management in their mature years, provided by those with the greatest aptitude for philosophical study who will have had ten years of mathematics and five of dialectics. It perhaps should be said in passing that Plato's Academy was attended by men who shared few or none of his political views and went off to govern states possessing a variety of political arrangements. There were a very few women students, too. In *kallipolis* all will specialize in what they are best suited to do. Their skills will be based on natural talent, but they need development, and the education of an elite based on natural talent is the most important task the state has to perform. Those who dislike Plato complain that almost his first move is to expel all poets and artists from his polis. Even those who do not dislike him flinch. Plato's case is simple; the first stage of education is what the Greeks called "music"—*mousike* is wider in scope than "music" and includes dance, poetry, and celebratory ritual. Like Socrates, Plato thought early training had a profound impact on the souls of children, and he wanted it to instill courage and a regard for truth. Socrates died for saying that traditional Greek poetry defamed the gods by depicting them as lecherous, deceitful, vain, and worse. Neither denied the beauty of Greek poetry, and Plato was himself a considerable poet, but he thought most art was a form of attractive lying. Lying has no place in the philosophical state—a proposition the critical reader might think comes awkwardly from the inventor of the idea of "the Golden Lie"—so the poets will be garlanded and loaded with honors, escorted to the city boundaries, and sent to ply their trade elsewhere. There will be poetry, drama, and dance in early education, but it will be on decidedly Spartan principles.

Plato's understanding of art is not our subject, except in this respect. Plato's theory of knowledge, on which the arguments of *Republic* depend, explained the empirical world of everyday appearance as a distorted picture of the world of Truth. True knowledge is knowledge of the world of the Forms, the essences that make things what they are; they are unchanging and eternal, in contrast to the transitory objects we find around us. This is explained in the Allegory of the Cave that features in Plato's explanation of why philosophers will not wish to rule, and why they cannot rule in states as they are actually constituted. Art is a double misrepresentation, since it paints deceitful pictures of what is already a deceitful picture. It is an engaging feature of Plato's argument that he uses all the artful devices of the poets and painters in arguing against their activities. It is not merely that he employs every rhetorical device he possesses in the course of denouncing rhetoric; he does it so blatantly that he leaves readers at a loss to know what to take literally and what to read as ironic. One deeply disconcerting issue is that Plato, like Socrates, thought that if we did attain knowledge of the True, the Good, and the Beautiful, we would not be able to *say* what we knew. It seems that we must inevitably rely on allegories, parables, devices that point us toward the truth, but do not literally say what it is. More than once, in other dialogues, Socrates says that it is not he who is speaking but a force beyond his control, and in *Republic* his discussion of philosophical truth is invariably allegorical and contrastive, emphasizing its difference from empirical conjecture. We know more about what it is *not* than about what it *is*.

So far as the education of the ruling class is concerned, Plato seems to be wholly in earnest in his proposals, especially in his proposal that women should receive exactly the same education as men. One reason for taking him quite literally lies in the instructions for training young Spartans ascribed to Lycurgus. That was a more militarized version of the subjection of the individual child to the needs of the state than Plato puts forward, but the thrust of the training was the same: the unceasing repetition of lessons in self-discipline for the sake of political unity. What Plato puts forward in *Republic* echoes what Lycurgus was credited with creating in Sparta; and it is not hard to believe that someone whose family was attached to the pro-Spartan oligarchy that emerged at the end of the Peloponnesian War would have been attracted to Sparta's educational practice—except, and it is a very large exception, that in *Republic* it culminates in an education in philosophy, not in the creation of a hoplite infantry happy to die where it stood. What Plato's readers made of *Republic* is unknown, and impossible to guess. On the face of it, he was rash to put forward ideas with such an unmistakably Spartan ring. Athens continued to fight Sparta on and off in the fourth century as it had done in the fifth, and no Athenian democrat would forget that Plato's relatives had been members of the savage oligarchy installed by Sparta in 404.

Nonetheless, Plato did not despise the arts. Because they have such a powerful effect, he tried to ensure that they preached the right message: that the gods are always good and always virtuous. Some of his injunctions seem ludicrous, such as the prohibition on allowing children to play the roles of cowards and weaklings for fear it will rot their characters; but these strictures are squarely Spartan in origin and in line with the views of Cato the Censor and Jean-Jacques Rousseau among later writers. We are asked to imagine an education that will first inculcate virtue through a tightly constrained syllabus of poetry and drama, and will then take the young men and women and train them in gymnastics and the arts of warfare. It is worth emphasizing that girls will receive the same training; that was another un-Athenian but not un-Spartan thought. What counted for Plato was *character*; a person's sex was immaterial, though the Spartans did not expect women to fight alongside men. Eventually, the most apt will receive the philosophical training that will enable them to rule wisely and justly in utopia.

In arguing for the necessity of training a virtuous elite, Plato presents two arguments. The first concerns the different kinds of soul that human beings possess, and sets out the "Golden Lie" that citizens will be taught as an allegorical account of the hierarchy of talent; the second argument draws on the first and eventually yields the answer to the questions of what justice *is*. We must think of souls as bronze, silver, and golden; the possessors of bronze souls are the workers, of silver the soldiers—what Plato calls auxiliaries—and of golden souls the guardians, the philosopher-kings. He imagines a flawlessly meritocratic system for selecting the elite and proposes elaborate mechanisms to ensure that elite parents breed elite children; but he also expects ordinary people to need a picture of its basis that they can readily grasp. Readers of Aldous Huxley's *Brave New World* will recognize the ambition; "I'm awfully glad I'm a Beta," says the antenatally conditioned worker, who thinks the Alphas are much too clever and work terribly hard.[14] Bertrand Russell thought that Huxley had stolen the idea of brave new world from him; Russell feared that modern science would enable mankind to destroy itself in a new and terminal world war, and he looked to eugenic science to produce a pacified population. Huxley produces a ghastly parody of utopia. It makes all the difference in the world that Plato did not think that his elite was conditioning the people into believing that they were naturally what they had been genetically engineered into being. Plato's myth is a "golden" lie because it contains a deep truth. So we shall tell the populace that we are born with various metals in our souls and that our social position reflects the preponderance of these metals. This is the Golden Lie, the necessary myth. Plato does not argue for the assumption that makes the Golden Lie a deeper truth: the existence of a cosmic symmetry between the order of the ideal society and the order of nature. He assumes as a premise that we are naturally suited to different sorts of social roles, and that one of many things wrong with democratic Athens is that the wrong people end up occupying positions of power.

What reconciles *physis* and *nomos* is the thought that we can create a society whose social structure mirrors the natural harmony of the universe. It is an axiom of Plato's philosophy that we can be happy and fulfilled when we occupy a social position that reflects, or encapsulates, the position that our innate character fits us to occupy. Absent this vision of a harmonious natural hierarchy, the argument of *Republic* loses its appeal. Meritocracy is attractive if we believe both that society will be properly led only when natural leaders are in charge and that the rank and file will be happier in a subordinate position than in positions of power and responsibility. This provided another reason for combating the views of Callicles and Thrasymachus; they assumed that everyone would wish to exercise power, because everyone would wish to enjoy the payoffs from doing so. The rowers in the fleet hoped to profit from successful wars on their neighbors and valued their political power in the Assembly because it enabled them to force a warlike policy on their leaders. They failed to display the virtue of temperance that Plato thinks especially appropriate to the working classes. Writing two thousand years later, in the aftermath of the English Civil War, Thomas Hobbes, who translated Thucydides and was himself deeply hostile to democracy, made the revolutionary claim that we are by nature equal, not unequal, that there is no natural aristocracy, no natural division into workers and rulers, and that *all* political hierarchy is a contrivance.[15] We should give unhesitating obedience to our rulers, for the sake of peace, not because they were given us by nature. But Plato's cosmology was shared by Aristotle and other classical writers; it subsequently reinforced Christian ideas about the divine ordering of the universe and was reinforced by them, with obvious implications for social and political order.

Plato's case could be made differently. It could be argued as a flatly sociological proposition that a polis—or a modern state—functions best when there is a clear class structure with powerless workers, a military caste that knows its business, and an educated governing class whose right to rule is taken for granted. It would not be impossible to present modern China as evidence in favor of the thought. This is a sociological claim that needs no philosophical backing beyond the empirical evidence. If it is true at all, it is a truth of social science. Conversely, such a perfectly structured society can be presented as a dystopia rather than a utopia, something to avoid at all costs. In *Brave New World* Aldous Huxley created just that.

Justice Defined

With our three class structure before us, we can now see justice itself. The cardinal virtues are temperance, courage, reason, and justice, and we know which class embodies which. The virtue appropriate to the workers is temperance; they are, as it were, the stomach of the society, looking after its fleshly aspect, keeping it in operation as a physical enterprise. Their virtue is self-control. The virtue appropriate to the auxiliaries is courage; they are the heart of the society, and must be brave hearts. The virtue appropriate to the guardians is wisdom; they are the society's mind, and the virtue of the mind is wisdom. The discovery of three classes and three virtues seems to have exhausted the discussion; where, then, is justice? The answer is that justice is the overarching virtue that governs the whole. When all are in their proper place and each person and each class does its proper job and no other, there is justice.

This strikes us—modern readers—as implausible, because we think of justice as one among several virtues, whereas Plato uses the term to mean something very like "overall rightness." We have already seen that

the Greek *dike* embraces more than our idea of justice; Aristotle took
pains to distinguish two kinds of justice, one embracing overall rightness and the other justice in the narrower and more usual sense. The
view that there may be a conflict between justice and mercy, for example,
involves the narrower sense and not the wider sense with which Plato is
concerned. In the wider sense there cannot be a conflict between justice
and mercy; the "right" outcome is the "just" outcome. Plato believed
that the ultimate criterion of "rightness" is that our souls are in order,
that we are acting as our nature requires, contributing as we should to
the order of the universe and of society. Nothing could be more at odds
with modern liberalism.

Socrates's case for a philosophically based dictatorship is not a
defense of aristocratic rule in the ordinary sense. The rulers get no
earthly rewards from ruling, and exercising power is an exercise in self-
abnegation. Readers of *Republic* have always been struck by the details of
the domestic lives of Plato's ruling elite and how bleak their lives appear.
Plato's guardians have no property; they have no families. Their children
are the children of the whole class; Plato argues that in the absence of
money or private property they will see the whole polis as "theirs" and
will think only in collective terms. There will be no "I" and "mine,"
only "we" and "ours." Their interests are subservient to the interests
of the whole, not vice versa. Glaucon and Adeimantus wonder whether
the guardians can be happy, and Socrates has to take two bites at the
answer—first, that the happiness of the guardians is less significant than
that of the whole society; second, that they will be happy because they
will be fulfilling their natures in doing their duty. Aristotle thought
neither answer would do.

This is the moment to emphasize again the *unpolitical* or *antipolitical*
nature of these thoughts about justice. There are two crucial thoughts
about justice that Plato refuses to entertain, the first about the rule of law,
and the second about political competition. The first holds that a major
reason for the existence of government is to ensure that individuals are
treated justly: that they are not robbed or assaulted, that their property
is secure, and that their lives are regulated by rules rather than the whims
of the powerful. Law vanishes in Plato's *Republic*. Once philosopher-kings

rule, the conflicts that law regulates vanish. So therefore does a central aspect of justice. A second and related sense of justice in political contexts concerns the fair allocation of power—whether the wellborn or the many should rule, for instance. That question is answered by Plato: philosophers must rule, and nobody can have any interest in having his affairs run by the ignorant and ill informed, even if that includes himself. The idea that "the many" might have a legitimate interest in running their own lives just because they wish to is not one Plato entertains. This is an *unpolitical* politics, because the idea of legitimate but conflicting interests has no place. The task of the rulers is to know what the correct allocation of tasks and rewards is, and to institute it.

Last Thoughts

Much of the last two-thirds of *Republic* is a fabulously interesting exposition of Plato's metaphysical convictions; these are not directly relevant here, and we must neglect them. But three later arguments concern us. The first is why philosophers can and must rule, the second why the perfect state cannot endure forever, and the third Plato's final attempt to show that the just man is always happier than the unjust man. The rule of the philosopher is required because Plato has turned the ordinary political argument in favor of stability into a philosophical argument about the need to create a polis that reflects the order of nature. Since it is a philosophical skill to discern the divine order, the polis can be perfected only when put under the aegis of philosophy. For unphilosophical readers, the interest of the argument lies less in the details of Plato's ideas about the natural order than in the similarity between his argument for the rule of the philosopher and later arguments in favor of assorted kinds of theocratic government.

If the premise is accepted that the crucial task of politics is to align the social, economic, and political order with a divinely appointed natural order, a central role must be found for whoever understands that order, if not as the day-to-day ruler of a society, then as a spiritual guardian of the day-to-day ruler. How that authority is to be exercised is a question that roiled medieval Christendom and remains unanswered in the Muslim world. In medieval Europe the question whether popes could depose kings was one aspect of it; in the modern world Iran is an avowed theocracy, while Israel is avowedly but uneasily not one. Britain has an established church but is strikingly more secular than the United States, whose Constitution prohibits any establishment of religion, but whose politicians compete assiduously for the votes of the devout. Plato's answer was that philosophers must be kings and kings must be philosophers. One major difficulty was that on his own showing, philosophers would be unwilling to do the job. In the Allegory of the Cave, Plato likens the human condition to that of men sitting in a dark cave able to see only directly ahead; on the wall in front of them are the flickering shadows cast by people walking behind them, and these shadows will be taken for reality. Out of the cave, the philosopher is first dazzled by the sun, then sees things as they are. Will the philosopher who has engaged in a long and arduous search for Truth and has finally found it really be willing to return to the world of illusion? Surely not. Such reluctance is highly desirable, because government is best entrusted to men who are not consumed by ambition. On the other hand, it suggests that, outside utopia, philosophers may not be successful rulers.

In utopia government will not be complicated. A defect of Plato's utopia in the eyes of critics, but a virtue in the eyes of Plato himself, is that nothing much happens. It is too poor to excite the greed of neighbors, and its soldiers are tough enough to deter them; because everyone is doing what nature fits him to do, nobody will have any desire to do anything different, and novel tastes will be unknown. The guardians will organize the breeding of the ruling elite in such a way that the right people are born into the right positions—just what the calculations are that they perform and how they do it, Plato sadly leaves mysterious, although he gestures toward some barely intelligible equations. So long as they get the calculations right, timeless tranquillity rules.

Two large questions about the common, or "bronze-souled," people remain. One is whether they live just lives. We may think that they cannot, because their souls are of bronze, and their guiding virtue is therefore temperance; we may equally think that they do, because if they occupy the right social position and do what persons like themselves are intended to do, they live rightly or justly. They stick to their lasts. With both thoughts in mind, we may suppose that they *share* in justice, but not as fully as the philosopher does; even this may strike some of us as a repulsive conclusion in suggesting that moral capacity is class related. The other large question is what the common people do. The answer appears to be that they live as they would anywhere else, but undisturbed by political uproar. They do not have to fight; they cannot take part in politics, not least because there is none to take part in. Presumably, they farm, engage in handicrafts, look after their families, and are uncomplicatedly happy because they are secure and not out of their depth. They are not the helots of Messenia kept down by the brutality of Spartan overlords, but an invisible laboring class.

Decaying States

If utopia could be created, surely it would endure forever. Not so, says Plato. Something will go wrong. The mathematics of procreation may be miscalculated, or some other cause may lead to the guardians' losing their skills or commitment, and a cycle of political change would begin. Decay follows a cyclical path. First, honor supersedes wisdom as the basis of authority; the wise elite will become a "timocracy," or an aristocracy based on honor; this in turn will degenerate into an oligarchy where rich men oppress their inferiors. The timocracy is Sparta, as the text itself makes clear; this is the second-best state, moving away from perfection rather than toward it. Just as our souls mirror the condition of utopia, so the soul of the timocratic man will mirror the values of the timocratic state. The same will be true of oligarchy and the oligarchs; they are degenerate timocrats who have replaced the search for honor with the search for wealth. The oligarchical state is not one state but two, the state of the rich and the state of the poor, at war with each other. The inevitable revolution ushers in democracy.

The principle of democracy is freedom, and Plato is unabashedly hostile to it. The Athenian concept of political or democratic freedom was *isegoria*, or the equal right of all qualified citizens to speak in the Assembly; the term *eleutheria* had the more general meaning of having no master, not being enslaved. It was *eleutheria* that the Greeks defended against the Persians, and *isegoria* that Athenian democrats thought they particularly possessed. Plato complains that democracy is the rule of pure license, where everyone does just what he pleases. Slaves are insolent, and donkeys jostle citizens on the sidewalks. Finally it leads to the lowest point of the cycle when its excesses alienate the better-off and powerful and lead to the rise of the tyrant. Tyranny, the worst of all forms of government, might be transcended if the tyrant was somehow to become a philosopher and begin the cycle anew. Other than in utopia, philosophers should keep clear of politics, but perhaps a philosopher might teach the child of a tyrant to be a philosopher-king. When Plato went to Syracuse to try the experiment, he barely escaped with his life.

The enthusiasm for cyclical theories of history is a recurrent feature of the history of political thinking. They have little to be said for them as contributions to the analysis of political change, but Plato's cyclical story served other purposes. His account of "timocracy" is a nod toward Sparta, as if Sparta is far from perfect but only in the first stage of degeneration; that timocracies degenerate when aristocrats become obsessed with money was true enough of Sparta, and the distinction between the rule of the better sort and the rule of the greedy rich needed little elaboration to a Greek audience. The description of democracy as a regime addicted to liberty, where everyone does exactly as he pleases is mostly simple abuse of Athens and wholly unfair; it was, however, common coin in upper-class complaints, with Plato's complaints sounding very like those of the author known as "the Old Oligarch." It is also an inadvertent tribute to Pericles's account of the city whose citizens did not feel that they had to mind everyone else's business because they had interesting lives of their own to get on with. Plato's assault also fails in the eyes of modern readers because it makes Athenian democracy sound like such fun. It is the account of tyranny that we must take most seriously; for it provides Plato with the final vital link in his case for preferring justice to injustice.

Plato's premise is that the souls of the citizens mirror the character of the state. Democratic citizens are half-crazy with a passion for novel-ties, never making up their minds what to do, and never sticking with a decision; hence the disasters of the Peloponnesian War, and hence the imprudent overreaching that led to the war in the first place. The tyrant is Thrasymachus's hero, the man who can do whatever he likes because nobody can stop him. Plato paints a wonderful picture of the true horror of his situation. He can ascend to power only by murder and deception; and the maintenance of his rule depends upon exciting fear in his sub-jects. That means that he also excites hatred. He is, and knows he is, an enemy to the world and the world is an enemy to him. He cannot have a moment's peace of mind. His food may be poisoned; he may be stabbed in the night; old friends he has not murdered on his way to the top may turn out to be the assassins he fears. His life is not worth living, and he will probably meet the fate he fears sooner rather than later. The tyrant's life is a bad bargain even in this-worldly terms. As always, the critical reader will complain that Plato paints an exaggerated picture, but that is hardly the main point.

Plato concludes, first with an oddly interpolated rehearsal of the quarrel between philosophy and poetry, and then, as at the end of *Gorgias*, with an account of the fate of the just and the unjust man in the afterlife, where their souls will finally be assessed and they will receive their eternal rewards. This is where the ultimate payoff for the just and unjust life is received. Cicero built on the passage for "Scipio's Dream" in book 6 of *De republica*, to suggest that the Roman statesman who serves his republic unswervingly will be blessed with immortality, and Scipio's Dream served as the launchpad for discussions of reincarnation and the compatibility of Christian and Platonic cosmology for many centuries. There is, however, little to be said about the bearing of the myth of Er in the narrow context of the ostensible argument of *Republic* other than that it shows that Plato fails to answer Thrasymachus's challenge, or that if he has met Thrasymachus's challenge, he has not met Glaucon's: he has failed to show that a cool, calm, and collected tyrant (supposing such a person to be psychologically possible) would do worse *in this world* than his victims. As Immanuel Kant observed, we hanker for an afterlife pre-cisely because virtue and happiness are so poorly correlated in this life.

More to the point in political terms, perhaps, is that although Plato fails on that score, as he surely must, he is entirely persuasive on the worthlessness of the tyrant's life. Contemplating the lives of Hitler and Stalin, we are not moved by envy; and that is enough to defeat Thrasymachus, if not to prove Socrates's case, which in its own fashion is as extreme as Thrasymachus's.

The final thought that *Republic* inspires is that Plato's account of the ideal polity belongs to soul craft rather than to statecraft; it is not a picture of political life at all. There is no economic life to regulate, no crime to suppress, no conflicting interests to balance, no competing views on policy to reconcile, no conflicts of value to assuage, accommodate, or suppress. To the question "How can we live together in spite of not being of one mind about so many important matters?" Plato's answer is to deny the premise. "Let us always be of only one mind about all important questions" is the response. *Brave New World* is a parodic commentary on the corrupt form the Platonic utopia would take in the twentieth century; Hobbes's *Leviathan* is an exploration of how far we must *make* ourselves agree if there is to be peace. From Aristotle onward, it has been recognized that Plato did not so much solve the problem of establishing a just polity as dissolve it. Plato's genius was, in part, to show so clearly how far our hankering after harmony—and how could we not hanker after harmony?—is at odds with making everyday politics work more productively. Pursuing that point, Aristotle set out to show what sort of justice we might achieve in a nonutopian polity, and to him we now turn.

CHAPTER 3

Aristotle: Politics Is Not Philosophy

Life and Times

UNLIKE PLATO, ARISTOTLE WAS embroiled in the politics of his day; indeed, he died in exile because the Athenians suspected his loyalty when they revolted against Macedonian rule in 323 BCE. He tutored Alexander the Great and was the father-in-law of Antipater, the Macedonian general whom Alexander installed as regent to keep Greece in order when he left to conquer the Persian Empire in 334. The ancient historians do not suggest Aristotle was devoted to his former pupil; Plutarch credits him with supplying the poison that may or may not have been the cause of Alexander's untimely death. (It was rumored that Antipater feared that Alexander had turned against him and was likely to have him executed; so Antipater preempted him.) Aristotle was born in 384 in the small town of Stagira, on the borders of Greece and Macedon—slightly east of the modern Salonica. He came to Athens in 367 to join Plato's Academy and spent the next twenty years there. The forty-five years between his arrival in Athens and his death in 322 saw Athens's revival after the destruction of the Peloponnesian War, and then the extinction of the Greek city-states' political independence following their defeat by Macedonian forces, first at the Battle of Chaeronea in 338 and when the death of Alexander the Great in 323 prompted Athens to revolt, at the naval battle of Amorgos in 322.

Aristotle's career at the Academy suffered a hiatus after the death of Plato. He and his friend Xenocrates left Athens when the Academy fell under the leadership of men whom Aristotle disliked. He spent time on Lesbos, where he was supported by the tyrant Hermias, a former slave of great ability who had gone on to buy the rulership of the city of Atarneus from the king of Persia. Hermias had spent time at the Academy and was reputedly an excellent philosopher; Aristotle later married Hermias's niece, after her uncle had been tortured and executed on the orders of the great king on suspicion of plotting to assist a Macedonian invasion of Persia. Whether Hermias brought Aristotle to the attention of Philip of Macedon is unclear, but in 342 Aristotle was summoned to Pella to become tutor to the young Alexander, a position he filled until 336. It must soon have been a part-time post, since as early as 340 Alexander was governing Macedonia in his father's absence, while two years later he commanded part of his father's army at the Battle of Chaeronea.

In 335 Aristotle returned to Athens to found his own school, the Lyceum. This was in the immediate aftermath of the second unsuccessful revolt of the Athenians against Macedonian rule. Surprisingly, neither Philip nor Alexander meted out to the Athenians the punishment meted out to Thebes, which was razed to the ground. Demosthenes, the most intransigent leader of the anti-Macedonian elements, was allowed to remain in Athens and not forced into exile. Xenocrates was now head of the Academy, but there is no suggestion that Aristotle set up in competition with his friend. There was no disloyalty in establishing his own school, and his school had a distinctive character. It was marked by an enthusiasm for empirical investigation; among other things, Aristotle founded the empirical discipline of politics by setting his students to describe and analyze 158 Greek constitutions. The "naturalism" of Aristotle's philosophy struck a balance between what we would recognize as a scientific, empirical, experimental approach to understanding the world, and a more nearly religious approach that regarded nature as the source of a beauty and order that human contrivance could not match. One result is that his political analysis is an engrossing mixture of practical wisdom and an almost Platonic attempt to show that the best state is best "by nature."

Aristotle's life in Athens after his return was not tranquil. The majority of Athenians were bitterly hostile to the hegemony of Macedon. Athenian politics until Demosthenes's death by suicide in 322 was dominated by the question of whether and how far the hegemony of Macedon could be resisted. Antipater was as unpopular as the head of an army of occupation is likely to be; and Aristotle felt himself not only a foreigner but an unwelcome one. The awkwardness was for a time reduced by Aristotle's friendship with Lycurgus, a student of both Plato and Isocrates, and now in charge of the finances of Athens and the upkeep of the city; Lycurgus was a nominal democrat and an ally of Demosthenes, but was the sort of moderate aristocratic politician praised in his *Politics*, who safeguarded the economic interests of the propertied classes and ensured they were kept friendly to the democratic constitution. Nonetheless, Aristotle's position eventually became untenable. In June 323 Alexander's unexpected death in Babylon at the age of thirty-two, whether from malaria, liver failure, or poison, provoked open revolt. Aristotle retired to Chalcis, on Euboea. He died there a year later, just as Antipater's victory at Amorgos destroyed Athenian hopes of recovering political and military independence.

Aristotle's Political Prejudices

Modern readers find several of Aristotle's views deeply repugnant. The two most obvious are his views on slavery and his views on the intellectual and political capacity of women.[1] Unsurprisingly, these are connected. The relation of master to inferior—of the male head of household to wife and slaves—is a basic and natural human relationship. For Aristotle the household of a man qualified to be a citizen is a family unit where slaves do the menial work: menial work unfits a man for political life; slaves and common laborers liberate the citizen for political life. The head of a household governs his family partly politically and partly not. The relation of citizen to citizen is that of equal to equal. The relation of master to slave, husband to wife, or parent to child is not one between equals, although wives are certainly free persons, whereas slaves are not.[2] Fathers exercise "royal" rule over children and "constitutional" rule over wives, but there is no suggestion that husbands and wives take turns in governing the household as citizens do the polity. We shall see how Aristotle argues for the justice of these relationships. It is worth pausing to notice two things. The first is the alarming suggestion that the acquisition of slaves is a branch of the art of war or hunting.[3] The ancient world was heavily dependent on slavery; and there were states, or pirate kingdoms, that regarded "man hunting" as a legitimate business and their own distinctive way of making a living. For villagers living within reach of their raids or for anyone forced to travel a long distance by sea, the danger of being seized and sold into slavery was very real. Aristotle suggests ways of regulating the practice of seizing captives in war and selling them into slavery, but the practice itself he does not criticize. Since he admits that many writers think slavery is unjust and contrary to nature, he certainly had the chance to do so.

The second thing to notice is that when Aristotle seeks a justification in the natural order for the existence of slavery, he appeals to the gulf in the capacity for self-government that—in his view—separates natural slaves from their masters. What he made of Hermias, the former slave, who was one of his students as well as his protector, a man to whom he dedicated a memorial and whose niece he married after her uncle's untimely death, one can only imagine. Hermias's last words were said to have been "I have done nothing unworthy of a philosopher." Along the same lines, Aristotle maintains that women are rational enough to fulfill the subordinate role in the family that he assigns to them, but have too little rational capacity to give their own independent judgment in the political arena. Women, slaves, and children belong within the well-ordered household, not in the agora or *ecclesia*. It is worth considering why readers are so often outraged that Aristotle held views that were entirely commonplace in the ancient Greek world. It is surely because so much of what he writes is strikingly down-to-earth and shows an attention to how politics is in fact conducted that is quite absent from Plato's sweeping rejection of political life in toto. Aristotle talked to many intelligent women and had every chance to change his mind; he had every opportunity to reflect on what the existence of Hermias implied for the justice of slavery. In short, modern readers might think that the remedy for Aristotle's blind spots is a more diligent application of the empirical methods he himself advocated.

Teleology: Nature and Politics

Aristotle would have been unmoved by our anachronistic advice. His conception of "nature" was not like ours, and the search for the natural order of things was not straightforwardly empirical. Hermias was transparently not a "slave by nature," but that did not mean there were no slaves by nature. Aristotle famously wrote that "it is evident that the state is a creation of nature, and that man is by nature a political animal."[4] We must, therefore, start from Aristotle's idea of nature. Aristotle is known for the doctrine of the four causes: the matter of what is to be explained; its form; the efficient cause, or how it is produced; and its final cause. The behavior of entities such as plants, animals, persons, and institutions was explained by their telos, or "end"—their goal or purpose or point. This is teleological explanation, explanation in terms of goals or purposes. The scientific revolution of the seventeenth century expelled teleological explanation from the physical sciences. Our idea of a physical cause is essentially that of the antecedent conditions that make something happen; we do not think that there is some state of affairs "proper" to physical nature, and the modern conception of nature is thus very different from Aristotle's. We use the term "natural" to describe the way things are when not affected by human contrivance—think of "natural blonde"—but Aristotle included human contrivance among the things that had their "natural" and their "unnatural" forms. A society like our own, where women have equal political rights with men, is "unnatural." "Natural" forms of life were good because they fulfilled their natural purpose. Today this Aristotelian view survives in the teaching of the Roman Catholic Church, where it is underpinned by the thought that God is the author of nature and that natural law and divine law reinforce each other. Aristotle did not think in terms of a deity who authored nature; nature itself was divine. He is therefore very exposed to the skeptical view that "natural" and "unnatural" are synonyms for "usual" and "unusual," or for "morally good" and "morally bad."

Throughout his *Politics* it is taken for granted that nature is the ground of social norms. When Aristotle asks whether there are slaves "by nature," he wants to know whether there are persons whose proper place in the world is to serve as slaves to others. If there are, it explains *both* why there is slavery *and* why it is good for (natural) slaves to be slaves. Discovering what is "natural" uncovers both the way things are and how they should be. Moreover, nature is hierarchical; everything aims at some good, and the highest things aim at the highest good. Human beings are at the top of the hierarchy of living creatures, and we must understand human behavior in the light of how we are meant to pursue the highest good. Allowances made for his prejudices, Aristotle did not simply impose a model of the good polity upon the evidence; investigating the way people do govern themselves shows how they should govern themselves.

The way to discover what nature aims to achieve is to observe what nature actually does. Nature does not always achieve the good she aims at: there are stunted trees, sickly children, unhappy marriages, and states that collapse into civil war. But we discover the standards embodied in words such as "stunted" and "diseased" by looking at what happens when things turn out well. Political science is thus a form of natural history with a strongly normative flavor. Aristotle set out the standards that explanation has to meet in his *Physics*, and they remained canonical for two millennia. The four kinds of cause—form, matter, purpose, and origin—all have their place in political analysis. The form of a state is its constitution, its matter is its citizens, its purpose is to allow us to live the best life in common, the cause of its coming into being appears from the first chapters of *Politics* to be the search for self-sufficiency; and Aristotle's discussion of revolution in later books of *Politics* is both an account of the causes of a state's ceasing to be and an account of the causes of its persistence as a going concern.

Aristotle did not share Plato's belief that all real knowledge must resemble geometry or mathematics. Plato condemned the world of sense as a poor shadow of reality. Sufficiently fine measurement will show that no equilateral triangle drawn by human hands is *perfectly* equilateral; measured sufficiently precisely, one side will be greater than another and the angles of the sides unequal. For Plato the empirical world itself was a botched copy of a transempirical reality; geometry studies perfect geometrical figures. Aristotle did not impugn the world of observation. The world is as we perceive it, though our senses can sometimes deceive us; a man with jaundice will see things as yellow when they are not. Successful explanation should "save the appearances"; it must explain why the world we see, hear, feel, taste, and smell appears as it does. In the seventeenth century Galileo, among others, persuaded his contemporaries that the earth rotated about the sun. Although he overturned Aristotelian astronomy and physics, he professed himself a disciple of Aristotle and accepted the obligation to explain why it *looked* as though the sun moved around the earth. He rejected much of Aristotle's physics—Aristotle thought the earth was truly the center of the universe—but he accepted Aristotle's claim that a successful explanation must explain why things look the way they do.

The study of politics is a form of natural history. Thomas Hobbes loathed Aristotle's politics, and in *Leviathan* followed Plato in modeling politics on geometry; but he admired Aristotle's biology. One consequence of that "biological" style is important, not only because it was at odds with Hobbes's—and Plato's—hankering after political geometry. Aristotle claimed that political analysis should aim only "at as much precision as the subject matter permits." Political wisdom cannot aspire to the precision of geometry, and must not pretend to. Aboriculture suggests an analogy: most trees grow best in firm soil with a moderate water supply; a few thrive with their roots in mud and water. Scientists achieve deeper understanding by analyzing the differences between the trees that do the one and those that do the other. This may or may not assist the farmer, and Aristotle's writings on ethics and politics suggest that it is the farmer's needs—which is to say, in politics, the statesman's and citizen's needs—that are important. In ethics and politics we seek knowledge for the sake of action. Aristotle complains that Plato treated all knowledge as if it served the same goals, but in ethics and politics we seek the truth for the sake of knowing what to do. They are practical disciplines. We try to improve our ethical understanding by reflecting on the way we praise and blame certain actions and characters and ways of life; but we do it to live better, not to gratify curiosity.

One final aspect of this view of nature and science matters to us. Most of us today begin by thinking about the rights or the needs of individuals, and ask what sort of state has a legitimate claim on their allegiance or will best promote their welfare. That is, the individual is—to use Aristotle's terminology—"prior" to the state. Not for Aristotle. The individual is intended by nature to live and thrive in a polis, so the polis is "prior" to the individual. This has the consequence that politics is the master science or the master art, since it aims to discover the conditions under which the best state can come into being and flourish. Just as the hand is explained by its role in enabling its owner, a human person, to flourish, the qualities of citizens are explained by their role in enabling the state to flourish. An analogy might be taken from the theater. Any actor longs to play Lear or Hamlet, the first because Lear is one of the greatest tragic heroes in all drama, and the second because every skill an actor might possess is needed to display Hamlet's agonies of indecision. King Lear and Prince Hamlet are characters in Shakespeare's plays. We understand them by understanding the plays. We understand citizens by understanding the polis, and just as any actor wishes to play Hamlet or Lear, any autonomous and intelligent being would wish to play the part of a citizen in an Aristotelian polis.

Ethics and *The Politics*

Aristotle claimed that the polis existed "by nature" because nature means us to live a good life in common. We must therefore start with his view of the good life; and because the central virtue of the polis is justice, we must see how different Aristotle's views of justice and of our motives for being just are from Plato's. In *Politics* Aristotle relies on the account of justice he gave in the *Nicomachean Ethics*. Ethics is the study of "living well." To know how to live well, we need to know the goal of human life, since knowing how well any activity has gone is a matter of knowing how far it has achieved its goal. Human life, says Aristotle, goes well when we achieve happiness, but only happiness of a certain sort, namely, happiness approved by reason. Only then are we exercising the capacities that nature intends us to exercise, and "living well." If I am a Mafia boss, and I have just murdered the entire family of a rival, men, women, and children alike, I may be happy; but I am happy because I have a vile character. No reasonable man wants to be made happy by a massacre.

Nature intends us to enjoy the happiness of a good person. This argument seems circular: we ask what the good life is and are told it is a happy life; we ask what happiness is and are told it is pleasure achieved in the right way by the right sort of person; we ask what the right sort of person is and are told it is someone who lives a life of virtue according to reason; and when we ask about the virtues, we are told that they are those habits of thought and action whose practice gives happiness to the person who has acquired the right kind of character. The argument is indeed circular but not viciously circular. To make progress, we must examine the particular virtues—reason, temperance, fidelity, courage, justice, and so on—and discover how they contribute to the good life. This is what Aristotle does. The fact that practicing the virtues can be shown to fit together in a well-conducted life gives Aristotle confidence in the framework. Once again it is worth noticing that our notions of morality and Aristotle's ideas about ethics are not quite on all fours. Many excellences that he thinks a well-found polis would encourage are not ones that we would call moral: being well-educated, having good taste, knowing how to bear ourselves in public. They are important in cementing a certain sort of social life, which is in turn important in preserving the cohesion of the polis, but they are not in the modern sense moral qualities.

Aristotle agrees with Plato that a successful polis must be built on justice, but his understanding of justice is not Plato's. The *Nicomachean Ethics* criticizes Plato for collapsing all the virtues into justice; Aristotle contrasts the justice that is one virtue among others with "justice" conceived of as virtue in general. "All-in rightness" is one thing; but justice in the usual sense is concerned with the distribution of goods and bads according to merit, giving everyone what is due. In a political context,

this means the distribution of authority and power according to political
virtue. A just state must have just inhabitants; states are just only if their
citizens lead just lives. It would be a defect in Plato's utopia if philosophers alone could be truly just. We must therefore be able to show that
an ordinary reasonable person can practice justice and will wish to do
so; but it is enough if such a person wishes to be just only under nonex-
traordinary conditions. *Republic* lost sight of the limits of argumentative
possibility in defending the view that justice profits its practitioners *no
matter what.* Plato's argument was heroic but unpersuasive because the conception of happiness to which he appealed in arguing that the just man is
inevitably happier than the unjust man is too unlike ordinary happiness;
Aristotle repairs the defects in Plato's case.

A just man will wish to be just as one aspect of living a good life.
It is rational to be just and to acquire a just character, but there can be
no guarantee that the just man will always do better than the unjust
man. Nature means the just to flourish, but a given individual may be
unlucky and be brought low by behaving well. A society of just persons
will always do better than a society of unjust persons, and a rational man
will wish to belong to such a society; but it cannot be guaranteed that
every individual in such a society will thrive. Doing justice comes more
easily when supported by the other virtues. A generous man will think
of his family and friends and wish them to live in a just society, and that
will make it easier for him to be just. Even the least-just person believes
in justice to the extent of wanting everyone else to behave justly: the bur-
glar does not wish to be burgled, nor the robber to be robbed. But a good
person wants to be just for its own sake. He is made happy by being just,
and being just is indispensable to the happiness he wants: he wants the
trust of his friends and the respect of his peers, and these are logically
connected with his being a just person, that is, the sort of person who
rightly excites trust and respect.

It can be difficult to see how right Aristotle is. If we think that the
deep truth about human beings is that they are self-centered "utility
maximizers," it is hard to see how they can interact except by treating
one another as a means to their own selfish happiness. This is the worldview of Polus, Callicles, and Thrasymachus. Aristotle did not think we

are the maximizers of anything in particular. We pursue many goals, each with its own point. There is still a hierarchy of goals: a rational man subordinates the search for worldly goods to the search for excellence of character, for instance. He hopes to be honored as such, and he will care very much what others think of him; but he is not only just instrumentally. "Greed is good" is not consistent with Aristotle's view, but each genuine good has its place in a well-conducted life. There is no *general* problem of the form "Why should essentially selfish creatures care about justice, honesty, or any other virtue that benefits other people rather than themselves?" The premise of the question is false.

Human beings seek their own well-being, but not always effectively. When they fail, something has gone wrong. What is good for us is *connected* with what we want, inasmuch as the well-balanced man wants what is good for himself. But what is good for us is not *defined* as what we want, as it was by Thrasymachus; the wrong wants (think of addiction to drugs or alcohol or gambling) are disconnected from the good. Misguided wants undermine the pursuit of our good. So does simple error, as when I drink poison, believing it to be a tonic, and die when I mean to restore my health. We may make more elaborate mistakes, as when we think that harshness toward defeated enemies will make them more cooperative rather than less, or jump to conclusions, as when we succeed once in intimidating our enemies and conclude that we shall always so succeed. Other mistakes stem from deficiencies in character; a coward misreads situations as being more dangerous than they in fact are, *and* fails to see the point of courage.

Political Analysis

The correct mode of political analysis seems inescapable. We should inspect whatever political regimes we can, and determine what makes for success and failure; we can distinguish corrupt governments from good governments; we can ascertain which regimes promote good political character and which the reverse; we can discover why different peoples adopt different kinds of regimes, and why what we call "politics" flourishes in some but not all societies. Aristotle sent students to discover the constitutional arrangements of Greek cities, although only *The Constitution of Athens* survives; it is itself something of a jumble and may or may not have been written by Aristotle himself rather than a student, but is fascinating nonetheless.

Politics consists of eight books, the two last very unlike their predecessors. These provide a picture of the ideal state and its educational system, a task that earlier books seemed to dismiss as a waste of time. They are also very incomplete; the final book amounts to a handful of pages devoted to the education of the young. The first six books form a well-organized argument; the first book distinguishes political associations from all others, and distinguishes their organizing principles from those of the family and the domestic household; the second discusses ideal states in theory and in practice; books 3 and 4 tackle the connected topics of forms of constitution and qualification for citizenship; and books 5 and 6 cover the connected topics of revolutionary upheaval and the construction of constitutional arrangements that will prevent or divert or defuse such upheaval.

Nonetheless, *Politics* is a sprawling work, and many issues come up for discussion more than once. The nature of citizenship is a running theme, for instance. It is discussed in the context of forms of authority in the first book, when citizen–citizen relations are distinguished from master–slave, husband–wife, parent–children relations; that launches the repudiation of Plato's model of the polity in the second book. Qualifications for citizenship are the topic of the third and fourth books, and that subject recurs in books 5 and 6 in the context of rethinking what sorts of people should have access to political power. The pleasures of brooding on these recurrent discussions are to be had by reading *Politics* slowly. What follows here selects rather brutally, with an eye to the discussion of Plato's *Republic*, and to what others made of Aristotle in the next two millennia. My discussion does not follow Aristotle's own sequence; it initially skirts book 2, in order to end with Aristotle's attack on ideal state theory in that book, and his later ventures into that field.[5]

Political Man

Almost at the beginning of his *Politics* Aristotle declares that man is a creature intended by nature to live in a polis. Before he does so, he makes three only slightly less famous observations. First, he claims that all associations exist for a purpose and that, as the most inclusive association, the polis exists for the most inclusive purpose. It is the ultimate form of human organization and exists to satisfy the highest goals of social life. Second, other associations need the shelter of a polis, but it requires no other association above it; it is self-sufficient and sustains a complete life for its members. Third, the correct way of governing such an association is peculiar to it; it alone should be governed "politically." Aristotle criticizes writers who conflate the authority of "statesmen"—constitutional rulers—with that of conquerors, husbands, fathers, or owners of slaves. Plato is the target. Authority in a polis is specific to it, not to be confused with authority in other relationships. A state is not a large family, and a family is not a small state. States may have begun as monarchies because they grew out of patriarchally governed clans; but if they grew out of clans, their goals are not a clan's goals. An association is to be understood in terms of its purpose rather than its origin; the purpose of the state is not that of a family or clan. The polis, he says, "grows for the sake of mere life, but it *exists* for the sake of a good life."

Aristotle has in mind the Greek city-state. Much of what he writes seems to be applicable to any state, and surprisingly often is; what he himself was concerned with was the successful functioning of the kind of state that the Athenians had created in the late sixth century, and its Greek peers. When he goes on to say that man is meant by nature to live in a polis, he means that the polis provides the environment in which human beings can best fulfill their potential and in which they can live the good life to the full. This appears on its face to contradict what he says elsewhere (and even in *Politics* itself) when claiming that the best of human lives is the philosopher's life of contemplation.[6] Aristotle has two plausible ways of resolving this tension, and his students would very likely have invoked both.

The first is to notice that few people will wish to follow the route that the philosopher follows. It may be true that *if* one has the tastes and aptitudes that philosophy demands, the life of the philosopher is uniquely fulfilling, and that nobody who has followed the life of the philosopher would wish to follow any other. Not many people have those tastes and aptitudes, and most people will find that the polis provides the environment in which they can lead the best life for them. Nor is this to say that they are "inferior" people. Their lives display virtues such as courage, justice, fidelity, honesty, and temperance; they live the best possible active rather than the best contemplative life. Nor is it a simple truth that the *vita contemplativa* is better than the *vita activa*, if it is a truth at all. The second move is to observe that the fulfillment of the philosopher is slightly odd. Aristotle claims that the man who does not need the polis is either a beast or a god; animals cannot form political societies, since they lack speech and reason, while gods are individually self-sufficient and do not need political association.[7] The philosopher aims to think God's thoughts, and if he succeeds, he also is so self-sufficient that the assessment of the success of his life escapes the usual categories. Whether this is a condition one would wish to be in, unless so irresistibly called to it as to have no choice in the matter, is a deep question not to be tackled here. It suggests yet again a tension between philosophy's search for absolutes and the political search for the modus vivendi, for ways of living together.

Aristotle devotes the first book of his *Politics* to following out the implications of this approach. Since a polis is an association of villages— he may have had in mind the demes of Athens—and a village is an association of households, he first analyzes the nature of households, with an eye to the relationship between economic and political life, always looking to differentiate the kind of authority exercised in these different spheres from political authority. Within the family, a male head governs women and children. Aristotle did not say that women were imperfect men, but he thought they were less well governed by their own reason than an educated man would be. It is therefore good for them to be governed by their husbands, and it would be bad for them to live public lives as male citizens do. A man exercises domestic authority as the head of a household, over wife, children, and slaves. As husband/father his authority is not based on force or exercised in his own narrow interests; his authority over slaves, however, is literally despotic: *despotis* means "master." The aim of his rule is to ensure that the family flourishes as a family. Aristotle bequeaths to posterity the thought that the extent and the nature of the authority that sustains human associations are determined by the functions for which the association exists, that is, by the nature of the association. Locke's analysis of the authority of government in his *Second Treatise*, published in 1690, relies on just this thought two millennia later; whether through Locke's influence or by some other route, the thought itself is enshrined in the American Constitution with its commitment to limited government, and the measuring of authority by the goals to be sought.[8]

Slavery

The insistence that authority follows function extends to the relationship that most troubles Aristotle's readers, slavery. Aristotle assumed that if a man (and it is only men he has in mind) was to have leisure to play a role in the political life of his society, slaves must do the manual labor that is beneath the dignity of citizens. The defenders of slavery in the antebellum American South sometimes relied on that argument, though they were more likely to draw on biblical than on philosophical inspiration, or simply to point to the miseries of "free labor" in the North, an argumentative resource not available to Aristotle. He very bleakly describes slaves as "animated tools," instruments to be set to work to achieve what their owners require of them. Greek slavery was mostly, but not always, less horrible than the plantation slavery of the southern United States and the Roman latifundia. It was easy for men, women, and children alike to end up enslaved after military defeat, with the result that many slaves were better educated than their owners, and the condition of household slaves was often tolerable. We may recall

Plato's complaint that in Athens one could not distinguish slaves from citizens, or the depiction of cheerfully idle household slaves in any of Aristophanes's comedies. The same could not be said of slaves working in the silver mines at Laurium, on which Athenian prosperity depended and where miners died of overwork and lead poisoning; but the Athenians had been on the receiving end of the same treatment when they were defeated at Syracuse and set to work in the Sicilian quarries, and they neither complained on their own behalf nor softened their treatment of others. Broad humanitarianism was no more current in the classical Greek world than in the Roman world.

The view that the slave is a living implement did not imply that the owner could do with a slave anything that he might do with a plow or a spade. It was rather that *if* the relationship between master and slave is founded in nature, the disparity between the intelligence of the master and that of the slave should be of such a degree that the slave has intelligence enough only to follow instructions, and needs the master's intelligence to direct him. It would be good if masters and slaves were physically unlike as well. Nature, says Aristotle, intends slaves to have strong but unattractive bodies meant for manual labor and their masters to have attractive and athletic but less strong bodies. Sadly, nature often fails.[9] Aristotle half admits that slavery is for the most part "conventional" and that many slaves, perhaps even most, may be wrongly enslaved. He avoids undermining slavery: slavery was necessary, if politics as Aristotle understood it was to be possible. If all went well, there could even be a form of friendship between master and slave, since the master would treat the slave in ways that conduced to the slave's well-being. Unsurprisingly, when Aristotle draws up the design for an ideal state, he suggests a compromise. Greeks should not enslave Greeks, only non-Greeks, since they have servile natures, whereas Hellenes do not.[10] These remarks, which remain quite undeveloped, indicate the distance between Aristotle's casual assumption of the ethnic superiority of the Greeks over all their neighbors and modern racism, and how little intellectual pressure he was under to provide an elaborate justification of an institution that was taken for granted until the Enlightenment.

The oddity of Aristotle's views, which explains why readers so often hope that he might really be meaning to undermine the institution, is that he contradicts himself in a way he rarely does elsewhere. The thought that a slave is an animated tool suggests the slave's owner need take only the interest in the slave's welfare that he would take in the well-being of a spade. A spade needs cleaning and sharpening to be fit for digging; but nobody thinks we could be friendly with a spade. The recognition that masters and slaves often existed on good terms undermines the thought that slaves are merely tools. This is not the only contradiction; Aristotle holds, as he must, that for those who are slaves by nature, slavery is good. Yet when he discusses the ideal state, Aristotle argues that slaves should be offered the prospect of manumission, although this would not be doing them a good turn if they were suited only to slavery. Defenders of antebellum slavery were more consistent in arguing that the freed slaves would be unable to survive. If freedom would be good for them, only captives taken prisoner in a just war are rightly enslaved; and their enslavement is a punishment brought to an end by manumission. Aristotle has the same difficulties with slavery as with the authority of husband over wife. If the relationship is not arbitrary and based on brute force, the superior party must be more rational than the inferior; but not only is the inferior likely to be as rational as the superior; it is implicit in the theory that the inferior must be intelligent enough to be governed as a rational human being. If slaves and women are intellectually indistinguishable from their owners and husbands, Aristotle's framework is threatened. His mode of justification creates more problems than he can admit to. It may suggest some residual unease that he says that if, *per impossibile*, plows could act of themselves, slaves would be unnecessary.[11] It does not, of course, follow that everyone who could employ machinery in place of slaves would choose to do so; it took the American Civil War to persuade the southern states to give up their slaves. It was not obviously and indisputably irrational of the southern slave owners to make some sacrifice of economic efficiency for the sake of preserving what they saw as an aristocratic way of life.

One explanation of Aristotle's persistence in the face of difficulty lies in a different aspect of the nature of politics. When he turns to defining politics for a second time in book 7, he says that there are climatic and cultural-cum-economic reasons why only some peoples can practice politics. In the cold and barren country of the Scythians, life is so hard that it leaves no time for public debate and for the give-and-take of politics. Peoples whose energies are consumed by staying alive can practice nothing properly called politics. They live off the land, they do not form settled communities, and their tribal organization cannot sustain political life. Conversely, people who live in too hot and enervating a climate cannot sustain the vigorous debate that politics requires; they will find themselves living under a despotism. The Persians, for instance, do not govern themselves politically. They are doubly non-self-governing. They do not govern themselves, since their lives are managed by the satraps of the Persian king; and the process whereby the satraps decide how to manage the people under their control are not public processes of debate and discussion, but secret and unaccountable. Aristotle does not quite say that we cannot talk of the "politics" of the Persian monarchy; but he makes a sharp contrast between the ways events are controlled and initiated in Persia and among the Greeks. Unsurprisingly, in view of Aristotle's habit of looking for the proper course of action in the mean between two extremes, he finds the Greeks uniquely suited by nature, climate, and economy to practice politics. In Greece there is, or can be, freedom without anarchy, and order without tyranny.[12]

Economic Activity

The economic activities that permit political life to flourish can also threaten it. Aristotle considers what sort of production and consumption best sustains citizenship. As one might expect, he seeks the mean between excessive austerity and riotous moneymaking and consumerism. The Spartans were obsessed with the dangers posed by the helots whom they enslaved and kept down by murder and brutality, and with the danger of their own citizens' becoming corrupted by soft living; they kept foreign trade to a minimum and made their young men eat at military messes, so that commensality would maintain public spirit and prevent them from hankering after a comfortable private life. It worked only partially. Spartans were notoriously rapacious once away from the repressive discipline of their own city. Spartan education and militarism were not successful in internalizing the desired morality. The Spartans turned their city into a boot camp; it produced soldiers willing to die for good, bad, or indifferent reasons, but not an intelligent devotion to duty. Spartans were easy to bribe; they also lacked the cultural refinements of less militaristic states.

Aristotle shared the aims of Plato and the Spartans: to create public-spirited citizens and avoid the subversion of public spirit by private economic activity, but he hoped to achieve them by nondrastic measures. Plato admired the Spartan contempt for physical comfort; Aristotle did not. More importantly, he was skeptical of Plato's obsession with abolishing private property. He agreed that *use in common* in the context of public feasts and festivals encouraged public spirit, but he denied that production in common could be efficient. He mocked Plato's belief that the community of wives, children, and property would encourage people to transfer the sentiments ordinarily attached to "my family" and "my property" to "our" common family and property. He saw a truth that the state of much public space reinforces today; we do not think that what belongs to all of us belongs to each of us; we think it belongs to nobody, and we neglect it. For a man to have an incentive to provide for his family, he must think of it as *his* family; to have an incentive to look after his farm and crops in the most productive way, he must see them as his. Aristotle argues for private production and common use.

Even more deeply embedded is the thought that some work is intrinsically degrading and bad for the character of those who do it; and some kinds of economic activity are wrong in themselves. The basic thought is familiar. Nature tells us what we need: what food and drink, what shelter and clothing. We need enough but not too much food, drink, shelter, and comfort, as any properly brought-up person understands. We may not be able to give a very detailed account of these needs, but we do not have to. We know what work is degrading even if we cannot say exactly why; and we know that a decent person would engage in some occupations and not in others even if we cannot say exactly why. Modern economists do not ask, as Aristotle and medieval writers did, about the *proper* end or goal or purpose of economic activity; we do not talk as they did about the just price of things, though we do have a strong, if not very clear, sense that some prices and some incomes are unconscionably high or low. Trade unions have always been committed to a fair day's pay for a fair day's work, which is not so different from Aristotle's economics. Aristotle thought that our natural needs set the bounds of acceptability. We work to provide food, drink, clothing, and shelter; the aim of production is consumption. Money is therefore problematic. Official coinage was a fairly recent invention in Greek society, the oldest surviving coins dating from around 600 BCE, and was regarded with suspicion by conservative moralists such as Plato and Aristotle. The way money is "worth" things to which it bears no physical or other relationship is "unnatural." When one considers that a pair of shoes is worth or costs $175, and that this is what a hundred loaves cost or are worth, it is tempting to think that something must underpin their shared value. Whatever underpins it, it is not the fact that people will give us pieces of silver for shoes or bread; the value of money itself is what needs explanation.

Two plausible views have dominated purported explanations from that day to this. One relies on the thought that what we use requires human effort to make, catch, dig up, or find; the other relies instead on the fact that what we purchase reflects what we *want*. The first measures value by the efforts of the producers; the second measures value by the desires of the purchasers. Neither works well in all circumstances, and certainly not on its own, though they work well in combination; if I am a terrible shoemaker, my shoes will cost me much effort, but have little value in the marketplace since nobody will want to wear them. If I stumble across a diamond, it will sell for a great deal, but it will not have cost me much effort. The two thoughts together suggest that the price of anything measures its scarcity relative to the demand for it. We all need bread for survival and diamonds only when our hunger is sated; but bread is easy to produce in quantity and diamonds are not.

Aristotle began the tradition of thinking that behind the prices of goods in the marketplace there lies a true or natural value that should determine those prices. His discussion of money and usury had an enormous influence on later economic thought; most importantly, he inspired the medieval condemnation of moneylending and usury, though not of course its anti-Semitic aspects. Those flowed from the fact that Christians were supposedly prohibited from lending money at interest, and Jews were shut out of most economic activity, with the result that the Jews became moneylenders and loathed in consequence. Aristotle does not denounce gouging or excessively high interest rates; using the biological metaphors that came so easily to him, he argued that things really useful to life were organic and that their creation and use are part of the natural cycle of production and consumption. Money is helpful when it promotes that cycle. It itself is barren, mere metal that cannot produce offspring as trees and plants do. Usury is therefore unnatural. The man who made his living by lending money at interest was setting barren metal to breed. As an unnatural way of making a living, it was to be deplored.[13]

Aristotle might be thought to be attacking the nouveaux riches. His complaints are rather more than social polemics, however. Most productive activities have a natural cycle; first we create and then we consume what we have made. Making money has no such beginning and ending. It has no natural terminus. Banking and moneymaking are solvents of social order, a point made by poets, playwrights, and social theorists ever since money was invented, and one that is made today whenever the excesses of operators in the financial marketplace threaten to impoverish everyone else.

Given Aristotle's views about economic activity, and his praise of self-sufficiency, it is unsurprising that he thought the polis is best governed by moderately well-off men who draw their livelihood from farms on which they themselves do not do so much work, or work of the wrong sort, that they unfit themselves for public life. Speaking of a regime in which farmers and the moderately wealthy form the citizen body, he suggests that they should have some but not too much leisure; if they cannot spend too much time in the agora "politicking," they will have to rely on standing regulations, that is, on the rule of law. Aristotle is the first writer to wish for the "government of laws not of men." When Aristotle speaks of "farmers" in that context, he means small landowners or tenants, who owned a slave or two with whose assistance they worked their farms;[14] at other times he means by "farmers" those who actually labor in the fields, and in the ideal state they would be slaves, some owned by private individuals and some by the state.[15] Having distinguished the domestic arts from politics as the master art concerned to create the conditions of a good life in common, he turns aside in book 2 to discuss ideal states. But he has laid the foundations for what most concerns him: citizenship, constitutional order, and the avoidance of stasis, and we can follow that discussion before turning back to the ideal state.

Citizenship and Constitution

With the ground cleared of ideal states and utopian experiments, Aristotle advances on the topics that have kept his work alive for two and a half thousand years: the nature of citizenship, the qualities of good constitutions, the causes of revolution, and prophylactics against upheaval. Their connection is that constitutions distribute power among citizens; the rules governing the gaining and use of political power are the central element of any constitution; and whether the inhabitants of a political community are content with the allocation of political rights and obligations is decisive in whether the community is stable or conflict ridden. Ways of allocating rights, obligations, and power that are least likely to provoke discontent are what we are seeking.

The subject raises questions about the connection between the qualities of the citizen as a member of a community and his qualities as an individual: loyalty, for instance, is a virtue in individuals and in the members of groups, but if the group is devoted to bad purposes, loyalty to the group is less obviously a virtue, because it will help the group achieve its (bad) goals. Criminologists suggest that there is in fact rather little honor among thieves, but our belief that there must be reflects the obvious thought that thieves who were honorable among themselves could prey on the rest of us more effectively. Whether a man can be a good citizen only by being a good man was hotly debated for the next two millennia. Among writers who drew their inspiration from ancient ideals, Machiavelli insisted that the man who is loyal to his country must often behave in ways a good man would flinch from, while Rousseau feared that Machiavelli was right and followed Plato in urging the merits of a small, simple, isolated, and uncommercial republic whose near-isolation from its neighbors would prevent the military and other entanglements that lead us into the temptation to sacrifice humanity and a wider justice to a patriotism that amounts to individual selflessness and collective selfishness. The modern nation-state has not rendered these anxieties obsolete; we are all too familiar with the fact that we know how to train young men to serve in our armed forces but do not know how to retrain them for civilian life.

Aristotle's ideas about the qualities needed by citizens reflect the assumptions of well-off Athenians about the members of different social classes as well as a hardheaded view of the way economic interests affect political behavior. Citizenship for Aristotle is not the modern world's notion, which is that of an entitlement to benefit from the protection of a particular government, and to exercise such political rights as that system confers. In most modern states, resident aliens can be expelled for misconduct; citizens cannot. Greek city-states habitually exiled their own leading citizens. Conversely, Swiss women were until recently unable to vote, but they were Swiss citizens in the modern sense of the word, since they carried Swiss passports and enjoyed the usual legal rights of inhabitants of modern states. In Aristotle's terms, they were free—not slaves—but not fully citizens. It is the right of political (but not economic) equals *to rule and be ruled in turn* that constitutes citizenship as he discusses it. Mere membership of a polity is not his central concern; nor was it to Greeks generally, living as they did in a world devoid of passports, and without the welfare arrangements that raise questions about our identities and entitlements. That is not to say that membership was unimportant; when the Athenians murdered the male inhabitants of Melos and enslaved their wives and children, membership was no light matter.

Aristotle keeps his eye on the question of who can safely be given the right to rule and be ruled in turn; and to that question his predilection for finding virtue in a mean is relevant. Since men are neither beasts nor gods, their social arrangements must suit an existence lying in a mean between the invulnerable self-sufficiency of gods and the mindless self-sufficiency of beasts. Political existence rests on a form of equality (or inequality) among men. Thinking of the constitutional arrangements that determine citizenship, he is impelled toward a familiar position. *If there were such a difference between one man and all others as there is between God and men or between men and animals, that man should have absolute authority.*[16] There is no such difference. Conversely, if there were no difference between rich and poor, slave and free, men and women, adults and children, natives and foreigners, all could be citizens of whatever city they found themselves in. But there are important differences between them. The equality that citizenship implies is to be found in the mean position.

Aristotle did not argue that since everyone needs the protection of the laws, everyone should have the rights of (modern) citizenship. Slaves, foreigners, and women were entitled to much less than Athenian citizens, and Aristotle had no difficulties with that, even though he was himself only a resident alien in Athens. Indeed, the calmness with which he describes people in his own position is astonishing: "we call them citizens only in a qualified sense, as we might apply the term to children who are too young to be on the register, or to old men who have been relieved from state duties."[17] Nor did he suggest that human beings possess common attributes that should ground a human right to citizenship in whatever state one happened to be born in. The Stoics later argued something close to this, and it is a commonplace of liberal democratic theory, but Aristotle did not. He took it for granted that there are better and worse candidates for citizenship and that properly educated, economically independent, native-born, free men are the best. Nature meant women to be ruled by their husbands, so it would be against nature to admit women to citizenship. Men employed in repetitive manual labor where they did not exercise their own judgment were unfit to give their views on political matters. He did not argue, like later opponents of female suffrage, that women do not bear men's military burdens and therefore cannot claim the same political status; nor did he suggest that regardless of mental capacity and occupation, the fact that we are all at risk from the errors of government entitles us to a say in their activities. His test was whether a person was naturally "autonomous." Someone who was not self-governing domestically could not be part of the self-governing political community.

No Athenian believed that a Greek could be uninterested in politics. At the very least, self-defense demanded that a man keep a close eye on the holders of power; they understood what Trotsky observed twenty-five hundred years later. "You say you are not interested in politics; but politics is interested in you." The uninterest in politics and the ignorance about both politicians and political institutions displayed by British or American "citizens" of the present day would have been incomprehensible. It would also have been very surprising in such small, face-to-face communities. Within the polis politics was often class warfare; it was understood that the upper classes would try to restrict eligibility for citizenship to protect their wealth and status, and that the lower classes would try to extend their political power in self-defense. The prehistory of Athenian democracy was a long struggle to open the right to participate and hold office to those not already entitled by wealth and birth; once Athenian democracy was instituted, it remained a struggle in which the common people tried to extend their grip on the political process and the oligarchically minded tried to roll back the gains of their opponents. These struggles were sometimes conducted with a degree of savagery that no political system could readily contain; Thucydides's account of the massacres that took place all over Greece when the war between Athens and the Peloponnesian League sparked off civil wars elsewhere makes it clear that rich and poor were ready to bring in outsiders to settle local scores, and settle them violently.[18] The violence of the Thirty Tyrants during their short-lived regime was notorious, and they were violently overthrown in turn, but atrocities were commonplace all over Greece. Aristotle's obsession with political moderation is all the more compelling given the long history of immoderate behavior that constituted Greek political life. Unsurprisingly, he wants moderate persons to be citizens and institutional mechanisms to moderate conflict.

Who is to be a citizen is the obverse of the question of the best form of constitution. The nature of a constitution in Aristotle's understanding of it is very like the modern understanding: the set of rules adopted by a polis that allocates functions to institutions, and lays down who possesses the right to participate in political decision making, and how decisions affecting their polis are to be made. Aristotle felt, but resisted, the temptation to which Plato succumbed. If "the best" could rule, everyone would do well to obey them. If there was one best man, there should be a *panbasileus*, a single ruler with no check on his authority. Since by definition he would always do what was best, there could be no reason to hold him back. More plausibly, there might be a group of individuals who were "the best," and if so there should be an ideal aristocracy. Aristotle muddies the waters by assuming that "the best" would be intended by nature to form a *hereditary* ruling elite and that nature would try to ensure that the appropriate qualities would be passed down from one generation to the next. The difficulty, as the history of Athens and everywhere else attests, was that the genetic transmission of political wisdom and political flair cannot be relied on. The puzzle that obsessed Plato—why virtuous men have wicked sons—did not obsess Aristotle, but he noted the contrast between the heritability of desirable qualities that breeders could readily achieve in animals and the absence of any similar inheritance of good character in humans. To his credit, he also noticed that the "naturalness" of aristocratic rule was less obvious to nonaristocrats than to the upper classes themselves.

Aristotle came very close to the solution that would have resolved his anxieties. He had the right premises: the talent for political rule is not widely distributed, so politics is intrinsically "aristocratic"; the talent is not reliably inherited, so *hereditary* aristocracy is imperfect. Many people who do not possess political talent can recognize its presence in others; they can choose a nonhereditary aristocracy. This is modern representative government. The reason he did not suggest it is instructive. The premises were in place. Aristotle firmly believed that although the wearer of a pair of shoes may not know how to make a pair of shoes, he knows where the shoe pinches. He also went out of his way to point out that in many contexts many heads are wiser than one. He lived two millennia before the invention of modern representative government; but representative government essentially allows a democratic citizen base to choose its own rulers. It is, when it works as we hope, the device for producing an elective aristocracy that Aristotle needed in order to unite the common sense of the many with the talent of the few. James Madison and James Mill, writing within two decades of each other in the late eighteenth and early nineteenth centuries, thought that representation was the great discovery of the modern age. It allowed democratic, or more exactly popular, government on a large scale. Aristotle thought a state in which citizens did not know each other by sight was no state at all; a state was necessarily limited in size. If there were no more than a few thousand citizens, they did not need representative arrangements, and the only purpose of election would be, as at Athens, to choose the occupants of official positions. His discussion of the correct size of the citizen body implies that Athens is far too large. The idea of representative democracy did not come easily to modern thinkers; representative institutions existed centuries before they were seen as a way of creating a form of democracy, namely, "representative democracy." Rousseau proposed elective aristocracy as the best of all forms of government, but denounced the idea of representation on which the modern version of elective aristocracy rests. A few years later, Madison saw the modern argument clearly, as did Jefferson when he distinguished "pure" and "representative" forms of democracy.

Aristotle's Classification of Constitutions

Aristocracy is in principle the best form of government: there the best men rule because they possess judgment, courage, justice, and moderation in the highest degree. They display excellence as citizens, and a constitution that places power in their hands achieves excellence as a constitution. A true aristocracy is the constitutional regime in which the few best rule in the interest of the whole. Yet experience shows that aristocracies have a regrettable habit of becoming oligarchies in which class pride, not public spirit, rules the day, and in which moderation gives way to the oppression of other social classes. To see how Aristotle resolved the difficulties as he understood them, we must turn to what he is best remembered for, the sexpartite distinction between forms of government

according to the numbers who participate in them, on the one hand, and
their goodness or corruption, on the other.

The three virtuous forms of government are kingship, aristocracy,
and *politeia*, in which one, a few, or many persons possess ultimate power,
and employ it to govern for the sake of the common good; the corrupt forms are tyranny, oligarchy, and democracy, in which one man,
a few men, or the poor many govern in their own narrow interests.[19]
When "democracy" became the preferred label for modern representative government, the fashion sprang up to call the bad form of popular
government "ochlocracy," or mob rule; Aristotle had no such qualms.
The *demos* are the "poor many," and like all Greek thinkers he assumed
that the poor many would use political power in their own interest. The
problem in designing a constitution is to distribute power so as to give
every incentive to those who have it to use it for the common good, not
in their narrow class interest. Democrats believed that poverty and the
practice of mean occupations should not disqualify a man from active
citizenship; Aristotle thought them doubly wrong. Poor men and practitioners of the banausic trades cannot raise their heads to contemplate
the good of the whole society; as a class, the poor resent the better-off
and will try to seize their wealth by whatever means they can. The "narrow democracy" or "expanded aristocracy" of the well-balanced *politeia* is
the remedy. A narrow democracy would be a more restrictive version of
the democracy that Cleisthenes had instituted, where the lowest social
class was not yet permitted to hold most offices; conversely, an expanded
aristocracy would be a system in which the requirements of birth and
wealth were not as onerous as oligarchical parties wanted to institute.
The thought is not complicated: too restrictive a constitution arouses
resentment; too broad a constitution also does so. Somewhere in the
middle ground lies the answer.

It is now clear how Aristotle connects the excellence of citizens
with the excellence of the constitutional form. Although some men are
undeniably superior to others, nobody is so unequivocally superior to
every other man that his fellows will obey him unquestioningly. A virtuous man is more likely to be corrupted by absolute power than to

become wiser and more virtuous; and untrammeled monarchical rule will turn tyrannical. Unbridled democratic government will so frighten the better-off that it will cause civil war. If it does not, it may become a collective tyranny. What is needed is what later came to be called checks and balances, and a selection process for political office that secures the service of people whose characters are adequate to the task. Nonetheless, Aristotle's perspective is not ours. Modern political discussion is imbued with a concern for individual human rights; we look to institutions to hold accountable those who wield power over their fellows, so that the rights of individuals are respected. Aristotle does not. Because he sees the world in teleological terms, he asks—as Plato did—how we can ensure that the state functions as it should. The excellence of the citizenry and the excellence of the constitution are understood in that light. Hence, of course, Aristotle's focus on the collective intelligence and collective good sense of collectives; if "the many" are not to be trusted, it remains true that many heads are better than one.

One way in which Aristotle surprises modern readers whose conception of democracy is tied to the existence of representative institutions and occasional visits to the polling booth by around half the electorate is his acceptance of the radical democratic view that *the* democratic mode of choice is the lottery.[20] Something else that surprises modern readers who reflect a little is how right he is. *If* what we wish to achieve is equal influence for all, and an equal share in the governing authority, choosing the occupants of political positions by a random procedure—a lottery—is uniquely effective. The fact that most people flinch from that conclusion suggests that—like Aristotle—they do not wish for equality of political influence above all else. They wish to secure both the benefits of aristocracy and the benefits of democracy without the defects of either. If we achieve this, we shall have created a *politeia*, the state that Aristotle claims is "on the whole best" and most likely to survive the problems that beset a political community.

The Avoidance of Stasis

Aristotle seems to set his sights very high in arguing that the polis exists to provide the best life in common for man. But his eyes were also firmly fixed on the need to avoid revolution. The fact that *politeia* is the best practicable state is not a small matter; practicality is a central virtue in a state. Aristotle's theory of revolution, or perhaps one should say his theory of the avoidance of revolution, is interesting for innumerable reasons, of which one is that it is intrinsically highly persuasive and makes excellent sense two and a half millennia later. Aristotle's conception of revolution has two parts. It refers, on the one hand, to what he termed stasis, the situation in which political life simply could not go on any longer, and, on the other, to the bloody civil war to which this kind of breakdown could easily lead.

Stasis in the first sense is the antithesis of what every British civil servant is trained to regard as his purpose in life: "keeping the show on the road." Stasis occurs when the show is decisively off the road. But the struggle for power does not stop when matters come to a grinding halt. When an existing ruling elite, or single ruler, loses the confidence of the populace and loses the capacity to hold their attention and to coerce dissenters into obedience, it is invariably replaced by another ruler or rulers, immediately or after a period of civil war. So the other face of Aristotle's interest is in what later theorists summarized as "an unconstitutional change of constitution," not just matters coming to a grinding halt but some new ruling group seizing power. This conception of revolution embraces both what Marx and other thinkers have taught us to think of as "real" revolutions, involving insurrection, bloodshed, and the mass mobilization of the populace, and what Marx's disciples dismiss as mere coups d'état, in which no mobilization occurs and one elite is displaced by another, probably violently, but without popular involvement.

Aristotle was concerned with two situations above all, and about them he was extremely acute. The first was the tension between democratic and oligarchical factions. His interest was unsurprising, since it was this tension that marked Greek city-state politics and led to the most violent and prolonged bloodshed. He had an interesting, if schematic, view of what was at stake. His first insight was that revolution was provoked not only by a conflict of economic and social interests but also by a sense of injustice. Aristotle added the thought that two distinct conceptions of justice were at issue. The democratic conception of justice fueled the argument that men with equal political rights should be equal in their economic advantages. This suggests that revolution in democracies is essentially economic, driven by the needs of the poor or by a desire to be better-off. Unlike Marx, Aristotle did not think that the many are driven to revolt by sheer need. He thought it a brute fact about democracy that men who say to themselves that since they are equal in political status, they should be equal in everything, will turn to the elimination of economic inequality as their revolutionary project. Aristotle had no sympathy with an aspiration for economic equality. His politics is founded on the belief that nature provides for differences in intellectual and other virtues, and therefore in desert, and he did not doubt that the better-off were generally entitled to their wealth and social position. The point was to meet everyone's aspirations sufficiently to preserve political stability.

If the democratic conception of justice might lead to an economic revolution among people who have the same political rights as their economic superiors, an oligarchical revolution proceeds in exactly the opposite way. The oligarchical notion of justice was that men who were unequal in wealth ought to be unequal in everything, that they should remove the political rights of the many and monopolize power as well as wealth. The history of Athens would have seemed to Aristotle sufficient evidence for this thought; but he could have drawn on innumerable other examples. The Peloponnesian War had been marked by savage struggles between oligarchs and democrats all over Greece and throughout the Aegean, and city-states were torn apart as oligarchs in one city aided their counterparts in another and democrats came to the aid of democrats.

Aristotle's delicacy of touch comes out in his recipes for holding off the evils of stasis. Even relatively bad states can profit from the intelligent application of the rules of self-preservation. Aristotle was happy even to advise tyrannical regimes on preserving their power. His advice has been echoed through the ages, and makes a great deal of sense. It is simple enough, though hard to follow. Since what disables a tyrant is either the simple illegitimacy of his rule or the wickedness of his behavior, and the first of these is by definition irremediable, he must adopt a double strategy; on the one hand, he must keep his opponents divided, so that they do not unite against him, and on the other, try to behave as a decent monarch who had come to power by constitutional means would do: moderately and virtuously. Pre-echoing Machiavelli and other advisers to princes ever since, Aristotle advises against undue greed and self-indulgence; the rationally self-interested tyrant, to employ the idiom of a much later day, will sacrifice the pleasures of the flesh and the satisfaction of personal grudges, to protect his hold on power. In particular, he should be careful to eschew sexual advances to the wives and children of upper-class men. It is one thing to deprive others of their rightful share in the government of their society, quite another to affront their family pride and their honor by assaulting the chastity of their wives and daughters. The same advice evidently applies to seizing their property. The tyrant whom Polus imagines in *Gorgias* would be short-lived.

The advice suggests Aristotle's concern to analyze how a state could function smoothly rather than to moralize from the sidelines about the wickedness of tyrants. The modern tendency to restrict the term "tyrant" to murderous dictators in the mold of Idi Amin makes Aristotle's willingness to give advice to tyrants on how to preserve their position seem more shocking than it is. Aristotle's patron and father-in-law, Hermias, was a good man but technically a tyrant. Not everyone was as unlucky as Plato in Sicily. Moreover, in Aristotle's day there was no such disparity between rulers and ruled in their access to murderous military power as there is today. Tyrants were uneasier then than now and had to watch their step in a way their modern successors do not have to, as long as they can preserve the allegiance of their armed forces.

Given his advice to tyrants, it is easy to guess that Aristotle advises other regimes to look to their strengths and avoid their weaknesses. Democracies are in danger of provoking revolution if they add to the distress caused to the traditional ruling elite when it was forced to yield power to the poor; so attempts to create an equality of wealth as well as an equality of power should be eschewed. The temptation to load all the burdens of public life onto the backs of the well-off should be resisted. Moreover, the better-off ought to be allowed a proper place in the political system; the more democracy counterbalances itself with the characteristics of aristocracy, the safer and longer lasting the regime will be. The converse holds good for oligarchies; they must strengthen those features that will make them less repugnant to democrats, and should endeavor to avoid the risk of a revolution in which the poor many revolt against being reduced to near-slavery.

In offering this advice, Aristotle began a tradition of empirically minded constitutional theorizing often described as the theory of the mixed constitution; his place in that tradition, however, is not easy to characterize. Commonly, theories of the mixed constitution set out to provide a recipe for achieving the advantages of monarchy, aristocracy, and democracy within one "mixed" constitution. Two centuries later, Polybius praised the Romans for adopting the recipe. More recently, much self-congratulatory thinking about British politics has pointed to the mixture of crown, Lords, and Commons as such a mixed system, matched by American self-congratulation on the subject of the virtues of a separation of powers and the ability of executive, legislative, and judiciary to check and balance one another. Aristotle was interested in something different. His recipe for a stable governmental system relied on matching political power and economic interest, and it anticipated the findings of twentieth-century political science. A political system that gives political power to the majority of the citizens so long as they also possess the majority of society's wealth is uniquely likely to be stable. This requires what sociologists called a "lozenge-shaped" distribution of wealth; if there are few very poor people, few very rich people, and a substantial majority of "comfortably off" people in a society, the middling sort with much to lose will outvote the poor and not ally with them to expropriate the rich; conversely, they will be sufficiently numerous to deter the rich from trying to encroach upon the rights and wealth of their inferiors. American political sociologists explained the resilience of American democracy by noting the United States' achievement of this happy condition after World War II. This is not an account of a mixed constitution in the sense of a regime that combines elements of monarchy, aristocracy, and democracy, but an argument about the economic basis of political stability. Nonetheless, both it and the genuinely mixed regime reflect Aristotle's search for a mean between extremes, as he acknowledges. He admits that commentators praise the mixed regime; it certainly benefits from being a mixture, just as bronze is stronger than the metals of which it is an alloy, but Aristotle's interest is really in what to do if we cannot simply rely on "the best men."

One-man rule degenerates too easily into tyranny, and democracy into mob rule; dictators are proud and prone to run amok, and the poor are ignorant and prone to be misled by demagogues. One difficulty Aristotle faced in giving unequivocal assent to the virtues of the mixed regime in the strict sense was that the system was made famous by Sparta; and Sparta failed in the task of encouraging the widest range of excellences among its citizens because it was devoted to one excellence only, military prowess. Aristotle relies instead on the good sense and steadiness of the middling sort, and his *politeia* allows the middling sort to exercise a preponderance of power that should ensure that things never get out of hand. This is why the distribution of wealth and income must support the distribution of political power. In 1961 Seymour Martin Lipset published a justly famous account of the conditions for stable liberal democratic government, freely acknowledging his debts to Aristotle and entitling the volume in which his argument appeared *Political Man.*[21] Dante's description of Aristotle as "the master of the wise" holds up very well six centuries after Dante.

A modern treatment of the subject would emphasize that if the middle class outnumbers the poor, as it is said to do in most prosperous modern economies, there is little advantage to be had in reducing the poor to beggary; even if the poor have some resources to exploit, the payoff for each member of the middle classes is too small to provide an incentive for misbehavior. Aristotle does not argue in those terms; he focuses rather on the effects of occupying a middle-class position on the character of middle-class people. The moderate social and economic condition of their lives would create a corresponding moderation in their desires; they would not wish to tear down their betters or to oppress their inferiors. Once again, we have to remember the principle that in all subjects we should aim only at as much precision as the subject affords. Aristotle's views do not apply to all times and all places, or to all sorts of economy. The middle class in modern liberal democracies is not exactly the middle ranks of Greeks society, nor should we extrapolate from a small, poor agricultural economy to a modern industrial economy with an elaborate and extensive public sector. The panic-stricken middle class that has been accused of bringing Hitler to power, described by Marxists as the *wildgewordene Kleinbürger,* is not what Aristotle had in mind. While we may admire the ingenuity of Aristotle's analysis, we cannot simply "apply" it to ourselves. Nonetheless, it remains astonishingly suggestive.

Ideal States

Aristotle's genius was for showing the ways in which we might construct the "best practicable state." This was not *mere* practicality; the goals of political life are not wholly mundane. The polity comes into existence for the sake of mere life, but it continues to exist for the sake of the good life. The good life is richly characterized, involving as it does the pursuit of justice, the expansion of the human capacities used in political debate, and the development of all the public and private virtues that a successful state can shelter—military courage, marital fidelity, devotion to the physical and psychological welfare of our children, and so on indefinitely. For this project to be successful, the state must practice what Aristotle regarded as politics in its essence. This essence is the bringing together of a diversity of people with a diversity of interests—to the degree that a community of Greeks from the fourth century BCE is not anachronistically described in such terms.

One of Aristotle's most famous distinctions was the one he drew between the mere gregariousness of bees and cattle and the *political* character of human beings. Recent evolutionary theory suggests that he may have underestimated the complexity of the social lives of bees and ants, but the distinction he had in mind holds up well enough. Gregarious animals come together without speech; their need for one another brooks no discussion. People unite in a political society only by agreement on the *justice* of the terms on which they do so. This agreement invites a lot of discussion. This is a thought that Hobbes later twisted to his own ends, claiming, quite falsely, that Aristotle had described ants and bees as naturally political, and going on to argue that humans were not naturally political precisely because they had to establish political communities by agreement on principles of justice.[22] The power of Aristotle's argument is perhaps attested by Hobbes's need to misrepresent it while stealing it for his own purposes.

The fact that politics achieves unity out of a plurality of interests and beliefs without suppressing them is the moral that Aristotle draws from his glancing discussion of Plato's *Laws* and *Republic* in book 2. The book discusses the theory and practice of ideal communities, but Plato's picture of utopia receives the most attention. If it is really true that Aristotle had worked with Plato on the writing of *Laws* when he was a student in the Academy, it would explain the similarities between the ideal state that Aristotle sets out in books 7 and 8 and the polity of *Laws*. In book 2, however, Aristotle criticizes *Republic* and *Laws* very severely. Plato, says Aristotle, was obsessed with disunity. This was not unreasonable. Athens was always on the verge of civil war; social class was set against social class; and the city's self-esteem was fueled by constant wars with its neighbors. The attractions of social cohesion, and of a society that did not keep peace at home by waging war abroad, were obvious. Still, Plato's attempt to secure peace by making the polis an archetype of a unitary order is a mistake.

It is a mistake because it turns a city into something other than a city. It is of the essence of the city that it is a compound of parts that have to be kept in a constantly changing but orderly relation to one another. Aristotle was the first critic to level against Plato the charge that has a particular resonance today as a criticism both of a certain sort of overly rationalistic politics and of the totalitarian state to which that kind of politics can lead. Plato does not provide for a better politics but for a society with no politics. He has purified politics to death. Nonetheless, Aristotle felt the attraction of this mode of thinking. At the heart of the attraction was the impulse to self-sufficiency. The centrality of self-sufficiency to Aristotle's analysis is evident. The polis is logically prior to the individual as being the more self-sufficient of the two; individuals must live in a polis because they are not individually self-sufficient. This is not merely a matter of physical survival; it is a moral matter as well. Without mutual discipline, men become worse than animals. The being with no need of a city is either a God or a beast. The temptation is to think that the more complete the unity of the city, the greater the degree of self-sufficiency, and the greater its immunity to the ravages of time and conflict.

Both the larger claim that Plato abolishes politics by overemphasizing unity and Aristotle's particular criticisms of Plato's work are well taken. We have already seen his defense of the family, his acceptance of the need for private property, and his skepticism whether Plato's abolition of family life for the guardians would mean their loyalties were transferred to the city. No doubt, some sorts of moneymaking are unnatural, and property for use is more natural than property for exchange and acquisition, but that does not impugn the desirability of private property as such. Aristotle approved of the Spartan tradition of making their young men dine in common messes, without thinking that it implied the end of private ownership or that Spartan austerity was good for us. Aristotle finally produced a devastating objection to Plato's belief that the society described in *Republic* would be happy. Plato had said that in spite of the deprivation of property, family, and private life, the guardians would be happy serving the polis; but he backed away from that claim and argued that the *city* would be happy—implicitly admitting that many of the citizens would not be. To which Aristotle replied that happiness was not the sort of thing that could exist in the whole without existing in the parts. If the citizens were not happy, the polis was unhappy.

Yet Aristotle ends his *Politics* by setting up his own version of an ideal state. Exactly what is happening in books 7 and 8 is obscure, in the sense that, even more than elsewhere in *Politics*, Aristotle recurs to themes tackled elsewhere, in ways that threaten the consistency of the work. The dismissive treatment of the construction of utopias in book 2 casts doubt on whether the project of books 7 and 8 makes much sense. That book's insistence that politics is the art of constructing a setting for the good life against the background of difficulties that can be controlled but never eliminated suggests that constructing ideal states is a dubious undertaking, suffering the problems suggested by the famous joke against the economist on a desert island who responds to the absence of a can opener with which to open the canned food washed up with himself and his companions with the sentence "Let x be a can opener."

Nonetheless, the last two books of *Politics* have an interest as revealing what Aristotle thought perfection would look like. Like Plato, Aristotle turns a central problem of politics on its head; abandoning the question "Given the frailties and imperfections of human character, how does a statesman preserve order and pursue the common good?" to answer the question "How does a statesman ensure that the citizens are of good and amenable character?" Aristotle produces the town planner's ideal state. The ideal polis will have no more than ten thousand citizens, so that all citizens can know one another, and in this context Aristotle makes his famous observation that a state can be neither too little nor too large, and rashly appeals to the obviousness of the fact that a ship cannot be five feet long or five hundred. Readers may wonder what we should call supertankers or the Chinese state. The citizens will be supported by an agricultural economy in which slaves will supply the workers needed for the farms, and the citizens will be fed at common tables. The detail into which Aristotle goes when discussing where the common tables should be established and especially where the common tables sponsored by the officials of the city should be located is surprising in itself and an indicator of the grip that Sparta exercised on his imagination as well as Plato's. It may also reflect his friendship with Lycurgus, who was responsible for the organization of festivals and the like.

More importantly, it reminds us that Aristotle's emphasis on the plurality of legitimate interests that politics exists to reconcile is not the ancestor of the social, moral, and religious pluralism of modern political liberalism. For although Aristotle acknowledges that different elements in a community will have strong views about the justice of their share of the benefits and burdens of social and political life, he does not acknowledge that they might legitimately have different and irreconcilable views about the nature of justice or the nature of the good life. The perspective is authoritarian. One aspect of this is Aristotle's uninterest in any such concept as that of privacy. For Aristotle, it is perfectly proper for the state to regulate the sexual and family lives of its citizens; he sets down strict rules governing the ages at which men and women should have children, and provides for compulsory abortion where women become pregnant in a way that might imperil population policy or produce unhealthy children. In the process, he begins a long history of controversy by suggesting that when miscarriages are induced, it should be before the fetus has life and sense, which he puts at the time of quickening.

In short, Aristotle's conceptions of a free society, political freedom, and the free man are not wholly foreign to us, but they are not ours. One can see this vividly in his fragmentary remarks about education at the very end of *Politics*. Aristotle is perhaps the first author of a theory of liberal education, which is to say, an account of the value of an education devoted to knowing things that are worth knowing for their own sake, and calculated to make the young man who learns them a gentleman. The definition of a liberal education as a *gentleman's* education persisted into modern times; when Cardinal Newman wrote *The Idea of a University* in the middle of the nineteenth century, he declared that the object of a university was to turn out "gentlemen." Conversely, Locke's more utilitarian and vocational account of education had made an impact a century and a half earlier precisely because it subverted the older Aristotelian picture. But "liberal" in this context has nothing to do with political liberalism. It means "nonvocational" or "suited to a free spirit," and its social connotations are unabashedly aristocratic.

A piece of advice that strikes oddly on the modern ear is that well-bred young people ought to learn to play a musical instrument but not with such skill that they might be mistaken for professional musicians. This was not simple snobbery, or a matter of urging that a violinist of good family ensure he was not mistaken for Menuhin or Heifetz. Professional musicians were in demand in places of ill repute, hired in for parties at which prostitutes provided the entertainment. Today we would not expect a stag party to hire both strippers and a string quartet. Nonetheless, Aristotle's enthusiasm for the preservation of social distinction and his emphasis on the social position of the "high-souled" man remind us that even in his favored *politeia*, with as many respectable and steady men of the middle class admitted to political participation as is possible, Aristotle hankered after the rule of true, that is, *natural* aristocrats. If that attitude is not unknown two and a half millennia later, his unconcern with those left out of this vision of the world—women, ordinary working people, foreigners, slaves—is happily rather less common. But we shall not see much sympathy for ordinary lives and ordinary happiness for many centuries yet, certainly not in the work of Cicero.

CHAPTER 4

Roman Insights: Polybius and Cicero

Polybius and Cicero

NEITHER OF THE SUBJECTS of this chapter was primarily a philosopher; Cicero was a statesman, although he was a more accomplished
philosopher and a less accomplished statesman than he supposed. Polybius was a soldier, a diplomat, and the third of the great Greek historians
after Herodotus and Thucydides. His intellectual successors as writers
of political and military history are the Roman historians Tacitus and
Livy. Polybius's work entitled *The Rise of the Roman Empire* has survived only
in part; but his explanation of the extraordinary political and military
success of the Romans provided Cicero and writers thereafter with their
understanding of the Roman or "mixed" republican constitution, and
the dangers to which such a mixed republic might succumb. Since the
constitutions of modern republics owe more to Roman republican inspiration than to Athenian democracy, we are ourselves his heirs. Polybius
was a highly educated Greek aristocrat from Achaea, in the northwestern
Peloponnese, and as a young man was active in the military and political
life of his homeland. He was born at the beginning of the second century, sometime after 200 BCE and before 190. Roman military power
had by then reduced the kingdom of Macedon to client status, in spite
of attempts by kings of Macedon to recover their independence. At the

end of the last of these Macedonian Wars in 168, he was one of many upper-class Achaeans taken off to Italy for interrogation and to be kept as a hostage.

He was in exile for eighteen years, during which time he had the good fortune to become close friends with Scipio Africanus the Younger, whom he served as tutor and whose lifelong friend he remained. Scipio was the son of the Roman general who had won the decisive Battle of Pydna against the Macedonians, where the younger Scipio had also fought. Grandson by adoption of Scipio Africanus the conqueror of Hannibal, he was responsible for the final destruction of Carthage in 146. That is the terminus ad quem of Polybius's *Rise of the Roman Empire*. Scipio the Younger plays the central—fictional—role in Cicero's *De republica*, articulating the values of Roman republicanism in its final years of glory before the republic's institutions decayed and civil war overtook them. Polybius spent his exile in Rome, where he served his friend as secretary and learned all there was to know about the workings of the Roman republic. In 150 he was allowed home, although he remained close to Scipio, accompanied him during the Third Punic War, and witnessed the destruction of Carthage. Polybius later served his homeland well by acting as a mediator with the Romans after another ill-judged rebellion ended as badly as rebellions against Rome usually did: he did such an excellent job that after his death a remarkable number of statues was erected in his honor all over Greece. The fate of Carthage, sacked, put to the flames, and razed to the ground, suggests the value of his services. His last years are obscure, but he is said to have died after a fall from his horse at the age of eighty-two in 118. The tale attests to a temperament more friendly to soldiers and statesmen than to speculative philosophers.

Cicero was ninety years younger than Polybius. He was born in 106 in Arpinum, a city not far from Rome. His family were prosperous provincial aristocrats, but not members of the senatorial elite; they belonged to the class of the *equites*, the "knightly" rank that reflected a man's ability to provide himself with a horse as well as the other equipment of a soldier—as it later did in medieval Europe. By this time the label picked out people who were simply well-to-do. Membership of the Senate was confined to men who had occupied one of the magistracies—high judicial and administrative positions; membership entailed restrictions on the senators' economic activities, so persons who were well-off but not very wealthy might think twice about embarking on the *cursus honorum*, the prescribed path to high office. However, Cicero's father was ambitious for his son, and sent him to Rome to learn how to advance himself in a world where he was a *homo novus*—a "new man" and the first in his family to aspire to public office. At sixteen, he served as a soldier in the Social War of 90, the war between Rome and its Italian allies, or *socios*, but he always meant to make his name in the courts and politics. He learned rhetoric from the best orators in Rome, Athens, and Rhodes and met some notable philosophers, including the leading Stoic, Diodotus, whose old age he later made comfortable by taking him into his home. His passion for philosophy and his philosophical talent are indisputable, but he emphasized the way his training in philosophy made him a great forensic orator. Studying rhetoric in Athens in 79–77, he encountered the rival philosophical schools of the Peripatetics and Academics, and acquired the ability to refute any argument of either side. He drew the moral that in the absence of certainty we should defend whatever doctrine seemed most persuasive on any given occasion. It is easy to see why critics doubted his honesty.

Cicero was vain and self-regarding; he was immensely ambitious, saw himself as potentially the savior of the Roman Republic, wrote like an angel, and in private life was a generous friend and a devoted father, even if always on the lookout for ways of advancing himself politically. Initially, his political rise was meteoric; he secured the offices of quaestor in 75, praetor in 66, and consul in 63, on each occasion at the earliest permissible age; but the republic itself was already in its protracted death throes. By the time he became quaestor, Rome had experienced two bouts of civil war and the bloodletting that accompanied the dictatorship of the hugely successful general Cornelius Lucius Sulla in 82. Sulla had revived the office of dictatorship, which had lapsed after the defeat of Hannibal more than a century before; and he revived it in a form that presaged the principate of Caesar Augustus. Previously, the dictatorship was instituted for six months only. In 82 Sulla had himself

made dictator without time limit. Surprisingly, he stepped down voluntarily after instituting some short-lived constitutional reforms. They had
less effect than the example of his success in turning his troops against
the city they were pledged to serve.

Cicero was quaestor in Sicily, where he earned a reputation as a prudent administrator of the province's finances, and later became famous
when he prosecuted Verres, the governor of the island, for extortion. It
was typical of Cicero's career that he scored a triumph—Verres was so
unnerved by Cicero's prosecution that he went into exile before the case
was decided—and that his opponents claimed Cicero had been bribed
to ask for a smaller penalty than Verres deserved. In fact, it was unprecedented for such a prosecution to succeed at all; such cases were heard by
a jury composed of members of the senatorial class who were expected
to acquit one of their own.

Many equestrian families took several generations before one of
their members moved on from the office of quaestor; but Cicero became
praetor, in charge of a financial court, at the age of forty and consul at
the age of forty-three. As consul, he was faced with the attempted insurrection of Catiline and his coconspirators. Catiline was a man of great
personal bravery but politically, financially, and sexually rapacious, even
if most stories about him were urban myths. He had previously been
tried for the rape of a vestal virgin; this was the most shocking of crimes,
since the vestal virgins were the keepers of the sacred flame in the temple
of Vesta, the goddess of the hearth, and committed to lifelong chastity.
He had been acquitted; by paying a bribe, said his enemies. Catiline not
only planned to seize power and make himself dictator, but boasted
that he had planned the murder of senators and officials who opposed
him. When Cicero secured his condemnation by the Senate, Catiline
fled Rome and assembled an army. In his absence, Cicero persuaded the
Senate to agree to the summary execution of those conspirators they
could lay hands on. This was flagrantly and doubly illegal; the Senate
had no authority to try capital cases, and it was conviction and execution
without due process. Yet with civil war brewing, action was needed, and,
as Cicero said, *inter armas silent leges*—the laws are silent amid the clash of
weapons. Hailed by his supporters as the savior of the republic, he spent

the rest of his life reminding his readers and hearers of his triumph: *non sine causa, sed sine fine*, "not without cause, but without end," said Seneca.[1] Catiline himself fled, not out of cowardice, but to raise an army against the republic. He may have been a thoroughly bad character, but he was also a very brave man. When his militia confronted the army raised by Cicero, he died heroically on the battlefield, far in front of his own soldiers and surrounded by the bodies of the enemy.

He was mourned by the *populares*, the leaders of the poorer Romans whose support Catiline had secured by proposing the forgiveness of their debts. Cicero belonged to the party of the *optimates*, the defenders of the upper classes who were opposed to any measures of debt forgiveness or anything that smacked of the equalization of property. Cicero was not savagely reactionary, but a conservative who thought Rome's troubles had begun when the Gracchi—Tiberius and Gaius Gracchus—brought in agrarian reforms to benefit the poor. Cicero praised their assassins, but in none of his works does he show much understanding of the social and economic causes of the republic's collapse. He was a moralist for whom the personal qualities of statesmen and citizens were everything, not a sociologist concerned with the economic and cultural conditions of political stability.

The Senate was not united behind Cicero, and once he was no longer consul, his opponents gathered. When Caesar, Pompey, and Crassus established the triumvirate in 60, he refused to be the fourth member of their group; they looked for the support of the *populares*, and Cicero allied himself with Cato the Younger, the leader of the *optimates*. He was exiled by the tribune Clodius in 58 and his property confiscated but was almost immediately brought back by Pompey and his property restored. The triumvirate had little use for him. Leadership at Rome depended on the ability to mobilize armies against the city and assemble mobs within it to intimidate the Senate and leading politicians. Cicero's skills as an advocate were not very relevant, nor was his political judgment astute. Like many others, he consistently backed the losing side: he was a protégé of Pompey, with whom he sided against Julius Caesar during the civil war of the late 50s. Pompey was defeated in 48, and Cicero was pardoned by Caesar in 46. As a notable writer himself, Caesar greatly admired Cicero's literary abilities. Cicero was not reconciled; he was not one of the conspirators who assassinated Caesar in 44—the conspirators knew he could not keep a secret and would have betrayed the plot out of sheer garrulousness—but he approved of the deed.

Caesar's assassins intended to rescue the republic from one-man rule. They succeeded in destroying the republic instead, sparking a series of civil wars that ended only when Caesar's adopted heir, Octavian, defeated Mark Antony at the Battle of Actium in 31 BCE. That was the end of the struggle between Caesar's most notable supporters, Mark Antony, who had been his lieutenant for two decades, and the boy—Octavian was only eighteen when Caesar was murdered—he had named as his heir. As to his assassins, they had underestimated Caesar's popularity with the Roman poor and were themselves nearly killed at once in the disturbances that accompanied his funeral. Cicero was killed not long afterward. Seeing Mark Antony as the greatest continuing threat to the restoration of the republic, he made a series of violent speeches against him in the Senate; the *Philippics* were modeled on Demosthenes's polemics against Philip of Macedon, and they cost Cicero his life. Mark Antony formed a short-lived alliance with Octavian—the future Caesar Augustus—in 43, and each gave the other a free hand in murdering his enemies. They concluded, reasonably enough, that Caesar's leniency toward his enemies after the civil war had allowed them to conspire against him and in the end to kill him. They were not going to repeat the mistake. They also wanted to seize the property of wealthy men to reward their supporters, and the bloodletting was considerable. It is said that three hundred senators and two thousand *equites* were killed. In Cicero's case, Antony indulged himself in some notable brutality; he had Cicero's head and hands cut off and nailed to the speaker's rostrum in the Senate to remind everyone of the perils of speaking out against tyranny. Cicero died bravely; attempting to flee, he was overtaken by his enemies. He put his head out of the curtains of the litter in which he was being carried, stretched out his neck, and told his murderers to do their job quickly. As his life and death suggest, Cicero was addicted to Roman politics; he wrote beautifully about the pleasures of a quiet life in the countryside, but hankered for the hurly-burly of the Senate and the courts.² His political theory is reflective but far from dispassionate.

Politics for Statesmen, Not Philosophers

To turn from Plato and Aristotle to Polybius and Cicero is to turn to a different way of thinking about politics. Put much too simply, it is the move from philosophy to statecraft; it is much too simple, because Cicero takes more than the titles of his works from Plato—*De republica* and *De legibus.* He says that *De officiis*—on duty—is modeled on the work of the Greek philosopher Panaetius, and indeed there is great deal of moral philosophy in it. Nonetheless, Cicero is less interested in what philosophers care about, the foundations of their view of the world, than in the use that a statesman, or a Roman politician, can make of the ideas of Greek sages. Plato and Aristotle disagreed about the nature of politics, but they were unequivocally philosophers. To call them "career philoso-phers" is anachronistic, but they spent their lives teaching philosophy and thinking about its problems. When Plato gave advice to Dionysius I and Dionysius II in Sicily—if he did—he taught them philosophy. He was not concerned to impart the techniques of keeping the show on the road. The distinction is not absolute, as Aristotle's readiness to give advice on keeping imperfect shows on the road demonstrates; by the same token, when Cicero claims that the most important aspect of state-craft is to secure the good character of our leading citizens and embarks on an account of the virtues, he blurs the distinction.

If political theory is a mixture of philosophical analysis, moral judg-ment, constitutional speculation, and practical advice, it is the extreme cases that sharpen the distinction between statecraft and philosophy. Hobbes's *Leviathan*, like Plato's *Republic*, is an unusually pure work of polit-ical philosophy, Polybius's *Rise of the Roman Empire* and Machiavelli's *Prince* unusually insistent on practicality, history, experience; Plato and Hobbes offer to show us how to escape from the rough-and-ready solutions to problems that politicians provide. Neither suggests that we can learn only from experience, and neither suggests that all we can learn is rules of thumb. Statecraft, by contrast, is focused on the political practitioner, politician, statesman, or ruler, and on the viability of the constitutional arrangements within which he is supposed to operate; experience is all-important, and the wise man accepts that its lessons will be valid "more or less." Philosophy looks at the statesman to assess the morality of his actions, and at a constitution to assess the legitimacy of different forms of rule. Statecraft has a strongly empirical bias, because it teaches the lessons of experience. Machiavelli's *Prince* and *Discourses* mock philosophers and emphasize the teachings of experience; Polybius has no time for utopias that nobody has tried to put into practice. "As for Plato's celebrated republic," he observes, "I do not think it admissible that this should be brought into the argument about constitutions. For just as we do not allow artists or athletes who are not duly registered or have not been in training to take part in festivals or games, so we should not admit the Platonic constitution to this contest for the prize of merit unless some example can be provided of it in action."[3]

In this light, Plato's dialogue *Statesman* is an ironic commentary on statecraft, not a contribution to it. The participants in Plato's dialogue discuss the definition of the statesman, and what he must know to be the master of his art. But that art is not that of preserving the republic against its corruption by ambitious men such as Alcibiades or Sulla or Caesar; and the Socratic statesman's argumentative skills are not devoted to persuading the Roman Senate to agree to the execution of Catiline's fellow conspirators on the basis that *salus populi suprema lex est*—the preservation of the republic legitimates an otherwise illegal act. The statesman of Plato's imagination is the godlike superior of the human herd or flock that he superintends, and Socratic statecraft is the tending of souls. Socrates did not expect to carry conviction in *Gorgias* when he described himself as the only true statesman in Athens. In the sense at issue here, his craft is not statecraft at all, and he is not a statesman.[4]

Aristotle advised tyrants and oligarchs on how to preserve their position in the face of hostile public opinion; but the *Politics* was not a treatise on statecraft, and his advice is generally very unlike Machiavelli's unabashed recommendation of violence and deceit. *Politics* was a treatise on the nature of the Greek polis, framed by a philosophical account of the nature of the good life. It explained why the skills and temperament of the statesman were useful, but it does not discuss them in detail or encourage the reader to acquire them. Aristotle's ideal was, as he said, the rule of laws, not men.[5] He theorized the political life, not the skills of statecraft. He made a persuasive case for the autonomy of the political realm, and for more everyday and down-to-earth values than those that Plato cared for; he provided a philosophical justification for the existence of statesmen and an account of why we should not seek to replace political leaders with philosopher-kings. Once he had explained the deficiencies of Plato's attempted purification of political life, he needed no elaborate account of the role of philosophy in practical life, since his account of ethics and politics in the *Nicomachean Ethics* supplied it, along with a caution that such inquiries were not for young men but for those whose blood had cooled a little.[6] Unlike Plato, he did not dismiss rhetoric as the art of making a bad case look good, but he made nothing of it in the *Politics*. The writer who made oratory central was Cicero.

Cicero wished to teach his Roman compatriots what Plato and the Stoics had to say about justice, courage, temperance, and wisdom, but insisted that he was imparting Greek wisdom and that he was himself only a student and instructor. The purpose of imparting the philosophical wisdom of the Greeks to his Roman contemporaries was political. The young men he wanted to teach were to be statesmen, not philosophers, and the value of philosophy was its usefulness to the republic—a training in the best thought of the Greeks would improve the young men's characters, and they would not behave with the greed, cruelty, vanity, and shortsightedness that were bringing the Roman Republic to its knees. *De officiis* is addressed to his son, Marcus, a very ordinary young man from whom Cicero hoped for great things. This little treatise on the virtues was commended to Christians by Saint Ambrose and much copied and commented on in medieval Europe; both Erasmus's and Luther's great ally Philipp Melanchthon encouraged the creation of pocket editions of the work; and either in the original Latin or in translation it remained an influential educational handbook for upper-class young men until the nineteenth century. It confessedly borrowed from Plato, Aristotle, and

the Stoics, but its target was upper-class Romans; when European ruling elites centuries later modeled themselves on their Roman predecessors, they professed—whether or not they practiced—the virtues Cicero
taught. It helped that Cicero's Latin is both beautiful and readable, a
model for anyone studying the classics. The political treatises that share
the name of Plato's political tracts—*Republic* and *Laws*—are only fragmentary, but in the same way they are Greek in inspiration and Roman
in purpose, and their character is what that suggests.

The Originality of Polybius

To make better sense of Cicero's aims and beliefs, we must first consider
what was probably the first articulate account of Roman political institutions and their success, provided by Polybius in one short book of *The
Rise of the Roman Empire;*[7] then we should place Cicero's political writings in
the context of his own tumultuous and catastrophic career. The Romans
were the military superiors of their immediate neighbors. Nonetheless,
they were one small Italian tribe among many others, and their rise to
supremacy in the known—Mediterranean—world was initially slow.
Until the third century they were preoccupied with their own internal
struggles between the upper (patrician) and lower (plebeian) classes and
had their work cut out to handle the military problems posed by their
rivals on the Italian peninsula and by Gauls invading from the north.
Only in the third century did they secure a firm grip on Italy from the
Alps in the north to the Strait of Messina opposite Sicily in the south.
Anyone with a taste for speculation may wonder what might have happened if Alexander had turned his attention to western Europe rather
than Persia.

The Romans' arrival within a stone's throw of Sicily brought them
into conflict with Carthage, the most powerful state in the western Mediterranean. So comprehensive was Rome's destruction of Carthage in 146
that no Carthaginian account of its history survived. Polybius's history
of the rise of Rome to mastery of the known world is the history of the
118 years between the outbreak of the First Punic War in 264 and the

city's destruction in 146. Carthage was a maritime power and a great trading city, and at various times it controlled Sicily, Sardinia, Corsica, much of North Africa, and southern Spain. Its constitutional arrangements seem to have been not unlike those of Rome, which is to say an aristocratic oligarchy with a substantial, but carefully controlled, role for a popular assembly. In the Second Punic War (218–202), the Carthaginian Hannibal was a better general than any Roman, with the possible exception of Scipio Africanus; but he demonstrated, like Napoleon and Hitler much later, that fighting far from home with insecure supply lines is the road to ruin. Carthage was enfeebled, and Rome now controlled Spain and North Africa. The final destruction of Carthage took place long afterward, in 146, after a revolt against the relentless erosion of Carthage's independence. This was the Third Punic War. The First Punic War brought Rome into hostile contact with the Greek eastern Mediterranean, the Hellenistic kingdoms that divided the legacy of Alexander the Great after his death in 323 BCE. Carthage was in origin a colony from Greek Asia Minor; fighting Rome, Carthage allied with Philip V of Macedon, while Rome formed alliances with Greek states hostile to Macedon. After the last of a series of Macedonian Wars, in 168, Rome had an empire in the eastern Mediterranean, and the Greek kingdoms were shattered. Rome was an imperial power.

These events are the subject of Polybius's *Rise of the Roman Empire*; our concern is with book 6, where he explains why the Roman Republic is superior to all other forms of government. The explanation lies in a theory of mixed government that was anticipated but not developed by Aristotle, and that has influenced thinkers down to the framers of the American Constitution. John Adams was a particular admirer. The Constitution of the United States is the most impressive tribute to the theory that Polybius laid out, though not, of course, Polybius alone. Indeed, he is never mentioned in *The Federalist*. Polybius traced the principles of the mixed constitution to the establishment of the Spartan constitution in the eighth century, and treated Lycurgus as the creator both of the theory and of the first mixed constitution; Lycurgus's fame as the founding father of Spartan stability is only slightly diminished by the uncertainty whether he really existed. Aristotle refers to the virtues of Sparta's constitution: "Some, indeed, say that the best constitution is made up of all existing forms, and they praise the Lacedaemonian because it is made up of oligarchy, monarchy and democracy. . . ."[8] Absent in Aristotle's mention of the mixed constitution is an account of what its strengths stemmed from, and Aristotle himself had little reason to develop the theory, since his own ideal was the rule of the "best men," a genuine aristocracy, even if the best practicable state was a *politeia* in which citizenship was extended more widely than in a pure aristocracy.[9]

Aristotle did not elaborate as Polybius did on the view that mixed government is superior to any single form. The theory of the mixed republic, strictly speaking, holds that the best government incorporates elements of monarchy, aristocracy, and democracy within one set of constitutional arrangements. This was Polybius's theory, and Cicero's. Aristotle's favored system of government—*politeia*, or "polity"—is a widened aristocracy (or tightly restricted democracy) that allows more men from humble backgrounds into the circle of "the best men" than a pure aristocracy (but many fewer than in a more radical democracy). Aristotle's account of *politeia* was tailored to a Greek context. He was writing for a people whose conception of citizenship was entitlement to hold office, "ruling and being ruled in turn," and who set store by being treated as political equals. Excluding fewer competent and well-qualified citizens than an aristocracy, while admitting fewer incompetents than a pure democracy, avoids the class conflict that commonly leads to revolution. This is mixed only in the sense in which all constitutions are mixtures— monarchs have advisory councils, assemblies have executive committees and chairmen, and so on.

He wrote as though mixtures were commonly stronger than their pure constituents. The existence of bronze, an alloy that is a great deal tougher than its component tin and copper, provided a potent argument that mixtures were stronger than what they were mixtures of. This was true not only of metals: mules are much tougher than horses and donkeys. This raises two questions: first, what the strengths of the mixed constitution are and, second, why we should expect that a mixture of constitutional forms will combine the strengths of the pure forms rather than their weaknesses. One might suppose that the strength of monarchy lies in the decisiveness that one man can bring to the making of policy, while the strength of democracy lies in the variety of opinions that will be presented, and in the greater likelihood that good sense will emerge among them; Cicero argues just that. If all goes well, and the strengths of both are combined, the decisive decision maker will be assisted by the collective wisdom of the many. What if it goes badly? Might we not find the fickleness and fecklessness of the many exacerbated by the arrogance and ambition of the man who leads them, as Plato thought happened when democratic Athens fell for a demagogue; and if things go only somewhat badly, might not a decisive leader be rendered impotent by indecisive followers? Polybius asked exactly this question; the value of his account lies in the way he explains how the Roman mixture checked the defects of the pure forms without losing their virtues. He turned what might have been an account of the Romans' success in solving local problems into a general theory of stable government.

He made life more difficult for himself and his readers by placing the theory of mixed government within a cyclical theory of constitutional change such as Plato set out in *Republic*. The difficulty is this: one might content oneself with explaining why mixed governments, combining elements of monarchy, aristocracy, and democracy were especially stable—because they accommodated different interests and therefore helped keep the show on the road—or especially legitimate—because they allowed each element of society to contribute as justice suggested it should. It would be perfectly proper to leave matters at that and defer to another occasion questions about the conditions under which such a form of government can be established in the first place. However, Polybius inherited the classical view that change is decay. An inference that he and many successors drew was that no matter what constitution we establish, we must get it right at the outset. All political arrangements deteriorate over time, and if we begin with a botched job, we shall have nothing but trouble. We must seek a Lycurgus, or hope that one turns up. That is another trope that endures to this day, reflected in the popular American view that there was a "miracle in Philadelphia" and that the founders were men of superhuman wisdom.

Polybius mentions Plato's theory, but his picture of the transformation of good constitutions into bad is more Aristotelian: the good forms—monarchy, aristocracy, *politeia*—turn into their bad opposites—tyranny, oligarchy, mob rule. Polybius had no interest in the search for a philosopher-king and was not concerned to explain why perfection could not last forever. Utopia was uninteresting; since it never existed, it could teach no lessons. Polybius knew that the works of man are imperfect; sooner or later even the Roman Empire will decay, probably sooner rather than later. The destruction of Carthage brought tears to Scipio's eyes, even as he ordered its completion; and Virgil's *Aeneid* is surely a reflection on the theme of Troy, Carthage—and Rome? The question was how the Romans had thus far escaped what seemed to be their inevitable fate. They had begun with a botched constitution: they established elected kings with few checks. Nonetheless, their ancient kings had not become tyrants; they had been expelled. Even then a mixed constitution was not instituted by a Roman Lycurgus, and all of a piece, but evolved by trial and error. How had the Romans done it? Prompted by Livy, who himself was much in debt to Polybius, Machiavelli asked just that question.[10] The question remains important even after we reject cyclical (indeed any or all) theories of history; states can recover from unpromising beginnings, and it is worth knowing how they do it. It was obvious to Polybius that Rome had done it; his problem was to square the facts with the theory.

Like many writers charmed by the analogy between the human body and the body politic, Polybius officially held the view that a healthy start is indispensable. Sickly children did not make healthy adults. Lycurgus was famous for getting the Spartan constitution right once and for all: "Lycurgus's legislation and the foresight which he displayed were so admirable that one can only regard his wisdom as something divine rather than human."[11] Polybius was nonetheless an astute critic of the inadequacies of Sparta's economic arrangements. They could preserve social peace and support a formidable defensive army, but anyone looking for economic arrangements that allow expansion and the conquest of the known world would find the Roman hospitality to trade and the accumulation of wealth essential.[12] The Spartans won the Peloponnesian War with Persian money not their own.

The belief that the founding moment is decisive dies hard. When the framers of the Constitution of the United States set out to construct "a machine that would go of itself," they expressed the inherited conviction that their new country's constitution would determine its future, and the belief that a Polybian recipe was needed. Neither peace nor prosperity would be secure if the constitution gave the demos absolute power; but class warfare would be inevitable if a wealthy upper class monopolized political power and exploited the lower classes. As for leadership, one man must be the focus of allegiance and the source of leadership as George Washington had been during the war, or the country would be rudderless; but if Washington was tempted to rule as George III had tried to, the United States would become a tyranny for which a second revolution would be the only cure. Not everyone took the analogy between the body politic and the human body so seriously as to think that an ill-made constitution could not sustain a long-lived and healthy regime merely because a sickly baby was unlikely to become a healthy and long-lived adult human being. Still, a surprising number of people did, and do.

The Romans broke the rules and prospered; indeed, they conquered the whole (known) world. They did not institute the best constitution at the beginning, but reached it through trial and error and flirtations with civil war. Class conflict was endemic; only in the middle of the fourth century did the patricians give up their hereditary monopoly of the highest positions in the Roman state. Machiavelli dwelled on this point at length, because it was so striking an exception to the general rule that an ill-founded state cannot achieve greatness. Sparta was the great example of the benefits of initial perfection, invoked even by those who were unsure Lycurgus had even existed. Cicero argued both sides; with Scipio Africanus as his mouthpiece, he quotes Cato the Elder's observation that Rome "was not shaped by one man's talent but that of many, and not in one person's lifetime but over many generations,"[13] but he cannot resist suggesting that Romulus's original constitution had been the same mixed constitution as Lycurgus's. Elsewhere he ascribes the success of Lysander, who led Sparta to victory in the Peloponnesian War, to the constitution created by Lycurgus four centuries before. Sparta's institutions were invariably credited to Lycurgus's genius alone. Lycurgus set up constitutional arrangements that mingled monarchical, aristocratic, and democratic elements; a pair of hereditary kings were advised by a council of mature men—the *gerousia*—with their decisions subject to the assent of five ephors, and with ultimate authority lying in the hands of a popular assembly. Variations on that model appealed to the enemies of pure democracy on one side and to those of pure monarchy on the other for the next two millennia.

The Peculiarities of Rome Explained

Polybius was an excellent historian, Thucydidean in his determination to gets things right. He therefore approached the history of the Roman constitution with caution, half apologizing indeed to his readers for keeping them waiting for his explanation of the role of Rome's political arrangements in facilitating its rise to world domination. The *Histories* were forty-eight books long; most of them are lost to us, but it hardly seems a great unkindness to readers to keep them waiting until the sixth book of forty-eight. But Polybius was right to be hesitant; how Rome rose to glory is not clear, and what will happen next less clear. He begins by demurring at the usual division of constitutional types into kingship, aristocracy, and democracy, arguing like Aristotle that only good forms of one-man rule can be called kingship, while the others are tyranny or despotism; by the same token, rule by the best is aristocracy, and is otherwise mere minority rule or oligarchy, while rule by the whole people under law is democracy, but lawless and fickle popular government mob rule. That introduces the cycle of degeneration in which monarchy becomes tyranny, aristocracy mere oligarchy, and democracy mob rule. Polybius complicates his account by distinguishing between "monarchy" as a generic form of one-man rule dependent on the leader's personal qualities of strength and bravery and "kingship" as the specific form of one-man rule that depends on the voluntary assent of the community and is constrained by law, what we might call constitutional monarchy. It is a useful distinction and worth making, and becomes important when tribal forms of one-man rule give way to legally structured forms, but it is one we can overlook here.

Polybius's picture of the motors of political change is persuasive if not taken rigidly, and it provides a rationalization of Roman history: leaders who rise by their talents will (at least initially) live like their fellows and arouse no hostility, while those who inherit a throne will separate themselves from everyone else and arouse envy. They will be opposed by men of the upper class affronted by the insolence of their king—or kings, since Polybius knew that Sparta and Rome had been ruled by a collective monarchy. When they are overthrown, their aristocratic supplanters will rule in their stead. That aristocracies degenerate into oligarchies is the most common complaint against aristocratic governments, and often leveled at their modern descendants, the elected aristocrats who occupy the seats of power in the modern democratic world. Readers will find less persuasive Polybius's claim that when an oligarchy is overturned, democracy invariably follows. He says that the memory of the tyranny of kings will be too fresh in everyone's mind for there to be a reversal of the cycle from oligarchy to monarchy, but this is empirically unconvincing; it turns the unusual experience of Athens and Rome into a principle. We are all too familiar with situations in which a disgusted public turns to a dictator, though it has to be said in Polybius's favor that "oligarchy-democracy-dictatorship" is perhaps the most common cycle of all.

The spectacle of the populace's following a single leader in a way that appeared to contradict its democratic attachments was familiar long before Julius Caesar charmed the Roman populace. Nor was it always a bad thing. Thucydides said that Athens was a democracy in name but a monarchy in fact when Pericles was in charge of its affairs, and he was not complaining. When the Athenians fell for Alcibiades, the problem was not that the demos followed one man but that Alcibiades was a crook. At the end of the Peloponnesian War the Athenian Assembly would surely have agreed to save itself from a pro-Spartan oligarchy by handing power to one man, if a Solon or Cleisthenes or Pericles had been available. Sadly, there was not. It is plausible that the Romans accepted that outcome in the hope of putting a stop to murder and civil war when

Octavian established the principate in 27 BCE as Caesar Augustus. Nor is an example taken 120 years later irrelevant to Polybius's analysis. The danger to the republic that led to its extinction was visible much earlier. Rome's conquests in the eastern Mediterranean put enormous wealth in the hands of the political and social elite and raised the specter of a military leader's using that wealth to secure the backing of his army in the field and the mob in the city, and seize power by brute force. The possibility of a successful coup by a rich and bold leader—Julius Caesar, say—was obvious; and the Roman populace might well have thought it would be better off as the prey of one man than as the prey of a large class of aristocratic exploiters. The possibility of political predation of that kind alarmed Polybius; Cicero complained that it had been realized by the time he wrote *De officiis* in 44 BCE.

Roman Success

At the moment of its greatest glory, Rome briefly achieved equipoise. Its armies were the most formidable in the world; its upper classes were public-spirited and nonrapacious; its ordinary people were prosperous. This raises two questions: how the Roman system *in fact* operated, and how plausible the presentation of the Roman system by Polybius and others is. The answers to these questions overlap at the most important point: the Roman understanding of Roman liberty and its role in secur- ing the legitimacy of the Roman state. We must take one step backward to recapitulate why. The mixed republic secured stability; but it was the stability of free institutions, not the stability of, say, the Persian Empire of three centuries earlier. In Rome, neither tyrants, nor oligarchs, nor mobs threatened the liberty of their fellows. Roman citizens were not slaves; they were ruled by law, not the whim of tyrants. Their freedom gave all Romans something they would fight to preserve, just as Demera- tus had told Darius that the Spartans would die to preserve their free- dom. It was freedom, not license, liberty under law, and both Rome and Sparta were fierce in instilling the self-discipline that free institutions required. Because Sparta and Rome were highly militarized societies, we might think that the discipline of the Romans was simply that of well-trained soldiers. Aristotle sometimes said as much of the Spartans. In principle, it was much more, a self-discipline that sustained the rule of law. The Roman conception of *libertas* as freedom under law became a model for republicans from the Renaissance onward; it animates Machiavelli's discussion of the greatness of Rome in his *Discorsi* and inspires his exhortation to the Medici to liberate Italy from the barbarians at the end of *The Prince*. The freedom he longs for the Italians to recapture is the freedom that the Romans lost when they lost their republic. It was invoked in the American and French revolutions and explains a good deal about modern republican institutions.

What freedom was not is quite as important as what it was; it was not the modern notion of individual liberty or the modern notion of laissez-faire, laissez-aller. Nor was it the freedom of Athenian democracy. Roman writers were sure that direct rule by the common people led to chaos; the Athenians classified their citizens by wealth, but the Romans carried the process to an extreme. Even the lowest class had some political rights, but beyond the formal right to vote for magistrates and laws, they were few. Eligibility for office was confined to the richest class, the *equites*. Moreover, the republic itself was free inasmuch as it was not subject to any other state; it was free of external domination, so its inhabitants were free citizens of a free state. The individual Roman was free from personal oppression by any other Roman; the story of Saint Paul's dealings with the Roman legal authorities in Acts of the Apostles suggests how important that was. Slaves were paradigmatically unfree, but their presence sharpened the importance of the fact that every free man could rely on immunity to arbitrary ill-treatment by anyone else. Even those citizens in the provinces who had no voting rights in Rome and were *cives sine suffragio* were free. In the modern, liberal, individualist sense, Roman society was far from free. The state's demands were not light. No sharp line protected the private realm from public demands, and the *censor morum* could deprive a Roman of office and even of citizenship for disgraceful conduct. But all free Romans possessed a form of what we have come to call *negative* liberty—they were not vulnerable to anything other than legally prescribed penalties for misconduct; and according to their status they might have one form of *positive* liberty, namely, an entitlement to occupy office and make the laws that governed the Roman state.[14] The sovereignty of Rome with regard to other states was untouched when the republic collapsed, but although many of the forms of republican government were preserved under the empire, they became dead letters. The central distinction between slave and free remained as important as ever, although many citizens were manumitted slaves.

Polybius held, and generations followed him, that within the Roman constitution the consuls represented the monarchical element, the Senate the aristocratic element, and the popular assemblies the democratic element in the constitution. A modern American reader will project the U.S. Constitution back onto this account; but wariness is needed. Polybius was not thinking of the modern separation of powers into executive, judicial, and legislative branches; he certainly thought in terms of the checks and balances that the modern doctrine of the separation of powers is supposed to reinforce, but he had no thought that particular institutions should exercise distinct powers. Nor was the Roman constitution organized along the lines of an executive that answered to a legislature composed of an upper and a lower house, with a separate and independent judiciary. What was mixed were the monarchical, aristocratic, and democratic elements within one untidy system; our notion of executive, legislative, and judicial functions was not theirs—indeed, the idea of the separation of powers as now understood was not clear until Montesquieu, and perhaps not quite clear even to him.

Even Polybius thought the Roman constitution was untidy. The consuls were elected for one year only; they were two in number; each could veto the acts of the other; and their role was to command the Roman armies in the field. They could also veto any of the acts of the magistrates subordinate to themselves. Becoming consul was the pinnacle of Roman ambition, and one of the most contentious issues in the long struggle between patricians and plebeians in the early days of the republic was the eligibility of plebeians for the consulship. It was an elective office, so although few Romans were eligible for the office, they were to an extent answerable to the common people. Regulating the contest for the consulship was the *cursus honorum*, or permitted path to the highest office; it required a man to hold the lower offices of quaestor and praetor before he could stand for the consulship, ensuring that there was orderly competition and that the holders of the highest office had proved themselves and were old enough to behave with some discretion. Nonetheless, there were more men of ambition than positions for them to fill, and behind-the-scenes negotiations between leading families to fix the elections were common.

The Senate was composed of members of the highest social rank who had held one or more of the magistracies; they were appointed, initially by the kings of Rome, then by the consuls. It began with a hundred members, but in the late republic, it was first expanded to three hundred and then to nine hundred members when Caesar was dictator. This last step was a sign of the contempt in which Julius Caesar held the Senate, since so large a body could not perform the executive duties that the Senate had performed throughout its history. Senators were unpaid and restricted in the economic activities they could undertake without losing their status; initially, this meant they had to be landowners, not merchants; later it meant that only rich men became senators. The Senate exercised complete executive power when the consuls were absent from Rome, supervised the raising and expenditure of taxes, and dealt with foreign relations; military and foreign relations were its main concern for most of its history. So recent is the modern understanding of the division of powers between different institutions that James Madison imagined that the Senate of the United States would exercise such executive functions as late as the early days of the Philadelphia convention of 1787 that created the U.S. Constitution.[15] A general in the field who was on bad terms with the Senate would grow short of supplies and reinforcements and find himself harassed at all points. In the last resort, the Senate could withdraw his command; but senators were vulnerable to charges of unpatriotic conduct if they did it without good reason. The Senate did not in theory possess either legislative or judicial power, although its advisory judgments—the senatus consulta—had the force of law unless overridden. The Senate proposed legislation to the popular assemblies that were summoned by the tribunes of the people, and whose assent was required before proposed legislation became law. Criminal cases were tried by the assembly, not the Senate: the Senate laid a decree requiring a trial in a capital case before the assembly, which had to agree to hear it. In narrowly legal terms, Polybius was right to say that the Roman people possessed ultimate authority and that this was part of their freedom. They elected the magistrates, approved the laws, and conducted criminal trials (civil cases were held before specially appointed juries of well-off citizens). Yet, the more important point, as Polybius emphasized, was that every element in the constitution needed the concurrence of the others to perform effectively. Consuls could not antagonize the Senate; the people had no spontaneous authority, but their choices in elections decided whose career advanced and whose did not; the Senate would cover itself in ignominy if it made life impossible for soldiers in the field, and so on. A balance between the elements was the constitution's most striking feature.

Citizens

Many modern readers will know Saint Paul's assertion of his citizen-ship "civis Romanus sum," when he was faced with scourging, and infer that the rights of citizens included immunity to brutality at the hands of soldiers enforcing law and order. Others will recall images of sturdy Roman legionaries from the cinema and innumerable historical paint-ings. The Roman citizen features prominently in the history of political ideas, usually with little regard to the intricacies of the various rights and duties attached to citizenship, or to the different statuses that citizens might enjoy. This is not surprising. Roman historians wrote about a tiny elite, and the ordinary citizen is almost invisible except as an anonymous soldier, farmer, member of an urban mob. Polybius was writing for read-ers who understood Roman citizenship, and no thumbnail sketch can do justice to a system that evolved over several centuries. Two or three key elements must be picked out, however. The Romans knew they had achieved what the Greek city-states failed to do; as they expanded their rule from Rome and its hinterland first to Italy and then to the whole known world, they incorporated conquered peoples into their system of

citizen rights and duties. This achieved two things; negatively, it protected the incorporated from a degree of exploitation by the Roman state
that would have led to resentment, tax evasion, even outright rebellion
and insurrection; positively, it opened military and political careers to
ambitious provincials ready to be loyal to Rome and possessed of talents
that Rome could use.

Although the Romans understood the merits of the policy of offering citizenship to the inhabitants of conquered cities, they were cautious
about it. Roman citizenship, like that of Greek city-states, was based in
the state's military and financial needs. All male citizens between the ages
of seventeen and sixty were liable for military service. Because Roman
armies were citizen militias, not standing armies, and not mercenary
armies, legions were raised as needed, but once conscripted, a man might
find himself serving for as long as eighteen years. He was not a volunteer,
although late in the life of the republic when manpower shortages were
acute there was a call for volunteers; in an emergency even slaves were
enrolled by their masters. Citizens were enumerated in periodic censuses.

Allowances made for changes over time, in outline there were three
"orders" of citizens, or *ordines*: senatorial, equestrian, and popular. The
senators and *equites* formed an aristocracy of wealth, education, and ambition; below them were the common people, or *populus*. The patricians
had been a hereditary aristocracy monopolizing political power, but had
been forced to concede to the formerly powerless plebeians the *ius suffragii*
and the *ius honorum*, the rights to vote and to hold office. By the time of
Cicero, few Romans could claim patrician origin, and it meant nothing
politically. The *populus* was divided into five classes, reflecting financial
standing, and taxable and military capacity. This was the task of the censors, whose ability to affect a Roman's status was considerable; a member
of the *equites* might be demoted for any number of reasons, including
cowardice, reluctance to meet his duties, or general bad character. It was
very rare for a citizen to lose his citizenship entirely, but not unheard of.
The censors also allocated citizens to the thirty-five tribes, which were
the basis of the military draft, as well as of the electoral, legislative, and,
for some purposes, the judicial systems. They were geographically based,
and each was further divided into 10 centuries, by financial standing and

by age. The senior centuries embraced those aged forty-six and older. To these 350 centuries were added 18 centuries of *equites*. The system combined popular and oligarchical features: each century voted as a unit, casting one vote according to a simple majority within the century. The best-off centuries had fewer members than the worse-off, so each well-to-do citizen's vote was worth more than that of a poorer citizen. His military burdens were much greater.

Soldiers provided their own armor and weapons and, in appropriate cases, horses. They were supposed to be self-sufficient, and although they received pay, their subsistence was deducted from it. Rome resembled Greek states in which the upper classes formed the hoplite, heavy-armed infantry. In a Roman legion the heavy-armed troops formed the front ranks of the infantry, and they needed the courage of a Spartan. The connection between military service and politics was very direct; to stand for office, a man had first to undertake military service. The military system also demonstrated Roman conservatism in ways that echo to this day. Most generals preferred to recruit their troops from the countryside rather than from the urban tribes; the image of the sturdy yeoman under arms was a legacy from Rome to Britain and thence to the United States. The "well-regulated militia" spoken of in the Second Amendment to the U.S. Constitution was a Roman militia; the modern army of professional soldiers recruited from the poorest members of society was what the Romans wished to escape, and until late in the second century BCE did. Of course, the fighting forces were accompanied by civilians engaged in every imaginable occupation, including that of the purchasers of the loot collected on a successful campaign.

The system of a carefully graduated citizenship survived until late in the second century BCE. In addition, cities that Rome subdued were often admitted at first *sine suffragio*, which is to say their inhabitants had the civil rights of citizens but no voting rights at Rome. This allowed Rome to assimilate its nearest neighbors first, and then extend citizenship to the rest of Italy. Some cities preserved many of their own institutions, and their inhabitants had a form of dual nationality, which worried some observers, much as "hyphenated Americans" worried some observers in the late nineteenth and early twentieth centuries. Others, including Cicero, thought it enhanced a citizen's sense of belonging to have two *patriae* rather than one to attach himself to. Cicero's native city of Arpinum was admitted *sine suffragio* in 316, and its inhabitants were admitted to full citizenship only in 188. This allowed Cicero's many enemies to mock him as a provincial and not a "real" Roman. Their mockery, though not to be taken seriously, reveals the depth of Roman conservatism, and the extent of the Roman obsession with the pedigree of laws, institutions, and individuals.

The system was radically changed as late as 212 CE, when the emperor Caracalla extended citizenship to every free person within the empire. His motive was surely to widen the tax base, rather than to emphasize the blessings of Roman citizenship or the liberality of the imperial administration. It mattered very much to be a citizen, not only in the sense of not being a slave but also in the sense of having the full range of civil and, until the principate, political rights of a citizen. Women had the same civil rights as male citizens, but could not vote or stand for office. They could own property in their own right and dispose of it according to law, by sale or by testament. Because Roman politics depended so heavily on personal connection, heiresses were important, and marriage—or divorce—for political and financial reasons was a prominent feature of Roman politics, along with the device of adoption.

A citizen's political rights were the right to vote and the right to hold office; citizens who had these rights were *optimo iure*—as one might say "first-class citizens." A citizen *sine suffragio* or *minore iure*—a second-class citizen—nonetheless had important rights: one especially valued was the *ius provocationis*, which was the right to appeal to the assembly against a magistrate's sentence in a criminal case. When Saint Paul asserted his citizenship and was told, "You have appealed to Caesar, to Caesar you shall go," it was his *ius provocationis* that he exercised. Among the other privileges that citizenship carried were the rights not to be subjected to crucifixion, not to be tortured when asked to be give evidence, and not to be scourged. One might, upon conviction and after the failure of an appeal, be beaten with rods and beheaded, but that was another matter.

Less dramatically, citizenship carried rights to engage in trade, to marry, to use the civil courts in litigation, and to bequeath property by will. If the concept of politics is Greek, the concept of a legal system is Roman.

All this must be set against the background of the feature of Roman life that we find most alien, the institution of the *patria potestas*, or the absolute authority of the male head of the household over its members. In law, this "paternal power" was held by a father over his unmarried children, no matter what age they were; it embraced power over both their persons and their property. A woman left the *manus*—literally the "hand"—of her father on marriage and was then under the authority of her husband, though divorce was not difficult. Her children were his, however. It goes without saying that the power of a paterfamilias over his slaves was unchallengeable. In principle, but not in practice, a father might sell his children into slavery, or kill them for any reason that seemed good to him. An interesting contrast with Athens was that women were not excluded from the social life of the wider society, and though they were used as pawns in political games, daughters were much loved—if we can trust the evidence of poets and orators. Accustomed as we are to living into our seventies and eighties, we find the thought of children and grandchildren remaining under the sway of their fathers and grandfathers into their middle age hard to grasp. Life expectancy in the ancient world meant that few fathers survived to tyrannize over middle-aged sons. The patriarchal character of family life was a natural accompaniment to the practice of "clientelage," whereby the less well-off attached themselves to well-off men who needed their services.

Cicero

Together with the histories of Polybius and Livy, Cicero's polemical speeches and writings, and his personal correspondence, form some of the most important historical resources for understanding the Roman legal and political system. Here we focus only on his political theory narrowly construed, part of his program to adapt Greek philosophy to Roman social and political purposes, bypassing even the extended defense of the role of oratory in political life that became something like a handbook for the study of rhetoric. *De republica* and *De legibus* were written during the 50s BCE when Cicero was sidelined by the triumvirate of Pompey, Crassus, and Caesar; *De officiis* is the product of the aftermath of the assassination of Caesar. These works had very different and, in the first two cases, complicated histories. The *Laws* was never finished, and found no audience in antiquity, but was well-known during the Middle Ages, when Cicero was a resource for the education of humanists and legal scholars. *De republica* was well-known in antiquity; then vanished. Fragments were rescued in the nineteenth century; they were recovered from a manuscript of a work by Saint Augustine. It was a remarkable early feat of recovering a text from a palimpsest, but the work itself was dismissed by the great Roman historian Theodor Mommsen as a work of no political judgment and no intellectual interest. What kept the audience that Cicero sought was *De officiis* (*On Duties*). Cicero's skill was to combine ideas about virtue from Stoic, Platonic, and Aristotelian sources while glossing over their differences, and to make them applicable not only to the Roman statesman but to the citizen of the world. The idea that human beings are citizens of the world, governed by the laws of nature and of peoples, as well as citizens of an earthly state, was Stoic in origin; but so appealing to Christian Europe was its formulation in Cicero's work that he all but became an honorary father of the church. Augustine credited Cicero with first turning his mind toward God.

Cicero bent Greek ideas to his vision of the idealized Roman Republic, and his understanding of the *mores*—the morality and social attachments—of the gentlemanly statesmen who would hold power in a just republic. Readers familiar with Machiavelli's *Prince* will hear curious echoes of that work in Cicero's advice; curious because the pieties of Cicero's advice to the would-be statesman were satirized by Machiavelli sixteen hundred years later. If his philosophy was Greek and eclectic, Cicero owed his constitutional theory to Polybius; he was born soon after Polybius died, and read his history. And Cicero greatly admired Polybius's friend and employer Scipio the Younger. There are obvious differences of tone. Polybius celebrated Rome's achievement of equipoise, while Cicero lamented the ruin of the republic. Cicero's account of republican politics veers between a "constitutional" emphasis on the way that good institutions allow a state to function by recruiting men of good but not superhuman character, and a "heroic" emphasis on the role of truly great men in reconstituting the state when it has come to ruin.

Cicero's vanity was so notorious that everyone knew he had himself in mind as this hero—had he not saved the republic before when he quelled the conspiracy of Catiline?

The rhetorical tension so visible in Cicero continued to mark the tradition. It emphasizes *both* heroic founders and refounders *and* stable, predictable government; heroic founders set up the mixed republic with its balanced constitution, but lesser mortals make it work. Republican writers were not obsessed with leadership in the modern sense. Many modern writers are convinced that politics exists in a state of continuous crisis, either because this is the natural condition of the political world, or because leaders engineer crises to justify their hold on power. Republican theorists were obsessed with foundation and persistence. In many accounts of the foundation of republics, particularly the numerous near-mythical ones, the founder vanishes from the scene as soon as affairs are settled, as if to emphasize that after a successful founding new founders are not required. Sulla had role models when he stepped down from the dictatorship.

De republica and *De legibus* are fragmentary and hard to read as consecutive texts. Their interest lies in the way Cicero unites Greek philosophy and Polybius's theory of the mixed constitution to formulate a recipe for stable republican government. In so doing, he does something that scores highly on bravado and poorly on persuasiveness by insisting that the Roman *mos maiorum*, "the custom of our ancestors," incorporates the wisdom of Plato, Aristotle, and the Stoics. Given the anti-intellectual character of the early Roman Republic, the ancestors whose wisdom he praises might not have liked the compliment, but it allows Cicero to slide gracefully away from his philosophical allegiances. Virtue having had her due, the maintenance of republican institutions can be looked at without preconceptions. In *De republica* he hands the chief speaker, Scipio Africanus the Younger, the task of providing a *histoire raisonnée* of the Roman Republic at its best. The focus switches from a philosophical concern with the ideal state to a historical account of the creation of the best actual state. In Scipio's account, Plato is rebuked, though not by name, for an obsession with building utopias; it is easy to believe that Scipio had as a matter of historical fact shared Polybius's prejudices against such speculation. Cicero does not say in his own voice that the subject of politics is not the ideal but the best practicable, and that the method is not philosophical first principles but the historical analysis of prudent conduct. His hero does. *De republica* ends, however, with an extraordinary passage, Scipio's Dream, in which Scipio imagines himself taken up to heaven by his grandfather Scipio Africanus. This is a reworking of the Myth of Er from Plato's *Republic*. In a very un-Platonic fashion, Scipio is encouraged to be brave, to devote himself to his country, and to win the glory that will come from the destruction of Carthage; but at the same time he is urged to remember that the earth is vast, that he is unknown to most of mankind, and that the only good really worth having is to be had in heaven amid the music of the spheres. It goes without saying that the theme of the vanity of earthly success resonated with Cicero's Christian readers; until the nineteenth century, Scipio's Dream was the only portion of *De republica* that survived from late antiquity. It did so for entirely unpolitical reasons; the pagan philosopher and anthologist Macrobius, a contemporary of Augustine, devoted a long commentary to the work that focuses on the numerological aspects of Platonic and Ciceronian cosmology. We shall shortly see what Augustine made of Cicero.

Cicero's claims regarding the nature of the republic and the aims of political life defined the republican tradition once and for all, which was no small achievement. His definition of the nature of a commonwealth became canonical. The *res publica* is the *res populi*. *Res publica* almost defies translation; "the public thing" is neither elegant nor self-explanatory, to say the least. In essence the *res publica* gestures toward the entire set of institutional arrangements and the *mores* that sustain them in the task of pursuing the good of everyone. That is why the *res publica* is the *res populi*—the people's state. Unless the people "own" the republic, there is no republic. Cicero goes further than Polybius in making justice the defining feature of a republic that is truly a republic at all, and anticipates Augustine's famous remark that without justice a state is simply a large gang of thieves: a corrupt state is no commonwealth at all. There can be no *res publica* if the institutions of government are perverted to serve private interests. This raises an obvious question, What conditions must be in place if there is to be a *res populi*, that is to say a common good that belongs to the whole people and whose promotion is the task of politics?

Following Aristotle, Cicero says the common good is the pursuit of happiness according to reason; politics must foster its social, economic, and political conditions. He rejects Plato's instrumental account of society and follows Aristotle and the Stoics in saying that human beings are sociable by nature and take pleasure in one another's company independently of the practical returns from cooperating with one another. We all share a common good and an interest in its pursuit. Nonetheless, we also have private interests that may be at odds with other individuals' interests and with the common interest. Good institutions protect the common interest against erosion by private interests and prevent conflicts of private interest from becoming destructive. What those institutions must be is the subject matter of political theory.

De republica is less concerned to provide a general theory than to celebrate the success of the Roman Republic at its best, which is to say down to 133, and what it celebrates are the virtues of the mixed constitution. It was in 133 BCE that Tiberius Gracchus's agrarian reforms, pushed through by none too scrupulous methods, led to Tiberius's assassination; this, the first serious violence in domestic politics for many decades, marked the beginning of the conflict that ended with the death of the republic itself. Cicero's account has strengths that Polybius's lacks. Because Scipio is given space to narrate the history of the expulsion of the Tarquin monarchy and the development of the institutions of the classical republic, Cicero can claim that Rome fared better than Sparta because Rome had the chance to learn by trial and error which institutions would best work for the Roman people. How this squares with Cicero's praise of Lycurgus is unclear. Nonetheless, Scipio makes an excellent case. One great man will achieve more than a squabbling and disorganized multitude, but an orderly process of experiment brings a variety of perspectives to bear on problems and reveals truths that a great man may overlook. This thought must have underlain Polybius's account, since he simultaneously declared himself puzzled by Rome's success and gave a perfectly plausible trial-and-error explanation of what he claimed not to understand. But, like Polybius and others who are obsessed with the work of the founding figure, Cicero was tempted to think the founder had to get things right at the moment of foundation if success was to be ensured.

Sentimental though he often is, Cicero provides a more hard-headed account of Roman politics than Polybius. Polybius's emphasis on the democratic element in the mixture of monarchy, aristocracy, and democracy exaggerated the real power of the ordinary Roman. Cicero's mouthpiece Scipio makes no bones about the way the first Roman census organized the voting units of the assembly—the so-called centuries. Individuals did not vote as individuals; votes were taken century by century; and each century cast one vote. The centuries were so organized that the small number of wealthy citizens were divided into a sufficient number of centuries to outvote the much more numerous poor citizens. Since voting stopped when a majority of the centuries had been achieved, the lower classes rarely voted. Rome was a plutocracy. Given his approval of this device, it is not surprising that Scipio repeatedly observes that he would think monarchy the best of all governments if it were not so difficult to ensure that kings did not turn into tyrants, but since monarchy is the most dangerous form of government, it is not a candidate for the best practicable form. How committed Cicero is to all the doctrines he puts in Scipio's mouth is obscure. In any event, plutocracy or no plutocracy, Cicero has Scipio claim that when the people desire liberty, which Cicero and Scipio certainly approve, they want not a good master but no master. Even if the ordinary Roman had less opportunity to participate in politics than the ordinary Athenian, Roman *libertas* required the people to be self-governing. That forbids the return of kings to Rome; and indeed, no Roman emperor dared call himself *rex*.

Cicero's other improvement on Polybius's account of the merits of mixed government is a more detailed explanation of its positive advantages. Polybius concentrated on its negative virtues, the way one element of the governmental mechanism can prevent another element from getting out of hand. Mixed governments avert—or slow—the cycle of degeneration. Kings who require the assent of an aristocratic council less readily turn into tyrants; a judicial council that may have its decisions vetoed by another institution, as did the Spartan ephorate, is less tempted to give arbitrary decisions or to act from spite; if the fundamental rules must be ratified by a popular assembly, the rich hesitate to fix the rules governing property (and particularly debt) in ways that oppress the common people and make insurrection likely. This is the theory of checks and balances, and not to be despised; without an account of checks and balances, neither the later theory of the separation of powers nor the traditional theory of mixed government make much sense.

Checks and balances do not include the positive component that Cicero adds. There are advantages to rule by one person—decisiveness and an absence of divided counsels; there are advantages to rule by a true aristocracy—discussion without indecision, and the opportunity to secure the services of an elite devoted to politics as a career; and there are advantages to rule by the many—all views can be canvassed, decisions will have the support of a majority of the active population, selfish interests will have less opportunity to pervert decisions. The question is whether we can secure the desirable elements of each of these forms of government, and not merely fend off their disadvantages. Cicero's view is that a well-constructed mixed government secures the decisiveness of the one, the expertise of the few, and the common sense and loyalty of the many. His view has been repeated for two millennia; but before concluding that it is a two-thousand-year-old cliché, we should remember that the modern version of the doctrine is strikingly more inclusive of "the many." Cicero's emphasis on keeping the many under the tutelage of the wealthy and wellborn has simply disappeared in the modern world. Our conception of a government in which a president or prime minister, assisted and checked by a cabinet, answers to a parliament or congress, which in turn represents and answers to the whole adult population, is infinitely more open to the ordinary person than Cicero could have imagined.

Good Law and the Good Citizen

If the best of all practicable governments is the Roman Republic before it was pulled apart by class war and the feuding of warlords, two issues need to be addressed. The nature of law and the rule of law is tackled in *De republica* and *De legibus*; who must play an active part in politics and what virtues he needs is answered in *De officiis*. The answers to "What is law?" and "Who should govern?" run seamlessly into each other, partly because they rest on Cicero's Stoic conception of natural law, and partly because of Cicero's expository skill. Cicero did not have the modern view of law. Although he is one of the originators of modern discussions of the relationship between the positive law of particular states and an overarching natural law (as well as the law of peoples, or jus gentium), and although he was a sharp critic of the chaotic and archaic quality of Roman jurisprudence, he did not work with the modern notion of legislative authority or with our sharp distinction between the work of the legislator and the work of the judge. Nor were his interests in *De legibus* quite what one would expect; the great bulk of what we have concerns the regulation of religious and ritual conduct.

Because *De legibus* is fragmentary, we cannot tell how conscious Cicero was of how different his enterprise was from the work on which it was modeled. Plato's *Laws* answers the question of how to create a second-best state if the ideal state of *Republic* cannot be had. Cicero's *De legibus* focuses on the relationship between the law of nature—which Cicero equates with moral law or divine law—and the law of a particular state. Even then, he never explains quite how the nature of law as such illuminates the detailed Roman regulations to which he adverts. His account of the nature of law is Stoic in origin and the basis of endless later analysis: law is the deliverance of right reason; it rests on the natural sociability of mankind; it treats everyone equally; the mere say-so of any particular group of people does not suffice to make their decrees law. This last claim is the crux of Cicero's natural law theory. Laws must be made properly and for the right reasons to be laws at all. It became the basis of one of the most important—and hotly disputed—claims of medieval and subsequent jurisprudence: *injusta lex nulla lex est*. A law that violates justice is not a law at all. It is the view that sustains the claim that Nazi legislation depriving Jews of all civil and political rights *could not* have been valid law, because it was too unjust to count as law at all, a view that contrasts very starkly with the so-called positivist view that whatever a recognized legal system accepts as law is law, no matter how wicked or misconceived. Disappointingly, Cicero seems not to have meant anything so far-reaching; it appears that he had in mind particular cases of bad law in a Roman context, not the general claim that bad law is no law at all.

Given the fragmentary quality of both *De republica* and *De legibus*, it is not surprising that later generations seized on *De officiis*. It induces mixed feelings in a modern reader. It is a crisply written and cogent statement of an eclectic, mostly Stoic vision of the virtues and their social and political purpose; but it is hard not to feel sorry for Cicero's son, Marcus, the avowed target of the moral instruction and political advice that Cicero offers. He must have found his father's boasting a frightful burden. The cogency of the work, however, explains why it was embraced so warmly by Christian writers. It relies on the view that Cicero often expresses: most disputes between philosophers are terminological, and we should attend to what their doctrines have in common because that is what is true in each of them. The notion of "one truth, many formulations" has an obvious value, not only for pre-Christian Romans conscious that they lived in a multiethnic empire but eventually for Christians conscious that they must coexist with non-Christians and with Christians who interpret their common faith with different nuances. It is a highly political work, because it presupposes throughout that the young man to whom advice is being given will be a public-spirited, upper-class citizen ready to serve the republic to the best of his abilities.

Cicero set out to give an account of our duties that keeps duty and self-interest sufficiently separate while acknowledging that morality must also have a nonmoral point for the individual. He was hostile to the Epicureans because—he thought—they failed to do this; they collapsed morality into self-interest and explained our duties as whatever we find useful to ourselves. The beneficial is not identical with the honorable; the commonsensical view that we do not always benefit ourselves by being just or brave is prima facie right. Nonetheless, there is no deep or irresolvable conflict between the useful and the honorable; the morally good life is naturally attractive to us. Cicero provides an account of the four cardinal virtues—wisdom, justice, "greatness of spirit" or courage, and moderation—an account of the legitimate acquisition of whatever we value for ourselves, and an account of how to handle conflicts between duty and inclination. It can never be in our *ultimate* interest to act unjustly, and the conflict of virtue and utility is in the very last resort only apparent. Nevertheless, he sufficiently respects the realities of everyday life to do much more than dismiss the conflict out of hand. That is the other face of his rejection of Plato's claim that philosophical contemplation is the ultimate blessedness. He concedes that one might accept it as a religious doctrine; but he never retreats from the view that wise action is better than theoretical knowledge and that wise action is action in a community.

The foundations of ethics are reason and natural sociability. Reason is unique to human beings. We alone inquire into the nature of things, and we alone can reflect on our own nature and on the duties that stem from it. Cicero is even more eloquent on the subject of sociability. We are not drawn to each other to compensate for our weaknesses, but because we want the company of friends for their own sake. Although Cicero thinks of duties as including duties to ourselves as well as to others, *De officiis* is interesting above all as an account of the demands of justice. The arguments that become so important to later writers first emerge in a distinctive shape in these pages. For instance, Cicero quotes Plato's observation that we are not born for ourselves alone, but turns it into the thought that we are born for our friends, our country, and humanity, which Plato would never have done. Where Plato sees us pulled toward the depths of philosophical truth, Cicero embeds us in concentric circles of social connection.

Justice is the desire to give each man his own, to preserve as common what is common, and to keep as private what is private; and Cicero raises all the still familiar questions about how we should distinguish between

justice and benevolence—the line between giving people what they are
entitled to as opposed to giving them what they are not entitled to but
what we are prompted to give them out of generosity. Characteristically,
he reminds us that we must not be generous with what is not our own,
nor even so generous with what *is* our own that we imperil our future
ability to do good. He writes always with an eye to the way in which
the way we behave will look to other people, and the notion of what is
honorable or decorous is constantly to the fore. We do not behave justly
for merely selfish reasons, but we should remember that being just is one
way to make sure that we are well thought of by everyone else. It is a very
Ciceronian thought that being well thought of is something to aim at—
as long as the people who think well of us are people who judge rightly.
The praise of the misguided or eccentric we can do without.

Cicero once more assimilates the philosophical arguments of the
Greeks to the *mos maiorum* of the Romans. Roman history and contemporary Roman politics are everywhere visible, with all the usual targets receiving the usual rebukes. In the same vein, when he engages in a
lengthy discussion of the stringency of the demands of honesty, he cites
cases he would have come across as praetor, and one gets glimpses of his
talents as an advocate. The most strenuous defense of traditional Roman
values comes, however, when Cicero discusses the fate of Regulus. Marcus Atilius Regulus was consul and a Roman general during the First
Punic War; after several victories he was defeated and captured in 255.
He was held for several years, and the story has it that in 250 he was
sent to Rome by the Carthaginians to arrange an exchange of prisoners,
having given his parole to return to Carthage if he was unsuccessful in
arranging the exchange. At Rome he argued against the exchange and
urged his compatriots to continue the fight against Carthage. He then
returned to Carthage in accordance with his oath and was tortured to
death, either by being put in a barrel with a spiked interior and rolled
down a hill, or by having his eyelids cut off and being exposed to the
light of the sun. Cicero rather alarmingly insists that he did no more
than his duty; even promises made under duress to an enemy must be
kept. Regulus was right to return to the Carthaginians and face martyrdom because he had promised the Carthaginians that he would do

so; conversely, the hostages taken at Cannae were wrong to try to evade their duty to return to their captors. Indeed, says Cicero, Regulus does not deserve great praise for his actions, because it was the republic that made them possible and inevitable.[16] This sets the price at which we *might* be asked to do our duty very high. Not all the links between high principle and Roman practice demand such sacrifice. When Cicero considers generosity, he takes for granted Roman clientelage: we owe most to those who have done most for us in the past. His political anxieties make an appearance when he observes that unusual generosity to strangers suggests that the seemingly generous man may be moved by ulterior motives and may—for instance—be cultivating political support for an improper purpose.

Cicero's style is a key to the success of *De officiis*, and not just the literary style, but the political and intellectual style. Regulus aside, the demands of duty generally stretch only as far as the well-educated, well-to-do man is likely to follow. Thus, he insists, in a famous metaphor that Machiavelli later stood on its head, that courage is necessary but the courage of a human being is not the ferocity of the lion, just as wisdom is necessary but the intelligence of the human being is not the cunning of the fox.[17] Sulla was said to combine the cunning of the fox with the ferocity of the lion, and Machiavelli famously held that the prince must know how to do so.[18] Cicero held that we are not to model ourselves on the lesser animals, but to ask always what the distinctively human form of conduct must be. Although reason links us to the gods, these are not injunctions for philosophers but recipes for good—that is, decorous, honorable, and reputable—conduct on the part of men of good family who are conscious of their duties to friends, family, class, and locality. Compared with the philosophical heights of Plato, Cicero is parochial; but this is one of many reasons why he talks to us in ways we still find persuasive.

What he was not and could not be was the savior of the Roman Republic. There is a valedictory note about Cicero's reflections on Roman politics which reminds us that the future lay not with a revived republic but with the Roman Empire, and that the spiritual and moral future lay not with the *mos maiorum* and traditional Roman piety but with Christianity. Christians who initially lived in expectation of an imminent Second

Coming had little to say about the politics of a world that offered them no more than grudging toleration when they were lucky and martyrdom when they were not. Nor did the conversion of Constantine in 311 see a sudden flowering of a distinctive Christian political philosophy, not least because Christianity did not become the "official" religion of the empire until the emperor Theodosius outlawed pagan cults in 382. That makes it the more astonishing that the first sustained account of a Christian's attitude to earthly politics is a work whose vitality continues after sixteen centuries. Augustine's *City of God against the Pagans* is very much more than a masterpiece of Christian political theology; but it is that, and Cicero was one of its targets.

CHAPTER 5

Augustine's Two Cities

Augustine's Life and Times

AUGUSTINE'S IMPORTANCE TO THE subsequent history of Europe is impossible to exaggerate. His political theory, which is all we focus on here, was a very small part of what he wrote in some 113 books and innumerable letters and sermons. Nonetheless, it is pregnant with arguments that racked not only Christian Europe but the modern world: how seriously should a Christian with his eyes on eternity take the politics of this earthly life; is it the duty of the state to protect the church, repress heresy, and ensure that its citizens adhere to the one true faith; absent a Christian ruler, are we absolved of the duty to obey our rulers, or must we follow Saint Paul's injunction to "obey the powers that be"?[1] More generally, Augustine articulated distinctive and long-lived thoughts on matters that remain controversial: the nature of just war, the illegitimacy of the death penalty, the limits of earthly justice. The fact that his views on all these matters were embedded in a theology of some bleakness does not mean that they do not survive on their own merits. One needs only the barest sympathy with the thought that we are fallen creatures to find many of his views deeply appealing, far from cheerful as they may be.

Augustine was a Roman citizen, born at Thagaste, in North Africa, in 354. It is generally assumed that he was ethnically a Berber. His father was a minor official, a decurion; the rank was initially a military rank in the auxiliary forces with which Rome kept order in the provinces; the civilian equivalent was a town manager. The family's curial rank mattered less than that his parents were just prosperous enough to send Augustine to boarding school at the age of eleven. His mother, Monica, was a devout but uneducated Christian, his father a non-Christian who may or may not have converted on his deathbed. Catholic Christianity had recently become the official religion of the Roman Empire, the final great persecution of the Christians having taken place under Diocletian in 305–6. Augustine was not baptized as a child, but infant baptism was far from universal. He claimed that he had a wholly miserable childhood. In *The City of God* he says that he would rather die than live his childhood over again; but the claim comes in one of his many descriptions of human life as a long journey through a vale of suffering, and is not conclusive evidence that his childhood was more miserable than most childhoods or than his subsequent life. Indeed, he does not suggest that it was, since he asks rhetorically, "If anyone were offered the choice of suffering death or becoming a child again, who would not recoil from the second alternative and choose to die?"[2]

He claimed that as a child he disliked learning and preferred the pain of punishment for refusing to learn Greek to the pain of the lessons. He also says, perfectly sensibly, that Latin came easily because everyone around him spoke it, but Greek did not, because it was a foreign language. Many of us have thought as much about the languages we have tried to learn. He was certainly very clever and perhaps as willful as he claimed; how much Greek he learned is unclear, but it seems likely that he could read it without great difficulty but much preferred Latin. He initially intended to advance himself with a career in the imperial administration. This required a training in the skills of the orator, and at sixteen he went to Carthage to learn rhetoric. While there, he took a mistress by whom he had a son, Adeodatus. In retrospect, he was appalled by these youthful yieldings to the urgings of the flesh. Modern readers of his *Confessions* find them wholly forgivable and are much more appalled that he never tells us the name of his mistress, and that he abandoned her a dozen years later—as anyone of his class and upbringing would have done—when he was minded to marry an heiress to advance his career.[3]

He taught rhetoric in North Africa, then Rome, and when he was thirty secured a distinguished position as professor of rhetoric in Milan, which was a stepping-stone to a provincial governorship. By this time Rome was no longer the imperial capital. Early in the fourth century Diocletian had established his eastern capital at Byzantium and his western capital in Milan. Under Constantine the imperial capital was Byzantium, now renamed Constantinople, but late in the century the empire became de facto an eastern and western empire, with the western capital at Milan, and later at Ravenna. When teaching in Milan, Augustine arranged to make an advantageous marriage, essential to membership of the Roman aristocracy, but after much mental anguish he renounced these ambitions, was baptized as a Christian in 386, and devoted himself to the service of the church. He was baptized by Ambrose, bishop of Milan, the most intellectually and politically powerful churchman of his day, but it was devout lay friends who had done the work of conversion, or reconversion, since he had been brought up as a Christian as a child and had abandoned his faith in Carthage. He had by this time explored many of the religious and quasi-religious resources of the late classical world. He was for a time a Manichaean "hearer" or acolyte, but found Manichaeanism intellectually unpersuasive and littered with superstition and myth. He was then attracted by the austere Neoplatonism of the pagan philosopher Plotinus, which was a very plausible gateway to the Christian faith. Once he had become a Christian, he returned to North Africa, first to Thagaste, where he set up a little community of celibate Christians, and then to Hippo, where he was inducted as a priest in 391 and made bishop in 395, taking up office in 396. He spent the second half of his life as bishop of Hippo, in continual controversy with movements he thought heretical or otherwise a danger to the church, and writing a stream of books and pamphlets to defend his view of the true church and the true faith.

One of the first things he wrote as bishop was a book that defies categorization, the *Confessions*, written in 397–400 and read with passionate interest ever since. Although it is a record of the route by which he came to his Christian faith, it is not an autobiography in the modern, or even in the ancient, sense. It is more nearly a continuous prayer to the God who had saved him, accompanied by lengthy passages of self-recrimination based loosely on his recollection of particular episodes of wrongdoing. It is made unforgettable by Augustine's extended reflections on the sheer mysteriousness of human existence. The first ten books are a loosely chronological *apologia pro vita sua*; the last three discuss time, the Trinity, and the Creation. Even readers who find Augustine's emotional style overpowering find it deeply engrossing, atheists as much as Christians.[4]

A bishop was not a grand figure in the church of the late fourth century. There were seven hundred bishops in the African church alone. He was nonetheless a central figure in the ordinary secular administration of his region, called on to exercise judicial functions and much else. Although such a life was not entirely thankless, it was exhausting, and Augustine lived it against the background of a steady decline in the western Roman Empire's ability to defend itself and protect its subjects. In 410 came the shattering event that launched Augustine on the task that occupied him for much of the rest of his life: writing *The City of God against the Pagans*, begun in 413 and completed after many interruptions in 427. When Alaric and his Visigoths sacked Rome in 410, the Eternal City was revealed as the indefensible former capital of the crumbling, and less important, western portion of the Roman Empire. The event was less important militarily than symbolically, but its symbolic importance was vast. Although Augustine does not mention it, Roman rule was decaying in North Africa as it was elsewhere. Roman control was increasingly fragile away from the coastal cities, and the military units meant to keep the peace on Rome's behalf were decreasingly under the control of the imperial administration, adding another danger to the incursions of barbarian tribes. In the last years of Augustine's life, the Vandals who had seized Spain realized that the province of Africa was at their mercy, and crossed the narrow straits to seize their prey. Augustine died in 430, with Hippo a besieged city full of refugees from the surrounding country. It was sacked and burned the following year.

In spite of the innumerable Renaissance paintings of Augustine at his desk, his daily round as a bishop was not spent in the study. He spent most mornings giving judgment in litigation over land, inheritances, and the other business of everyday life. His pastoral mission involved keeping his clergy even more than the laity on the straight and narrow, and managing intense relationships with the most spiritually aware of his congregation. Through his writings, Augustine would be second only to Saint Paul in his impact on the history of Christianity, but not only could he not have guessed this might happen; it would have been incredible to anyone else. The intellectual life of the Christian churches was still more Greek than Roman; Ambrose and Augustine were among the first Latin fathers, but that retrospective status was not something they set out to acquire. Greek was the language of philosophy, and Augustine's knowledge of Greek philosophy was secondhand, acquired from Cicero and from Latin translations of the Neoplatonist Plotinus. The churches of Constantinople or Jerusalem would have seemed much more likely sources of a Christian theology with real intellectual power.

As a Roman of the western empire, Augustine was not a natural intellectual leader of the Catholic Church. As an African, he was a provincial; the African church was provincial, too. It had a more austere view of the demands of Christianity than did the church in Italy; it did not accept the aristocratic laissez-faire that allowed Roman families to be partly pagan and partly Christian in their practice, and it was intolerant of doctrinal looseness. Retrospectively, we can see Catholic doctrine crystallizing into an orthodoxy; Augustine's contemporaries would have thought it was an open question where Christianity would settle on issues such as the freedom of the will, predestination, original sin, and the requirements for salvation. Augustine's vast and unwieldy masterpiece, *The City of God*, takes such firm and uncompromising views on all these issues that we are not surprised they triumphed; they have an unmatched intellectual power. Yet the price—intellectual, emotional, and moral—that must be paid for holding Augustine's views is so high that it is equally surprising that they made any headway.

Augustine excoriated himself for ever holding his pre-Christian beliefs. Nonetheless, they greatly influenced his view of the world as a Christian. To say that he remained a Neoplatonist or a Manichee would be foolish; to say that in temperament and in intellectual style he remained the man who found Manichaeanism and Neoplatonism attractive is the bare truth. This was not only a matter of Augustine's temperament and intellect. Christian doctrine was much affected both by the mysticism of the oriental mystery religions and by the rationalism of Greek philosophy. We can find our way into, and perhaps out of, Augustine's *City of God* most readily if we start with the dilemmas that any devout Christian must face when contemplating earthly politics, wrestle first with Augustine's youthful opinions, and enter *The City of God* by way of his confrontation with Cicero's *De republica*. This will involve a perhaps surprising degree of attention to the doctrinal pressures on Augustine, but much as Plato thought that only the truth as he saw it could redeem earthly societies, so Augustine, who thought that nothing but the grace of God could redeem anything mortal, thought that the truth inherent in his Christian faith contained the key to the value, limited as it was, of our earthly politics, as well as the explanation of the chasm that separated those politics from the nonpolitics of the true kingdom of God. Where philosophers and theologians are convinced that their ideas stand or fall as a systematic whole, there is nothing for us to do but to explore the edifice they have constructed.

Politics and Religion

Between the death of Cicero in 43 BCE and the birth of Augustine four centuries later, enormous changes had occurred. The most immediately momentous was the collapse of the Roman Republic and its gradual transformation into an empire. No thumbnail sketch of the following four centuries is possible here; but the crucial transformations can be briefly outlined. After the civil wars that followed the assassination of Julius Caesar, Caesar's adoptive grandson, Octavian, emerged victorious and established the "principate" that was recognized as the institution of one-man rule. The Roman hostility to the concept of a "king" remained as intense as ever, and for a surprisingly long time the forms of republican institutions were preserved. What we now think of as the imperial structure of administration and government was very late in coming.

Only when the entire empire was threatened by military disasters and economic and administrative chaos during the third century was there a radical transformation of its political structure that kept the empire alive for another century in the west and another millennium in the east.

A succession of emperors who gained power by military prowess created the centralized, bureaucratic, and uniform system of administration that we think of as defining the imperial system. The empire's ambition to rule the known world remained, even if the western empire was increasingly a patchwork of local regimes whose subordination to the empire was a legal fiction. At a doctrinal level, the Roman ideology of consensus, honored in the breach as it had always been, yielded to an emphasis on obedience and order. In terms of the contrast we began with, citizens gave way to subjects, and as emperors were increasingly drawn from the eastern empire, a more "Persian" view of a ruler's status crystallized. Christian rulers could not receive divine honors, but their pagan predecessors did, and the elaborate ceremonial of the court at Constantinople under Christian emperors was scarcely different.

The transformation of the pagan empire into the Christian empire that Constantine began to create and that became solidly established when Theodosius, the last emperor to reign over both the eastern and the western empires, outlawed pagan cults late in the fourth century, was in the long run even more momentous. The Christianization of the regions and peoples that composed the Roman Empire survived the decay of the western empire and ensured that the "barbarian" kingdoms that succeeded the western empire were Christian societies, just as the Byzantine Empire was. Somewhat fortuitously the Christianization of barbarian Europe fostered the process by which the pope ceased to be one bishop among many and became the head of the entire western church. The only language of law and culture they possessed in common was Latin— the language of western but not Greek Christianity—and Latin thus became the universal language of Western culture and gave the western Catholic Church a distinct identity.

Until Pippin and Charlemagne established the kingdom of the Franks in the eighth century, the Catholic Church was the only institution whose authority aspired to the geographical reach of the western empire. This sustained the concept of the universality of Roman rule while spiritualizing it in a way republican Romans would have found strange. It need not have happened. In retrospect the preeminence of the pope as the heir of Saint Peter seems inevitable, but when Constantine made Christianity the religion of the empire, it was to his city that eyes turned rather than to Rome. Thereafter, Milan and Ravenna were as important as Rome. Looking back, we see the ingredients assembled for the creation of the distinctive institutions of church and state, cooperating but serving different ends, and always in danger of coming into conflict either over doctrine or over the privileges of the clergy or over the different loyalties they appealed to. But if the western and eastern halves of the Roman Empire had not gone their separate ways, the history of Christianity would have been very different, and our ideas about the naturalness of a division of labor between religious and secular institutions would have been very different, too.[5]

The theoretical analysis of the role of religion in politics or of the politics of religion in all its forms is made harder by the ambiguity of both concepts. Politics and religion resist simple definition; nor can we wish these ambiguities away. It is of the essence of both religion and politics that it is an open question what is and is not a religious consideration or a political one. Politics as a simple struggle for power is not politics as Aristotle conceived it—the citizens of a polis ruling and being ruled in turn; and the politics of a society that seeks to find a "godly ruler" is not like either. The boundaries of the concept of religion are so porous that we habitually distinguish between "organized religion" and a "religious" view of the world more generally, with many writers thinking the first an enemy of the second.[6] The crucial contrast for our immediate purposes is between Christian politics and pagan politics: between the political implications of a theologically complex, fiercely monotheistic Christianity and the political implications of the theologically casual, polytheistic, "civic" religions of the Greek and Roman world. The contrast sheds light on the difficulties that pagan rulers had with the unwillingness of Jews and Christians to sacrifice to the local deities and on the very thin sense in which their persecutions were "religious" in motivation, and it also illuminates the first and most important articulation of Christian political theology.[7]

The very idea of a Christian political theology is problematic. If human beings are only transitorily on earth, and earth is but a vale of tears through which we must pass on our way to paradise, earthly politics loses almost all value. Life in the polis cannot be the good life for man, since fulfillment lies in the hereafter; here below, we must prepare for eternity. Earthly happiness for rational persons consists in whatever confidence they may entertain about the life hereafter. This "abstentionist" vision is in some ways at odds with the involvement of Christ in the everyday life of the community in which he spent his short life. He may not have taken part in "politics," and he certainly insisted that his kingdom was "not of this world." But he healed the sick, preached to large crowds, and taught an ethical system that would have made a deep political impact on any society open to his teaching. Roman Judaea was not wholly deaf to it, which may well have been one reason for his execution. In the first two centuries after the death of Christ, Christianity might well have been thought un- or apolitical, however. The belief that Christ's return was imminent undermined a concern with earthly politics, and Christianity initially appealed mainly to the poor, to slaves, and to outsiders with no role in Roman political and public life. In the innumerable cities of the Greek east that preserved their earlier institutions by Roman concession, there was "local politics" still. There was also a great deal of public life both in the administration of justice and the provision of the usual services of government, and in semicompulsory public duties incumbent on the upper classes, such as laying on games and paying for sacrifices. As a religion of the poor, Christianity had nothing to offer public life.

Both in Rome and in the provinces, the civic life of the empire certainly impinged on Christians, however; they faced punishments up to and including hideous forms of death for refusing to sacrifice to the emperor of the day or to the Roman gods, and they might at any time be made scapegoats for a famine or some other misfortune. When persecutions became infrequent and when Christianity began to appeal to the

higher social classes, who were bound to accept their share of public obligations, the question of how Christians should relate to the state became
harder to evade. Finally, when the emperor Constantine converted to
Christianity and the empire became Christian, all the questions so familiar to us about how the state should support religion, and how Christians should support a Christian or a non-Christian state, demanded
answers. Christian thinkers had to form a view on vexed issues: how did
God's law relate to civic law, and beyond that to the law of nature—*lex
naturae*—and the law of peoples—the jus gentium? Could a Christian
shed blood as a judge imposing the death penalty? Should Christians
serve in an army? Early Christianity was overwhelmingly pacifist, but
Constantine's Christianity was the reverse. What moral sacrifices, and
how many, could a Christian make to be a good citizen? Augustine neither raised nor answered all these questions, but he provided the intellectual apparatus with which subsequent generations did.

Manichaeanism

The story is rich in paradox. Augustine was a fierce critic of pagan philosophy and adamant that only in Christianity could salvation be found;
but he found his way to an intellectually cogent Christianity by way of
Cicero's philosophical works and Neoplatonism. His conception of the
two cities was foreshadowed in Scipio's Dream, with which Cicero's *De
republica* concludes, just as Scipio's Dream was foreshadowed in Plato's
contrast between the two realms in which the philosopher finds himself: the earthly republic and the reality revealed by philosophy. Initially,
Augustine was tempted by Manichaeanism.

He began his search for faith as a Manichaean "hearer," a spiritual
fellow traveler who served the adepts of the faith—the illuminati—and
prepared their food. Manichaeanism was not then the reviled heresy it
became; there was no unified and authoritative source of Christian belief,
such as the papacy became in medieval western Europe, and no authority able to impose a single view of orthodoxy and heresy. This did not
encourage toleration, and it did not reflect a belief in the separateness of

secular and spiritual authority; no premodern society entertained such a view. Churches and secular authorities repressed ideas they did not like, in a sporadic and inconsistent fashion; where they either could not do it or had no particular reason to do it, they were tolerant by accident rather than design. Manichaeanism was the creation of a third-century Persian sage, Mani, who described himself as the apostle of Christ.[8] Its one, very important intellectual strength was its answer to the problem of evil. The problem is simply stated: if God is both loving and omnipotent, why is there suffering in the world? Augustine eventually held that suffering exists because humanity is sinful, an answer built on an unflinching acceptance of the doctrine of original sin and the heritability of the taint of Adam. Pagan polytheisms did not face the problem. Evil was a brute fact, and accepted as such, unclouded by any idea that the gods might have intended there to be less of it.

Manichaeanism relied on one non-Christian—and non-Judaic—premise. It was dualistic. The material world is evil, as is all matter; that is why the world we live in is a realm of pain and suffering. The God revealed in the Old Testament is good, and is pure spirit; but contrary to Genesis, the physical world is not his creation but the work of the devil. For this reason, Manichaeanism held a negative view of sexual passion, both human and other. The created world is evil, as is our physical nature and sexual reproduction. This was one reason for the Manichaean commitment to vegetarianism, although the Manichaeanism of Augustine's day was independently committed to the virtues of fruits such as melons, which were identified with the sun, the supposed dwelling place of God. Sun worship was Zoroastrian, and the Zoroastrian element in Manichaeanism swiftly alienated Augustine. Mani's writings also made claims about stars and planets and phenomena such as eclipses that were patently false. When Augustine found that pagan writers had made careful celestial observations of eclipses and similar phenomena, and that their predictions were invariably right and Mani's wrong, his faith gave way.[9]

Nonetheless, the attractions of Manichaeanism are powerful. It does not blame innocent suffering on God. Innocent suffering is the rock on which Christianity is always in danger of shipwreck; critics of the Christian belief that this imperfect world is the creation of a benign omnipotence always point to the painful deaths of little children as clinching evidence that it cannot be. Either God is not omnipotent or he is not benign; few wish to bite the bullet and accept the third possibility— that tiny children are sinful and merit their suffering. Augustine bit the bullet, eventually arguing that we all enter the world tainted with the sin of Adam and deserve what we suffer.[10] One might think that the Manichaean view that God is the source of goodness, but unable to make headway against the devil, is less alarming. The persistence of Manichaeanism into the late Middle Ages suggests that many people have thought so.

Augustine's mother, the devout Monica, forbade Augustine the house while he was a hearer. Nonetheless, Manichees and Christians had a lot in common; and that was not surprising in an age when pagan philosophers numbered Christ among the wonder-workers and magi they admired, while rejecting as absurd the idea that a human could be literally the son of God, and dismissing the doctrine of the resurrection of the body as preposterous. Manichees saw Christ as the Gnostic heretics did: Christ was a great teacher. Like others who embodied great doctrines, he emanated from God, but was not literally his son. Nor could he have suffered bodily torment on the cross; the appearance that he did so was an illusion. Christ was pure spirit, and the human body that observers saw was the appearance that the divine spirit wore for temporary purposes. The point of Christ's mission was to spread enlightenment, and his work as a teacher was central to his life. The Resurrection was the emancipation of Christ's spirit from its earthly appearance, and resurrection for anyone else would similarly be the escape of the spirit from the body.

Gnostic sects were innumerable and various, and Manichaeanism embraced many local varieties, so it is impossible to give a more precise account of what Augustine believed than the one he gave in his *Confessions*. There are no competing accounts to set against his. The triumph of Christianity everywhere west of Persia and the dislike that political rulers felt for the anarchist implications of Manichaeanism mean that the literary remains of Manichaeanism are sparse. Precision is not necessary; once Christian orthodoxy embraced the Incarnation and the Resurrection of the body, Gnosticism was at odds with the two central items of the faith. The struggles internal to Christianity between Trinitarian and non-Trinitarian accounts of the divine nature were violent; but they were between Christians who shared precisely the doctrines that Manichees and Gnostics rejected.

Most religious faith owes less to its intellectual coherence, narrowly considered, than to two other elements. One is its ability to provide a lightning rod for powerful emotions; the other, the persuasiveness of the picture of the human condition it offers. For Augustine, Manichaean-ism appealed to a powerful element in his character, his sense that he was full of bad desires. This was his personal "problem of evil"; his religious sensibility focused on that sense of sin with lasting political consequences. Only when he found inspiration in Saint Paul, who had a similar sensibility to his own, did he find a more satisfying answer than Manichaeanism provided.

A last persuasive feature of Manichaeanism was that it offered a "two-tier" doctrine of the spiritual life that could readily migrate to a Christian worldview. Manichaeanism seems on its face to demand a suicidal hostility to the material world. If the flesh is evil and the spirit good, then taking leave of the flesh by suicide seems to be the route to felicity, or at least to emancipation from earthly evil. In practice, it was held to be sufficient even for the most devout to reduce the fleshliness of existence—by sexual abstinence, eating a sparse vegetarian diet, drink-ing water, wearing linen garments, and avoiding the use of animal hides and fur. In the Middle Ages the Manichaean elite, the *perfecti*, followed this regime; only those who felt themselves to be particularly called to live such lives were under any obligation to do so. Most people could continue to live their usual lives: so long as we are trapped here on the material earth, we do not sin if we do not succumb unduly to greed, lust, anger, and the other sins of the flesh. Elements of this acceptance of the limits of the demands we may make on ordinary life recur throughout *The City of God*.

From Manichaeanism to Christianity

Augustine's account of his escape from Manichaeanism to Christianity gives Neoplatonic philosophy pride of place in making him seek non-superstitious intelligibility in the human predicament. It is not easy to distinguish the part played by Cicero from the part played by the Neoplatonists Plotinus and Porphyry. It is easy to believe that the deep impact of the latter was greater; they were obsessed with the same problems as Plato and reacted in the same intense, determined, and detailed way. Cicero's writings certainly had the greater impact on Augustine's ideas about politics. At nineteen he read a work of Cicero's that has long been lost and whose contents are unknown—*Hortensius*—but *The City of God* draws explicitly on Cicero's political writings: Augustine's criticism of Rome was that it suffered from the *libido dominationis*—a lust for power for its own sake that is inimical to the pursuit of even earthly justice, a complaint that comes straight from Cicero's *De republica*. In *The City of God*, the most "political" discussions come many books apart, and many years apart in their writing, when Augustine so to speak returns to the argument with Cicero that he begins in book 2 and concludes in book 21, but the argumentative method is the same: to hold Rome to Cicero's standards.

What Augustine learned from the Neoplatonists was how to reconcile the goodness of ultimate reality with the miseries of the world of everyday experience. This world is inevitably a vale of tears, for it is a shadow of the true world illuminated by the light of the divine mind. Stripped of Mani's absurd cosmogenic myths, the thought became acceptable that ultimate reality is one, perfect, indivisible, and unshakable, while the world in which we dwell is fragmentary and chaotic and incessantly shaken by disasters both natural and contrived by passionate and unwise humanity. Evil is privation, not a positive force in the world. The notion that the ultimate misfortune for humanity is separation from God is a thought of the same kind. There was room for a dialogue at least between adherents of the Christian and Jewish faith in a strongly personal God and Neoplatonists attached to the idea of a central Mind or Intelligence animating the world. Augustine himself observed that he found in his philosophical reading the insight that begins Saint John's gospel: "In the beginning was the Word, and the Word was with God, and the Word was God."[11]

Still, Augustine was converted—or reconverted—by reading Saint Paul. He had become increasingly unhappy and unsure of himself. He finally convinced himself that he had received a divine message to open the Bible and read what it commanded. He opened the book, read a passage from the Epistles, and took it as a direct injunction to arm himself with the Lord Jesus Christ. The sharpness of the break was greater at an emotional than an intellectual level, but at the emotional level it struck like a thunderbolt, which is just the impression his *Confessions* conveys. All the same, conversion implied nothing about whether Augustine should do something other than climb the career ladder to a provincial governorship. Most Christians were laymen and laywomen going about their ordinary lives; only a few became recluses or members of monastic communities. Augustine was initially inclined to become a recluse and adopt a Christian version of the quiet life led by Plotinus when he retired into the country to think. Nor did his return to Africa after the death of Monica lead immediately to the priesthood; he established a small community in Thagaste before being more or less strong-armed into the priesthood by the congregation at Hippo.

Practical Politics and Theoretical Politics: The Provocation for *The City of God*

His reluctance to give up the quiet life of the scholar was genuine. Augustine would happily have kept away from the world of politics. He was combative, and his work is polemical; but the fights he picked were with those who committed intellectual, moral, and spiritual errors. He was a warrior in the cause of theological truth. This means, inter alia, that although *The City of God* is an enormous book, "a loose, baggy monster," as it has been called,[12] it is not Augustine's "political theory." That is an intellectual construction of later ages, not something Augustine created. Most of *The City of God* is concerned with theological controversies and large philosophical issues. Some of it is historical controversy. Some things that the modern world would think part of a political theory, even things one would have thought central to a Christian political theory, such as an account of the right of the state to enforce religious uniformity, hardly feature in *The City of God*. They hardly feature, because Augustine takes it for granted that it is a good thing if an earthly ruler is imbued with the true faith and is willing to bring his people to that faith. He had scruples about the means used; he did not, for instance, wish to see torture employed against the Donatists, the North African sect that threatened his church in the early 400s, even though the Donatists were themselves physically violent. But he took it for granted that earthly rulers should bring their subjects to God if they could. What else were they to do?[13]

The provocation for writing *The City of God* was the sack of Rome in 410. This did not mark "the fall of the Roman Empire"; the western empire had been militarily on the defensive for two centuries, the last emperor, the sixteen-year-old Romulus Augustus, was deposed only in 476, and elements of Roman administration persisted for another century in the west. The Byzantine Empire endured until 1453. Nor was the physical damage done to Rome by Alaric and the Visigoths particularly severe; this was not the Romans sacking Carthage. The psychological shock was another matter. Moreover, it provoked the argument about the role of Christianity in the destruction of Rome that Augustine responded to. When Christians were persecuted in earlier centuries, before the emergence of Christianity as the official religion of the empire, the reason was that their unwillingness to sacrifice to the traditional gods imperiled the state. Pagan religion ascribed earthly misfortune to the malice of gods who had been insulted or slighted, so the Christian unwillingness to sacrifice to the gods was a literal threat to the well-being of their fellow citizens.[14] It was rarely suggested that they posed any other threat—although Nero, seeking a scapegoat for the burning of Rome, latched onto the Christians as an unpopular group on whom to pin responsibility, as others did thereafter in face of a variety of disasters.

Augustine was not quick to respond to the suggestion that Christian hostility to the old gods was the deathknell for Rome. He began to write *The City of God* in 413, three years after Alaric's invaders had ransacked Rome. Whatever his immediate purposes, it turned out to be a fruitful provocation. Augustine created a Christian political theology by turning Cicero inside out. At the end of *De republica*, Cicero placed the fantasy of Scipio's Dream, a few lyrical pages that purport to record the encounter of Scipio Africanus the Younger with the first Scipio Africanus in the heavens where his spirit now dwelled. The older Scipio gave an account of the afterlife very like that which Plato provides at the end of *Republic*, and rehearsed many of the ideas on which Stoics and Neoplatonists agreed—the vanity of earthly desire, the transitoriness of human glory, and the triviality of the life of the body, among them. The passage illuminates the tension that Augustine had to handle throughout *The City of God*, though he, like Macrobius, was interested in Scipio's Dream only as a source of reflection on such topics as the transmigration of souls. In *The City of God*, it is Scipio's account of the history of Rome and his account of a true *res publica* that Augustine criticizes. Scipio the Younger was the leading speaker in *De republica*; he sets out the standards for a true *res publica* and the conditions necessary if there is to be a true *populus*, a people whose common good is served by a republic practicing earthly justice. If there is no justice, there is no *res populi*, and therefore no *res republica*. The standards of justice are universal; they are given in natural law; and natural law is known to all mankind who consult their reason. The key ideas are justice and reason; the republic is founded on justice, and the requirements of justice are known to reason. Man is distinguished from the beasts by the possession of reason, and from other gregarious creatures by being able to found a community on the practice of justice rather than sociability alone.[15]

Augustine subverts these claims by accepting them. He does not deny that man possesses reason, but by the time he began to write *The City of God*, he had ceased to believe that reason was capable of motivating human beings to behave as they ought; we have only a very limited degree of free will, and in general, he says, reason merely assists us to choose one more or less sinful course over another. Nor does Augustine deny that Cicero's account of justice is an accurate account of the nature of justice:

a settled intention to give everyone his due is what justice is. What he denies is that *any* state on earth ever was, is now, or ever will be a true *res publica* in the Ciceronian sense, and therefore that any actual people can be a *populus* in the Ciceronian sense of a political community practicing real justice. *The City of God* makes two claims, one more difficult than the other. The simpler claim is that no pagan state practices Ciceronian justice, because no pagan state gives the one true God his due. By the same token, no pagan state can have a true common good, so no pagan state can be a true *res populi*. This seems an unfair and ad hoc argument, since justice between members of a political community hardly seems on all fours with justice toward God. Nonetheless, it is a useful part of a case against those who accused the Christians of bringing about the downfall of Rome by forbidding the worship of the old gods. Their complaint was that the Christian emperors who forbade the worship of the old gods had treated the old gods unjustly by depriving them of the worship that was their due; so the old gods had retaliated by withdrawing their protection from Rome. One of Augustine's best, and wholly effective, retorts was that the old gods had never kept their side of the bargain; they had never protected any state, however devotedly their adherents had kept up their cults. He lists the innumerable disasters that Rome suffered when most attached to the old cults; throughout *The City of God* he insists that good and bad fortune falls upon the just and the unjust alike.[16]

The more difficult claim is that it is not clear that even a Christian state can practice true justice, though it obviously clears the hurdle at which pagan states must, on this view, fall at once. It can give God his due by worshipping the one true God and no others. But since real justice is giving everyone what is really due to him or her, and the only being who knows what that is is God, true earthly justice is beyond us, or, at least, we cannot know whether we have achieved it. If justice is not the foundation of human affairs, what is? The reply is *love*, but love in a very difficult sense; it is tempting, though cowardly, to leave the word in Augustine's Latin, *libido*. Love, in Augustine's usage, embraces love in the ordinary sense of strong affection, and it certainly embraces sexual desire; but it also embraces the mathematician's desire to discover an elegant proof of a difficult theorem and the general's wish to win a victory. Nor is Augustine saying anything so banal as that we do what we do because we *want* to. That is true, but uninteresting. Love in Augustine's sense is an active force in the world, as we see when he claims that in any loving relationship between two people there are three agents in action: the lover, the beloved, and "love itself." *Libido*, or active desire, makes the world move, and especially the social and political world. It is important, too, that it is an active force that can take possession of us; the Rome whose misfortunes provoked the writing of *The City of God* was animated by a *libido dominandi*—a desire for conquest—that then dominated Rome herself. Just as sexual passion can become addictive, so can the desire for glory.

Augustine escaped the clutches of the Manichaean view that evil was an active force when he accepted Plotinus's view that evil is privation, a loss of good, and not a positive force. Understanding evil as estrangement from God and his grace was a Christian rendering of the Neoplatonists' claim that the world is the more evil and the more unreal the farther away it is from the One and the True. Nonetheless, Augustine did not empty the world of forces that would, if misdirected, get humanity into trouble. Love was the most important of them. Their existence did not undermine individual agency. Indeed, Augustine emphasized the individual will in ways the ancient world had not. For Augustine the problem of the will was central. He was a strong-willed person by anyone's standards; and he possessed an acute sense that he had when young deliberately willed to do wrong. This was a breach with the Platonic tradition every bit as great as identifying the impersonal "one" of Neoplatonism with the very personal God of the Old Testament. Socrates surprised his contemporaries by insisting that we do evil only in error and that it is a lack of knowledge of the good that explains human wickedness. Augustine articulated what is implicit in Saint Paul; we sin against the light because we have a will do evil.

Some commentators have been puzzled by one of the stories that Augustine retailed in his *Confessions*.[17] When he was a boy, he and some friends stole pears from a neighbor's orchard. It was a pointless theft. The pears were no good; he had no need of them; he and his companions gave them to the pigs. The misdemeanor was doubly symbolic. It was a willful crime, committed not to get the pears but out of sheer devilment;

he wanted to break the rules and committed a pointless theft to gratify that desire. Adam had no need of the apple; he said he was beguiled by Eve, but that was an evasion. He wanted to break the most important of the few rules that God had laid down for him. Why might we, or Adam, or Augustine want to behave like this? Two reasons occur to Augustine: first, simple pride. We are creatures who not only have wills but wish to make those wills effective. Why else does God afflict Job with all sorts of unmerited misfortune save to humble his pride? Not until Thomas Hobbes twelve centuries later does another thinker appear with the same eagle-eyed insight into the role of the will and the centrality of pride in our misfortunes.

The second reason is to keep company with others. Adam was not so much "beguiled" by Eve as ready to do whatever it took to remain in her good books. We cannot survive without company. Augustine wanted the approval of the local hoodlums and joined in their wickedness. He had a surer grasp of what motivates rioters and looters in the contemporary world than commentators looking for the deep causes of unrest. He is unflinching about the fact that he chose to do what he did and that he enjoyed it. This is non-Manichaean—it was *he*, not his body, who acted—and non-Platonic—it was not a mistake but willed misbehavior. Augustine's view of the freedom of the will is difficult, and its intricacies must be evaded here; but it is worth noting that true freedom of the will, that is, the ability to choose between good and evil at will, belonged to Adam, and only between the Creation and the Fall.[18] Fallen men can only choose between evils unless they receive divine grace, and that is the unearned gift of God. Nonetheless, we make choices, and it is we who make them.

Armed with these insights, Augustine can make short work of his opponents, though he allowed himself fourteen years, twenty-two books, and twelve hundred pages of text to do it. The fall of Rome is not to be laid at the door of the Christians; Rome did not fall because the Romans' neglect of the old gods led to the gods' rejection of Rome. Much of *The City of God* focuses on that issue, though the reader is hard put to it to remember the fact, when Augustine is pursuing Roman historians through the last recesses of their narratives of the glory of Rome. He ignores innumerable traditional issues. He nowhere bothers to discuss the merits of different forms of government; Polybian or Aristotelian classification does not interest him, and he is not interested in Aristotle's great concern, the prevention of stasis. One might have expected him to be, but Augustine's world was not the Athenian polis, with its restless citizenry, but the bureaucratic empire; the empire might come to grief at the hands of invading barbarians, but it would not succumb to anything resembling stasis. In any event, trying to build an eternal polity is futile. Peace is better than war, in general and with necessary exceptions; but the preservation of perpetual peace is beyond mortal men, and they must live with that fact. Indeed, they must look only for the consolation of knowing that, in the eternal scheme of things, it is of small account whether they perish this year or in a decade's time. This deflates Roman glory, and especially Roman *libertas*: "As far as this mortal life is concerned, which is spent and finished in a few days, what difference does it make under what rule a man lives who is soon to die, provided only that those who rule him do not compel him to what is impious and wicked?"[19] Rome may have done the peoples it subjugated no real harm by conquering them, but by the same token, the glory the Romans got did them no real good.

The Citizens of the City of God

We must, to make complete sense of all this, start with the most obvious question. What is the city of God and who are its citizens, and what is the earthly city and who are its citizens? Augustine's answer is that the citizens of the city of God are those whom God by his grace has admitted to the company of the saved. The earthly city is defined by exclusion as the company of all the rest. The "earthly city," as much as the "city of God," is a conceptual rather than a geographical entity; Old Testament saints are citizens of the heavenly city, and so are those yet unborn who will receive God's grace in future. The population of a physical earthly city contains both the elect and the nonelect, and earthly judgment cannot be sure which is which. Election is not something we can discern

with mortal eyes, or something we can earn by good behavior. We are all
sinners, and God might justly have condemned all of us to eternal punishment: Augustine uses an argument that the violently reactionary critic
of the French Revolution Joseph de Maistre found invaluable fourteen
centuries later. Voltaire had asked why God chose to destroy Lisbon in
the earthquake of 1755; was there not dancing and misbehavior in Paris
too? Maistre's reply is Augustine's. None of us is innocent of the sin of
Adam. A godless pride is built into us at birth. We talk of childish innocence, but babies are not innocent. They are weak; the red-faced baby
longing for its mother's breast and bawling fit to burst its lungs is powerless to wreak upon the world the violence it would like to wreak in its
frustration.[20] The content of its desires is as bad as could be. When God
saves some but allows many to suffer eternal punishment, it is not his sin
but theirs that explains why they are punished. We should be grateful
that he has spared some when he might in justice have punished all.

We mortal spectators here below cannot know who is a member
of the city of God; not the least powerful of the implications is that
political relationships cannot be based on distinguishing the saved and
the elect. Augustine's insistence on the mixed nature of all human communities was a powerful argument in the local conflicts of his own day,
but equally important in explaining the nature of Christian politics. In
insisting that any ruler who provided the limited earthly goods that a
state could provide was entitled to our obedience, Augustine provided
the foundations of two famous arguments, both controversial. The first
was the view of Aquinas that Christians must obey non-Christian rulers;
the second was what became in seventeenth-century Europe the highly
unpopular claim that a Christian commonwealth should be governed
in the same way as any other commonwealth.[21] The local problems that
provoked him were specific to his time and region. The great threat to
the unity of the Catholic Church in Africa was posed by the so-called
Donatists, named after a bishop of Carthage—Donatus the Great—
who was their leader in the mid-fourth century. They were extreme rigorists, who wanted a church of the elect alone. Their standard of election
was a person's conduct during the last of the persecutions. They denied

that anyone who had succumbed to persecution was entitled to give the sacraments; and they insisted on rebaptizing members of their sect.

The Donatists were condemned many times by imperial edicts and church councils, became more extreme in the face of persecution, and by the end of the fourth century convinced themselves they were the only Christian church in all the world, and entitled to convert dissenters by force. They occupied twenty years of Augustine's time as bishop and were a sore trial to his spirit. They also made him more ready to employ the brute force of the state to bring heretics to obedience than when he first took office. They were not the only unamenable sect to plague Augustine; the Circumcellions—the name means simply "those who live in the neighboring villages"—were a still more violent offshoot of the Donatists. Their political interest is that they forced him to articulate clearly the view that it is the sacrament, not the minister, that is efficacious: what matters is the sacrament being administered and not the moral purity of the minister. This is not a directly political view, but it has clear political implications: if what matters is the law and its effects, we should not inquire into the character of political leaders but look to their impact on the lives of their subjects.

Augustine's doctrine of the mixed quality of all human communities— the Catholic Church included—meant that no earthly body could claim to be "the city of God on earth" and that although Christian asceticism was acceptable—he himself lived with a community of celibates from the moment he became a priest—it did nothing to lessen the contrast between the mixed earthly community and the city of the saved. A community of ascetics could not lay claim to be a community of the elect. This had large implications for the authority of the church vis-à-vis the state. Augustine had no doubt that it was the task of the church to warn rulers as well as their subjects when they were acting immorally; not to do so was to commit an injustice toward them, since admonition was their due.[22] In general, however, the church ought not to exercise earthly responsibilities. This did not mean that the functionaries of the church might not also have to perform secular administrative duties. Augustine knew that de facto the empire could not function unless bishops took responsibility for hearing civil cases in their dioceses, and since emperors had placed this burden upon them, they were obliged to discharge these duties to the extent consistent with the Christian faith. It meant that the church as an institution should attend primarily to its one unique function, caring for the souls of its members, although caring for the unfortunate and the destitute was a Christian duty, too.

Augustine had to steer a careful path. Christ told his followers to render unto Caesar the things that were Caesar's. They were to pay taxes and obey the civil authorities in everything not contrary to the direct injunctions of Christ; by the time of Augustine, the pacifism of the early church had been transcended, and it was agreed that if Christians were recruited to fight in the imperial armies, they must do so. Nonetheless, they were not to embroil themselves in politics. They were not to resist tyrants, nor were they to disobey their lawful rulers except under very extreme circumstances, and then only by passive disobedience. Only when they were given a command that in effect amounted to the requirement to deny Christ, might they refuse. Martyrdom occurred in all persecutions when those suspected of Christian attachments were required to sacrifice to the pagan Gods and eat the sacrificial meat, or required to swear allegiance to the cult of the emperor. Swearing allegiance to the emperor's cult was regarded by the civic authorities as the *least* demanding declaration of civic loyalty they could ask of a Roman subject, but it was a sticking point for both Jews and Christians. Augustine thought that if they were so required, they had to, if they had the strength, refuse and endure the consequences. On no account were they to engage in rebellion, incite tyrannicide, or disturb the earthly peace of the empire.[23]

One need only recall the way in which Cicero's writings are replete with praise for tyrannicides, including the murderers of the Gracchi, himself in the case of Catiline's followers, and subsequently the murderers of Julius Caesar, to see the gulf that has opened up between the classical and the Christian political universe. The reasons need no rehearsing, but vast as these differences are, we must not exaggerate their implications. Cicero's thinking is this-worldly, Augustine's other-worldly; Cicero's republic is worthy of respect, admiration, and loyalty, and its glory is a great good, but Augustine thinks all earthly states are the playgrounds of violent and self-deluded men, and earthly glory mere vanity. The temptation that we must resist is to conclude that Augustine has nothing good to say about earthly life and that the state is to be regarded with contempt.

Politics as a Limited Good

This is wrong. The world is God's creation. To despise it is blasphemous. Augustine did not follow classical philosophers in their wholesale contempt for the body. They elevated mind and, in so doing, deprecated body. Given his extraordinary intelligence, he had no need to do the first, and he was not tempted to do the second. He was certainly curious about the body. One of the things that has given rise to the belief that he was obsessed with sex is his recurrent discussion of the contrast between pre-Fall Adam, who would have had sexual intercourse with Eve for the sake of friendship and mutual affection, and would have had an erect penis when and only when he wanted one, and fallen man, who is driven by lust, has erections when he does not want them, and cannot have them when he wants them.[24] He was not in fact as concerned with sexual continence to anything like the extent to which he was concerned with deceit, malice, and plain brutality.

What the curious case of the male sexual organs demonstrates is the way in which we—that is, the fallen male we—cannot control what we very much want to control. The disunity of mind and body is a fact of deep significance. Nor did he confine these thoughts to the case of men. He made a point of arguing that the women who were raped by Alaric's Visigoths in the sack of Rome were not violated and not dishonored; there was all the difference in the world between being the victim of rape and the instigator of fornication. Even if some of them had found themselves sexually excited against their will, they were not to feel ashamed— this is one of the cases where the body acts of its own accord. As to the Roman heroine Lucretia, who committed suicide after being raped by Tarquin, Augustine claimed that she was doubly wrong—wrong to think herself dishonored by the rape and wrong to kill herself. Raped, she was an innocent victim of assault; in committing suicide, she had killed an innocent woman and was a real murderess. Augustine discussed Lucretia at what even he agreed was perhaps excessive length, but uses this, and many other examples where Roman historians and poets had praised a suicide, to argue that suicide was murder—not to be admired but deplored.[25]

The earthly kingdom exists to promote peace in this world. The goods of this world are as nothing to the ultimate good of union with God, but they are not to be despised. Peace on earth is as nothing to the peace we shall enjoy in the company of God, but peace is a very great good. We and the world we live in are God's creations. While we live here below, we must accommodate ourselves to its reality. One such reality is the impotence of religion to fend off earthly evil. The Christians were not responsible for the downfall of Rome, and Mars was not responsible for Rome's glory. Earthly success and failure have earthly causes. God's misfortunes rightly fall upon the just and the unjust alike, and to seek the proximate cause of disaster in local wickedness is an error. The larger claim, one to which Augustine recurs throughout *The City of God*, is that even the success of Rome was not something to glory in. States exist because we care for earthly things and require earthly arrangements to satisfy that desire. Property, to take the central worldly institution that the state protects, has a limited but real value. Without laws governing *meum et tuum*, there would be dissension and bloodshed, and starvation into the bargain. All the same, property has a relative value only, and its side effects are unattractive, including as they do greed and cupidity and opportunities for theft.[26] Without a state there could be no stable ownership, so the existence of political and legal arrangements of the minimal kind required to sustain the rule of law, and an economy adequate to keep us fed and sheltered, is desirable.

Such a regime cannot achieve *ultimate* justice; that is, it does not give to everyone what is really due to him or her, not least because that will not be known until the last judgment; but as institutions built on our love of earthly things and taking advantage of nothing more than our intelligence to coordinate our behavior in the interests of our long-run welfare rather than our short-run impulses, property and the legal institutions that maintain it are to be valued. If we may not kill ourselves, we ought not to neglect ourselves, either; so ordinary legal or conventional justice is to be valued and conscientiously pursued. Augustine makes life difficult for the reader because he moves back and forth between agreeing that "there was, of course, according to a more practicable definition, a commonwealth of a sort; and it was certainly better administered by the Romans of more ancient times than by those who have come after them,"[27] and reiterating his negative reply to the question "Whether there ever was a Roman commonwealth answering to the definitions proposed by Scipio in Cicero's dialogue."[28] The negative reply rests as always on the thought that no society can give a man his due if it takes him away from the worship of the one true God. A godless republic is no *res publica*. Since the only *res populi* that matters is the worship of the one true God, a polity devoted to the worship of demons has no *res populi*, and the multitude of whom it is composed is no true *populus*. Viewed in that light, the only true *populus* are the citizens of the city of God. Viewed more "practicably," earthly justice is self-evidently better than injustice.

Rome did not confine itself to the rational pursuit of earthly but not overrated interests; Rome conquered the world. Contrary to Polybius and Cicero, who thought the Roman Republic of the midsecond century BCE was the height of political success, Augustine almost invariably attacks the whole enterprise as driven by the *libido dominandi*, the lust for conquest. Like Plato, he thought imperial ambition was a self-destructive folly. If human beings had been rational, they would have created not empires but an enormous number of very small states—Augustine says *regna*, literally "kingdoms," but he means any set of political arrangements whatever. A multitude of tiny, harmless polities could have lived at peace among themselves and therefore at peace internally, just as a city contains innumerable households, none of which seeks to dominate the others, and all of which may be domestically at peace.[29] This was not the revival of Christian pacifism. Augustine freely admits that there are just wars and thinks it a grave sin not to fight them when we should. Nonetheless, it is a rather astonishing suggestion, even if one might think the example of the Greek city-states of antiquity suggests that large numbers of small states is not a reliable recipe for peaceful coexistence.

The State, Punishment, and Just War

The central feature of the state is that it wields coercive power. Private individuals can cajole and entreat; the state can issue orders and back up those orders by violence against the recalcitrant. Punishment serves two purposes. The threat of punishment gives bad people a motive to behave better. Their wills may only be amenable to earthly inducements, but against the attractions of misconduct we can set the dissuasion of earthly penalties and thereby promote peace. Since the Fall we have only limited free will, but Augustine does not underestimate the possibility that with appropriate aids we can avoid choosing the more obvious and antisocial evils. The ultimate cause of the existence of political societies is sin; absent the Fall, we might live in simple, egalitarian, communist communities with neither property, nor law, nor political authority. Our fallen nature needs regulation. Augustine's day-to-day conduct in his little celibate community certainly suggests that he thought that both reproof and encouragement could strengthen the wills of his fellows in the direction of good and away from evil, and that is what he argues in *The City of God*.[30] If threats fail, punishment may reform the criminal. Because Augustine hoped for the reformation of the criminal, he was hostile to the death penalty. He was unflinching about the brutality of the Roman state, but his understanding of the purpose of punishment made the death penalty simply wrong. The infliction of punishment is an educative process. Like the father chastising his son to get him into the good habits that will regulate his conduct without the need for further chastisement, the state that imposes successful punishment will train the criminal into better behavior. If the better behavior becomes habitual, there will be no need for further punishment. To kill a man deprives him of the possibility of repentance.[31]

Augustine's argument goes deeper than this, with regard both to the criminal and to the court and the executioner. The criminal is supposed to be brought to a state of repentance, but Augustine thinks it almost impossible for him to die in a good frame of mind. Given the barbarity of

Roman executions, that seems all too plausible. The argument is backed by other considerations. In Roman criminal procedure, accused persons were commonly "put to the question," which is to say tortured until they gave what were perceived by their interrogators as honest answers; and material witnesses could expect the same treatment. The privilege that a Roman citizen most valued was that a citizen was not tortured for his evidence. Augustine was passionate that nobody should be condemned unjustly. He thought the judge's task was hideous at the best of times. Since certainty was not to be had, the judge could never be sure that he had done (earthly) justice. Sentencing a man to flogging or execution for a crime he had not committed was something that Augustine shuddered at. The same reasoning applied to the criminal. An innocent man might endure torture without incriminating himself, only to die of the torture; or he might incriminate himself falsely to spare himself the pain of further torture. To kill an innocent man or to force an innocent man to perjure himself was an appalling evil. These evils lay squarely on the conscience of the judge, and Augustine is more appalled by the impact of sin on our souls than by the torments inflicted upon the body.

This is not the expression of a modern humanitarian impulse. The extent of modern humanitarianism is in any case debatable; we have more in common with Romans who enjoyed seeing criminals torn to pieces by wild beasts than we like to acknowledge. Augustine did not flinch from physical suffering; and hypocrisy was wholly foreign to him. He did not flinch from the *fact* of the hangman or the soldier or the civilian police. It no doubt took a peculiar temperament to earn a living by butchering one's fellow human beings, but it did not follow that the hangman was not God's instrument. In this vale of sorrows, he is. Nor should we, looking back from a safe distance, ignore the fact that corporal and capital punishments are almost inescapable in societies where the expense of housing and feeding prisoners would be intolerable, and where only the better-off would have had the resources to pay fines—as they frequently did. The violent poor would suffer violence at the hands of the state, as would poor robbers and housebreakers. Augustine's fear was not that they would suffer but that they would suffer for what they had not done.

Given such a view of punishment, it was possible to imagine the state acting like a stern father, compelling a reluctant offspring to toe the line. This view of punishment provides the premises for Augustine's account of just war, which has been immensely influential, even though it partly rests on an analogy between the state's right to punish its own members and its right to punish other states, an analogy that the modern world largely rejects. The most familiar parts of the case are very familiar indeed. Self-defense is always a legitimate ground for fighting, and nobody should hesitate to fight back when attacked; self-defense is always a valid casus belli. Nor need we wait until the enemy is literally at the gates before we resist; we may frustrate his preparations for attack as well. These claims became part of the standard account of just war doctrine in the later Middle Ages and are enshrined in modern doctrine, to the extent of featuring in the Charter of the United Nations. The less usual claim is that in a just war a state punishes the crimes of another state and its people. On the face of it, this seems to involve a notion of collective guilt otherwise foreign to Augustine and a willingness to see the innocent die that seems at odds with his condemnation of the death penalty. The state acts, so to speak, in the name of global justice—due precaution taken about the extent to which we can achieve here below anything properly called justice, and how far Augustine thought that there was a law of peoples that conferred such a right—or duty.

A just war is motivated by the intention to give to each what is his due, in this case the punishment due to an aggressor. The idea that a state should act to promote justice was not at odds with Roman ideas; it was at odds with what Augustine thought had in fact motivated Rome. There was an old Roman tradition of not going to war in the absence of a casus belli, a quasi-legal justification for an attack, which was in reality an equally old tradition of manufacturing situations to produce the necessary excuse. There is an obvious rhetorical awkwardness in Augustine's insisting on the inadequacy of earthly justice while defending what we cannot but call a "just war," much as there is an awkwardness when he emphasizes that there is no *real* justice here below at the same time that he insists that we must play our part in the institutions that administer "justice," such as the courts, police, and prisons. But Augustine is, after all, talking of both the city of God, the community of the saved that is here on earth only as a "pilgrim," as well as the earthly city, and he quite rightly reminds us that this world is not just as the heavenly city will be just and that our capacity to determine the deserts of states and individuals is limited.[32]

There is a further twist to Augustine's position. Unlike his predecessors such as Cicero and almost equally bleak successors such as Thomas Hobbes, Augustine believed that we are sinners. Cicero thought many Romans behaved badly, but he did not discuss this in terms of "sin." Hobbes thought we were provoked into harming one another in the absence of secure government and often behaved badly for reasons such as pride; but he expressly repudiated the idea of original sin. For Augustine original sin is the most important fact about us. Some are saved and some are not, but all are sinners. This puts a distinctive complexion on what would in the absence of the framework provided by the doctrine of original sin be a grim, pessimistic, this-worldly, and empirically wholly plausible outlook on political authority and political life. In the absence of government, with its attendant apparatus of law and law enforcement, we cannot help behaving badly because we are terrified of being robbed, assaulted, or murdered by other people; where there is no government and no law enforcement, we are rationally tempted to make a preemptive strike and attack them before they can attack us—the knowledge of which increases their fear of us and makes it more likely that they will attack us preemptively. That is Hobbes.

Absent original sin, this vicious circle is broken by the institution of government. We shall not be afraid of others if we know that they are afraid of the law; and they will not fear us when they know that we, too, are afraid of the law. We are a threat to one another because we fear one another; when that fear is removed, we can become peaceful and cooperative creatures. Augustine anticipates every step of this (Hobbesian) argument, but he cannot stop there. One could say that he pauses there when he admits that, "in a practicable sense," Rome at its best practiced (a sort of) earthly justice; but if he pauses, he does not stop there. If humanity was as coolly and self-controlledly rational as this argument suggests, our history would be infinitely less unhappy than it has been.

Our problem is that we suffer from what one might call surplus motivation toward theft and violence—namely, the wickedness that stems from
original sin. The boy who stole pears out of devilment is a younger version of the men who rob their neighbors and invade other countries for
loot and for glory. This is the sin that Augustine identifies as the sin that
drove Adam to take the apple; the apple was neither here nor there. The
self-will that led to its taking was. Augustine praises the state for quell-
ing violence and robbery, but reminds us that the drive toward violence
and robbery is still there—not cured, only counteracted.

For Augustine, then, the sense that the earthly city is the city of
those driven by love of earthly things is pervasive; he had few reasons to
explain at length which earthly cities are better than which others, and
why, though it was clear that some were much better than others. It is
obvious that peace and good order are good; obvious that chaos and war
are bad. That almost exhausts the comparison. Relatively good earthly
cities are not in the deepest sense just, but "well ordered." This is a powerful thought, and an elegant kidnapping of an idea usually more at home
in the thinking of republicans. The "well-ordered" republic that Machiavelli and Rousseau longed for was an idealized version of the republic
described by Cicero, and hankered after by the founders of the American
Republic. In Augustine's discussion, mixed republics and well-founded
states are at no particular advantage. Augustine thinks *any* state can be
"well-ordered" so long as there is peace, agreements are kept, laws are
observed, and affairs are predictable. Rousseau's claim that when an
absolute monarchy achieves these things, we achieve the silence of the
graveyard would have struck Augustine as romantic nonsense.

To the modern eye, one further disconcerting and interesting element in Augustine's accounts of just war, of punishment, and of the
individual's relationship to the state is the insistence that the individual
must leave politics to the powers that be. Augustine's grounds for insisting that we must not resist our rulers under (almost) any circumstances
are interesting and, it must be said, dangerous. They are at odds with
almost everything other writers have said on the subject. Hobbes insisted
that we must obey our sovereign in anything that did not threaten our
lives; in what did threaten our lives, we must do what we could to save

ourselves. This is not a doctrine of *resistance*, as in Locke, let alone tyrannicide, as in Cicero. Locke allows us to resist the sovereign when he violates the compact that establishes his authority; Cicero think tyrants are
criminals and should be killed. Hobbes held the wholly secular view that
no state can survive if individuals are free to pick and choose which rules
to obey, so we must obey our rulers unless our life is imperiled. Augustine anticipates the secular argument, but his conviction that it does not
matter very much whether we die sooner or later means that he does not
rely on the right of self-defense to uphold a "last-ditch" right to disobey
our rulers. Augustine accepted the Pauline claim that the powers that be
are ordained by God and that disobedience—save under the conditions
spelled out earlier—is an affront to God.

Nonetheless, this is not a defense of the divine right of kings, and
not a defense of theocracy—not an argument for giving priests political
power. Augustine does not argue, as later writers did, that kings are the
Lord's anointed and that their right to govern is *personal*; his argument is
only that God has created rulers whose power is part of the providential
order, and must be accepted as such. The bleakness of the argument
is extreme. One can see how bleak it is by considering the famous tag
in book 4 of *The City of God*: "if justice is absent, what is a state other
than a large and successful band of robbers?" Augustine says that even
robbers must observe some of the rules of justice in order to prosecute
their schemes successfully; and robbers know as well as anyone else that
robbery is wrong and unjust, since they themselves do not wish to be
robbed. All this has led many commentators to draw the obvious inference that Augustine is following Cicero in arguing that what defines a
true state is that it is based on justice. Since orderly coordination even
for wicked purposes requires justice, how much more so an organization
created for good purposes?

If Augustine had gone down that track, he would have been more
plausible but less original and interesting than he was. Some states would
have been nothing more than *magna latrocinia*—large and successful bands
of robbers—and others would have been lawful regimes founded on
justice. The Nazi regime would have been the former and Britain and
the United States the latter. Augustine did not do the obvious thing. He

quoted with pleasure the brave—or foolhardy—response of a captured pirate to Alexander the Great. Asked by the great conqueror what he meant by his piracy, he replied that he meant just the same as Alexander, and that he took it amiss that just because Alexander had many ships and he had only one, he was condemned as a pirate and Alexander was praised as a hero. Augustine's view seems rather to be that states are by nature *magna latrocinia*, but that under their protection the limited goods of this earthly life can be pursued.

In short, the authentic Augustinian note is that states are organizations built to allow the earthly passions of human beings to be satisfied without excessive disorder. These passions always tend toward disorder, and no amount of law will put an end to that. Punishment and the threat of punishment can bend men's wills in the right direction, even though it is only because we care so much for life, liberty, and property that we are amenable to threats of death, imprisonment, and fines. Generally speaking, states are indeed much the same as large bands of robbers; substantial states get into wars and are animated by the lust for domination. More sensible and less passionate creatures than we would have lived in innumerable small, self-centered, and self-satisfied states and would not have got into the fights we have. But just as cowardly bishops can administer the sacraments, and we are not to inquire into their characters but accept the sacraments at their hands, earthly rulers must be obeyed because they are rulers and not because they are good men. If we have benign and merciful rulers, we are lucky; if not, we cannot complain. The deficiency of this view is that it offers no defense against genocidal madmen such as Hitler and Stalin other than the reflection that they will in due course come to grief: little consolation to their victims.

If he does not encourage resistance when one wishes that he had, Augustine equally takes no advantage of the potential for toleration and religious liberty inherent in his own ideas. Consider the way in which his distaste for the death penalty owed so much to his wish that in struggles between the Catholic Church and its rivals—especially the Donatists in Africa—the losing party should come around to the opinion of the victors and should be brought back into the fold by love and by argument. At a personal level, he seems eventually to have become exasperated with the Donatists. Who would not have lost patience with people who resorted to violence and intimidation to make converts and reduce the ranks of the Catholics, and who denied the right of the secular authorities to regulate their affairs while constantly appealing to the imperial authorities for judgment in their favor and refusing to take condemnation for an answer? The Circumcellions were worse. It is not surprising that he urged the secular authorities to suppress them.

The personal element in Augustine's reactions is not important. More important is this: Augustine's account of the limited utility of the earthly city, taken in conjunction with everything he says about the mixed nature of all earthly associations, including the church, leads naturally and readily to the thought that the task of the state is to care for externals—to keep the peace, to regulate property, and to perform useful tasks such as providing lawcourts to settle disputes. Deep matters, questions of the meaning of life and the ultimate rewards of virtue, must be settled elsewhere. Coercion is the natural and proper instrument of the state, but force is not an argument. We can frighten people into behaving as we wish, but we cannot frighten them into an unforced belief in what we wish. Eventually, this was the soil that nourished the Protestant conception of toleration; the church is a voluntary organization for worship in common and the discussion of matters of faith, while the state is a coercive and nonvoluntary organization for the regulation of external matters.

Augustine would have found these conclusions almost unintelligible. He was heir to the pagans who feared that Christian hostility to the cults of the gods would bring disaster upon the Roman state. He drew the line at employing extreme measures of coercion, and especially at employing the death penalty because of its terminal quality. Nonetheless, although one might regard him as the very remote founder of Protestantism, he never contemplated the suggestion that religion was in any way "off-limits" to state control. This was hardly surprising. The modern idea of toleration was more than a thousand years away, and it made headway as much because of European exhaustion after the religious wars of the sixteenth and seventeenth centuries as because of the acceptance of a new principle. Roman emperors automatically protected religious institutions, and the church had now become the beneficiary rather than the victim of the policy.

The dangerous novelty was the extension of coercion from enforcing outward observance to the suppression of heresy; neither Socrates nor the victims of God's wrath in the Old Testament had been accused of heresy. One could be put to death for blasphemy, for outraging the gods, and for worshipping the wrong gods; but the concept of heresy was a distinctively Christian invention. The danger it posed was that it allowed Christians to persecute one another with a clear conscience. Augustine took it for granted that being coerced into receiving the truth was a benefit, not a burden; it was a view one might expect from a man who thought that corporal punishment might be administered lovingly and with the intention to bring the offender to his senses. Whether it was consistent with the sharp line he drew between body and soul when arguing that the women who had been raped by Alaric's soldiers remained unviolated, because accidents to the body did not impugn the integrity of the soul, is another matter. Whether, indeed, it was a plausible view, coming from the pen of the man who remembered that he had been more willing to receive a savage beating than to learn Greek, is also another matter. It became part of Christian orthodoxy. The acceptability of coerced orthodoxy to Christians relied almost entirely on Christ's injunction to "compel them to come in," and the Augustine who strained to read Christ's injunction to "turn the other cheek" in a metaphorical and spiritual sense, in order to permit Christians to serve in the military with a good conscience, now strained to read the *cogere intrare* of the parable of the reluctant wedding guests in the most literal sense to explain why earthly rulers might—indeed must—compel orthodoxy among their subjects. It was a dangerous legacy: not only did it place the Christian subject at the mercy of his ruler's ideas about what was and was not heresy; it made it inevitable that the church would claim to police the Christian ruler's orthodoxy, and inevitable that rulers would resist.

PART II

⚜

THE CHRISTIAN
WORLD

Preface to Part II

G IVEN THE INFLUENCE OF Saint Augustine on subsequent Christian thinking, it may seem perverse to draw a line under classical
political thinking with his death. Should we not rather begin a consideration of Christian political thinking with him? There is no conclusive
response to this, but one fruitful way of looking at the history of political thinking runs as follows. Augustine's political world was that of the
Roman Empire. The empire was undeniably in decline in the west, dis-
mantled piecemeal by the incursions of innumerable "barbarian" warrior
tribes. It was not yet in decline in the east, and under the sixth-century
emperor Justinian it reconquered a good deal of the territory lost to the
invaders: North Africa, Italy, Sicily, Spain, and Dalmatia. This was a
short-lived triumph, however; Justinian was the last emperor whose first
language was Latin rather than Greek, and after his death his territorial
gains were soon lost. It was the western empire on which Augustine's
gaze was fixed. His polemical target, as we saw, was Cicero's conception of a legitimate republic, and apart from his astute observation that
the world might have been better-off without the imperial ambitions of
Rome, with humanity living in a multitude of small kingdoms—*regna*—

which kept the peace and left each other alone, it was the Roman conception of politics that he criticized.

In the long-drawn-out aftermath of the dissolution of the western empire, the one unifying force in western Europe was Catholic Christianity. Politically, Europe was for several centuries a patchwork of kingdoms where authority rested with leaders whom the modern world would have called warlords. Ironically, the modern image of a state as an entity whose essence is unified authority, exercised through law and focused on one man or a group of men who embody that authority and wield it with the assistance of subordinate officials, was fostered by the church rather than by lay authorities. It was the papacy, rather than the barbarian kingdoms that inherited the territory of the empire, that inherited the imperial conception of a state. This was not merely a matter of the papacy's mimicking the outward trappings of imperial office, although it did so. It was rather that the church was the means by which Roman notions of a law-governed political community were transmitted to medieval Europe.

This is not to say that secular political development was unimportant. One reason behind the relative ease with which William the Conqueror secured his position after the invasion of Britain in 1066 was that there already existed a centralized state that was both militarily effective and capable of enforcing law and order, securing property and personal rights, and governing in a recognizably modern fashion. Certainly, kingship carried an obligation to lead one's soldiers into battle, but this was not a barbarian horde but a feudal levy. By this time, of course, the Merovingian and Carolingian kingdoms had come and gone; Charlemagne had been crowned emperor in 800, and the Ottonian empire, which is often thought of as the "real" beginning of the Holy Roman Empire, had come into existence with the coronation of Otto I as emperor in 962.

Political thinking in the eight centuries between Augustine and Aquinas is resistant to analysis. Thinkers saw society as a Christianized whole, and they did not view politics as a distinct activity with its own rules and purpose. Trying to allocate different modern ideas to their medieval sources is more like trying to unbake a cake than like unraveling a sweater into lengths of colored wool. Nonetheless, the difficulty is not that the modern view of human nature is very different from that of the early Middle Ages. It is easy to think that it must be, because it is easy to think that if medieval political thinking was structured by religion, ours is defined by secularization, that the Middle Ages believed in God and original sin and we do not. Or in the alternative, we think we are obliged not to let our views about God and sin influence our views about politics, public policy, and the structure of government, whereas our medieval forebears could have made no sense of letting anything else dictate their political views.

That is not the true line of cleavage; whether or not we believe in original sin, everyone knows that the political arena tempts us to behave exactly as original sin would prompt us to do: to engage in pointless conflicts for the sheer pleasure of crushing opponents, to exploit our fellow citizens for our own benefit, to ventilate malice and cruelty, and to exhibit the *libido dominandi* that Augustine deplored. David Hume was a religious skeptic and a central figure in the eighteenth-century Enlightenment, but he insisted that it was "a just political maxim *that every man must be supposed a knave.*"[1] Bertrand Russell, a committed atheist, claimed that nobody should run a school who didn't have a deep conviction of the reality of original sin. He was not alluding to the Fall; he meant that the desire to commit pointlessly unkind, unjust, and treacherous acts is deeply ingrained in children and that teachers who do not acknowledge this grim truth will have a hard time.[2] Sigmund Freud shocked early twentieth-century readers by claiming that children were racked with sexual desire and that an amorphous but all-consuming need for sensual gratification was built into us at birth. Neither Russell nor Freud shared Augustine's religious beliefs, but they shared his view of human nature. Commentators often say that Augustine seems oddly "modern," but he was simply unblinkered. Politics is as constrained by dealing with fallen human nature as it ever was, and perhaps even more so, given the rewards offered by the modern world to those who behave badly and get away with it.

More alien is Augustine's belief that human nature properly speaking—the nature with which God endowed man at the creation—existed only in the period between Adam's creation and his transgression. What we ordinarily refer to as human nature without qualification is depraved, postlapsarian human nature. Fallen human nature is what politics has to deal with. The concept of a fall makes for a devaluation of earthly politics beyond anything that an acceptance that we often behave badly will do. The effect was that even when Christianity had become the established religion of the Roman Empire and Christians held office in the Roman administration, there was an arm's-length quality about the Christian insistence on the moral obligation to do such jobs and to do them conscientiously.

Christians take politics seriously as a realm in which imperfect but constructive motives check sinful and destructive motives, but as against the classical political philosophers and historians, Christianity devalues politics; if this life is merely a preface to our life elsewhere, politics is less important than religion, and the greatest service the state can render us is to help us live as good Christians. Modern liberalism may be contrasted with classical patriotism in the same way; if the ultimate values are those of the private realm of culture and personal relationships, the political realm is valuable only as a shelter for these private goods. The Christian devaluation of politics was never complete, however; after Aquinas had absorbed Aristotle's *Politics*, it was again possible to talk of the polity as the highest form of (secular) human association. Nonetheless, the Augustinian insistence that we are *peregrini*, pilgrims passing through the earthly life, undermines Aristotle's view that the political life is the life of the highest goodness. The earthly city is at best a pale reflection of the heavenly city to which the Christian's deepest allegiance is owed; when Augustine agrees that the Roman Republic admired by Polybius and Cicero exhibited a "certain goodness," he supposes that God intended it to show us how we should feel toward the true City of God.[3] In the early church the conviction that the Christian was a citizen of another city verged on antinomianism—the idea that Christians were not bound by the laws of the local state, because Christ had come to repeal the law—or anarchism—the idea that Christians should live in a Christian community and take no heed of the political world around them. During the Reformation the urge to recover the purity of the early church produced similar effects.

By then, however, the recovery of most of the literature and philosophy of the ancient world that we possess had occurred, the medieval revival of the classical city-state in the Italian republics had reached its apogee and was in decline, and the modern, bureaucratically managed monarchical state was emerging in northern Europe, delayed by religious conflict in the territories of the Holy Roman Empire, delayed in France by the aftermath of the Hundred Years' War and religious conflict, and in Britain by the dynastic conflict of the Wars of the Roses. But the direction of travel was clear enough. Whether the new monarchical regimes were to be more or less absolutist, whether they were to be Catholic or Protestant, only the balance of forces on the ground would decide. That this was the coming state form and all else peripheral was clear.

CHAPTER 6

Between Augustine and Aquinas

Did Medieval Political Theory Exist?

T HIS CHAPTER IS ONE of four whose theme is the impact of religion, and of Christianity in particular, on ideas about politics.
Unlike its immediate neighbors, it focuses less on individual thinkers
than on issues that preoccupied secular and religious authorities: the
authority of rulers and the obligations of subjects; the medieval view
of law, property, and slavery; and relations between church and state.
It ends with a short coda on what many commentators have seen as the
rebirth of distinctively *political* thinking with John of Salibury's *Policraticus*, published in 1159. To talk of the rebirth of *political* thinking implies
some doubt whether there was such a thing as medieval political thought.
Some writers have indeed denied that there was, and every commentator
agrees that what there was was unlike what went before and came after.
This is not a terminological issue. The Greeks, like the Romans until
the death of the republic, argued about the politics of city-states—*poleis*
in the strict sense. Their citizens did not speak the modern language of
individual human rights, but they had a strong sense of their entitlement
to play a role in the political life of their cities and states, and to be the
authors of the laws they lived under. There was room for argument about

the virtues of monarchy, aristocracy, and democracy and the dangers of tyranny, oligarchy, and mob rule; indeed, argument was inescapable.

The replacement of the Roman Republic by the Roman Empire after the principate of Caesar Augustus, established in 27 BCE, left one political model in command of the field, intellectually or doctrinally speaking, namely monarchy. Moreover, the empire, like its Hellenistic predecessor monarchies, adopted the Persian habit of worshipping its rulers as quasi-divinities. From the fourth century onward, the Christian emperors who followed Constantine could not have themselves deified as their pagan predecessors did, but they did everything short of it. Far from the western church checking the practice, the papacy copied the thrones, tiaras, and robes of the Roman Empire, and in the course of time, the cardinals, who were originally the assistants of the pope in matters of liturgy and care of the poor, came to form a College of Cardinals that replicated the Roman Senate. In the eastern empire, secular and spiritual authority were united in the emperor, whose right to appoint the patriarch of Constantinople was unquestioned; in the west, there was no settled view of the proper mode of appointment of the pope until 1059, when a reforming papacy insisted that election by the College of Cardinals was the only legitimate route. The existence of the one transnational institution of the papacy alongside a patchwork quilt of kingdoms and smaller entities raised a question with no classical antecedents—the relationship of secular and spiritual power. Were kings to appoint bishops or popes to appoint kings, or at least to bless their appointment?

For intellectual resources, thinkers still drew on classical philosophy, even if at second hand and, until the twelfth century, with no direct knowledge of the political writings of Plato and Aristotle. One consequence is that the political institutions of modern western Europe and the countries of European settlement have their institutional roots in the European Middle Ages, but we think about them in ways borrowed from the Greeks and Romans. The roots of modern representative government lie in medieval systems of legal administration and military recruitment—often described as feudalism and with a prehistory in older forms of tribal organization—but we talk about them in the language of Greek democracy and Roman republicanism. Representative government as we know it began in the Middle Ages with the representation of places and groups, and we still elect legislatures from geographical constituencies; but we now think of representation in terms of individual citizenship. British parliamentary government evolved from a monarchical "king and council" system, while the United States inserted the English system of representation into a framework derived from a very different tradition—a republic based on Ciceronian ideals and perhaps inspired in part by the example of the Lykian League. The paradox is only apparent: classical ideas illuminate medieval institutions, no matter that the ideas originated elsewhere. The Polybian view of mixed government aligns easily with the medieval idea that a king should rule with the advice of an aristocratic council and seek consent for taxation from a body representing the "commons." The Greeks operated representative institutions in the leagues for mutual defense they created in the fourth and third centuries, and the Lykian League did so for much longer. If the occasion had arisen, a fourth-century Athenian or a second-century Roman could have explained the Greek or Roman concept of citizenship to an Anglo-Saxon of the tenth century CE.

Medieval Conceptions of Authority

Some writers on medieval political ideas have made much of the distinction between *ascending* and *descending* theories of authority.[1] The ascending view sees political authority as something with which a ruler is invested by individuals, or groups, or "the people" in their entirety, while the descending view sees authority as inherent in the ruler, or as something with which he is endowed by a superior, as it might be God. The descending view seems more suited to monarchy and to a world in which God is seen as the King of Kings. Yet the feudal institutions of early medieval Europe combined ascending and descending conceptions in the contractual relationship between lord and liege. Republican institutions provide the paradigm case of an ascending model of authorization, but even the most extensive assertion of absolute authority could in principle derive that authority from a (once and for all) grant of authority from the people, and the emperor Justinian did it in fact in the early sixth century. There is no paradox in imagining a situation in which the citizenry grants absolute authority to a leader for shorter or longer periods, although it raises difficult questions about the revocability of the grant.

Between the deposition in 476 of the last emperor of the western Roman Empire, the sixteen-year-old Romulus Augustus, and the end of World War II, some form of one-man rule was the most common form of government in Europe, government by kings, princes, dukes, counts, bishops, and popes. There were others. The city-states of Italy and the Adriatic were republics that Cicero would have recognized. None practiced Athenian democracy, though some came close; most were ruled by aristocratic families who saw their right to govern as an inheritance rather than a conditional gift from the people, and many existed on sufferance from royal or papal overlords. Most political units were small but in 800 Pope Leo III crowned Charlemagne, who had been king of the Franks since 768, as emperor of the Romans. This first iteration of the Holy Roman Empire was short-lived; in 962 the German Otto became emperor, and the continuous history of an institution mocked by Voltaire as "neither Holy nor Roman nor an Empire" began. Its basis was Germany, but the emperor's status was elective, and the geographical Germany contained a multitude of diverse political entities, ranging from prince-bishoprics to kingdoms to free cities, that were finally swept away only in the nineteenth century when Germany was forcibly unified by Prussia.

Subordinate institutions, such as universities, guilds, and communes all over Europe, practiced various forms of self-government from around the millennium onward; these institutions were not political oddities, but the strength of the descending view of authority is suggested by the way their rights of self-government were so often rationalized as gifts or concessions from a superior authority. Marsilius of Padua provided a clear formulation of the doctrine that rulers rule by the consent of their subjects only in the fourteenth century, and even he argued that what the people do is choose a wise and worthy single man to rule them. The descending theory of government, in which authority comes from God and descends to popes and kings, and thence to their dependants, and so on downward, suited medieval rulers and the Christian understanding of the world. The Christian worldview rested on a hierarchical and hierocratic conception of authority that transcended the merely political: all authority came from God and was divinely ordained. Christ was a King like no other, but he was King, not chairman for a day of a governing committee on the Athenian model.[2]

When Diocletian became the first emperor from east of the Adriatic, in 284, he established a non-Christian cult of the emperor and backed it up by persecuting his Christian subjects. That kind of deification of the emperor was impossible once Constantine converted to Christianity, and established Christianity as the imperial religion in 324; nonetheless, Constantine and his successors went to all lengths short of reestablishing the cult of the emperor. These eventually included the use of elaborate stage machinery in the imperial palace in Constantinople to heighten the impression that visitors were entering the presence of a more than merely human being. He was emperor *Dei gratia*—by the grace of God. The impact of the Byzantine Empire on the west was limited, even though the empire based on Constantinople called itself *Rhum* and thought of itself as the (only) Roman Empire. Until around 1050 there was a faint prospect that the Byzantines might invade Italy, or rather, the *rest* of Italy, since Byzantium had held Sicily until displaced by Arab conquest in the eighth to tenth centuries, and still held enclaves in the south. Justinian had reconquered Italy from the Goths in the sixth century, and it was not wholly impossible that his successors might do so again. But much of Italy had fallen to Lombard invasion within a few years of Justinian's death, and the two Roman empires drifted farther apart. The Byzantine Empire spoke Greek; and the lingua franca of the west was Latin. New Rome was Greek, and increasingly alien.

After the coronation of Charlemagne as Roman emperor on Christmas Day, 800, western Europe claimed the inheritance of Rome. As the Byzantine Empire was slowly dismembered by Slav and Muslim enemies, its claim to be the inheritor of the universal empire of Rome became weaker, and its influence was further diminished because liturgically and doctrinally, the eastern church became increasingly unlike the western Catholic Church. Doctrinal differences were sometimes greater, sometimes lesser: western Christianity was emphatically Trinitarian, for instance, while Greek Christianity did not regard the Holy Spirit as a third "person." The two churches' reactions to the main issues of church politics were very different, too: the location of final authority in church and state, the duties of subjects and rulers, the allocation of tasks between secular and spiritual authorities. The final breach between the Roman Catholic and the Greek Orthodox churches occurred only in 1054, but earlier rifts over the veneration of statues and images of saints and the authority, if any, of pope over patriarch and vice versa presaged the breach, unhealed to this day, even though the excommunications and anathemata of 1054 have been rescinded.

Politically, the eastern emperor's appointment of the patriarch of Constantinople exemplified what the papacy wished to avoid. There was never any doubt that the Byzantine emperor held supreme authority; the patriarch of Constantinople was his appointee. In the west there were periods when the pope was *in fact* installed and removed by German kings and later by French ones, but these were aberrations; royal power was exercised by bullying, not by fiat. Indeed, in the fourteenth century the French monarchy took bullying to novel lengths by removing the papal court to Avignon, where it could better be kept under supervision. The papacy's constant aim was to preserve its freedom of political action, and it was helped by the fact that western kingdoms were numerous, generally small, and their rulers always poorer than the papacy. The Byzantine unification of all authority in one pair of hands was neither attractive nor feasible. Nor did the patriarch of Constantinople possess the authority over all Orthodox churches that the pope claimed over all Catholic churches. From a Roman perspective, he was too much the servant of his emperor and too little the master of his own church.

Passive Obedience and Political Obligation: Who Judges?

The Christian view of political authority rests on Saint Paul's declaration in Romans that the powers that be are ordained of God. They are to be obeyed for conscience's sake and for fear of hell fire. Not all questions are answered by that peremptory injunction. One that is not is the relationship between God's general government of the universe and any given monarch's title to rule. For Augustine government was necessitated by mankind's fallen nature; governments discipline the earthly desires of mankind by taking advantage of those desires to threaten earthly penalties and promise earthly rewards. Local variations of form or personnel were unimportant when set against the larger issue: classical philosophy saw self-sufficiency as the great good, and the polis as the most perfect institution because the most self-sufficient; Christians knew that man could never be self-sufficient on earth and would find true peace and justice only in God's kingdom. Here we must simply obey the powers that be.[3] How a given ruler came to be in charge was neither here nor there. This might satisfy the provincial subjects of the Roman Empire; it was not always a satisfactory answer for the more powerful subjects of the new kings and princely rulers of western Europe. Any one of them might think he had a better title to the throne than whoever happened to occupy it, and take up arms to vindicate his claim.

The powers that be are ordained of God; and we must obey our rulers for conscience's sake as well as from fear of punishment. Damnation is the lot of the disobedient. Kings are God's vice-regents, and the office of kingship is divinely instituted. Even if a given king is a pagan or a heretic, obedience is due. That position mirrored in the political sphere Augustine's insistence that in religious practice we respect the office and the sacrament, not the person of the officeholder.[4] It did not answer the question whether an incumbent ruler ruled by right. Some kings were tyrants; others attained their thrones by murdering their predecessors; Byzantine emperors routinely murdered their relatives upon accession. The office was divinely instituted, but this did not answer the question how far obedience to the present occupant of any particular throne was due. There was surely some point at which we should disobey. The conventional view down to the sixteenth century was that if a ruler required his subjects to repudiate Christ, they did not have to comply; short of that, they had to obey. The obligation not to comply implied no positive right to overthrow one's lawful rulers; the counterpart to passive obedience was passive disobedience. How much readiness to court martyrdom this required was disputed even after the persecutions under the Roman Empire had stopped. Rigorists held that a readiness to embrace martyrdom was obligatory for all Christians; their opponents held that it could not be. God would consider what was in our hearts rather than what was on our lips; we could repudiate Christ in speech, but keep our allegiance to him in our hearts. Augustine was anxious to distinguish martyrdom from the pagan suicides that he deplored.[5] Roman authorities indeed appear to have thought their Christian subjects were much too ready to get themselves martyred.[6]

If a direct assault on Christianity destroys the obligation to obey, but does not license rebellion, there is the issue of our duty to kings who do not attack the true faith. It was not obvious whether God institutes all of them or only those that gain their thrones by a legitimate route; or where a lawful pedigree is not at issue, whether God institutes only those who govern for good ends and not for their own or their henchmen's advantage. If the important question is whether a ruler does what rulers exist to do, the tyrant who governs lawlessly, murders his people, seduces their wives, and steals their property seems to be so far from serving the purposes of government that we might properly conclude that he has forfeited God's commission.[7] This raises the famously difficult question of who is to judge that a ruler lacks God's warrant, and who has the power to absolve subjects from their obedience to their rulers. In due course, popes claimed that they could release the subjects of a king from their allegiance on grounds of heresy or moral turpitude, and that if they excommunicated a king, his subjects' duty of obedience was at an end. The English king John discovered how powerful a papal interdict could be in the early thirteenth century; others discovered they could safely defy the pope. After the sixteenth-century Reformation, the English church became Protestant; in 1570 the pope declared Queen Elizabeth deposed for heresy. It did no harm to the queen. Nonetheless, it stiffened the English dislike for the Catholic Church's interference in politics, and following the revolution of 1688–89 the coronation oath of an English monarch required her or him to denounce as "heretical and impious" the "damnable doctrine" that a pope can depose a monarch for heresy.[8]

The extraconstitutional defense against tyrants is tyrannicide: political murder. The classical Roman view that tyrannicide is the act of a virtuous man was unattractive to anyone who believed in passive obedience. In any case, tyrannicide does not answer the question whether we may resist our ruler's commands in particular cases without denying the authority of the office and, perhaps, without denying our ruler's legitimacy. We might think a king had no right to command his subjects to subscribe to any particular religious faith, and they might disobey his orders *in that sphere* as best they could, without thinking they were entitled to kill him as a tyrant, or entitled to disobey him except in the sphere in which he had exceeded his authority. If the federal government commanded us to attend Episcopalian churches on Sundays, we would be entitled to take no notice, irrespective of the command's unconstitutional status; but as to everything from paying taxes to observing traffic regulations, we should surely continue to obey meticulously. The conspirators plotting to kill Hitler in 1944 were no less obliged to obey the ordinary law of the land because they had determined to kill the head of state. A nontyrant may act ultra vires in some area without being tyrannical more generally; and we should cooperate with bad regimes to the extent that we thereby serve good ends. Nor does the defense of tyrannicide tell us whether any earthly tribunal can say with authority when a king has forfeited his right to rule. The one thing that seemed incontestable to most medieval writers was that private individuals were not to make that judgment for themselves; Locke's insistence in the late seventeenth century that they had no choice but to do so was a real breach with that tradition.[9]

"Who judges?" gave rise to enduring controversies. If a king is answerable to a lay body, we need to decide who constitutes it; and what happens when its views and his are at odds, as they surely will be. The possibility of such a body was a plausible inference from Roman history: consuls could act only with the assent of the Senate and indeed of each other. Later examples abounded. Germanic tribes elected their military leaders and deposed them for incompetence; those who shared in their commander's leadership in war were entitled to judge his military competence, and perhaps other aspects of his leadership. Once the feudal system of land tenure was established, the idea that the authority of rulers existed on terms and by consent took root. A tenant swore allegiance and owed military service in return for the secure occupancy of his land and impartial justice from his lord. At the apex of this hierarchy was the king; his actions could perhaps be judged by the leading figures of a feudal kingdom. If he refused to accept their judgment, it was not obvious how to enforce their views without civil war. Maybe the king's most eminent feudal tenants—such as the English "barons" who extracted Magna Carta from King John in 1215—could in the last resort declare the king deposed and his subjects freed from their allegiance. Everyone flinched from that conclusion: it came too close to inciting rebellion and letting anarchy loose on the world. Nonetheless, by the end of the fourteenth century, the idea that not only a king but the pope also could be judged by those with whose advice and consent he governed was defended by thinkers who wanted the pope to be answerable to a council of the church. Answerability to a body with a Roman precursor was not an idea applicable only to one institution.

Popes and Kings

Feudal aristocrats were not the only candidates for the task of judging royal legitimacy; if secular rulers might be deposed for wickedness, the church surely had a role. The gospels were read to imply that Christ had given to Saint Peter the power to bind and loose; whatsoever he bound on earth would be bound in heaven, and whatsoever he loosed on earth would be loosed in heaven.[10] That suggested that decisions on the moral fitness, if not the practical competence, of kings and other lay authorities are for the church to make. Augustine tasked bishops with reproving sovereigns but not with removing them from office; discussing Saint Ambrose's famous insistence that the emperor Theodosius confess and repent before he entered Ambrose's basilica in Milan, he emphasizes Theodosius's goodness of heart rather than Ambrose's authority.[11] It is easy to press the argument to dangerous extremes. If anyone knows the terms on which God institutes the powers that be, and the conditions under which obedience is suspended, it should surely be senior figures in the church. Implicitly, this gave the pope authority to depose kings *ratione peccati*—for reasons of their sinfulness—and popes in due course claimed that authority. A danger of doing so from their point of view was that the thought that *all* authority comes from God can cut the other way. Christ was both king and priest; kings were anointed during their coronations to symbolize the divine origin of their authority. If kings are ordained of God, this suggests that kings may possess authority over, or within, the church. If popes may depose kings, *ratione peccati*, it opens the way to kings' deposing popes for breaches of canon law or mismanagement of the church. If kings and popes are thought to exercise a shared authority over both secular and ecclesiastical institutions, there is room for conflict over the source and extent of the bishops' authority over their clergy and the pope's over his bishops. A diocese is a geographical entity, and like many governments today, rulers regarded the earthly institution of the church as being under their authority. They might not rule on doctrine, though they frequently did, but the church as a property-owning institution was another matter.

The possibility of contriving a constitutional mechanism whereby individuals could be deposed, by peaceful and lawful means, was ignored for several centuries, and is ignored today in much of the world where rulers hang on to their positions by brute force and bribery and are forced out only at gunpoint. Many popes and kings were wicked or incompetent or both, and many kings and a few popes were removed from office by fair means or foul—but rarely after due process and because they had forfeited their authority for constitutionally enshrined reasons. Where a constitutional case was made against an individual, it was commonly by impugning his *acquisition* of the office, not by impugning his *performance*, save to the extent that the latter shed light on the former. Nor is it surprising that the papacy presented quite unusual difficulties in that regard. The pope presented an image of absolute and unconstrained authority that seemed to rule out a constitutional process of deposition; it even appeared to rule out resignation. The theory of papal authority was that each pope received his authority directly from Christ; he was the heir of Saint Peter, not of his predecessor as pope. Each pope was absolute. No pope could bind his successor, and concessions made by one pope could not bind another. At election, each pope acquired the *plenitudo potestatis* of

Saint Peter, the power to bind and loose that Christ had conferred. The
secular nobility, as distinct from the College of Cardinals, rejected the
idea that concessions made by a king did not bind his heirs. They had
an interest in constitutional rather than absolute monarchy. Cardinals
hoped themselves to become pope and had different incentives.

Natural Law and Conventional Law

Medieval legal history is a vast and fascinating subject not to be entered
on lightly, and here almost not at all. The evolution of law out of tribal
custom and the edicts of Germanic kings, the discovery of the work
of Justinian in the eleventh century, the establishment of institutions
to train canon and civil lawyers that began in Bologna in the eleventh
century, must all be ignored. The one question we cannot evade is the
impact of Christian ideas on arguments about law and its authority.
Whatever else the God of the Bible is, he is certainly a lawgiver, but the
doctrine of the Fall poses an obvious problem for our relation to all
forms of law, divine, natural, or conventional. It is not clear that fallen
man can know what the law is; if he can, it is not clear that he will obey
it rather than look for ways to avoid its requirements. Throughout the
Christian era, the problem of reconciling earthly law and the law given
by Christ has been exacerbated by the fact that Christ is reported both
as urging punctilious obedience to "Caesar" and as holding seemingly
antinomian views.[12] The easiest way to understand the medieval Christian view of law is through the problems posed by two central social and
legal institutions—slavery and property. Christian thinkers inherited
the classical question whether natural law lay behind conventional, local
law, but understood that question both in classical terms, as the relation
of the law of reason to local law, and in Christian terms, as the relation
between divine commandment and local law. Plato and Aristotle had
said that there was a natural law known to reason, antecedent to written
law, and binding on all human beings. "Some say there is one justice,
as fire burns here and in Persia," wrote Aristotle, and agreed.[13] Custom
relates to natural law in complicated ways. Different marriage customs

can fulfill similar tasks, but the welfare of children and the preservation of family property are morally desirable however achieved. Different customs can meet the universal demands of natural law. Not everyone who held that view shared the same conception of natural law, either in antiquity or later. Roman commentaries start with assertions of the natural equality of all mankind that Plato and Aristotle would have rejected, but that Stoics and Christians accepted.

The authority of local law poses problems with which we are still familiar. Is the law of a particular society law because it is the word of a local ruler, because it is local custom, or because it accords with natural law? When General Sir Charles Napier in the nineteenth century tried to prohibit the practice of suttee, or widow burning, in India, he was met with the reply that local custom demanded it; he responded by pointing out that British custom demanded the hanging of those who murdered women.[14] Augustine would doubtless have thought widows who willingly immolated themselves—if they did—were guilty of murder, too. The inherited tradition pointed medieval thinkers in the same directions as modern legal theory: on one view law is the word of a sovereign lawgiver, and on the other law follows the dictates of reason for the welfare of mankind. Justinian's *Corpus juris civilis* embodied the first view. His conception of authority, both his own and that of the law, was squarely "descending." He was the heir of Hellenistic conceptions of kingship: he was an autocrat—*autokrator* and *kosmokrator*, sole ruler of the world. Justinian's compilation described law as the reflection of the ruler's will; the validity of law was a matter of its pedigree in the will of the ruler. *Dicet rex et fiat lex*; when the king speaks, he makes law. That is the view that finds the lawfulness of law in the dictates of a sovereign legislator; and it is the view that most people today accept, with the necessary qualifications made for legal systems in which a written constitution constrains the legislature. The sovereign legislator may be a many-person sovereign legislature, but the thought that law gains its authority from the word of a person or body with authority to legislate is compelling.

However, the *Corpus* was a compilation based on the work of older authorities, and those authorities belonged to a different tradition. They were commentators from the second and third centuries. Although the republic was long dead, they recorded what they believed to be the traditional Roman view of law. Like Cicero, they thought that behind local law lay a law of nature (*lex naturae*) and a law of peoples (jus gentium) that set a standard to which law should conform. Cicero complained of the inscrutability and indeterminacy of the law that Roman officials had to apply; but its indeterminacy reflected an openness to such standards, and it gave judicial officials leeway in providing equitable relief where there was no other way of achieving justice. If those who were subject to the law were to have a moral as well as a legal obligation to obey it, the law had to meet appropriate moral standards. The difference between *lex naturae* and the jus gentium was not always made consistently, but the distinction is substantially that between a law intelligible to all rational creatures—the answer to the question "What rules would rational creatures agree to abide by for the sake of security, justice, and the better pursuit of the common good?"—and the common law of the society of nations, the answer to the question "What common principles regulate human societies?" The *ius civile* was the law of one particular society, Rome; it was the law that the *populus Romanus* had given to itself, and the inhabitants of western Christendom in due course came to see themselves as after a fashion a new *populus Romanus*, employing the *ius civile* to regulate their affairs.

The answer to the second question is not a flatly empirical "some societies do this and some societies do that." It sifts diverse practice in search of underlying rational principles, as does common law within a single society. The law of nature would dictate that there must be *some* rules governing the acquisition, use, and disposal of useful material things—laws of property. Property rights are thus mandated by the law of nature. The common practice of almost all societies acknowledges private property, recognizes acquisition by labor and by purchase, and makes specified members of an owner's family the heirs to his property ahead of others. These would be the dictates of the jus gentium. The closeness of fit of the laws of nature and the common law of peoples is not always so complete. On the legitimacy of slavery, the law of nature, understood as the Stoics understood it, declared that all men were equal and that nobody is naturally a slave. However, slavery is licit as part of the jus gentium; the law of peoples is law for people living in a state other than golden age innocence. The most detailed features of the jus gentium were those that nations adopted in their dealings with each other, such as the treatment of heralds and the return of prisoners of war, so that the jus gentium had features of an unwritten international law. This, too, would imply that slavery is part of the jus gentium, and not of the *lex naturae*, because so many accounts of slavery root it in the capture of prisoners in a just war.

What came down to medieval Europe was untidy, but philosophically provocative. Some commentators became interested in the question whether *all* creatures, irrational and rational, were governed by natural law. Aristotle had said that in a limited way they were; nonhuman animals followed instinctively the "laws" that led them to flourish in the way appointed for creatures of their kind. Since they did not understand the law they were following, they could not be said to be virtuous, but they did not break the law as humans did. A skeptic might think that the implication of Aristotle is that Adam's prelapsarian goodness was merely animal innocence. The more common view was that only creatures capable of recognizing the dictates of reason could follow natural law. On that view, the law of nature applies to rational creatures alone, thus only to human beings, since they alone can understand the law and follow or fail to follow it of their own volition. The Roman commentators whom Justinian's compilers exploited for the raw materials of his *Corpus juris civilis* were not of one mind. The most famous was the early third-century jurist and imperial adviser Ulpian; he had held that all creatures followed natural law, while human beings followed the jus gentium, the law of peoples. But the jus gentium so understood embraced much of what other writers described as natural law.

The Origins and Justification of Private Property

The earliest Christian communities expected an imminent Second Coming. They appear to have practiced a simple form of communism in which members put what they had into a common pool and took what they needed from it. If the Second Coming was indeed imminent, there was little room for a discussion of the nature of property. Once there were churches and monasteries, which received gifts and owned land and buildings, familiar questions about the nature of ownership needed to be answered. By the turn of the millennium, the papacy owned a great deal of property and was a powerful political institution. It was the most legally sophisticated institution in western Europe, and its administrative needs were a powerful force behind the revival of legal theorizing. The need for a secular theory of law is obvious. Whatever label such a theory wears is less important than that it should answer the questions that appeals to the laws of nature and the jus gentium answered. One of the most important was the nature of property and the justification of private ownership. To the modern eye, slavery, that is, property in human beings, is a particularly difficult issue, but slavery created less difficulty in early medieval thinking than private property generally. Before the Fall, slavery was impossible; at the other end of the historical process, in God's kingdom, there is neither Jew nor Gentile, slave nor free. In this vale of tears, slavery is one more unfortunate consequence of the Fall; the early churches employed slaves to till their fields. Monastic communities were forbidden to do so not because slavery was wrong but because labor was an essential part of monastic life. Little more was said than that slaves should obey their masters and masters should treat their slaves with kindness. Nor did criminal law pose the intellectual and political difficulties of civil law. It was debatable whether Christians should wield the sword of the executioner, and a Christian judge might wonder how sure he could be that he was not punishing the innocent. About the need for and the nature of the criminal law, there was no argument. When writers put the dictates of nature and the dictates of Christ together by assimilating natural law to the Golden Rule—"do as you would be done by, and do not do as you would not be done by"—it was easy to see that this ruled out physical assault, and equally easy to see that it ruled out theft *once there was private property*. It was not difficult to extract a view of punishment: we may defend ourselves against force and theft and exact from others what would appropriately be exacted from us. The deeper problem was to explain property rights in the first place.

The importance of property is obvious. People wish to know what is theirs and need to know how to acquire and transfer property, if they are to farm, to trade, and to leave property to their children or anyone else. Slightly less obviously, in societies that were never more than two bad harvests away from famine, an account of the duty of the haves to the have-nots is needed. I may own the corn in my granary, but if you are starving and I have plenty, do I own *all* of that corn; or do your rights diminish my ownership? Without a coherent account of the basis of property, it is hard to say what rights and what kind of rights owners and nonowners may have over the same things. For Christians, urged by Christ to sell all they had and give to the poor, it was and remained a problem to know what the proper limits of economic activity were; if nobody acquired anything, there would be nothing to dispose of charitably; but it was too easy for the greedy and the selfish to hide behind that platitude to accumulate wealth and never find the right moment to give even a small portion to the poor. As all students of Saint Paul remember, however, it is the *love* of money that is the root of all evil, not money itself; moderation in acquisition and generosity in charitable giving form the obvious basis for Christian economics.[15]

There was less agreement on the nature of ownership. Roman law distinguished sharply between *ius in rem* and *ius ad personam*, which is to say between rights in things and rights against persons. All rights are rights against persons in one sense, since only people can either respect or flout our rights; my ownership of my horse is a right *in rem*, but it takes another person to steal it, sell it fraudulently, ride it without my leave, and so on. Ownership is good against all the world. *Everyone* is obliged to respect my ownership. A right *in rem* and good against the world contrasts with rights that hold against particular other people. If I owe you money, it is only I whom you can sue for the debt, and you are the only person to whom I am obliged to repay it. The owner in Roman law is, so to speak, sovereign over the thing owned; its fate lies in his hands.

Under feudal arrangements, and the customary law that developed in northern and western Europe, ownership was less clear-cut. Some commentators have said that there was no such thing as ownership under feudalism, which is extreme. In one sense, the king owned all the territory he governed inasmuch as feudal tenures theoretically ran upward in such a way that the chain of tenant and lord terminated in the suzerain, the king who was the feudal superior of all. Tenants below the king had rights of possession and use over what they held of the king or of one of his tenants. Rights of disposal were another matter. In principle, they lay with the superior and could be exercised by his tenant only with his permission; in practice, this meant a payment in kind or in cash for his presumed acquiescence, his tenants paying a fee on disposal and the new tenant a fee on taking possession. Ownership thus embraced rights of use and occupation good against any other person's claims, but not the absolute right *in rem* of Roman law. In English law, this was true of freehold ownership of real property until 1925, and it remains true even now of real estate held without a registered title. Ownership meant having a "better right" than a competitor.

Such a title was always vulnerable to someone's appearing with a better right—a long-lost relative might always appear and establish a claim to be the rightful heir of whoever had held the property in the past; innumerable English plays and novels rely on the device, and title insurance companies exist to make everyday life less dramatic. The importance of different images of ownership becomes visible when arguments erupt over the duty of the rich to share their resources with the poor during times of hardship; commentators sometimes say that the starving poor *own* the grain in the rich man's granary, and sometimes draw a sharp line between the rich man's *ownership* and the entitlement of the poor to *charity*. Locke later said that the poor had a "right" to the rich man's surplus, while Hume said it hardly mattered since in the event of famine the political authorities would always break open the granaries.[16] One contentious problem throughout the medieval period was the property owned by the church. In the beginning many Christians were attracted to a mendicant way of life, taking literally Christ's injunction to take no thought for the morrow and living in the expectation of an imminent Second Coming. The church became an institution, and institutions notoriously cost money to run, so churches became dependent on their members' taxing themselves for the churches' benefit; laymen began to make gifts to their local churches, and the aristocracy began to make substantial gifts to the church in Rome and in capital cities such as Milan and Ravenna.

Some pressing questions now arose: should the church own anything, and who was "the church" for such purposes? The bishop of a diocese could not own the charitable gifts as his personal property, so it must be the church as a corporate owner. The appropriate persons to exercise the corporate body's rights of disposal by sale or exchange were the bishop or a group of deacons, a committee to act as steward of what its members owned collectively but not individually. This corporate model came to be the way the ownership of property by the church was thought of; the pope was the administrator of the church's property, not its owner. The classical world had been at ease with such arrangements in the case of publicly owned property. In a feudal setting the trouble that lay ahead was not conceptual but political. When laymen gave their property to the church, the gift deprived the layman's feudal superior of the "incidents" of ownership. When a lay tenant bequeathed his property to his heir, his heir inherited after a payment in cash or kind to the superior from whom he held his property. These payments were, in effect, payment for a lease, paid when the lease was renewed or a new lessee put into the lease.

The church was immortal; it had no heirs, its property never passed from one owner to another, and no feudal dues were paid. The landlord lost out; and the landlord most likely to take this amiss was the king. Moreover, there was a temptation to sharp practice; if someone gave his property to the church on the right terms, he could secure for his heirs an income and a substantial degree of control over the property, or a comfortable occupation in the church. This was not the only problem posed by the church's ownership of property. Two other issues were tithes and the church's exemption from ordinary taxation. Tithes were a tax levied on lay property for the church's benefit. It was not clear how the church had come by the right to levy the tax, conversely, since the secular government provided protection for the church, it seemed plausible to many secular rulers that they should be able to levy taxes on the church as well as on the laity. The exemption of the property of charities from ordinary taxation was not an issue that arose for the first time in the twentieth-century United States.

These issues poisoned church–state relations for centuries. They are capable of causing a frisson of unease even today, as witness the surprise that American students feel when they discover that most Germans pay taxes to the government for church purposes. The history of property rights, and devices such as the Statute of Mortmain (1279) that the English crown employed to make gifts to religious establishments less attractive to both donors and recipients does not concern us. What does is that these developments forced thinkers to give an account of the moral justification of property rights. It became orthodox doctrine that property had at first been held in common—not the view of the Roman lawyers, but of the Stoic philosophers.[17] God gave the world to mankind in common; reason and natural law concurred in seeing the world as a gift to mankind collectively, and not to anyone in particular. For reasons spelled out by Aristotle, but available to the common sense of those who never read him, it was right to divide the inheritance of the human race among individuals; it gave each person an incentive to care for what he held personally and whose product would go to him and his family. Still, this would be acceptable only if there was some overarching notion of the common good that property institutions served. If we could not quite say that the starving man *owned* the grain in the rich man's granary, we could certainly say that a rich man who thought he could let the poor man starve was mistaken. His rights lapsed if his behavior was intolerable.

Outside (Non)Influences

The history of the collapse of the western Roman Empire was in large part the history of invasions by Germanic tribes; and much of the subsequent history of western Christendom is the history of the kingdoms that emerged when formerly nomadic and seminomadic peoples settled in what became France, Germany, and England. But one phenomenon whose physical impact was as great as its impact on political thinking was slight was the rise of Islam. The presence of Islamic states in North Africa and the Near East colored European politics from the eighth century all the way to the present, whether by way of the Crusades of the late eleventh to the thirteenth century, the Spanish *reconquista* of the eleventh century to the late fifteenth, or the rise and fall of the Ottoman Empire, and the instability of the successor states that emerged from its ruins. Islam as a creed could have no impact on Western political thought. Islamic scholars had much to say about the political organization of Islamic communities and about the relations of Muslims and unbelievers, but these ideas could have no purchase outside Islam. Even if any Western thinker had been willing to pay attention to them, the Western distinction between the sacred and the secular has no place in Islam, and the Western anxiety about relations between church and state finds no purchase in a faith without the Western conception of a church. Western philosophy, medicine, and technology were all deeply indebted to Arab scholars, not least for preserving and translating Greek texts that would have otherwise have been lost; but finding new ideas about how to govern ourselves more effectively in the work of Arab scholars would have been implausible even if there had been an incentive to look.

The impact of Islam was military; the first wave of Islamic conquest overran not only Spain but much of southern France. Moorish warriors got as far north as Tours, on the Loire, where they were defeated by Charles Martel at the Battle of Poitiers in 732. This was the battle that inspired Gibbon to claim that if Charles Martel had been defeated, "the Arabian fleet might have sailed without a naval combat into the mouth of the Thames. Perhaps the interpretation of the Koran would now be taught in the schools of Oxford, and her pulpits might demonstrate to a circumcised people the sanctity and truth of the revelation of Mahomet."[18] Their conquests in North Africa were not reversed as they were in Sicily in the eleventh century, and in Spain only over several hundred years; nor was the slow destruction of the Byzantine Empire, which ended with the fall of Constantinople in 1453 ever halted. Islam remained entrenched in Greece and the Balkans until the end of World War I.

In the conquered territories non-Jews and non-Christians were offered a stark choice between conversion to Islam or death. Jews and

Christians as "peoples of the book" were tolerated if they accepted the
political authority of their Islamic rulers and paid extra taxes in recognition of their inferior status. The Islamic "solution" to the problem
of accommodating a variety of creeds and cultures under one political
umbrella—what became the millet system—had its virtues: Islamic rulers allowed their non-Muslim subjects a large measure of community
autonomy. Jews were much safer under Islam than in Christian Europe.
Nonetheless, Islamic pluralism did not generate political ideas that
would mean anything to a Western reader until it sparked an interest
many centuries later among those who contrasted Ottoman and Western forms of pluralism. The thinkers with whom we associate Islamic
philosophy—al-Farabi, Avicenna, and Averroës—were interested in the
metaphysics of Plato, Aristotle, and the Neoplatonists. Ibn Khaldun in
the fourteenth century was perhaps the first Islamic political writer of a
wider interest, and he depended on Aristotle for his moral and political
views. He was, if the anachronism is permissible, an original political
sociologist, among whose achievements was a persuasive account of what
later became known as the theory of the circulation of elites, but not an
original political thinker.[19]

Like their Arabic-speaking counterparts, Jewish scholars preserved,
translated, and wrote commentaries on the masterpieces of classical
Greek thinking, but had no reason to provide ideas about the authority
of kings, bishops, popes, and nobility that Western thinkers could use.
They transmitted medical and mathematical knowledge in advance of
anything generated in western Europe before the end of the first millennium; they did not provide what their Christian neighbors could
recognize as distinctive moral and political ideas. It would have been
astonishing if they had, and more astonishing if they had done so and
their Christian neighbors had made anything of them. The Jews of the
diaspora had little need to think about secular authority. Doomed to live
as barely tolerated outcasts under governments in which they had no say,
they had much to say to themselves about their survival as a righteous
community, and about such unnerving subjects as the moment at which
it was laudable to escape persecution by suicide, but nothing relevant to
the political dilemmas of their Christian persecutors.

Finally, we must remember something so obvious that it is easy to overlook. Medieval thinkers were almost always theologians first, philosophers second, and political speculators third and last. Augustine was a great political thinker, because he was a great thinker provoked by the political problems of the day, but it was the least of his achievements. One of the most influential figures in medieval thought was "Pseudo-Dionysius the Areopagite," a Syrian monk who lived shortly after Augustine; it was through him that Neoplatonic ideas came down to the twelfth and thirteenth centuries. Those ideas were eventually important for political theory because they reinforced the idea that the entire universe was hierarchically organized, and humanity part of a "great chain of being" that dictated the rights and duties of all creatures. These were ingredients in the synthesis of classical and Christian learning that Aquinas constructed in the third quarter of the thirteenth century. Nonetheless, the Pseudo-Dionysius belongs to the history of theology, and not to any but an unusually comprehensive history of political thought.[20]

Papal Absolutism and the Investiture Controversy

That said, one of the most important elements of the intellectual apparatus of early medieval political thinking was contributed by a late fifth-century pope in little more than two paragraphs of sharp prose. Gelasius I was pope for four years between 492 and 496, under conditions of extreme difficulty. The last Roman emperor in the west had abdicated sixteen years before; the Catholic Church was beset by heretics and pagans; Rome was stricken with plague; and the doctrinal authority of the pope over the patriarch of Constantinople was bitterly contested. The patriarch was protected by the emperor, whose appointee he was and who was naturally reluctant to concede papal authority over his appointee. The dispute provoked Gelasius's letter of 494 to the emperor Anastasius in which he laid down what became the doctrine of the two swords, and insisted on the superiority of the spiritual power to the secular. It was superior because in the last resort the pope answered to God for the morals of the emperor. The doctrine of the two swords is simple: God grants authority to both pope and emperor. Each is absolute in his own sphere. Each should sustain the other's authority. So far, so uncontentious. But the emperor in Constantinople thought his authority greater than either the patriarch's or the pope's. Gelasius held the opposite view.

The crucial passage of Gelasius's letter is two paragraphs in length. And the point on which so much turned was the second of two short opening sentences: "There are two powers, august Emperor, by which this world is chiefly ruled, namely, the sacred authority of the priests and the royal power. Of these that of the priests is the more weighty, since they have to render an account for even the kings of men in the divine judgment."[21] The letter went on to observe that there is a quid pro quo, with priests obeying the laws that the secular power made to preserve earthly peace and prosperity and the emperor being willing to acknowledge the authority of the pope in matters of faith. A later age sees this as the terms of a concordat between church and state; to Gelasius and popes down to the early thirteenth century, it meant something different. Certainly it was a statement of the division of labor that everyone accepted. More contentiously, it was a denial of the authority that the emperor unhesitatingly exercised in Constantinople, as well as an assertion of the autonomy of the papacy, and beyond that a claim by the pope to primacy over all other patriarchs—at Jerusalem, Antioch, and Constantinople. It was pregnant with trouble, since it claimed almost in passing the pope's right to judge the emperor's fitness for office, and by implication any other secular ruler's fitness, because one of the many juridical fictions that were half accepted until the late Middle Ages was that every ruler in Christendom was subordinate to the emperor, which later meant the elected Holy Roman Emperor.

The institutional conflict remained latent until it came to a head in the so-called investiture controversy in the mid-eleventh century. By this time, bishops were not only princes of the church; as the controllers of substantial territory and other property, they were also members of the feudal nobility. They were expected to provide military support to their secular overlords; some led their own forces into battle and died alongside them. Two practices grew up as the result of this meshing of roles; one was the creation of "proprietary churches," where the lay donor who had established a church and endowed it with property owned the church and installed as incumbent whomever he chose and on his own terms; the other practice was "lay investiture." A bishop was "invested" with his bishopric by a secular ruler in the same way that a feudal tenant received his fief from his lord. In effect, he did homage to the king for his diocese. Both devices made good sense for the secular authorities; when so many of the economic and military resources of troubled societies were in the hands of churchmen, their availability for secular purposes had to be guaranteed.

Pious nobles and princes founded or refounded monasteries and endowed them with land and buildings; but although these practices enhanced the authority of the church, they endangered its spiritual mission. A bishopric was a valuable piece of property, well worth purchasing—but buying ordination as a priest or bishop was the sin of simony and strenuously forbidden. It was also widely practiced. The papal tiara itself was frequently bought and sold. Simony became the target of reformers, as did the lifestyle of bishops who lived more like lay lords than priests. The reform movement built slowly, beginning with the reformation of monastic life in the tenth century and gathering momentum when a succession of reforming popes coincided with the accession of an underage emperor, Henry IV. Leo IX, pope from 1049 to 1054, Nicholas II, pope from 1059 to 1061, and Gregory VII, pope from 1073 to 1085, set out to achieve three things. The first was to ensure that popes were elected by the College of Cardinals and by nobody else. Leo IX laid the ground, and a Lateran Council called by Nicholas II decreed this mode of election in 1059. This was primarily aimed at reducing the influence of the Roman aristocracy, from whom the cardinals were largely recruited, but also at the influence of the emperor. The emperor was essentially a German king whose value to the papacy was his ability to control the Lombards, who periodically invaded northern and central Italy and threatened the territory of the papacy. The conflict of the 1070s between Gregory VII and Henry IV over lay investiture marked a paradoxical finale to a reform process that had begun when the emperor Henry III called a council to cure the scandal of the 1040s when three contenders claimed the title of pope. When the Council of Sutri in 1046 removed Benedict IX, Sylvester III, and Gregory VI, trouble was narrowly averted. The pious Henry III refused to receive his imperial crown from Gregory VI, because he had bought the papal tiara from Benedict IX and was therefore guilty of the sin of simony; but he installed his own choice as Clement II and was unwilling to give up the principle that just as the emperor in Constantinople appointed the patriarch, so the Holy Roman Emperor would nominate his choice for election as pope.

The second papal aim was to eliminate lay investiture. The object was to ensure that an archbishop or pope would invest a bishop with the regalia of his office, with no lay involvement. Henry IV resisted for the reasons suggested above. Gregory excommunicated him; there was near civil war in Italy and Germany. Gregory initially gained the upper hand, and in 1077 Henry had to humiliate himself, standing in the snow outside the pope's castle of Canossa to beg forgiveness. But Gregory overreached himself, was driven out of Rome, and died in exile. The dispute ended in the obvious compromise, enshrined in the Concordat of Worms of 1122 only after the deaths of both Gregory VII and Henry IV. The imperial side conceded the issue so far as investing the bishop with his office went, but ensured that the emperor or his representative would be present at the investing of bishops with their temporalities. The church secured control over the appointment of bishops, and the crown secured its rights over the land and property of the diocese. The concordat did not give either side all it wanted, but it established the papacy as a quasi-monarchical institution with the pope as the absolute head of the church in spiritual matters, and the papacy as a considerable secular power in central Italy. The papacy's third aim was to secure the primacy of the Catholic Church within Christendom. This met with total failure. Leo IX succeeded only in creating the breach with the church in Constantinople that remains unhealed to this day. In 1054, papal delegates traveled to Constantinople to secure the patriarch's acceptance of papal supremacy; when they did not get it, they excommunicated the patriarch Michael Cerularius, who anathematized them in turn. The papacy secured its political autonomy and its spiritual supremacy over a shrunken domain.

It is easy to represent medieval political thought as focused entirely on the conflicts of church and state, and generations of commentators have done so. This neglects the day-to-day evolution of political thinking forced upon both church and lay officials by the exigencies of their own institutional lives. Practicing lawyers in particular developed ideas about the ways in which superiors and inferiors related, and about the relationship between the will of a superior and the law. It was not from nowhere that institutions such as the English Parliament, which first met in 1265, developed, and not from nowhere that there arose in the church the so-called conciliar movement. Nonetheless, these developments belong more to the general historian than to the historian of ideas, precisely because they began as practical demands or responses to them. Conversely, one finds occasional outbreaks of intellectual originality that are hard to explain or to place and that have no impact as they occur, but are exploited long afterward.

John of Salisbury

One such was the writing of *Policraticus* by John of Salisbury. The fact that anyone could have written a work replete with ideas that we associate with the much later Middle Ages or with the modern world, as well as with the writings of classical political thinkers, suggests that similar ideas must have been in circulation from the end of antiquity without leaving any written evidence of their existence. Perhaps they were submerged by theological and ecclesiological discussion but remained part of an oral tradition. John was born in Salisbury around 1110 and ended his life as bishop of Chartres; he was a friend and confidant of Thomas à Becket and wrote a biography of the martyred archbishop. He was more than once exiled as a result of his ties to Becket and to Archbishop Theobald, Becket's predecessor as archbishop of Canterbury. He lived through one of the most intense periods of church–state conflict, but could take advantage of the new translations and epitomes of classical philosophy that had sparked the so-called twelfth-century renaissance.[22] He was not, however, a scholar in his own right, and relied very heavily on florilegia, anthologies of extracts.

Policraticus, "the book of the statesman," is in part a work in a familiar genre, a handbook addressed to rulers to remind them of their duty—in flattering rather than admonitory tones. Like Christine de Pizan's *Book of the Body Politic,* discussed in a later chapter, it relied heavily on *exempla,* illustrative stories from Greek, Roman, and biblical history, that emphasized the moral the author wanted to draw. The work became famous because it resurrected, or found room for, the ancient doctrine of tyrannicide. The argument was not complicated, but the conclusion was bold; John discusses over and over the crucial differences between the prince and the tyrant, and even introduces the novel category of the ecclesiastical tyrant.[23] The book's fundamental premise was that of all medieval thinkers. Political authority comes from God; the authority of a true king is divine and is rejected at the peril of our souls as well as our bodies. That this was not wholly a truism can be appreciated when it is remembered that even Justinian's *Corpus* first insisted that the word of the king is law, but went on to say that the law binds the king's subjects because the king had been given that authority by the *populus.* The tension between the claim to wield authority *Dei gratia* and as the expression of the vox populi is obvious, but was passed over by Justinian's compilers. John of Salisbury has no notion of the king's authority being bestowed on him by the people; it comes from God; that is why it is authority. This remained the conventional wisdom; four centuries later, Sir John Fortescue refers to England as a realm that is *regale et politicum,* "royal and political," which is to say, governed by a monarch in a constitutional fashion. Its laws are made with the assent of the people, and it is a body politic, because the common will of the people for their common good is what makes it a unity of which the king is the head. It is a *corpus mysticum* rather than a physical body, but that is hardly different from Cicero's insistence that a *res publica* is a "public thing" because it exists to secure a common good. The crucial difference is that the king's subjects are subjects, not citizens; they have no independent power of action.[24]

John holds that God gives kings authority only in order that they shall conduct themselves in a law-abiding fashion, serve law and justice, and attend to the welfare of the people over whom God has seen fit to place them. This is not constitutionalism, but it opens the door to an important distinction that John made much of. There is a vast difference between a king and a tyrant. This in itself was uncontentious. As the Carlyles pointed out in their monumental history of medieval political thought, Augustine's evasiveness about whether an earthly king can give true justice to his people stirred no doubts in subsequent writers in the Middle Ages. They universally came down on the side of supposing that when Augustine said that a state without justice was simply a large gang of bandits, he meant that a lawfully constituted state was not a gang of bandits but a realm in which justice could be done and be seen to be done. That was John of Salisbury's view.[25] It makes Augustine less interesting but more usable.

A true king practices justice and is to be obeyed. We are to obey him as the agent of God, but the mark of his being God's agent is that he does justice. God's conferral of authority is conditional on the king's practicing justice and doing those things for whose sake God institutes kings in the first place. This is more sensible, less anarchic, and less grim an account of politics than Augustine's; it is also less intellectually interesting and less morally demanding. The consequence that John draws is on its face dramatic. A ruler, or rather a purported ruler, who does not do justice is not a king but a tyrant. Lawful rule is monarchy; unjust rule is tyranny. Tyrants do not have God's authority behind them, and—here is the crux—if they are resisted and killed by their people, they have no legitimate complaint and their people have done no wrong.[26] The question is how far this thought is to be pressed. The answer is not simple. Recall Cicero: for him, the killing of a tyrant was not simply excusable but morally and politically meritorious, and tyrannicide was the positive duty of those who were in a position to effect it. Cicero rightly suppressed the followers of Catiline, and Brutus and his friends rightly killed Caesar. John also says that the killing of a "public tyrant" is a meritorious act.

Nonetheless, he was not trying to resurrect Roman republican ideals. His examples come from the Old Testament rather than Roman republican history, and when he discusses Nero, Caligula, and the like, he suggests that Christians were obliged to endure their tyranny. Even in the case of the Old Testament, he comes down on the side of thinking that Saul was a deserved affliction for the rebellion of the people of Israel against the word of God. John was milder and more moderate than the Roman tyrannicides. The ruler's word is law but only when it is (really) law. The prince's whim is not law; that would be a license for wickedness, but when the prince is guided by equity and justice, what he lays down for the good of his society is law. This is not constitutionalism, since it implies nothing about the institutions we might erect to ensure that kings and popes are so guided, but it is a defense of the rule of law. The pope is *servus servorum Dei*, the servant of the servants of God; the king is the servant of the common good according to law. He possesses genuine authority and is *legibus absolutus*, exempted from the law he gives to his subjects, but only insofar as that exemption serves the public good. There is no conflict between governing *Dei gratia* and governing according to law. God rules the universe by law; the king who serves God serves the law by which God governs his universe.[27]

This leaves John's understanding of tyrannicide somewhat up in the air. It is one thing to say that a prince who becomes a tyrant forfeits his authority and cannot complain if his people resist him or kill him. It is another to say that if a prince becomes a tyrant, it is somebody's duty to kill him and that doing so is an act of political virtue. John is torn between the Christian tradition of passive obedience and the classical tradition of tyrannicide. There is no doubt that he approves of past slayings of tyrants; he quite rightly invokes the Old Testament as well as Roman history to make the point that tyrannicides have been praised for their deeds. He certainly thought that tyrants forfeited their immunity to deposition. Nonetheless, the Christian framework, if not that of the Old Testament, sits uneasily with the classical doctrine. Tyrants may, after all, and as Augustine suggested, be God's punishment for our sins, and we may be intended not to resist evil but to suffer it patiently. The astonishing thing, even so, is John's readiness to extrapolate an argument that comes from republican writers of many centuries earlier to the position of clerical leaders. If it is lawful to kill tyrants; it must be lawful to kill clerical tyrants if there are such. Old Testament stories about the killing of the priests of Baal show that the wicked exercise of power by priests is to be punished.

In short, a writer like John in the twelfth century could draw on a great variety of intellectual resources to make some striking points about the conditionality of both secular and ecclesiastical authority and about the limits beyond which ordinary people were not to be pushed. There is an obvious moral to be drawn: we should neither exaggerate the closeness of such thinkers to ourselves nor treat them as though they were so distant in space and time that their ideas need decoding as if they were Mayan hieroglyphs concerned with a wholly inscrutable way of life.

CHAPTER 7

Aquinas and Synthesis

The Revival of Philosophy

AQUINAS DOMINATES THIS CHAPTER, but its theme is the impact on Christian political thinking of the rediscovery of classical philosophy and classical legal and political thought. Aquinas's situation was the reverse of Augustine's. Augustine lived in a Roman Empire that had only recently been Christianized. Its intellectual resources were largely pagan. The Europe of Aquinas was Christendom; its identity was Christian, and the eight centuries between Augustine's death and Aquinas's birth had seen a decline into and recovery from the chaos of the fall of the western empire. The unity of Europe was spiritual—Christian—not political. Its intellectual unity rested on the universality of Latin as a legal, scholarly, and spiritual language and on the existence of the church universal. Reinserting classical philosophy into that environment was quite unlike fighting the superstitions of the pagans.

Aquinas's attempt to integrate the insights of pagan philosophy with a Christianity that a rational man could commit himself to was a heroic undertaking. The church authorities were at best anxious about the rediscovery of Aristotle and at worst entirely hostile; his writings were condemned yet again in 1270, a bare four years before Aquinas's death. Aquinas's work was therefore decidedly brave. It rarely looks like that to modern readers in search of Aquinas's political ideas. They know that Aquinas became the "official" philosopher of the Catholic Church and look for something astonishing; and they are disappointed. This is partly because his thoughts on politics form a very small part of the enormous corpus of his work but more because those thoughts are almost invariably sensible, but often read like diluted Aristotle, offering excitement only when an Aristotelian view is so at odds with Christian orthodoxy that reconciliation is especially hard. The contrast with Augustine, who is often unnerving but never dull, could not be sharper. That, however, is the point. Augustine is unflinching in associating politics and the state with our sinful, fallen natures. Aquinas never disputes that we are fallen creatures, but—following Aristotle—thinks that the state shelters forms of social life that are at least relatively good. Unlike Aristotle, he does not believe that we can perfect ourselves within the political community; nonetheless, we can lead virtuous, happy, and fruitful lives. He is unsurprising in part because he so successfully erased Augustine's relentlessly negative view of earthly existence from ethical and political debate. If he did not himself advance much beyond Aristotle, apart from setting him in a Christian framework, others soon did.

The difficulties posed for the modern reader are exacerbated by the literary style of the *Summa Theologiae*. Under no conditions would Aquinas have been a stylish writer. Given that he was writing so much and so rapidly, on occasion dictating to as many as five scribes at a time, the "angelic doctor" would have been supernaturally blessed if he had written elegant and attractive prose. Much more problematic for modern readers is the style imposed by medieval Scholasticism. In any translation true to the original text and its organization, Aquinas's views are set out as answers to questions, followed by subquestions provoked by the answers, answers to those subquestions, and so on. The style reflects the lecturing (and learning) habits of medieval universities, not the reading habits of the twenty-first century. It is the style of Scholastic treatises, and its destruction was a goal of the critics of Catholic theology and medieval philosophy from the fifteenth century to the seventeenth who made "Scholastic" a term of abuse. They succeeded so well that a twenty-first-century reader is disabled from finding Aquinas easy going by almost every aspect of present-day education, in style, content, and argumentative method.[1] We must step back and ask what the project was within which such sensible political opinions, however expounded, found their place—remembering always that a Dominican, even one from an aristocratic family, put himself at risk whenever he put forward ideas, however "sensible" we may think them, which his superiors did not care for.

Aquinas's Life and Times

Aquinas was not long-lived. He was born in 1224 or 1225 and died in 1274. His family were aristocrats from Aquino, north of Naples; they owned a castle, Roccasecca, in which he was born, and where his siblings held him captive for a year when he was twenty in the hope of persuading him not to join the Dominican order. For the first stages of his education, he was sent as a child to the Benedictine monastery at Monte Cassino, where his uncle was abbot, and in 1238 went to Naples to the newly founded university. There he discovered the Dominicans. In 1244 he decided to join the order. His family had their sights set on his entering Monte Cassino as a Benedictine. The abbot of Monte Cassino was a great man in thirteenth-century Italy, and the position one to be coveted. Thomas's obstinacy was greater than his family's; after a year, they allowed him to leave for the University of Paris.

He studied for his novitiate with Albertus Magnus, a German theologian of immense learning, first in Paris and then in Cologne. His lecture notes on Albertus's lectures on Aristotle's *Ethics* survive, along with his notes on Albertus's lectures on the works of the Pseudo-Dionysius. Aquinas was a substantial young man—in later life, the table at which he sat was scooped out to accommodate his girth—and was jokingly called "the ox" by his colleagues. They saw he was extraordinarily intelligent, and Albertus observed that "the bellowing of that ox will be heard throughout the world," though he could hardly have foreseen that Thomism would eventually become the official philosophy of the Catholic Church. In 1252 Aquinas returned to Paris to work for his *licentium docendi*, which he received in 1256. One of the requirements for the degree was a commentary on Peter Lombard's *Sentences* both in a written form and delivered as lectures. Once licensed, he lectured and took part in disputations; and he began the first of his two summae, the *Summa contra Gentiles*, intended for use by missionaries attempting to convert Muslims and Jews. In spite of the chaotic conclusion to the Fourth Crusade (1215), whose only achievement was the sacking of Constantinople, the effort to proselytize in the Islamic world intensified in the thirteenth century, and the Dominicans were a proselytizing order.

After three years, he went to the Dominican house in Naples, and then to the Dominican priory attached to the papal court in Orvieto. In 1265 he opened a *studium generale* in Rome, and there wrote *De regimine principum* and began the *Summa Theologiae*. During these years, he worked with William of Moerbeke, who had begun to translate Aristotle out of the original Greek, bypassing the inaccuracies and infelicities introduced by translators who had turned Aristotle's work into Arabic and thence into Latin. In 1269 he returned to Paris as professor and for a time rector of the university. After three years he returned to Naples and in December 1273 suffered a collapse in health that led him to declare that he could write no more. "All that I have written seems like straw to me," he is reputed to have said.[2] He seems to have suffered a stroke, but that did not stop his superiors from sending him on a mission to the Council of Lyons. On the way he suffered an accident that led to his death on March 7, 1274. He was canonized in 1323, but Thomism became the official Catholic philosophy very slowly. It was only when the Protestant Reformation persuaded the papacy that it needed all the intellectual resources it could lay its hands on that Thomism became identified with philosophically sophisticated Catholicism.

The Dominican order had been founded in 1216. Whereas the Franciscans emphasized poverty and simplicity of life, and a ministry to the poor, the Dominicans were from the first a learned order. A Dominican was *canis Domini*, a hound of the Lord, and the order was the intellectual arm of the church militant, initially created to defend the church against heretics such as the Albigensians in southern France. The sword of the secular authorities was not enough; the Church required educated men who would go out and proselytize on behalf of the faith, and the Order of Preachers did so with enormous energy. The Dominicans were especially employed by the papacy to be preachers of crusades—crusades against heresy, against the Saracens, and against the emperor Frederick II during the struggle between pope and emperor. The order required that when not engaged in religious duties Dominicans were to study; they were initially confined to scriptural and theological inquiry, but this restriction was soon eased. They were notable linguists: members of the order became fluent in the languages of wherever they went as missionaries, and were soon preaching in Arabic and Hebrew as well as Greek. Aquinas's decision to become a Dominican was right.

Intellectual Life in Thirteenth-Century Europe

Much of Aquinas's life was spent teaching at the University of Paris. The universities of medieval Europe were initially founded by kings who needed competent lawyers, and in the beginning their intellectual life focused on the study of Roman law. The church had its own system of law, canon law, and highly trained lawyers; the secular authorities required skilled lawyers of their own. Bologna, founded in the ninth century, was the ancestor of all other European universities, including Paris and Oxford. Gradually, universities became communities of scholars devoted not only to law, medicine, and theology but also to a syllabus including mathematics and "natural philosophy"—physics and astronomy. A pattern emerged of lower-level and higher-level inquiries in a system that admitted students to advanced studies once they had attained proficiency at the "bachelor" level. At that point they achieved a *licentium studendi*, permission to study the higher disciplines; they were awarded a *licentium docendi*, permission to teach, once they demonstrated proficiency at the "master of arts" level. Canon and civil law remained central, along with medicine, and by the thirteenth century science and mathematics were thriving. Nonetheless, this was Christian Europe, and theology was the queen of the sciences and the crowning discipline of the academy. As ever, there was turf warfare, and the ownership of ethics and politics was disputed between the lawyers—particularly canon lawyers—philosophers, and theologians. One thing that did not trouble medieval universities was a conflict between vocational and nonvocational education. All study was vocational.

Theology was the queen of the sciences, but speculation was dangerous and so were non-Christian sources of reflection. The authorities feared the effect on undisciplined young minds of exposure to pagan thought; the boundaries beyond which unorthodox ideas would not be tolerated were unclear, but condemnation for heresy meant imprisonment or worse. Nonetheless, the rise of a philosophically informed approach to the Christian faith was unstoppable because so much of the received doctrine of the Christian church had been thrashed out by church fathers who had themselves employed the resources of Greek philosophy. The period between the death of Augustine and the beginning of the second millennium has often been labeled the Dark Ages, but outside northern Europe this is a libel. The intellectual resources of students were never as scanty as later ages thought. They were, however, lopsided and gave a distorted sense of the full range of Greek and Roman thought.

The empirical, scientific aspect of Greek thought was initially lost. The more mystical parts of Greek philosophy that strike modern readers as proto-Christian were known in part and always congenial to Christian Europe. Neoplatonism was given a new lease on life by Augustine and the Pseudo-Dionysius in the fourth and fifth centuries; and although only three of Plato's dialogues circulated in Latin translation, they included the *Timaeus,* so students knew the authentically metaphysical Plato. They did not know Plato's political writings. The church fathers were anthologized and widely read in the *Sentences* of Peter Lombard; these and the encyclopedic works of Saint Isidore of Seville provided access to the philosophical resources of the early church and empire. After 1100 Arab scholars who translated his works into Latin brought Aristotle to Western notice, and he swiftly acquired the status of "the philosopher." Aristotle was somewhat "Platonized" by translators whose interests were more religious than political or scientific, and when they commented on Aristotle's politics and ethics, it was in ways that diminished the distance between him and Plato. This was not a disaster: the Neoplatonist

Aristotle of Avicenna and Averroës was more easily assimilated than he would have been if he had been encountered whole and in Greek. Even so, the study of Aristotle was periodically forbidden by the church.

The works of Aristotle made their way into the universities during the twelfth century. They initially arrived in Latin translations of Arabic translations from the Greek; few scholars in the west could read Greek. When translations were made directly from Greek into Latin, Aquinas insisted on working with them. Aristotle's *Politics* was one of the first works translated directly from the Greek by William of Moerbeke, the fellow Dominican whom Aquinas recruited for the purpose. It was another two centuries before the ability to read Greek was common enough in western Europe for the texts to be widely used in the original language.

Reason versus Revelation: Faith and Philosophy

The importance of metaphysical and religious questions to the practice of politics is a political choice. Theocracies make religious orthodoxy the basis of political legitimacy, while modern secular states insist that a variety of religious convictions is consistent with political loyalty and political legitimacy. Societies where it is thought that there is only one true faith find it hard to believe that dissent in matters of religion will not have dire political consequences. Relaxedly secular polities see no difficulty in diversity. Taking Aristotle's metaphysics seriously posed spiritual, intellectual, and political difficulties for a Christian. The problems begin at the very beginning. Aristotle believed that the world was eternal and infinite and its existence rationally necessary. Christianity rested on the Jewish creation story, in which the creation of the world is a matter of divine will, and the world is in its essence a historical entity with a beginning in God's first creation, a history that starts with the Fall and attains its end with the Second Coming, the Last Judgment, and the restoration of God's kingdom. Platonic and Neoplatonic myths were more congenial than Aristotle's science.

Aristotle's philosophy was indisputably philosophy; Christianity is indisputably not. Like Judaism and Islam, it is a historical, particularistic creed and rests on revelation. Truth is divinely revealed to particular groups and individuals at particular moments in history. For a philosopher, the providential story set out in the Bible poses obvious difficulties. To a rational inquirer unaided by revelation, it was not obvious *why* God had created a world at all; to suppose that God had *had* to do so limits God's freedom of action, which is blasphemous, but to suppose the Creation was arbitrary seems to insult the divine intelligence, too. Aristotle had argued that an uncaused first cause was necessitated to create the world; but the first cause was not personal in the sense in which Yahweh was. Understanding what Aristotle had in mind has puzzled philosophers, but it does not raise unanswerable questions about the *motivation* of the entity to which it ascribes the origin of the universe.

Aquinas set out to reconcile Aristotle's metaphysics with Christian faith. The nuanced view of the relationship between Christianity and philosophy he provided was greatly needed. Too much reliance on faith opened the door to irrationalism; too much reliance on reason opened the door to skepticism. Reason is the light of nature, but natural reason can take us only so far. One of Aquinas's best-known remarks is *gratia naturam non tollit sed perfecit*—grace does not destroy nature but perfects it.[3] Human reason cannot uncover *everything* we need to know; but human reason is a God-given instrument to be employed effectively within its own limits. Aquinas's confidence in the use of reason within its proper sphere contrasts very sharply with the more extreme attitude of Augustine. Augustine more than once claimed that reason was essentially delusive, providing an example of the philosopher who argues brilliantly against brilliance in argument.

Aquinas avoided the skepticism of Augustine and the much more extreme skepticism of later writers like Hobbes, who held that we simply *had no idea* what it might be like to see the world sub specie aeternitatis and who thus deprived reason of any role in religious matters. Aquinas held the claims of faith and reason in balance. We can have *some* but not an *adequate* idea of the matters that faith dealt with. Reason can lead us to acknowledge the need for faith, and make it plausible that what we believe on faith is true; but the full revelation of the final mysteries of existence must await our vision of God in the afterlife. Until that time, we can only reason by analogy to what the ultimate truth *might* be.

Within philosophy and within Aquinas's *Summa Theologiae*, ethics and politics have a doubly subordinate place. They form a fraction of the concerns of a thinker whose chief topic is the nature of God, the nature of creation, and the relation of all God's creations to each other and to God. Moreover, they are not part of philosophy in its higher reaches. Philosophy tries to set out what is necessarily true; it explains why things *must* be the way they are, and not some other way. It aims at demonstrative truth. Aquinas followed Aristotle in thinking that we should aim only at as much certainty as a subject admits of; ethics and politics seek practical rather than theoretical knowledge, and their conclusions are true on the whole or for the most part, not demonstratively certain. It is the realm of prudence and good sense, not the realm of the geometricians. Aquinas wrote commentaries on Aristotle's *Nicomachean Ethics* and on his *Politics* for the benefit of his students in Paris in the early 1270s, but no work entirely devoted to politics. *De regimine principum* (On royal government) would have been such; it was intended as a gift to the king of Cyprus, but Aquinas wrote only the first chapter and part of the second chapter of the work before abandoning it when its dedicatee died. The book was expanded and completed by Ptolemy of Lucca. Aside from a letter to the duchess of Brabant in answer to her query about how heavily she could tax her Jewish subjects, everything else of interest comes from the two summae, the *Summa contra Gentiles* and the *Summa Theologiae*.

The Political Background: Church and Empire

Although politics and political theory were not Aquinas's major concern, it is surprising that the hostilities between papacy and empire that provided an unsettled backdrop to his life do not surface in his work. Emperor Frederick II was a distant relative, and the Dominicans were preachers of crusades, one of which was launched against Frederick II by Pope Innocent IV. No short, coherent account of the conflict between the papacy and successive emperors is possible; indeed, it is not clear that a wholly coherent account can be given at all. The political theorist may be tempted to see the diplomatic and military conflict between a succession of popes and emperors as inevitably arising from the problem raised in the previous chapter: *who* possesses the ultimate authority that Christ conferred on earthly rulers?[4] This would seriously overstate the role of ideas in conflicts of interest. The major cause of conflict was territorial and financial. The papacy was a powerful secular political entity in central Italy; the Papal States formed until the reunification of Italy in 1871 an S-shaped band of territory that stretched from Ravenna to in the northeast to Rome in the southwest. Frederick II was king of Sicily and the feudal overlord of much of northern Italy. His interest lay in extending his authority over central Italy, and the pope's lay in preventing him from doing so. The allegiance of allies depended overwhelmingly on bribery and coercion, but contending views of legitimacy came into play, too. The agreement that pope and emperor were absolute, each in his own *ordo*, or sphere, which was implicit in the creation of the Holy Roman Empire in 800, could hold only on the basis of an agreed view about where the boundaries of the two spheres lay. None was to be had, and each claimed the authority to depose the other in extremis.

Some views of political and ecclesiastical authority were equally unattractive to popes and emperors alike, because they appealed to secular and "ascending" theories of authority. Republican and natural law theories represented authority as something generated within a community that might legitimately adopt many different constitutional arrangements for creating law, clarifying it, and enforcing it. This was a bad basis for absolutism, whether papal or royal. Cicero's works were popular with civil lawyers and provided the most familiar and durable version of such an ascending theory: natural law sets the standards of communal justice, a *populus* invests an elite with the authority to make law in accordance with natural law, and the form of government matters less than that the form of government should suit the people who live under it and unite justice with the pursuit of the common good. The *populus* would be wise to establish a monarchy as all medieval writers agreed; nonetheless, the source of authority was rather too visibly the people.

This view had particular resonance in the numerous Italian city-states that practiced some form of self-government from the twelfth century to the sixteenth, and sometimes longer; the Venetian Republic endured until it was extinguished by Napoleon. Popes and emperors alike denied that the Italian city-states were truly autonomous; both insisted that they had only such rights of self-government as their papal or imperial overlord granted. The vexed question was the extent of papal authority over the emperor and vice versa. The papacy had no choice but to argue the extreme case that since the Holy Roman Empire had been a papal creation at the time of Sylvester III's coronation of Charlemagne, the emperor was subordinate to the pope. How it came about that the pope could create an emperor was a question answered by the supposed Donation of Constantine. Constantine had given the empire to the pope, who had, so to speak, granted it back to Constantine and his heirs.[5] Once his help to protect the territory of the papacy against invasion by the Lombards was no longer needed, the emperor was a threat to the papacy's political independence. To the south the emperor held the Kingdom of Sicily, embracing the island and much of the mainland ("the Kingdom of the Two Sicilies"), and to the north he was overlord of much of northern Italy, as the feudal superior of many of the city-states of the region. An emperor in control of southern Italy who could bring armies over the Alps and down through northern Italy could evict a hostile pope and install a friendly one. Indeed, even without a secure hold on southern Italy, an invader could make his way down the west coast of Italy to Rome; if the pope was driven out of Rome, it would not be hard to bully or bribe the College of Cardinals to declare him deposed.

The situation seemed to favor the emperor. It did not. The emperor was elected, and the papacy's most powerful weapon was the internal dissensions of the German princes who were the electors. Nor was the emperor welcome in northern Italy; the city-states valued their autonomy and were ready to defend it against their notional overlord. The early thirteenth-century pope Innocent III was a master of political maneuver. He threw his weight behind a friendly candidate for the imperial title, then betrayed him by engineering an alliance to prevent his adding Sicily to his German possessions and securing Sicily for the future Frederick II, who became king as a child of three. By the time he was an adult,

Frederick was the most intelligent, best-educated, and most engaging of all medieval kings, fluent in half a dozen languages, and a formidable enemy. Innocent secured a moral advantage by agreeing to crown Frederick king on condition that he do homage to the pope as his feudal superior and renounce the Kingdom of Sicily if elected emperor. He also got Frederick to promise to launch a crusade at some unspecified date; his grandfather the emperor Frederick Barbarossa had, after all, died on the Third Crusade in 1190, after many years of battling the papacy of Alexander III, and even if Frederick II survived, he would be distracted from the affairs of Italy. Frederick had no intention of treating the pope as his superior; after Innocent III's death, he had himself elected and crowned emperor in 1220 and announced his intention to unify Italy from Sicily to the Alps. He spent almost no time in Germany, where his authority was tenuous outside the south, and he never returned after 1237, claiming that nobody could govern a country where they spoke a language that resembled the barking of dogs and the croaking of frogs. His ambition was to establish a secular, polyglot kingdom in Italy based on Sicily and incorporating the papal and northern states.[6]

Frederick died in 1250, having very narrowly failed in the attempt and after exhausting his own and much of the papacy's resources; the imperial throne remained vacant for almost a quarter of a century. Within half a century the king of France became a more potent threat to the papacy's independence than the emperor had been. This was less significant in political theory than in political practice; only with Jean Bodin's *Six Books of the Commonwealth* of 1576 did anyone articulate the modern concept of a sovereign state and theorize its unity in terms of the indivisible sovereignty that encouraged a king to say, "*L'état, c'est moi.*" The medieval world was the world of Christendom, not the nation-state. The papacy's problem in the late thirteenth and early fourteenth centuries lay with the success of the Capetian monarchy in France; from a position in which the kings of France were weaker than their most powerful feudal vassals, successive monarchs had established themselves as their undoubted superiors. By the late thirteenth century Philip IV— Philip the Fair—could launch military and diplomatic initiatives that the papacy could not counter. Papal edicts of excommunication and deposition were effective if a king was unloved, not in command of his great nobles, not adequately funded, and unable to put effective armies in the field for long campaigns. Philip IV was not much loved, but he was in command of his nobles, his finances, and his armies, and therefore of events. Frederick II was not in command of the same resources, so his attempt to create the first secular state in Europe was stillborn. Philip's contemporary Edward I of England was as effective a monarch as Philip and equally unwilling to respond to papal financial and political demands, but fortunately for the papacy, the English crown had no interest in Italy.

Aquinas's Political Theory

Aquinas's writings were dictated not by local politics but by his aim to produce a synthesis and summary of the findings of theology and philosophy. At the highest level, where the Christian conception of divine law encounters classical notions of the natural law, the question is how divine law and natural law are related, and what their relation is to positive law. Of the institutions that human beings regulate by law, property is one of the most important, and against the background of the Franciscan criticism of wealth and its misuse, the crucial question is whether private ownership is legitimate and natural, and what its limits are—for instance, whether property in human beings, slavery, is legitimate. Against the background of Aristotle and the Bible, Aquinas could not avoid the question of what forms of political authority men can legitimately institute, and whether any are more natural—more legitimate, or more prudentially desirable—than others; and, in terms of the behavior of rulers and subjects, what difference the truth of Christianity makes to the conduct of politics.

This last question is obviously not one that could be addressed to Aristotle; but although classical political philosophers rarely took a view about the literal truth of religious claims, they invariably emphasized the political importance of religion. Aristotle was much concerned with the arrangements for the priesthood in both actual and ideal states. Nobody before the sixteenth century would have thought that secular authority could be indifferent to the religious practices of its subjects; a defense of toleration on the grounds that private religious practice was no business of the law would have been unintelligible. The Roman Empire accepted a great variety of religious practices where they were consistent with political unity, and where their practitioners could plausibly be thought to be cementing their loyalty to the state; but the idea that religion was not the state's business would have been scoffed at. Even Frederick II, who was famous for insisting that Jews and Muslims should practice their faith freely in the Kingdom of Sicily, had heretics burned at the stake in Lombardy.

In discussing natural law, Aquinas had to defuse the tension between a Christian view that separated the social arrangements of post-Fall mankind from those that would have been appropriate if we had never fallen and the pagan view that saw the social and political world as continuous with the natural world. This contrast was somewhat blurred by the popular classical view that mankind had once lived more simply, more rationally, and more happily in a golden age of innocence. In the golden age men had been free and equal and innocent; the Stoic vision of their subsequent corruption overlapped with the Christian vision of the Fall, at least to the extent of identifying the growth of sophistication with a loss of virtue. Nonetheless, the dramatic fall from grace imagined in Judaism and Christianity has no classical counterpart. There is no Stoic equivalent to the thought that death comes into the world only with sin, and no thought that the essence of the Fall is a revolt against God. Given the Stoic vision of God as the soul of the world, immanent in every part of creation, there hardly could be. The idea that each of us has a personal relationship with an angry but loving God is wholly unclassical; and the idea that only divine intervention—that is, grace—can save us from ourselves equally so. Nor can Christianity do anything with the Stoic doctrine of *apatheia*, detachment from desire. *Apatheia* frees us from bondage to the flesh and its disorganized urges and ensures that we are immune to threats and cajoling, and open only to reason; a Christian might think *apatheia* good to the extent that it clears our minds and hearts of obstructions to the voice of God. It cannot be a solution. Grace is the only solution, and Stoicism has no room for grace.

If the redemptive element in Christianity is the most striking difference from its classical antecedents, the Christian picture is not at odds with all classical natural law theories, but is so with anything one can easily find in Aristotle. One crux is the (non)naturalness of inequality. Christianity drew a sharp distinction between natural equality and conventional inequality; in Aristotelian natural law, the hierarchies visible throughout the natural world include the hierarchy of better and worse in society; aristocrats are by nature better than the rank and file, even if nature sometimes makes mistakes and upper-class children turn out worse than the children of the lower orders. One of Aristotle's most extreme assertions of the doctrine of natural inequality is the claim that there are slaves by nature whose servile condition benefits them as well as their masters.[7] In that respect, Stoicism was much closer to Christianity inasmuch as its starting point is the natural equality of all mankind and the nonnaturalness but inescapability of slavery.

Aquinas could not simply take over Aristotle's conception of nature, but he could readily accommodate himself to Aristotle's approach to the relations of nature and convention. He accepted contra Aristotle the orthodox Christian claim that God had given the world to man in common, so that in the strictest sense, there was neither property nor slavery nor political authority by nature.[8] But he had no problems with Aristotle's defense of private property. Indeed, he took over Aristotle's naturalism with regard to earthly affairs with no visible strain. Like Aristotle, he thought that within their proper limits, observation and reflection can tell us almost all we need to know about the conduct of everyday life. He found Aristotleian teleology especially illuminating. Almost more enthusiastically than Aristotle, Aquinas argues that everything is created to achieve some good proper to the sort of thing it is; apples, for example, exist to provide food of a certain sort, but they are also intended to grow to a proper roundness and redness in the process. We describe plants as "flourishing" and thus show that we understand them as having a destiny as *good* specimens of their kind.

So although Aquinas agreed with Christian orthodoxy that if we had never fallen into sin, we would not have needed to live in a political state at all, he went on to agree with Aristotle that the polity exists in order that we can live as good a life as possible on earth.[9] The coercive state may be necessitated by sin, but a well-ordered state is more than a regrettable necessity. We cannot achieve what Aristotle regarded as the greatest good, which is absolute self-sufficiency; for that, we must wait until we encounter God. Nonetheless, the Aristotelian view that the polis was the highest form of human association is *almost* accepted by Aquinas. It cannot be accepted in its entirety, for the good and sufficient reason that the highest community is the community of the Christian faithful. However, we are not mere *peregrini*, as Augustine described us, waiting until our time of tribulation is over. We are here to lead good lives, and, as Aristotle said, the individual needs others with whom to live the good life in common, just as families need the support of larger communities, and villages need a legal system to regulate the behavior of their inhabitants and their relations with other villages. A political system is required to secure all these things and make the good life possible.[10]

In *De regimine* Aquinas is concerned to argue that the best form of government is monarchy; in a treatise addressed to a king he could hardly do otherwise. Still, he does it at a high level of abstraction; kingship is not particularly personal. Rather, one man embodies the unity of the common good and the coherence of its pursuit more effectively than the multitude or a numerous body.[11] In *Summa Theologiae* Aquinas discusses Aristotle's account of *politeia*, the constitutional state that keeps the peace by doing justice to both the better- and the worse-off by blending aristocracy and democracy. Curiously, he does so in the context of a discussion of God's provision for the government of the Jews of the Old Testament, but he accepts without anxiety Aristotle's preference for *politeia* as the best practicable state.[12] Generally, he thinks, as did Aristotle in the abstract, that if it can be had, aristocracy is even better than *politeia*; but he goes further than Aristotle in preferring monarchy to aristocracy on grounds of efficiency. In the light of Aristotle's division of good and bad governments, democracy is to be preferred to tyranny on grounds of *inefficiency*: misrule by the many is less effectively evil than one-man misrule. In all, what is notable is the extreme matter-of-factness of the discussion.

One might ask whether this means that after all the state does exist "by nature," as Aristotle claimed. Yes and no. It is natural in the sense that it suits humanity to organize itself in this fashion, there are genuine goods that political organization shelters and encourages, and virtues that are required for and elicited by living a political life. It is not natural, in the sense that mankind would not have lived in a political community in the absence of the Fall. The argument is delicately set out. Adam neither needed nor exercised coercive authority of the kind that sets the state apart from informal associations; but Adam posssessed something a little like property and something a little like political authority. He had the right to use lower forms of creation for his own benefit, and if he had not sinned, he would have had the authority of a father over his wife and children even in the Garden of Eden. He would have been a patriarch with authority over an extended family whose members would have acknowledged that authority. Coercive law would not have been needed and would not have existed. Aquinas quotes and dissents from Augustine's claim that "God did not intend that His rational creature, made in His own image, should have lordship over any but irrational creatures: not man over man, but man over the beasts."[13] In so doing, he accepts something very like Aristotle's picture of natural hierarchy: parents govern children, husbands govern wives.

The Varieties of Law

Aquinas was fascinated by the taxonomic issues that any discussion of the law raises. He begins by arguing that there is an eternal law, implicit in the fact that God constructed the universe on rationally intelligible principles and for rationally endorsable ends. To the objection that there cannot be an eternal law, because God is the giver of law and preexisted the world, he replies that law is a principle of practical reason in the lawgiver, not a set of instructions the lawgiver issues to those subject to the law. God is eternal, and the principles inherent in God's plans for the universe are eternal also. However, the eternal law of reason is not identical with natural law. *Natural law*, strictly, is something that only human beings can follow, because it requires reason to discern it; animals following principles of action that lead to their own welfare follow natural law only analogically. Aquinas is happy to say that nonrational animals are guided by or governed by natural law, but the law is not "in them," and they do not follow it as we can.[14] As to the content of natural law, Aquinas insists that its precepts are simple and universal, reducing in the last resort to "seek good and eschew evil," or in the alternative to some variant of the Golden Rule, that we should do unto others as we would have them do to us and more especially *not* do unto others what we would wish them *not* to do to us. The simplicity of ultimate principles does not carry over to their implications; here common sense must come in, and casuistry in the nonabusive sense of reasoning to the particular case. Thus, the prima facie obligation to restore to another the possessions we have borrowed from him, which is the general rule, will fail if we have borrowed a weapon from a man who proposes to use it to fight against his country. Such considerations affect the legitimacy of private property, where the legitimacy of the institution takes one only a limited distance in deciding the rights of an individual in a particular case.

Aquinas introduces a further distinction between different forms of law. Jews and Christians have been given laws by God in a more direct, localized way. This is divine positive law. That the Jews were given laws by God Aquinas did not doubt; this was the old law. The question he took more pains to answer was whether there was one divine positive law or several. The answer could go in two different directions. One might say that God rules all mankind, is lawgiver to all mankind, and gives one law only. On the other hand, Christ said that he came to give a new law, and that implies that the old law and the new are two. Aquinas finds his way deftly between the horns of the dilemma. The sense in which the law is one is that it is given by one God; this anticipates nineteenth-century philosophers of law who explained the unity of a legal system in terms of its issuing from a single sovereign authority. The sense in which the law is more than one is that it is addressed, sequentially, to more than one community. Much as a human being is one and the same person when a boy and a full-grown man, even though the boy and the man may look very different, so the law is one law when it is given partially to the Jews in the Old Testament and fully to Christians later.[15]

Explaining why there has to be both divine law and eternal law, Aquinas argues that the eternal law, which is underwritten by reason as well as God, serves as a standard for any rational creature, but is silent on many issues that divine positive law speaks to. The new law contained in the gospel therefore contains within itself the natural law, but not vice versa. The same considerations dictated Aquinas's treatment of the question whether natural law is capable of change; the pro and contra are clear enough: on the one hand, the immutable principles of reason are just that, but, on the other, God gave particular instructions in the Old Testament that contradicted natural law, and human law introduces institutions such as private property that are not known to natural law. The resolution once again is that natural law is immutable as to first principles and not as to secondary consequences; where something is to be added or subtracted for the achievement of the law's purpose, there is both change and immutability.

This brings us to familiar issues, such as whether we could live without law, and whether positive human law must conform to one or other of eternal law, natural law, or divine law to be law properly speaking, and to command our obedience. This demands an account of what gives human law authority over us, and how its authority is constrained by the other forms of law to which we are subject. The medieval view held two possibilities in tension. On the one hand, rulers issued law in virtue of the authority that God conferred on them as rulers. This is the "top-down," or descending, view of authority, and no other seems (to almost anyone other than Hobbes) to make sense where *God's* law is at issue. On that view, law is the command of the sovereign. On the other hand, it was often claimed that rulers had received their authority to make law by grant from the people, or by concession of the community; this is a "bottom-up," or ascending, conception of authority and makes good sense of the authority of constitutional rulers. On that view, law expresses the will of the political community. The authority of natural law, which Cicero and Aristotle took to set the standard for positive law, must be accounted for differently; if we have a duty to pursue our own and the common good, we have a duty to obey those rules which minister to that good.

This still leaves the question of how far natural law constrains the legitimacy of human law. Aquinas consistently tries to apply the ideas of Aristotle, to whom modern conceptions of political obligation were foreign, and who provided no clear-cut answer to the question whether a law that fails the test of compatibility with natural law fails the test of being a law at all. The obvious, commonsensical view is to recur to the distinction between general rules binding on all rational creatures and the specification of what those rules require in particular conditions; purported laws that violate all the most important considerations that natural law rests on cannot possess any (morally) binding force, but if the complaint against them is that they are good-faith but incompetent attempts to implement natural law, the considerations that favor obedience will have greater force.

Nonetheless, Aquinas's views are not Aristotle's. Like any Christian writer, he has an unclassical sense of the gulf between the political world of sinful men and the prelapsarian world that preceded it. There is, he says, an indispensable role for human law in the fallen world in which we live. It is at the very least *useful*—though he means "indispensable"—to institute human law to supplement the other laws by which we are governed.[16] Aquinas's understanding of usefulness does not turn him into an eighteenth- or nineteenth-century utilitarian; the value of law is not exhausted by its usefulness in promoting ordinary happiness. Aquinas's view of the good life is much closer to Aristotle's than to Jeremy Bentham's, allowance made for Aquinas's dependence on Christian rather than classical ideas of virtue and what "the good life according to virtue" entailed. The purpose of human law is to make men behave virtuously, not merely to organize their relations with one another in a tidy fashion. Narrowly utilitarian considerations are not absent, but they are not central.

Aquinas quotes the observation of Isidore of Seville—he might have quoted Augustine and numerous others—that many men can be made to behave properly only by being threatened with punishment, and Aquinas agrees that this is a good reason to institute coercive law. Still, he does not appeal to many of the considerations that a modern writer would. We are as impressed as he by the usefulness of the criminal law in repressing antisocial and wicked behavior, but most of us are even more impressed by the usefulness of the civil law in assisting economic activity. Aquinas was not very interested in economic activity; he takes an Aristotelian view of moneymaking, is hostile to exchange for the sake of monetary gain, and is especially critical of usury;[17] he thinks like a thirteenth-century Dominican not an eighteenth-century classical economist. Even when Aquinas accepts Aristotle's observations about the need for human beings to cooperate with one another because they are not self-sufficient, the self-sufficiency he immediately discusses is self-sufficiency in leading the life of virtue. The service men do one another is less importantly that of cooperating to satisfy each other's physical needs than that of fulfilling "the need to receive from one another the discipline by which they arrive at virtue."[18]

Laws lose their authority by being unjust: *lex injusta nulla lex*. They also lose their authority when they cease to serve the purpose for which they are properly made. Aquinas's treatment of property rights illustrates the point. He took the Stoic-Christian view that by nature there is no private property. God gave the earth to mankind in common for the benefit of life, and but for our sinful natures there need be no rules of mine and thine. Aquinas has no interest in economic growth or ever-increasing prosperity; as a good Aristotelian, he thinks that we should aim to have "enough," not as much as possible. Aristotle's advocacy of the mean is Aquinas's touchstone; ascetics who starve themselves to death are as misguided as gluttons who eat themselves to death. The assumption of utility maximization that underpins modern economics implies a psychology alien to Aquinas.

The Virtues of Private Property

The morality of private property concerned Aquinas for the reasons it concerns ourselves—the contrast between the poverty of those who have too little and the greed of those who have too much—as well as for reasons remote from us. Dominicans and Franciscans took opposed views about property; the Franciscans claimed that they owned nothing, either individually or as an order, while the Dominicans took the view that the order, though not its individual members, owned what it seemed to own. The Franciscans were from the beginning, officially at any rate, more ascetic and self-denying than the Dominicans; they insisted that their order owned nothing and merely used what the pope allowed them. The distinction was important. In a Christian context, where the *amor habendi*, or desire for possessions, was held to be the root of all evil, the prelapsarian condition was seen as a time when Adam could use God's bounty, but owned nothing in the sense in which an individual's ownership entitles him to exclude everyone else from what he owns. It is easy to see the propaganda advantage accruing to the Fransciscans.

When he argues for the legitimacy of the private ownership of goods and land, Aquinas argues that we can accept some famous criticisms of property without concluding that all ownership is illicit. The argument runs briskly and persuasively. God is the sole lord of the world, so one form of dominion over the external world—better understood as sovereignty than as ownership—is simply not available. Nonetheless, God gave the world to mankind to use and to improve; and he gave mankind dominion over inferior creatures. It follows that there must be a right to appropriate whatever in the external world is useful for human life. As to the merits of individual, private property, he invokes the Aristotelian view that it is more efficient than other sorts of property both because people care more for their own than for common property and because we each know which things are our responsibility to care for. Perhaps more interestingly, he also says that an equitable distribution of property among individuals so that each is content with his own portion makes for peace. Dissension is more common where property is held in common than where it is held as private property. He may have had peasant communities in mind, but more probably he meant only that, in the absence of agreed rules, people will try to grab what they can.[19]

Use, on the other hand, should be as far as possible use in common. Aquinas bends an Aristotelian thought to Christian purposes. "Private ownership and common use" was Aristotle's attempt to secure the virtues of Sparta without a Spartan existence. The Spartan institution of military messes, where all males were supposed to eat together, was what Aristotle had in mind; but it was not at all what Aquinas was thinking of. Aquinas starts from the idea that law aims at the common good; property depends on the law for its legitimacy, and therefore the distribution of property should serve the common good, not the selfish interest of the legal owner. His defense of common use is an account of charity; a man can use his property as he chooses so long as he is ready to share with others in times of need. Sitting tight on his legal ownership and denying others the means of subsistence invalidates his ownership. This is farther from the Spartan messes in which Plato and Aristotle were interested than from the morality of the modern welfare state.

Aquinas recurs to the issue in discussing theft. Theft is self-evidently wrong. The essence of property is to be under the control of its owner, and its use should depend upon his permission; there cannot be property without rules against theft, so theft is transparently wrong. Aquinas considers the degrees of wrongness of theft under different conditions, but the crucial question is what we are to say about someone who commits theft only at the point where he will otherwise simply starve? Here Aquinas boldly says that the rich man's superfluity belongs to the starving man and that he commits no theft in taking what is his by right of necessity.[20] The argument reappears verbatim three centuries later in Locke's *First Treatise* on government.[21] It is a striking claim, but it is significant that Aquinas phrases it the way he does. The poor can be required to abstain from taking what they need from the stores of the rich only if the security of the possessions of the better-off is essential to the welfare of the poor themselves. Saint Basil had said that the rich man was like a man who comes into the theater and takes a seat and thus ensures that there is no seat for the next comer. If Saint Basil was wrong, it must be because the possessions of the rich do not prevent the poor from acquiring possessions of their own, and the wealth of the rich ensures that the poor can thrive.[22]

When that condition fails, the argument falls. The poor man is no longer obliged to keep his hands off the rich man's stores. In time of famine, the poor are entitled to help themselves if nobody else helps them. Aquinas seems to go further in saying that the superfluities of the rich "belonged" to the starving poor; ordinary speech does not suggest that the poor *own* the rich man's superfluities any more than patients own the public hospital that is obliged to treat them. Aquinas may have thought that in extreme necessity mankind was plunged back into a state of nature, where all things are common, or he may simply not have drawn such a sharp distinction as we do between one and another sort of "belonging." The latter suggestion is, however, at odds with the emphasis the Dominicans and Franciscans placed on exactly the distinction between ownership strictly speaking and a right of use, and the former thought is probably the right one.

War

Property is unimaginable without law to sustain it, and that involves criminal courts and punishment. It is also hard to imagine property existing without a state to protect it; but states are many rather than one, and they frequently engage in war with one another. Aquinas is one of the most influential theorists of justice in war, and he treats the justice of warfare, very plausibly, as part of the larger question of what entitles us to cause the deaths of other human beings. Since politics exists to preserve peace and unity, the state of war is the polar opposite of a properly political condition, but it can to some degree be regulated. Aquinas follows Augustine's account of the just war step by step, citing his authority at every turn. For war to be lawful, three things are needed: first, it must be official, declared by a person or persons authorized to do it; private revenge and banditry are not war and cannot be justified; individuals have courts to turn to for the redress of injustice and neither need to resort to war nor have the authority to do so.[23] Second, the cause of the war must be just; wars should be fought only in self-defense, but self-defense extends in one temporal direction to a preemptive strike to prevent imminent attack, and in the other to taking belated measures, for instance, to recover territory that has been unjustly seized and not returned. Third, the war must be fought with the right intention, with the aim of restoring peace and punishing the wicked always before our minds.[24]

Common sense marks the discussion. Aquinas goes on to argue against the active participation of bishops and priests on the battlefield, but does not suggest that they can play no part whatever in warfare; they may encourage the combatants and comfort the wounded. It was a live issue in medieval Europe, where bishops exercised secular authority and might lead a feudal host or their own militia into battle. In cases like this, Aquinas's attempts to extract firm principles from Aristotelian premises require a good deal of supplementation from without; like Aristotle, he believed that persons primarily engaged in one task were not to engage in others at odds with it, but he does not so much rely on the thought that a bishop who sometimes goes into battle will be a significantly worse bishop during times of peace as on the thought that "warlike tasks have a greatly unquiet character, and hence much distract the mind from the contemplation of Divine things and from praising God and offering prayers for the people, which belong to the duties of clerics.'[25] More obvious objections to bishops' fighting could be drawn from the gospels; but the injunction to turn the other cheek appears to forbid everyone to fight, not priests alone, and, following Augustine, Aquinas had defused that objection already.

The State and Christianity

For all his faith in Aristotle, Aquinas's account of politics is neither modern nor classical, but Christian and medieval. His Aristotelian resources fail him—as they must—at the point where he has to discuss the role of religion in politics in terms that make no sense outside a Christian setting: the secular authority of the pope, the allegiance we owe or do not owe to non-Christian rulers, the treatment of Jews, nonbelievers, and heretics. Aristotle did not advocate religious toleration, but the concept of heresy was foreign to him. The modern ideal of toleration, which is four centuries newer than Aquinas's ideas, requires the Christian obsession with heresy to give it purchase and to illuminate what the ideal requires. It is not merely that we—anyone likely to be reading this—think it better to tolerate heretics than to burn them, but that we are impressed by the conviction and commitment that leads heretics to prefer death at the stake to apostasy. It is because heretics care so passionately about their dissident ideas that we think their repression so evil.

Aquinas thought no such thing. The Christian polity can do what no pagan polity could do. It can bring its citizens to as much understanding of the truths of the Christian religion as mortal minds can possess, and it can make them comport themselves so as to have a hope of grace and life eternal. The Christian state cannot directly bring individuals to understanding or a proper moral outlook; that is for the church. The state can promote true religion by ensuring that the church is safeguarded against whatever evils assail it, and by following the guidance of the church in moral matters. That raises the question of the relation of secular and ecclesiastical authority. Aquinas's views are no more extreme here than elsewhere. He does not repudiate the papacy's claims of immunity for its clergy in criminal courts or its claim that church property may be taxed only with the church's agreement; but he does not suggest that the pope has any secular authority outside the Papal States.[26] Nonetheless, he claims that the church has secular authority over Jews and says that the church does not assert its rights over unbelievers as a concession.[27] In the everyday politics of a Christian polity, the church's authority is not in competition with that of the state; secular affairs must generally be left to the secular authorities. Where the pope has a standing in secular politics, it is *ratione peccati*, and the pope legitimately intervenes in politics when a moral issue of sufficient gravity arises. The commonest occasion is if a royal marriage must be dissolved and papal authorization is required. "Sin" is an elastic justification, and we might fear that *ratione peccati* could ground unbridled papal authority over secular princes; after all, most political controversies have a moral dimension. Aquinas was infinitely far from defending that sort of papalism; Boniface VIII asserted a sweeping jurisdiction over secular affairs thirty years after Aquinas's death and led the papacy to disaster. Aquinas provided no resources for such an expansion of the pope's role in secular affairs.

The reader may wonder why Aquinas did not press the point that the state exists to further our earthly interests, and the church to further our interest in the afterlife, and thus embrace the modern separation of the jurisdictions of church and state. One answer is that nobody did. Seventeenth-century ideas about toleration and the separation of church and state were not a thirteenth-century discovery. The thirteenth-century view was that there are distinguishable jurisdictions, but they are interlinked and overlapping. Americans deeply attached to the separation of church and state tolerate a lot of dubious jurisprudence to maintain the division; Aquinas took it for granted that states tried to foster virtue in their citizens. The nature of virtue is largely known by reason, but the Christian revelation has enlarged our understanding of it; a Christian ruler promotes virtue as understood by Christians. Moreover, it would be scandalous for a Christian ruler to allow Christian belief to loosen its hold on his subjects or allow confusion and disorder to seize the church within his domain. The doctrines around which he had to preserve unity were better understood by the church and its priests, including the bishop of Rome, than by the laity, so the secular ruler should generally accept the authority of the church in such matters. Things go better when everyone sticks to one job. A takeover of secular functions by the church made no more sense than monarchs setting themselves up as theological authorities; neither did a sharp line of separation between the spheres of authority of church and state. Kings should rule with the moral guidance of the church; the church should look to the salvation of souls with the earthly assistance of the state.

Aquinas took an equally moderate view regarding the right of unbelievers to exercise authority over Christians. De facto, Christians found themselves reliant on the protection of non-Christian governments if they traveled beyond the borders of western Europe; the interesting question was how far they were morally bound to obey non-Christian rulers, and on this Aquinas sided with the tradition that appealed to Christ's acceptance of the authority of the pagan Roman Empire. Aquinas did not share Augustine's relish for the thought that God places us under the dominion of wicked rulers to drive home the fact of our sinfulness, but he did note that the fathers of the church expected to deal with pagan

emperors. Saint Peter lived under the mad and wicked Nero without suggesting that the power to bind and loose that he had received from Christ
could be used to depose Nero.[28] The argument is simple: earthly rulers
are to be obeyed when they perform the functions that earthly rulers are
supposed to perform. When they do not, the situation becomes more
complicated, but the fundamental duty to do justice and act lawfully
implies that we must not resort to extralegal activity unless we shall do
more good than harm. The one exception to this is the much discussed
case where a ruler demands an action explicitly forbidden by Christian
teaching. Augustine held that we should engage in purely passive disobedience under such conditions. Aquinas held a more complicated view; he
says that such a ruler had forfeited his right to have us obey his orders,
and that we had returned to a state of nature in which we could legitimately do whatever was morally acceptable to restore a stable, lawful,
unoppressive regime. To see to the bottom of Aquinas's view, we should
first turn to two other aspects of the role of Christian faith in secular
politics and then to his discussion of the treatment of tyrants.

First, then, the question of heretics and, second, the treatment of the
Jews. Aquinas observes that there are many arguments against compelling unbelievers to adopt the Christian faith.[29] Faith is something we
must come to willingly, and forced professions are not faith. As often,
he argues from the symbolic interpretation of gospel texts: thus, Christ's
admonition to his disciples not to pull up the tares for fear of pulling
up the wheat with them is to be understood as an injunction not to
kill unbelievers for fear of killing potential Christians. The injunction
compelle intrare is also given much weight. The parable of the man who
gave a wedding feast and, lacking guests, told his servants to go out into
the highways and byways and "compel them to come in" led to a lot of
bloodshed over the centuries. It seems to enjoin Christians to force non-
Christians into the church. Aquinas trod carefully. We should certainly
stop unbelievers from subverting the faith of Christians. The Christian
ruler of a state containing a minority of nonbelievers may limit the nonbelievers' freedom of speech and action to avoid unsettling the faith of
the Christian majority.

It is not a license to kill unbelievers because they are unbelievers; kill-

ing the infidel is not good in itself. Nonetheless, Aquinas moves unnerv-
ingly from discussing the usefulness of mild coercion in bringing the
unbeliever to a Christian faith to considering their execution. The argument for mild forms of coercion is neither complicated nor implausible,
even if liberal readers will not much like it. Coercion works, and mild
coercion works best. Savage persecution arouses resistance, but mild measures of coercion do not. Many people say that they are glad to have been
made to observe the practices of the faith and that they regard themselves
as having been kept on the straight and narrow by such means. To use a
vulgar modern analogy, a man might be grateful that when he was intoxi-
cated his friends took away his car keys, though he put up a fight at the
time. The newly persuaded Christian will be grateful that he was enabled
to see the light by being forced to look in the right direction.

Heretics are another matter; they are not mere unbelievers. They are
backsliders and resilers from a faith they have adopted; they are in breach
of obligations freely made and must be forced to meet them. This does
not explain the savagery with which the church dealt with heresy, but
Aquinas is unflinching. The heretic has committed a mortal sin and has
condemned himself to eternal death; his crime is worse than that of the
forger and counterfeiter who is executed for his crime. Summary execution is warranted, even though it never happens in fact because the church
exercises a self-restraint and mercy appropriate to its mission, and never
seeks the death of a heretic until he has had several chances to repent and
return to the faith. Since heresy is so much worse than mere unbelief, it
follows that although an unbeliever who has never been a Christian may
exercise ordinary political authority over Christians, and Christians are
obliged to obey him and treat his laws as binding, the heretic is another
matter. He can be deposed for apostasy. Aquinas does not insist that he
must be deposed, but he does say that Gregory VII's deposition of the
emperor Henry IV was valid.[30] The pope was right to excommunicate
him, and an excommunicated ruler has no authority over his subjects.
One wonders what Aquinas thought of the fact that his distant relative
Frederick II, the emperor during the first twenty-five years of Aquinas's
life, was excommunicated no fewer than four times, including the time

he was first excommunicated for failing to go on crusade as promised and again for going on crusade while still excommunicate.

Among unbelievers who have never been Christians, the Jews form a special case. Aquinas accepts the canon law claim that Jews are "the slaves of the church," even though the church never acted on that claim even in the Papal States where it had the physical capacity to do so, and it was a canon that was contradicted by other canons. His acceptance comes the more oddly because Aquinas was not interested in the conversion of the Jews, and did not suggest they committed any crime merely by being non-Christians. If they convert to Christianity, they can be held to what they have promised, and relapses into their former faith can be punished. Otherwise, they should be allowed to live as they traditionally have done, partly because it is more trouble than it is worth to do anything else, and partly because they may serve a useful purpose as exemplifying the old imperfect faith that Christianity has perfected. This was not a display of friendship toward the Jews and their faith: his discussion of the need to tolerate their religious rites is reinforced by an appeal to one of Augustine's more surprising suggestions—that we permit prostitution to avoid the whole world's being consumed by lust.[31]

These thoughts are elaborated in Aquinas's response to a question posed by the duchess of Brabant on the lawfulness of exacting a tribute from the Jews. He responded with a letter on the government of the Jews.[32] He says that since the Jews are perpetual slaves, their property is their ruler's, and all of it can be taken save a bare subsistence. The duchess may have been less happy with his response to her claim that everything which the Jews in her jurisdiction possessed had been acquired by the practice of usury, and that since usury was illicit, she could seize the property on which the profits of usury had been spent and use it for her own purposes. He replied that it could legitimately be taken from the Jews, but should be returned to those who had paid the usurious interest. If they could not be located, it must be spent on charity. It must not be taken as tax revenue. Aquinas was not by the standards of his day severe or superstitious; he was far from suggesting that Jews might be killed just because they were Jews, or because they inherited the taint of those who had killed Christ, which was what medieval anti-Semitism often amounted to. He did not suggest that their rulers might treat them absolutely as they liked. Nonetheless, as with his acceptance of slavery and the division of the world into the better- and the worse-off, Aquinas demonstrates how easy it is to reconcile the natural equality and freedom of all mankind with the inequalities of the world as we have it.

Politeia, Kingship, Tyranny

De regimine principum provides a simple defense of moderate monarchy. The polity exists for the sake of peace and unity, and it is best ruled by a king. The unity of the larger is mirrored in the unity of the smaller, and one-man rule suits most polities. What a polity is for is constant: it must preserve peace and unity by means of law, and law aims at a common good, which is not an additive sum of the various private goods of the members of the society but the good of living in common the life of virtue. Aristotle might wonder where his concern for balancing social forces to fend off revolution has gone to, and the answer is that Aquinas is drawing on the authorities known to him—biblical, Ciceronian, Aristotelian, and the traditions of canon law—not in order to write political sociology but to write a mirror of princes. The genre is moral exhortation, not political theory.

Nonetheless, he does something important. Aquinas finesses the contrast between descending and ascending theories of legitimate authority, with no sleight of hand. The unity of a polity is best encapsulated in kingly rule; but the authority of the king is the authority of the political community. He takes it for granted that a wise king governs with the advice and consent of his nobles, and in conformity to the teaching of the church. This is not the Polybian theory of the mixed constitution, for Polybius's discussion is in the "sociological" mode of Aristotle's discussions of the avoidance of revolution. Aquinas was making the moral point that it is not the personal will of the king that makes his laws laws, but what we might—though Aquinas does not—call his representative will. Arbitrary will has no place in a constitutional polity. If a ruler is a source of disunity and scandal rather than unity and peace, his title to govern is undermined. Christian morality provides resources for a theory of constitutionally limited authority and an account of government as essentially representative government.

For Aquinas this provides a solution to the question of the deposition of tyrants and the praiseworthiness of tyrannicides. That tyrants may be deposed he does not doubt. One-man rule is the best form of government when it conforms to its own proper principles, but one-man misrule or tyranny is the worst form of government. The instrumental view of government that permeates *De regimine principum* provides a simple but adequate principle to govern the deposition of tyrants; if they can be got rid of, they should be, and enduring tyrannical rule is defensible only on the grounds that attempting the overthrow of the tyrant will create still worse evils. There is no Augustinian insistence on passive obedience or passive disobedience, nor a Ciceronian enthusiasm for political murder. Since the king's authority rests on the consensus of the community, his removal from office must be an act of the community, not of a single individual. This eminently sensible view raises a question that Aquinas did not address but others did: who speaks for the community? When Locke came to discuss revolution in 1680, he termed it an "appeal to heaven"—as did many American revolutionaries a century after that. Appealing to heaven may be something that a single individual has to do to start the revolutionary process, but it is done *on behalf of* a whole political community. Not surprisingly, commentators have seen Locke as a disciple of Aquinas.

The tyrant has forfeited the trust placed in him and should demit the office he has disgraced; if he will not do so willingly, he must be made to do so. What is needed is an account of who in particular may launch this process, and what we shall find is that once an answer is given, it becomes difficult not to go further and argue that the body or bodies that can approve and disapprove the conduct of kings ought themselves to be sovereign. If defenders of royal absolutism could argue that it was absurd to suppose that a sovereign might have a sovereign set above him, and equally absurd to suppose a "lower" body could have the right to dismiss him, critics could accept those premises and conclude that the body that could dismiss the sovereign must be the source of the sovereign's powers and that he could govern only as its agent. Down that path lay the conciliar movement within the church, the revival of republican theory in the city-states of Italy, and, very much farther down the path and a long time later, the rise of modern representative democracy.

CHAPTER 8

The Fourteenth-Century Interregnum

Roads Not Taken—Until Later

THE CONCERNS OF THREE fourteenth-century thinkers dominate this chapter: Dante's advocacy of universal monarchy, Marsilius of Padua's claim that representative and constitutional arrangements should govern both state and church, and Bartolus of Sassoferrato's analysis and defense of the semiautonomous city republics of northern Italy. The conciliar movement for church reform provides a very brief coda, while William of Ockham receives all too brief a discussion, as do Nicholas of Cusa and Jean Gerson, the theorists of conciliarism. In terms of their impact on the immediate political scene, all wrote in vain. The attempt to unify Italy under imperial rule that exhausted previous emperors had been abandoned by the first Habsburgs in the late thirteenth century, and the attempts of Henry of Luxemburg and Ludwig of Bavaria early in the fourteenth century met with no success. Ludwig's successor, Charles IV, was concerned only with his native Bohemia, and in accordance with a promise to the pope, he spent only one day in Rome when he was crowned emperor, by the prefect of the city rather than the pope. The vision of a new Roman empire with the political and military reach of the western Roman Empire died.

The city-states on which Marsilius and Bartolus focused their atten-

tion were increasingly dominated by their aristocratic and autocratic rulers, who were themselves increasingly dependent on the favor of popes or
foreign monarchs. Conciliarist pressures for a constitutionally governed
church were briefly successful in the early fifteenth century, then failed.
Thereafter they were overtaken by the Reformation of the sixteenth century, after which the Roman Catholic Church remained monarchical
and hierarchical, while the Protestant churches exhibited an almost infinite variety of political forms—though none that much resembled that
of the Roman Catholic Church.

Nonetheless, to dismiss the ideas discussed in this chapter merely as
"roads not taken" would be a mistake. These are roads taken in surprising ways a very long time afterward; Napoleon first, and Hitler more
terrifyingly, came close to establishing a European empire on the scale
that fired the imagination of Frederick II and Dante; the European
Union is sometimes accused of being on the way to doing so. Representative government as practiced throughout the Western world would
not wholly surprise Marsilius; and if it is overly imaginative to say that
the relationship between the individual states of the United States and
the federal government, or that between the European Union and its
constituent national states, would have been a fertile field of study for
Bartolus of Sassoferrato and the jurists who thought about the legal status of semi-independent city-states, it is not wholly fanciful. Conciliarism was almost entirely concerned with church government, not with
politics more broadly, but its advocates would not have been surprised by
representative democracy in the twenty-first century, and the theoretical
analysis of the voting systems we employ today (as well as some we do
not) began with Nicholas of Cusa.

Church and State

The background to the development of political thought at the turn of
the fourteenth century is the familiar conflict between church and state,
especially between papacy and empire: the conflicts between Pope Boniface VIII and Philip the Fair, king of France, and then yet again between

the papacy and the empire. Conflicts between successive popes and the kings of England, France, and Spain almost always had their origins in the desire of kings to tax the wealth of the church and were amenable to compromise. The conflict between papacy and empire was more nearly a zero-sum game. One or the other could dominate central Italy, but not both. Either the pope had a special role in the election of the emperor, or not; either the emperor had a special role with regard to the papacy, or not. This lent a sharper ideological, theoretical, and theological edge to disputes, which was one reason why they were drawn out and intractable. The Holy Roman Empire was a creation of the papacy, and the coronation of the emperor by the pope of the day was essential to the emperor's status as emperor, until Emperor Charles IV issued the so-called Golden Bull of 1356, which named the seven imperial electors and decreed that election by them was all that was required, and that a majority of the seven was sufficient for election.

Until that time, popes took the view that what they could confer they could take away; and they had some historical authority on their side; the election of Charlemagne's father, Pippin, as king of the Franks was preceded by a deputation of nobles to Rome to ask papal permission to depose Childeric, the last Merovingian king, not for sin or heresy but because he was "useless." The pope had concurred. One of Marsilius of Padua's many offenses in the eyes of the church was his tract *De translatione imperii* (On the transfer of power), which argued that the deposition of Childeric and the election of Pippin had been acknowledged by the pope, but was in itself legally valid and legitimate as the act of the appropriate members of the Frankish political society.[1] The doctrine of the two swords that Gelasius had laid down was much debated by both canon and civil lawyers, without a clear consensus emerging on the vexed question whether the superiority of the spiritual sword meant that its bearer could dictate to secular rulers and, if so, whether the pope could dictate to all, to the emperor in particular, and over what range of issues. It was never suggested that popes could supplant a secular ruler in his ordinary judicial and administrative roles; there were two swords, not one. Nor was it ever denied that the spiritual sword was "superior," in the same sense that the soul was superior to the body and heavenly concerns to earthly concerns. That settled none of the disputes about the rights of secular courts over the clergy, the coercive powers of ecclesiastical courts, or taxation.

At the end of the thirteenth century and the beginning of the fourteenth, it became clear that the papacy was all but impotent in secular politics outside Italy. It was a French king, not a German emperor, who made it obvious. When Aquinas died in 1274, this could not have been predicted; the imperial throne remained empty for two decades after Frederick II died frustrated in 1250. A new emperor was elected only in 1272. The papacy had won—or had drawn with the advantage on its side—every contest with lay rulers. In 1209 Innocent III imposed a papal interdict on England and forced King John to humiliate himself by acknowledging the pope as his feudal overlord. In the second quarter of the thirteenth century, Gregory IX and his successor Innocent IV had frustrated Frederick II's hopes of creating a secular Italian state stretching from Sicily to the Alps. But in the last years of the thirteenth century and the first years of the next, Philip IV of France decisively defeated Pope Boniface VIII. Indeed, the French monarchy kidnapped the papacy, physically and organizationally, relocating the papacy to Avignon and beginning the so-called Babylonian Captivity, which ended only in 1378. The territory of Avignon, the Comtat Venaissin, was, legally speaking, part of the Papal States until the French Revolution, but practically, the papal court was at the mercy of the French king. Whether this was worse than being at the mercy of rival Roman aristocrats is another matter.

The papacy's success in frustrating the efforts of successive emperors to unite Italy and make the unity of Europe a reality was deceptive. After King John had humbled himself before Innocent III, English kings were unaffected by the terms on which the excommunication had been lifted. The church was marginally more free to choose whom it wished as bishops, but a royal veto on elections persisted, and in spite of Innocent's insistence that the clergy could be taxed only by papal permission, the kings of both France and England continued to levy taxes on their clergy without waiting for it. The Catholic Church was a formidable force; it was wealthier than any single European state—owning perhaps a quarter of all the land and movables in Europe—and had a firmer grip on the loyalties of Christendom than most secular rulers. But these were wasting assets; bishops who lived like princes gave the lie to the claim that the church held its wealth in trust for the poor; and popes who spent taxes raised in France and England on fighting emperors in Italy ran into a growing sense of national identity and national loyalty. When Boniface VIII tried to emulate Innocent III and lay down the law to the kings of France and England, he violated the tacit compromise by which for eighty years the peace had been kept outside of the empire, and began a fight he could not win.

The weakness at the heart of the papacy was Rome itself. It was a city in incessant turmoil, where aristocratic families schemed, bribed, and fought each other to gain the papal tiara. The Gaetani and Colonna families were notorious for treating the papacy as a get-rich-quick scheme for themselves and their relatives. Popes had relied on the divisions of the German princes to undermine emperors from Henry IV to Frederick II. In the early 1300s, Philip IV played the same trick on the papacy, using the mutual loathing of the Colonna and the Gaetani to undermine the pope. Boniface VIII was a Gaetani. After his defeat the papacy contin- ued to wield military and political power over the papal territories until the nineteenth-century reunification of Italy; but the ability of the pope to challenge secular rulers on their own territory ended with the defeat of Boniface's pretensions, and the papal states looked increasingly like all the other Italian princely states.

Philip IV inflicted the decisive defeat in 1303, a decade before Dante wrote *De monarchia*. In 1294 Boniface VIII was elected under bizarre circumstances. From 1292 to 1294 the papal throne was vacant because the cardinals could not agree on whom to elect; the scandal was resolved by the election of the aged Peter Murrone, a simple hermit who took the title of Celestine V. He could not handle the demands of office and resigned after a few months. He was placed under arrest by his suc- cessor, escaped, was recaptured, and died in captivity ten months later. Boniface was elected to succeed him. He was old, suffered from pain- ful urinary ailments, and unsurprisingly had a vile temper; he was also astonishingly energetic and had extreme hierocratic views. The election was contentious. Celestine had no right to resign, and arguably there was no vacancy. To this day his is the only resignation in the history of the papacy. Dante placed Celestine in the lowest circle of hell for his cowardly refusal of the office ("che fece per viltate il gran rifiuto").[2] Dante's motive must surely have been that Celestine's abdication opened the way to the election of Boniface VIII, whose papacy saw the destruction of everything Dante cared for and brought about Dante's exile. Ever since then popes die miserably and uncomfortably in office rather than follow Celestine's example.

Boniface was immediately at odds with the English king Edward I and Philip IV over the taxation of the clergy. Each wished to raise the funds to make war on the other from their most prosperous subjects— the clergy. Whether motivated by a laudable desire to see peace restored or a less laudable desire to see the clergy's taxes in his own treasury, Boniface set out to starve the two monarchs of funds. He issued a papal bull, *Clericis laicos*, which restated Innocent III's claim that the clergy could be taxed only with papal permission and excommunicated clergy who paid taxes to lay authorities without permission. With the letter *Ausculta fili* addressed to Philip IV, and the subsequent bull *Unam sanctam*, it formed the clearest statement of Boniface's claim of legal authority over kings and emperors. Edward I ignored it. Philip went on the offensive and forbade the export of currency and precious metals from France. Fear of bankruptcy might have caused Boniface to retreat, but he had trouble close to home; the Colonna cardinals denied the validity of his election and in June 1297 accused him of having murdered his predecessor. Boniface backed down and agreed that in an emergency Philip could tax the clergy without papal permission. The papacy's finances were restored, and in 1300 a successful Jubilee was celebrated.

This may have made Boniface incautious when the next challenge occurred a year later. In 1301 Philip had the bishop of Pamiers arrested on charges of blasphemy, heresy, and treason, took him to Paris, tried him in a royal court, had him found guilty, and jailed him. This violated the long-standing "privilege of clergy" whereby clerics were tried only in church courts; to rub salt in the wound, Philip demanded that the pope endorse the proceedings. This reopened the old quarrel about the right of lay monarchs to appoint and depose bishops. The king was on solid ground in claiming that a secular ruler could not be impotent in the face of a bishop's treason, but the fact that the charges were both secular and religious seemed to imply that the king was assuming jurisdiction over spiritual offenses. As to the request for papal endorsement, it might in one light seem to accept that it was for the pope to press charges of heresy, but in another light suggest wholesale contempt for the pope's role within France.

Boniface was provoked to issue a papal bull, *Ausculta fili*. The literal translation "Listen, son" is infinitely too vulgar to catch the tone of pained regret with which Boniface tells the king that "although our merits are insufficient, God has set us over kings and kingdoms, and has imposed on us the yoke of apostolic service to root up and pull down, to waste and destroy, to build and to plant in his name and according to his teaching."[3] *Ausculta fili* did not in so many words assert that the pope had temporal jurisdiction over the king, but it came close enough to allow the king to claim that it did. He summoned a national council of clergy, nobles, and commons—an occasion of great importance as the first meeting of the Estates General—to repudiate the pope's claims and assert royal control over the church in France. He also engaged in a propaganda battle of extreme unscrupulousness, circulating forgeries of the pope's letters and a (forged) royal reply that addressed the pope as "your fatuity." A majority of the bishops and all the lay representatives supported the king. The pope insisted that he had well understood the doctrine of the two swords for more than forty years, and that the "fatuitas" and "insipientia" of claiming clerical jurisdiction over secular affairs had never crossed his mind.[4]

Matters did not immediately come to a head—the crushing defeat of the French forces in Flanders by the burghers of Courtrai in the summer of 1302 forced a pause. Then, in November, Boniface issued the bull *Unam sanctam*, in which he committed himself to the supremacy of the spiritual power in terms that could readily be misrepresented as a claim of lordship—though not the feudal suzerainty that Innocent III had forced Frederick II and John to acknowledge. It suited the king to pretend that the pope claimed to be his feudal overlord. Since *Unam Sanctam* drew on the writings of Aquinas among many others, it was inconceivable that the pope would have done so. What the pope claimed was the power to depose kings *ratione peccati*, for sin. This was the bottom line of Gelasius's claim for the spiritual authority of the papacy more than eight centuries before. The obvious difficulty with a claim to authority *ratione peccati* is that few actions of a government raise *no* moral questions; even such mundane enterprises as road traffic schemes may place unfair burdens on one or another group, and unfairness is a moral failing. The doctrine was generally held to apply only to monarchs of unusually vile character or blatantly heretical opinions. It was invoked in 1570 when Elizabeth I of England was declared deposed by Pope Pius V. She reigned for a further thirty-three years, but was provoked to judicially murder large numbers of her Catholic subjects by this seeming incitement to treason. Today the idea that a conservative pope might try to depose an American president *ratione peccati* is unthinkable, even if Catholic bishops may urge their flocks to vote against politicians who uphold abortion rights. *Unam sanctam* infuriated Philip, who promptly called another council; it declared Boniface's election invalid and the pope heretical; what its authority was in either case was unclear. On his side, the pope prepared to excommunicate the king.

Philip struck first. There were no French military forces near Rome, but mercenaries were easily hired for strong-arm tactics. When Boniface left Rome in the summer of 1303 for the Gaetani stronghold of Agnani, Philip's chief adviser, Guillaume de Nogaret, attacked the town with an army of mercenaries and Colonna troops. The assault brought about the pope's death. Boniface, very old and very ill, survived the terrifying experience for only a few weeks. Nogaret and Sciarra Colonna nearly lost their own lives, too: they were at a loss what to do after seizing the castle of Agnani with so little trouble, and spent a day quarreling over the next move. The outraged townspeople had time to organize an attack on the invaders, which they narrowly escaped. Nonetheless, Philip secured all he hoped. Boniface's immediate successor lived only a few months; and after his death, the cardinals elected Clement V, a Frenchman who never went to Rome but established the papal court at Avignon.

Papal weakness did not play into the hands of the emperor. French kings were old hands at stirring up trouble among the German princes who elected the emperor, so rendering an aggressive imperial policy impossible. For many years the electors could not agree on a candidate for emperor. After the death of Frederick II in 1250, there was an interregnum until Rudolph of Habsburg was elected in 1272; he had no Italian ambitions. The next emperor who did was Henry of Luxemburg (1308–13); he was the first emperor since Frederick II to be crowned in Rome—but not in St. Peter's and not by the pope. Henry's Italian expedition began well, but turned into a stalemate. His soldiers died of malaria or drifted away, and he fell sick and died. That expedition, on which Dante had hung his hopes for political change in Florence, was the inspiration of *De monarchia*.

Dante

Dante's place in European cultural history rests on his poetry, *La divina commedia*, above all.[5] Nonetheless, he was anything but apolitical. He was born in 1265, and as an ambitious young man joined one of the guilds that supplied candidates for civic office; in June 1300 he became one of the six "priors" who governed Florence—they held office for a year and presided for two months of it. In 1301 he went on a diplomatic mission to Rome; while he was away, a coup brought the so-called Black Guelphs to power; Dante was forced into exile on pain of death at the stake if he returned. Florence had always sided with the papacy against the empire and was thus Guelph, although the labels of Guelph and Ghibelline were loosely applied. With the election of Boniface VIII, the Florentine Guelphs split into factions; the White Guelphs—Dante's allies—were hostile to Boniface, while the Black Guelphs were papal clients.

Florentine politics were brutal, and Dante never forgave Boniface VIII his exile at the hands of the Black Guelphs. He found exile intolerable and safe haven hard to come by. His criticism of the papacy and its political meddling was public and savage, and giving him asylum was an invitation to revenge by the allies of the papacy. He was not impressed by his Florentine allies, nor they by him, and when peace was restored in Florence, he was never given honorable terms for a return, and died in exile in Verona in 1321. A tomb was later erected in Santa Croce in Florence, but Verona refused to return his body to his ungrateful mother city, and the tomb remains empty. The intensity of the description of the expulsion of Adam and Eve from paradise in the *Divine Comedy* is often said to reflect Dante's misery at his exile from Florence. *De monarchia* is his philosophical and political riposte to the theocratic ambitions that exiled him and a vision of the political world he longed for. *De monarchia* is divided into three books that argue the case for universal monarchy on three different bases: philosophy (that is to say, Aristotle), the history of Rome, and scripture. In argumentative terms, the first and third parts do the hard work; the middle portion adduces factual evidence in support of the arguments that precede and follow it.

About its merits commentators are divided. Dante scholars, for whom the *Divine Comedy* is Dante's great bequest to European culture, rarely have a good word to say for *De monarchia*, although their hostility has nothing to do with its politics. Dante wrote *De monarchia* in philosophical Latin, while in their eyes his achievement was to write great poetry in the Italian vernacular. Whatever language it was written in, it would resist sentence-by-sentence analysis, and it is hard to imagine that it can ever have seemed a very persuasive defense of the proposition that the only lawful political authority in the world was that of the emperor, and that all other powers, including the church, were subordinate to it. Dante's case was far from foolish, but it was utopian. His ultramonarchism did not mean that he thought that Henry of Luxemburg or his successors should conduct the day-to-day administration of Italian city-states such as Dante's native Florence, let alone the daily life of the church, and he had no thought that a universal monarch should aspire to govern the entire globe in detail. At the height of its power, Rome largely left the cities of the empire to attend to their own affairs in their own way, and Rome was the example that Dante had in mind. Nonetheless, Dante argued an extreme case: only a revived empire on the Roman model could provide the environment in which humanity could flourish. His negative target was the church's pretensions to secular authority, and unsurprisingly the book was loathed by the papacy; as soon as the Index of forbidden books was created in 1559, it was placed on it and removed only in 1891.

The extraordinary syllogistic form of the first book of *De monarchia* often misleads readers into thinking the tract is a theoretical exercise by an exiled poet, and a philosophical dream. Impractical it may be, and its treatment of the history of Rome in the second book is more akin to the elaboration of a myth than a rendition of Roman history; but the violence of the papal reaction shows that its enemies took it seriously. The first part justifies monarchy by the light of reason alone, and the third argues that there is no justification in scripture for papal supremacy over the temporal power. It is not the papacy's spiritual authority but its overreaching in secular matters that Dante condemns. Nor does he advocate the separation of church and state; even Marsilius's *Defensor pacis* does not go so far. As a good Christian, Dante thought the papacy should exercise an appropriate authority in secular matters, and gave a coherent account of it. What he repudiated was Boniface VIII's claim that the pope was the legal and political superior of the emperor and other earthly kings. The proper relationship was what Aquinas and innumerable others had spelled out: a morally upright monarch looked to a spiritually impressive pope for spiritual advice and used his own power to secure the church's earthly interests. The secular authority of the pope was the moral authority that an uncorrupt pope exercised over a righteous ruler. Endless misfortunes had fallen upon Italy in particular and the world more generally because the papacy had not kept within those limits.

Disentangled from the formality of its structure, Dante's argument is attractive. It contains ideas that five centuries later would underpin the philosophies of history of Kant, Hegel, and Marx. It seems astonishing that Dante derived them from an Aristotelian original to which the idea of historical development is wholly foreign, but the Christian conception of providence provided resources that Aristotle did not. Dante's premise is that the purpose of life in society is to allow the human species to manifest all distinctively human perfections; the two most important are the capacity of the individual to attain the life of reason and to govern himself by moral law. These perfections cannot be achieved in the absence of peace, and the preservation of peace is the fundamental duty of rulers. Like almost every thinker in that notably violent age, Dante longed for peace.[6] The supreme obligation of government is to govern justly so that the ruler's subjects can employ the blessings of peace to develop their abilities to the utmost. Peace and justice are the conditions of good government and a good life.

This is a deliberate echo of Aristotle's claim that the polity exists for the sake not of mere life but of the good life. The reader may wonder how Dante can extract a defense of the authority of the emperor from such premises; Aristotle held that the best life was led within the confines of the Greek city-state, and the best life was, in his view, available only to Greeks. Dante humanized the argument by adding a premise that was central to Kant's *Project for a Universal History with a Cosmopolitan Purpose* centuries later, and the works it influenced. The achievement of perfection cannot be the work of one person or group. It is the whole species that must accomplish it. We need each other's companionship and assistance to achieve anything, but when we aim at perfection we cannot stop with smaller and more limited associations. We must conceive of the whole of mankind as involved in the universal human striving after perfection. "There must needs be a vast number of individual people in the human race, through whom this potentiality can be actualised."[7] It is *universal* monarchy to which we owe our allegiance, not this or that king, count, or duke. One may wonder how Dante squared this thought with his all-consuming love of the city of Florence, but many thinkers have felt no tension between cosmopolitanism and deep affection for their own country.

The argument is encumbered by Dante's ostentatious logical demonstration of his case. Why he was so determined to show that he—almost alone—observed the rules of syllogistic inference, and committed none of the blunders that Aristotle had reproved, is hard to guess. It may simply reflect a passion for philosophy, which Dante had studied in depth in the 1290s. Having shown to his own satisfaction that universal monarchy is a demand of reason, Dante turns in the second book to showing that it was God's will that there should be a Roman Empire. The exercise induces unease; empirically considered, Dante's historical analysis is decidedly hit and miss. A caustic critic might complain that unreliable facts do little to support an intrinsically shaky conclusion. To understand what Dante was doing we must not complain that he was not a very good historian, but see him responding to anxieties about the role of providence in history.

Augustine's treatment of Rome in *The City of God* illuminates the project. Augustine argued that Rome had a place in God's providential scheme; the Roman Empire performed a limited service to fallen men, although at a high price in violence, while the rulers of Rome had themselves been dominated by their own lust for domination. Augustine did not think as his pagan contemporaries did: that the gods had favored Rome; and to the extent that a disbelief in a pagan providence admitted of degrees, he disbelieved even more strongly that Rome had benefited from the goodwill of particular gods. Like all political enterprises, Rome was a case of faute de mieux, a contrivance for making the lives of sinners less violent and painful than otherwise. Nonetheless, it was God's will that it existed, and the patriotism, courage, and honesty of the best of its citizens showed the virtues the citizens of the city of God should display.

Dante gave a much more positive role to government. He did not see Rome as only a large and successful example of doing the lesser evil to prevent the greater. Rather, he saw in Rome a manifestation of God's intention that humanity should develop all its capacities under the tutelage of a regime of peace and justice. The question was not whether *an* empire was a good; reason showed that it was. He had to argue that *this* empire was a good. Given the bloodiness and brutality that attended the rise of the Roman Empire, this was not easy for a squeamish thinker. Dante's boldest stroke was to claim that Rome had acquired power lawfully; it had done so by right of combat.[8] This was an oddly anachronistic argument: some historians say that trial by combat was not used during the Middle Ages, and is a literary invention, others that it was used occasionally; but classical history and mythology are full of occasions when two evenly matched armies decide not to hazard the lives of everyone but to allow two champions or two groups of champions to decide the matter. Dante combined the classical thought that the gods smiled on the success of heroes with a more Christian and juristic idea—not that might makes right, but that success under appropriate conditions is a mark of heaven's favor.

Since reason favored *an* imperial project and God acting through history endorsed the *Roman* imperial project, it remained for Dante to conclude his defense of the imperial project by demolishing the idea that scripture gave authority to the pope rather than the emperor. He did much more than this in the third book of *De monarchia*, however, because he also assaulted the historical claims of the papacy, in particular the papal appeal to the so-called Donation of Constantine, a notoriously implausible document concocted in the mid-eighth century or perhaps a century later. It purported to be a charter of the fourth century in which Constantine transferred authority over the western Roman Empire to Pope Sylvester I and his successors. The donation was widely taken to be a forgery, although the papacy defended its authenticity until the sixteenth century, by which time historical scholarship had utterly destroyed its credibility. The papacy was on much firmer ground in tracing its secular sovereignty over the papal states to grants by Pippin and Charlemagne, and subsequent confirmation by later emperors. Dante emphasized not the inauthenticity of the donation but its legal invalidity. In the *Divine Comedy*, he concentrates on its corrupting effect on the church. Here he claims that it is invalid because an emperor cannot divest himself of imperial authority; the act is self-negating. This is not the claim that an emperor cannot abdicate. An emperor could certainly abdicate and a new emperor be elected in his place. If that happened, the emperor would have renounced his imperial authority, and the process of election would transfer the imperial authority to a successor. What the emperor could not do by fiat was to alienate the imperial authority and deprive himself and his successors of it: "nobody has the right to do things because of an office he holds which are in conflict with that office, otherwise one and the same thing would oppose itself in its own nature, which is impossible." It is not an easy argument to assess; emperors could choose their successors, and they could and did divide the imperial authority between an eastern and a western emperor, and even establish a quadrumvirate. On the other hand, there is something incoherent about invoking imperial authority to validate the gift of that authority to a different institution.[9]

For the rest, Dante engages in standard New Testament exegesis; he insists that the passages adduced in defense of papal claims are reports of Jesus's attitude to political power and physical coercion, and cannot be read as deeply significant allegories. The famous "two swords" passage is flattened out: Christ had told his disciples that they should take steps to defend themselves in the face of his extreme unpopularity. That suggested that they should acquire a dozen swords, one apiece. When he asked how many they actually had, and they said "two," his reply, "it is enough," meant what it said: two swords would be enough to defend themselves if need be. Gelasius's contortion of the passage to argue that Christ had instituted both a secular and a spiritual power, and that the spiritual was superior, was ungrounded in the text. The conferral on Saint Peter of the power to bind and loose presents greater problems, but Dante dismisses them. Christ said to Peter that *whatsoever* he bound or loosed on earth was to be bound or loosed in heaven, which indeed sounds very like the gift of a *plenitudo potestatis*, or absolute authority. On the contrary, says Dante, all it means is that so far as all those things that he *could* do here on earth were concerned, his power was unlimited. There was much he could not do. Saint Peter could not even dissolve a validly contracted marriage by his simple say-so, and the idea that "whatsoever" included the deposition of emperors when it did not include the dissolution of a marriage was bizarre.[10] In any event, nobody at the time of Christ or at the time of the writing of the gospels had ever doubted that the emperor was in possession of freestanding political authority over the known world. Had Christ intended to deny it, he would have done so.

The sting in the tail from employing Aristotelian premises to defend royal authority against the pretensions of the papacy is that it implies that a political community is a good thing in its own right, and its preservation a duty. This diminishes the special position of monarchy. Nonetheless, it does not wholly undermine it. Neither Aristotle nor Aristotelianism was *anti*monarchical. Not only Aquinas but also John of Paris and most writers of the day assumed that one-man rule was generally better than any other. If Aristotle was right about the intrinsic value of political order, it remained true that its best form was monarchy. *All* constitutional regimes that consistently aimed at the common good were acceptable; one of them—monarchy—was best. *No* lawless regime that aimed only at the ruler's or rulers' private good was acceptable, and one of them—tyranny—was worst. Nonetheless, the thought was latent in Aristotle that the political community was prior to any particular form of constitution; and from this it seems with hindsight a short step to the thought that rulers should govern with the advice and consent of those they govern. Commentators have been surprised that the disciples of Aristotle discussed the communal governments of Italian city-states less often than monarchical government; but when the salient issue was the papacy's claims to secular authority, it is less surprising that it was the authority of secular monarchy they defended.

Marsilius of Padua

An attack on the pretensions of the papacy that caused even deeper outrage was that of Marsilius of Padua, set out at length in *Defensor pacis* (*The Defender of the Peace*) and more briefly in later works such as the *Defensor minor* (*The Shorter Defender*) and *De translatione imperii*. Marsilius was born in the late 1270s, in Padua. He belonged to a distinguished family of lawyers, the Mainardini, but himself studied medicine. His early years are obscure, but in 1313 he served as rector of the University of Paris for the usual three-month term, and thereafter he was frequently employed on the business of the Della Scala family of Verona and the Visconti of Milan. It is not clear when he began to write *Defensor pacis*; it is generally assumed that it must have been around 1315. It was published anonymously in 1324. When word of his authorship leaked out, Marsilius decided Paris was unsafe—with the pope and the French king reconciled to each other, he could look for no help from the secular authorities if the church took measures against him. He fled to the court of the emperor, Ludwig of Bavaria. He took part in Ludwig's inconclusive Italian expedition of 1327–28 and was briefly Ludwig's vice-gerent in Rome. He remained close to the royal court, without exercising much influence throughout the 1330s. Around 1340 he wrote the *Defensor minor,* to answer Ludwig's need for a defense of his actions in dissolving the marriage of the countess of Tyrol and remarrying her to his son, and to restate the main ideas of the *Defensor pacis.* He died soon afterward, probably in 1342.

The Defender of the Peace is a long book—some 500 pages in most translations. It was so fiercely antipapal that Pope John XXII declared it heretical on five counts even before reading it; it provided for the first time a theory of secular authority carefully distinguished from the account of spiritual authority by which it was accompanied; and the view of authority in both spheres rested on the doctrine of government by consent. Almost as important, the account of government by consent was backed by a theory of representation. As with most works of political theory, the question of *cui bono?*—for whose benefit was it written?—is an interesting one, but no easier to answer in this case than usually. Although Marsilius spent a long time in the service of Ludwig of Bavaria, and the treatise is dedicated to him, the work was written before Ludwig established himself as emperor in 1328. After the death of Henry of Luxemburg in 1313, it took a ten-year civil war to settle the succession. *De monarchia* was an antipapal and imperial tract; *Defensor pacis* is an antipapal tract, but not an imperial tract, although two later works, *Defensor minor* and *De translatione imperii,* certainly were.

The book makes a *negative* case, in that it argues *against* the absolute authority of the pope over the church, and against the papacy's role in secular politics. Marsilius's argument is not anticlerical or anti-ecclesiastical. His long and densely argued treatise set out to base secular authority on the consent of the governed; this consent was to be given through representative devices familiar in northern European cities as well as Italian city-states. Marsilius's bolder claim was that since this is the way to govern cities and kingdoms, it is also the way to govern the church. Heretical as this seemed to John XXII, it was not wholly groundbreaking. The early church held innumerable councils to resolve doctrinal and other issues, and some of them—such as the Council of Nicaea—became particularly famous as the occasion when the church settled deep and intractable questions—such as the nature of the Trinity. Most councils had been summoned by secular rulers, but the implications of that fact for church government were not agreed. The one indisputable fact was that accountability to a council and the suggestion that it was up to lay rulers to create such councils were unattractive to any pope.

The innovation was not the claim that a system of government that engaged numerous representatives could solve many practical problems. The novelty was Marsilius's use of the Aristotelian theory of government to claim that authority is morally legitimate only when founded on the consent of a people. He was perhaps the first writer to make that thought do some real work. The thought that hierarchical and populist theories of authority can be reconciled, intellectually at least, was familiar. Many writers held that authority was *generated* in the community and then *vested* in the ruler, much as Justinian had held that his authority had originated in the people and been transferred to the emperor without reservation and without the possibility of revocation. Justinian was an absolute sovereign, but the sovereignty had been the people's before they transferred it. On the theory embodied in the forged Donation of Constantine, sovereignty over the empire had been Constantine's; he had then transferred it to the pope; the pope had then charged him with the management of the empire's secular affairs. It was entirely possible to argue that authority had first been "in the people," became the emperor's by transfer from the people, then the pope's by transfer from the emperor, then the emperor's by delegation from the pope. Others had argued that God was the sole source of authority, but that God's grant to a ruler was valid only when a good man governed wisely and with the assent of his people. Election, which permeated that very hierarchical institution, the Catholic Church, could readily be understood as a process in which God made known his choice by inspiring the voices of those charged with the election: *vox populi, vox Dei*. It was God's authority even though we could discover where God bestowed it only through the voice of the people. Pure divine right theory, where God is not only the fount of authority but directly appoints the earthly ruler, is one of many possibilities.

Marsilius constructs the first of the three discourses that make up *Defensor pacis* by appealing to what he takes to be self-evident: men come together in a political community to live a self-sufficient life. The state—*regnum*—is the highest form of association because it is the only one that achieves self-sufficiency. This is pure Aristotle, as is his claim that we associate for the sake of life but practice politics for the sake of the good life. Aquinas had followed Aristotle so far. Marsilius goes further. *Ultimate* self-sufficiency is for the hereafter, but "civil happiness" is earthly self-sufficiency. What could have no roots in Aristotle and would have outraged Aquinas is Marsilius's claim that the great threat to peace and civil happiness is the papacy. The purpose of the book, he says at the outset, is to demonstrate a cause of strife and disorder that Aristotle could have known nothing of, because it came into the world so long after his time.[11] Marsilius also goes beyond Aristotle in analyzing the components of a polity in functional terms: the chief components, he says, are judicial, military, and religious. Book I of Aristotle's *Politics* analyzes the polity by distinguishing it from more-limited forms of association. This is an extension of that thought. Marsilius maintains that secular rule has a religious function because the secular ruler must secure the spiritual as well as the physical well-being of the citizenry. The priestly function is one of the functions of any well-conducted polity. This was not a surprising thought. Aristotle discussed the establishment of the priesthood in his design for an ideal polis, and Cicero, whom Marsilius cites, assumed that a properly constituted priesthood is needed by a successful polity. But the analysis of the functions of different sorts of authority and institutions is the beginning of institutional analysis as we understand it today.

Marsilius set out to defend what he termed "temperate" rule.[12] He says that the word "state" has several meanings, all of them in Aristotle, and he intends to discuss what is common to "temperate" regimes generally. There is no suggestion that a temperate monarchy is an implausible aspiration. Temperate government was not limited government in the modern sense. The modern conception of limited government holds both that there are things that no government is entitled to do and that there is a limited range of activities for which the coercive powers of the state are necessary and useful, beyond which its authority lapses. Medieval writers certainly thought there were things that governments were not entitled to do, but these were mostly defined by religion; a ruler who commanded his subjects to deny Christ must be disobeyed, and a ruler who led his people away from the true faith lost his title to rule. But the teleological framework within which medieval writers wrote after the recovery of Aristotle meant that they were disinclined to set the rights of subjects against the rights of rulers. The task of government was to do all the good it could. Controversialists often claimed that some particular ruler could not act in certain ways because his actions were contrary to the known and agreed custom and law of his polity; but the thought that subjects had rights that limited the authority of any government whatever was foreign to them. Marsilius argued that a "temperate monarchy" must act according to law, as Aristotle had done when defending the thought that "laws not men" should govern; but he did not hold the modern view that there are areas of life about which the law must be silent.

This difference affects Marsilius's explanation of representative institutions and systems of election. In the modern world they are devices to keep government within bounds, by holding government to account. This is not Marsilius's justification; he thinks the point is to ensure that the wisest rule. It is obvious upon reflection that there is no necessary connection between elections and limited government; *what* authority a person may wield is one thing, *how* they acquire it another. Popes were elected, but claimed a *plenitudo potestatis*, absolute authority. Marsilius wanted wise government, not limited government. Nineteenth- and twentieth-century dictators secured their authority in plebiscites. Marsilius wants not dictators but temperate rulers. The wise will be temperate, and the purpose of enlightened institutional arrangements is to secure wise rulers. What Marsilius discusses throughout the first part of *Defensor pacis* is how to secure government by the wise.

Nor is his idea of election quite the same as ours. Marsilius has struck many readers as very bold when he claimed that not only is popular consent the "efficient cause" of government—that government had originated in the agreement of a community to be governed—but that the community's continuing consent makes law law. In other formulations, that claim was not unprecedented, and with a little ingenuity could be extracted from Cicero; but it was unprecedented in the voluntaristic form that Marsilius gave it. He held that continuing consent was essential to legality. The thought that a well-conducted polity makes law for the common good, according to the will of the people, and with their consent is not surprising. It was a central element in the Roman self-image. It becomes bolder once Marsilius asks whose consent is to count, and replies that it is consent of everyone other than the vicious and undiscerning and those so poor they have no stake in the society at all. To the usual aristocratic and hierarchical claim that the multitude is vicious and undiscerning, he retorts that "most citizens are neither vicious nor undiscerning most of the time" and points out, as Aristotle had before him, that a citizen who cannot craft legislation himself can judge its merits when it is presented to him.[13]

If he recruits Aristotle to the cause of basing legitimacy on consent in a fashion that might have surprised him, Marsilius picks up Aristotle's argument for *politeia*—good government by many, but not "the many"—with perfect accuracy. Having begun boldly, he moves a very short distance toward a democratic conception of consent. Like others, he argues that many heads are better than one, that a wise ruler needs counsel, and that the best government involves many persons. To borrow a modern coinage, it is *polyarchy*.[14] This supports the governments found in Italian city-states such as Padua, and parliamentary or conciliar forms of government in other places, and is an argument for employing these forms of government in institutions other than secular states—such as the church. In any case, support for persons and policies will be greater the more directly it is based on the choice of the people. The "people" in this connection means enough people, and particularly enough of the more important people to provide a representative and powerful expression of public opinion. The term Marsilius uses as a synonym for enough of the right people is the *valentior pars*, literally the "more powerful part." It is not an argument that the will of the majority is binding on the whole people, but an argument for involving enough of the people who count. "Enough" can be a very small number; the imperial electors suffice to constitute the *valentior pars*, when the question is the legitimacy of the emperor. Marsilius was greatly indebted to Ludwig of Bavaria, Holy Roman Emperor by election. Nor would it be an implausible thought that Marsilius's influence was to be seen in the 1338 declaration by six of the imperial electors that the imperial title was conferred by a majority of the electors and needed no papal confirmation, the view enshrined in the Golden Bull of 1365.

The argument, then, is that the way to secure a "temperate" regime is by the rule of a lawful ruler over free citizens; citizens are those who play an active role in the affairs of their polity. This would be very like the Aristotelian theory of *politeia*, except that it is almost always couched in terms of securing moderate one-man rule. In Aristotle's *politeia* the citizens are engaged in "ruling and being ruled in turn," but Marsilius spends so much time discussing "temperate monarchy" that it often seems that the only question that concerns him is how to rest one-man rule on the consent of the better-off, wiser, and steadier members of the community.

He was, of course, primarily attacking his bête noire. What occupied more than three times as much space in *Defensor pacis* as the theory of legitimate state authority in general was his assault on the political power of the papacy. He was repetitive, savage, comprehensive, and persuasive. The unpersuaded were outraged; the hostility of the Catholic Church persists to this day. Marsilius began at the beginning by attacking the first step in the papacy's claim to authority, Christ's gift to Saint Peter of the power to bind and loose. He was not the first to argue that Christ gave no such power to Peter alone; others had argued that Christ's authority was given to the apostles equally. If the apostolic succession inhered in bishops and priests generally, authority within the church should be shared, and this was an argument for a conciliar form of church government.[15] Not content with undermining the papacy's claim to a plenitude of power, Marsilius went on to argue that the church was not entitled to the vast wealth it had acquired. Like the radical Franciscans, he argued that the apostles' reliance on their followers to provide shelter and support was the proper model for the fourteenth-century church.

The upshot was radical. The church had no legitimate coercive authority. Like almost everyone, Marsilius thought the power to coerce was the essential mark of legislative capacity; if the church had no right to coerce, it could not legislate. This meant that canon law was not strictly law at all. The church had a power over the faithful that all agreed on: the power to excommunicate. However, where others both before and after thought the church had the right to ask the secular arm to impose additional sanctions on the excommunicate, Marsilius did not. Even the limited sanction of excommunication belonged to the church rather than the pope. The final blow to the papacy's claims to secular power was decisive. Marsilius broke new ground by arguing that the power that Christ had conferred on the disciples was the power to teach and advise, not to rule. We are very close to the view of the nature of a church that John Locke argued for in his *Letter Concerning Toleration* 350 years later: a church is a voluntary association held together by the agreement of its members on articles of faith; its object is to allow its members to worship and encourage and instruct one another in the faith and its consequences for conduct. The demand for the commitment to poverty in the church, to which Locke paid no attention, is justified here by the thought that the moral authority of those who preach chastity, unworldliness, and contempt for the pleasures of the world, the flesh, and the devil is diminished by wealth.

Bartolus and the Italian City-State

Unlike freestanding kingdoms such as England or France, the states and cities of northern and central Italy were at least notionally dependencies of either the empire or the church. De facto, they resisted attempts by their nominal overlords to establish a tighter hold, especially attempts by successive emperors to assert their authority over the city-states of Lombardy. The political arrangements and legal status of the city-states of central and northern Italy were hard for contemporaries to analyze; their history and politics defy description. If the shifts by which the cities defended their independence against emperors with the help of the papacy, and against the papacy with the help of emperors, and against everyone with the help of outsiders hoping to profit by their meddling, are hard to describe, their predicament is not. The *regnum Italicum* covered the area conquered by the Lombards and liberated by German kings on the urging of the papacy in the ninth and tenth centuries. Technically, most of the cities and their inhabitants were subjects of the empire; those in the Papal States were subject to the papacy, strictly speaking as the result of a grant of suzerainty from empire to papacy, subsequently on the basis of direct rule, or rule by an agent installed by the papacy, a "papal vicar." For our purposes, the point is that the source of the legal competence of cities such as Milan, Pisa, Arezzo, or Perugia was the universal sovereignty of the emperor, but his actual authority was slight to nonexistent.

From the twelfth century most cities under nominal imperial over-lordship were not under the emperor's effective control and had no inten-tion of being. Each cared for its own freedom of action; none cared about neighboring cities; they cooperated when threatened by an impe-rial expedition to enforce the emperor's authority, and otherwise acted with the mixture of rivalry and distrust that had marked the Greek city-states one and a half millennia before. In the following centuries, and aided by successive popes, they defeated the threats to their inde-pendence from Frederick Barbarossa, Frederick II, and their successors. The popes' interest was obvious; if the German emperor controlled the Kingdom of Sicily and the *regnum Italicum*, the Papal States were held in a vice. Nobody supposed that the independence of the city-states held any other appeal to the pope. More interesting was the ideology of the city-states themselves. They claimed to be defending their liberty, which they held to be the *libertas* that the Roman Republic had enjoyed, and Romans had lost when the republic became an empire. Minimally, it meant they were autonomous in the literal sense, that is, entitled to make laws for themselves. This meant legal independence of the empire and a capac-ity to make their own laws. We shall see how Bartolus of Sassoferrato argued that they were so entitled, but on the face of it, anyone who held a narrowly legalistic view of the right to make law could not have seen them as sovereign states, but as having only a devolved legal capacity by permission of the emperor pro tem.

If one adopts the perspective of Justinian's *Digest*, there was one legit-imate lawmaker for the entire world, and that was the emperor. All other jurisdictions must in some fashion be legislating by tacit permission. The absurdity of insisting on such a narrow understanding—which implied among other things that France and England had their own legal systems either by dispensation from the emperor or by usurpation—made no difference when emperors wanted to insist on their authority over the Italian cities. But emperors had their own problems; they wanted the law on their side against the cities, but did not want canon lawyers claiming that the pope had a legal authority that trumped the emperor's. A canon lawyer might agree that city-states had no autonomous legislative capacity, but then argue that the emperor derived his legislative capacity only from his coronation as emperor by the pope; that was what Marsilius and Dante denied.

The cities needed a coherent account of their legal status and an affirmation of their sovereignty. They also needed forms of government that served their administrative and economic purposes. In the eleventh century they reinvented many features of the early Roman Republic, in particular the appointment of magistrates to very short periods of office as a defense against tyranny. When they evicted their kings, the Romans had elected consuls for a year at a time only, and consuls were what Pisa, Milan, and Arezzo began by giving themselves. These city-states were in many respects genuine revivals of the city-state of antiquity. An essential condition of their existence was that they controlled their rural hinterland; their *contadini* were not tenants of feudal landlords but small farmers who owned their own farms or were tenants of landowners from the city. Twelfth-century observers were struck by the absence of great lords, the feudal magnates of France, Germany, and England; when that changed, it undermined their political systems, as mercantile and banking wealth was converted into aristocratic status, and wealth and status into power. The cities faced problems familiar to their antique precursors: the prevention of tyranny, on the one hand, and the avoidance of class warfare and confiscatory projects, on the other. Their devices for preventing the rise of tyrants brought familiar negative effects: rapid turnover of leaders made consistency of policy hard to achieve, and competition for office led to extreme factionalism and zero-sum politics.

The solution devised for a lack of expertise was almost invariably a council, with whose assent the podesta ruled; a common pattern was a double council, one with many members that met in public and had few powers beyond the veto, and one with fewer members that met in secret and made policy. The problem of factionalism was rarely solved except at the cost of the liberty the city valued so much. The cities wanted, or late in the day discovered that they wanted, Roman *libertas*, which is to say stable constitutional government, the rule of law, independence of other authorities, and greatness for their city. Like Rome, they discovered that faction fights between aristocratic rivals for high office end in the exhausted or enthusiastic acceptance of one-man rule. With the exception of Venice, the greatest and most successful of all city-states, where the city established a hereditary mercantile aristocracy as early as 1279, their eventual fate was to be governed by hereditary dukes or counts, who were frequently themselves kept in power by powerful outside forces such as the papacy, the empire, or in due course the French or Spanish monarchy. The similarities with the Greek city-states and their fate at the hands of Macedon and Rome were not lost on observers.

Nonetheless, their fate was not so inevitable that an intelligent and passionate participant and thinker like Machiavelli was foolish to hope at the end of the fifteenth century that Florence could renew its populist energies and become a new Rome. Whatever one thinks of Machiavelli's hopes, for four centuries, from the eleventh to the early sixteenth, the city-state revived aspects of the political life of the ancient world, good and bad. Given their systems of government, it is unsurprising that Marsilius should have taken Aristotle's *Politics* as his guide in analyzing temperate government. Given, too, that he was fighting the papacy's pretensions to secular authority and its fondness for worldly wealth, it is not odd that he should have devoted so much effort to rebutting the scriptural interpretations of papal apologists. What puzzles modern readers rather more is the attention that writers in the fourteenth and fifteenth centuries devoted to the implications of civil law for the legitimacy of the city-states of Italy. It is less odd than it seems; modern American politics revolves around issues of legitimacy hardly less complicated. Not only the intersection of canon and civil law but the divergent practices of different cities needed legal resolution. The intellectual training of the most highly educated Italians took them into canon and civil law, and the practical needs of governments and merchants alike ensured a market for their services.

The most distinguished of legal theorists was Bartolus of Sassoferrato. He was born in 1313 and died in 1357, and was, one might say, born to be a professor of law; he studied at Perugia and Bologna, taught at Pisa, and then at Perugia, where he died at the early age of forty-three. He wrote lengthy commentaries on most aspects of Roman law and most of Justinian's *Corpus juris civilis.* He is still thought of as the great founder of the study of the conflict of laws. Political theorists remember him mostly for a very brief but influential discussion of tyranny, but his views on the legal status of semiautonomous states are full of good sense and pregnant with ideas that become important centuries later. Bartolus's position was elegant and straightforward. The German emperor had lost de facto control over the cities of northern Italy. A true sovereign united in one pair of hands both de facto power and the de jure authority that entitled him to wield it. To assert de jure authority when a long period had elapsed in which those over whom it was asserted had taken no notice of the assertion was nugatory. This sounds very like what later ages knew as legal positivism; law in any particular place is whatever the accepted local process of law creation says it is, and what confers legitimacy on a lawmaking authority is effectiveness. Bartolus was more delicate than that; he was a Roman lawyer and could not easily reject the idea that the one lawmaking community was the heirs of the *populus Romanus* in whose name Roman law was made. The legal systems of Roman law countries, essentially most of Europe other than England, were indebted to him for centuries, until the codification of civil law at the end of the eighteenth century and after.

Although the claims of the emperor could largely be ignored, as a matter of political practice, not every city governed itself without owing (or admitting) allegiance to an overlord, including the emperor. Not all were what Bartolus elegantly called *civitas princeps suae.* By the time Bartolus wrote, many cities in the Romagna willingly or unwillingly acknowledged the pope as overlord; and the invasion of Henry of Luxemburg at the time of Bartolus's birth came close to putting the *regnum Italicum* back under the authority of the German emperor. It was no easy task to discuss divided sovereignty; civil law was built on Justinian's *Digest* and inhospitable to the thought that custom could be a source of law in its own right. The admiration of historians is wholly justified, though the technicalities of Bartolus's treatment are rebarbative.

His short essay on "the government of cities," *De regimine civitatis,* is interesting for two main reasons. The first is that it provides an Aristotelian account of politics that explains how a city can be an autonomous lawmaking entity: a city exists when a people gives itself laws. This echoed Cicero's claim that a *res publica* exists only when there is a *populus,* that is, a people whose good is pursued by constitutional means; from Cicero also came the definition of the justice that a good king must practice: "a constant and perpetual will which renders to each one his due." Like Aquinas and Marsilius, Bartolus reads Aristotle as saying that monarchical government is the absolutely best, where it can be instituted, and for much the same reason, that the unity of will of one man is a greater security for peace and good order than the precarious unity of a multitude. It is "monarchical" government that he defends; "kingship" covers numerous forms of one-man rule, ranging from the emperor who claims universal lordship to the duke or count who rules a city and its hinterland.

Bartolus says much that comes as no surprise to readers of Aristotle, but that served a distinctive purpose. He revived Aristotle's concept of *politeia,* under the label of *policratia,* to describe a government in which most of those who have the attributes of citizenship play an active role, and which is directed toward the common good. He had a commonsense enthusiasm for popular governments where they could be instituted, that is, governments where neither the magnates nor the indigent wielded absolute power, but men with a solid stake in the city did. Like Aristotle, he finds six forms of government, and a seventh, un-Aristotelian "monstrosity" to be discussed shortly, divided according to Aristotle's own principles. Good forms aim at the common good, bad forms at the interests of the ruling party; the best is monarchy and the worst is tyranny. Given that Italy was full of tyrants in the narrowest and most literal sense, single rulers who had acquired power by unconstitutional methods, the pressing issue was obviously how to avert tyranny, selfish and lawless rule by a single ruler.

Thinking like a lawyer about legitimacy, Bartolus argues that kingship by election is closest to what is divinely approved; behind that thought lies distaste for the way tyrants installed their nearest relatives to create hereditary ruling families. As to how a ruler is to live up to the high standards of wisdom and justice that he has laid down, Bartolus shelters behind the (rather persuasive) views of Giles of Rome (Egidius Colonna): what a single ruler needs is wise advice, sage counselors, an independent council to keep him wise and honest. Since a ruler must retain a constant and unalterable will to be governed by justice and legality, it is important that he can rely on collective wisdom, but the unity of the city requires a single focus of authority—nowhere more obviously than in an Italian city-state.

The most fascinating aspect of Bartolus's essay is his hostility toward the anarchic condition of contemporary Rome. Rome was not even badly governed; it was a monstrosity—all government supposed some degree of unity in the polity, but in Rome there was none. Whether a government was popular, aristocratic, or kingly, it required a head, a person or institution that answered the question of what the laws were and what policies were to be pursued. Rome was a chaos of competing tyrants, with an entirely ineffectual notional ruler or city prefect. Machiavelli made himself deeply unpopular in the early sixteenth century by ascribing the chaotic condition of Italian politics to the misdeeds of the papacy, but at this point in the fourteenth century, the pope himself was in Avignon, firmly under the control of the French monarchy, and governing the church with the assistance of a college of cardinals who were overwhelmingly French. It was less the presence than the absence of the pope and cardinals that was to blame.

Bartolus was appalled by the condition of Rome for some of the same reasons of historical nostalgia as Machiavelli; the great stabilizing force of the ancient Mediterranean world was now a source of weakness and disorder. Toward the papacy itself, Bartolus displayed no animus. In a tract on tyranny written shortly before he died, at a time when the papal legate Egidio Albornoz was engaged in a very deft operation to turn the tyrants of north and central Italy into "vicars of the church," Bartolus dwelled at length on the legal issues raised by tyrannical governments operating in the territories over which the papacy claimed lordship, and more briefly on the possibility of "legitimation after the event."

He anticipated Machiavelli in arguing that tyranny could be acceptable as a transitional government, as it was when pope or emperor later made a regime lawful by turning a tyrant into a "vicar"—a vice-regent. Discussing city government, Bartolus treated tyranny as the corruption of monarchy and condemned it, but this did not answer the practical question of how to regard the acts of a long-lasting tyrant. If a tyrant—defined narrowly as someone who had acquired power without a title—governed well for a substantial period, it would be absurd to say that every agreement made under his power was de jure invalid. His acts lacked complete legitimacy, but not all were illegitimate. Oppression, iniquitous and unjust taxation—with which Bartolus was much concerned—and the unjust exile and ill-treatment of all opponents was another matter; and those who had profited from extortion should not benefit from legal amnesia.

He was not enthusiastic about the papal and imperial policy of converting tyrants into vicars, but, faute de mieux, it might be justified. "For as a careful sailor throws overboard his less valuable cargo in order to save the more precious, and as the prudent householder makes a choice of his more valuable goods to rescue, so a just overlord comes to terms with a tyrant and makes him his vicar in order to accomplish great and pressing reforms." The welfare of a tyrant's subjects might require such a measure, much as the doctor may prescribe life-threatening treatment to avert certain death. The tone is disapproving; the ideal of the ruler who secures office through proper procedures of election and governs for the common good casts a glaring light on the defective title of tyrants. And the insidiousness of tyranny is such that it might even be invisible; someone occupying no official position could exercise lawless power and be a tyrant. Bartolus thought that the factionalism of Italian city politics—he wrote a tract on the Guelphs and Ghibellines—meant that faction leaders might have such a hold over the officials notionally in charge that they were the true powers in the city and, if unjust, then tyrants. The modern Mafia springs to mind.

The world to which Bartolus was speaking is easily imagined by anyone who has seen Ambrogio Lorenzetti's allegories of good and bad government, painted a few years before Bartolus wrote about city government. Under good government, Justice reigns, aided by the virtues: peace, courage, temperance, and magnanimity; above Justice seated on her throne floats wisdom; under bad government injustice rules in the form of the Tyrant, depicted as the devil himself, and the vices that assist tyranny are anger, avarice, divisiveness, treachery, and cruelty. The payoff of a just regime is prosperity, willing taxpayers, and a successful state respected by its neighbors; the payoff of an unjust regime is famine and death. When the frescoes were painted in 1338–39, the Sienese were congratulating themselves on having regained their liberties after a tyrannical interlude; to the political theorist, the interest of the frescoes lies in the way in which Christian, Aristotelian, Stoic, and Ciceronian ideas about the demands of stable and peaceful government are all invoked without any sense that they are embarrassingly disparate. But those were the fourteenth century's intellectual resources; naturally, they are all employed when they concur in what they commend and deplore. Trouble ensues only when one or the other loses credibility or one tradition leads in dramatically different directions from the others.

Conciliarism and Ockham

We have seen how readily one or another version of the doctrine of government by consent could be applied to the government of the church. In historical fact, the conciliar movement was the product of the appalling state into which the papacy fell at the end of its "Babylonian exile" in Avignon. The papacy's capacity to influence European politics was obviously undermined by its being so firmly under the thumb of the French monarchy. Thus, its ability to mitigate the horrors of the Hundred Years' War between France and England was almost nil when the English regarded the pope as a far from impartial mediator. The papacy was also unpopular because it was seen as increasingly authoritarian, centralized, and corrupt. When the papacy returned to Rome in 1377–78, at the end of the pontificate of Gregory XI, the city was in its usual turbulent state, and the aristocracy of the city aggressively hostile to the non-Italian cardinals. Most would happily have returned to Avignon, but Gregory XI died soon after the return to Rome, and his successor Urban VI refused to leave. This provoked a revolt by the French cardinals, who declared Urban's election invalid and elected Clement VII as antipope. They were driven out of Italy and returned to Avignon. There were now two popes. France, the Kingdom of Naples, and the Spanish kingdoms of Leon and Aragon adhered to Avignon; England, the empire, and northern Italy, to Rome.

The obvious way to heal the schism was to call a council of the whole church to restore peace and unity. In practice, it took the secular monarchies almost seven decades to achieve a final settlement; and a movement that might have established constitutional, representative government as the European norm ended by enhancing the power of bureaucratically organized absolute monarchies. The intellectual interest of the conciliar movement is greater than its practical (in)effectiveness. The urgent but unanswerable question that needed an immediate answer was who had the authority to call a council of the church. Neither the pope at Rome nor the antipope at Avignon wished to call a council that might declare him deposed; the emperor was parti pris. An account was needed of where authority lay in the church as a whole.

An obvious source was Marsilius. Indeed, he was *the* obvious source and widely appealed to. If a political community was by its nature a body that generated the authority that it delegated to rulers by some process of representation, it took little imagination to argue—as he had—that this was true of the church. The arguments needed were negative arguments to show that Christ had not conferred on Saint Peter and thereafter on successive popes an absolute authority that shut out the representative principle. If there was no obstacle to the church as a community exercising its innate authority by delegation, a council was the obvious device to overcome the scandal of schism. William of Ockham was an equally usable source, but although he was less intransigent than Marsilius in his hatred of the papacy, he was intellectually more radical. Ockham was English, born in the 1280s. He became a Franciscan friar, studied and taught in Oxford, but when he was summoned to account for his work before Pope John XXII in Avignon, he like Marsilius took refuge in the court of Ludwig of Bavaria, where he wrote antipapal tracts on Ludwig's behalf.[16] He was a philosophical empiricist and took a markedly skeptical view of the doctrine that the church (like any other corporation) was a *corpus mysticum*, or mystical body, arguing that in reality it is simply a collection of individual believers. Popes do not represent the mystical unity of the church; if there is to be representation, it must be by delegation from the individuals whom we call, collectively, the church.

Pressure to call a council to resolve the schism had very mixed results. The first council, held in Pisa in 1409, failed to persuade either of the rival popes to resign; it added to the confusion by electing a second antipope, Alexander V, who died soon afterward and was succeeded by John XXIII. A few years later, the Council of Constance (1414–18) succeeded in deposing all three popes and electing Martin V, eventually accepted as the one legitimate pope. The success of Constance was a tribute to Jean Gerson (1363–1429), who had spent almost twenty years arguing the moderates' case, which was not to assert the authority of the whole over the part, or the community over its head, as Marsilius and Ockham and all radicals did, but simply to recommend giving authority in emergency to a council of the whole. The council itself took the radical view, and in *Hanc sanctam* declared that it had its authority directly from Christ and not from a pope. In fact, it owed its efficacy to the support of the emperor Sigismund, who had many reasons for wanting to see unity in the church, of which not the least was the Hussite rebellion in his native Bohemia. Nonetheless, the council declared itself the supreme governing body of the church and insisted that councils meet frequently.

They did not. The successor to the Council of Constance was the Council of Basel (1431–49), and although it provoked an important tract from Nicholas of Cusa (1401–64), *De concordantia catholica*,[17] the council itself ended ignominiously by splitting in two. Nicholas's work attempted to balance the two competing principles at stake, the consent of all Christians and the pope's position as head of the church. It was not a "political" work, in that it did not try to set out institutional arrangements that might have satisfied all sides, a hopeless task in any case, but a philosophical reflection on the various ways in which individuals can represent persons, ideas, or principles. Theologically, Nicholas was a mystic, but he was technically adept enough to devise a voting system for the election of the Holy Roman Emperor that was rediscovered three hundred years later and is much used today, known as the "Borda count" method of weighing preferences. After the Council of Basel, the papacy returned to its autocratic and hierarchical style. Whether a different outcome would have headed off the Reformation of the sixteenth century is doubtful. Ockham and Marsilius wanted a reformed church, but at Constance, Gerson prosecuted Jan Hus, whose views on church reform prefigured those of the Reformation a century later, and Nicholas attended Basel to reinforce his claims to a bishopric. They wanted unity in the church, not dramatic change.

CHAPTER 9

Humanism

What Was Humanism?

THE NEXT THREE CHAPTERS consider from three different angles the political ideas of one period of time within a single, chaotic context. The late fifteenth and early sixteenth centuries are the last time we can talk of western Christendom as a single entity. After the middle of the sixteenth century, there was a confessional divide between Catholic and Protestant Europe that remains unclosed. The violence of earlier centuries has disappeared, though by no means all of the distrust. The political history and political aspirations of Catholic and Protestant Europe diverged, too, although the connection between the confessional and the political history was less close than Protestant propagandists claimed. Two of the themes pursued in these chapters are familiar; no account of the origins of our own political ideas could ignore Machiavelli on the one side and Luther and Calvin on the other. The third has been less explored until recently. We begin with it.

Analysis of humanism and its bearing on politics is not easy. Commentators divide. Some have detected a political movement they call "civic humanism," sparked by the reading of classical moral and political texts, and committed to a revival of republican virtue.[1] The revival was centered on Florence, and an aspect of Florence's self-image as a self-governing republic rather than a princely despotism or a papal or imperial client, as well as a reaction against the tightening grip of the Florentine merchant princes on the city's politics. Critics of the idea that humanism and republicanism were born twins have observed that most humanists were less interested in politics than in establishing reliable texts of Latin and Greek literature, identifying their authors, and distinguishing genuine writings from fakes. Forgeries were rife, and the textual criticism that revealed them as forgeries marked the beginning of modern historical scholarship. The connection with an enthusiasm for republican virtue is not obvious. A plausible "elective affinity" is that an interest in classical antiquity might reinforce the sense that Italian politics in the fourteenth and fifteenth centuries presented an embarrassing contrast with the politics of republican Rome. Still, the connection is tenuous; such a reaction was equally strong in Marsilius, who was attached to the Scholastic and syllogistic style of reasoning that humanists disliked, and Machiavelli, whose views on the "virtue"—or *virtù*—that a prince should display were shockingly at odds with conventional humanist views.[2] Humanist credentials were neither necessary nor sufficient to inspire an enthusiasm for republics; many humanists admired tradition and hierarchy, and the most characteristic political product of a humanist was a "mirror of princes," or a tract on princely education.[3]

Humanism originated in the need for educated lawyers. Technical and formal instruction in the law was not concerned with the literary graces; but the so-called *dictatores*, men who drafted documents, drew up contracts for merchants and others, and handled the governmental correspondence of the Italian cities, had to write well. They needed an education in humane letters, and such an education also became part of the prelegal education of lawyers. Familiarity with literary texts bred an interest in their quality as literature, and a more sophisticated historical and philological approach to authorship and interpretation rapidly followed. The possession of literary and linguistic skills became a source of pride even among aristocratic and royal families. Princes and princesses were forced to learn the Greek that Saint Augustine had balked at; Queen Elizabeth I, to take one famous instance, was a more than competent scholar.

A close analysis of humanism would draw distinctions ignored here—for instance, the differences between earlier Italian humanism and later northern European humanism—and would distinguish the very varied political allegiances of literary humanists. All we can do here is explore some ways in which humanist writers discussed political issues, not least by the use of novel literary forms. The playful use of political utopias was one novelty, as was the invention of the short polemical essay. While the Protestant Reformation gave new life to Augustine's conviction of the depth of original sin, and reform theologians were emphasizing that good works (let alone papal indulgences) could not secure salvation, other thinkers were inspired by the utopian speculations of the Greeks. Humanism also begat interestingly nonhumanist variants on its themes. Machiavelli did not share the humanists' views about how princes should behave, but he was capable of utopian speculation; his hopes for a revival in Florence of the civic virtue of the Roman Republic were utopian in both the abusive and the nonabusive senses of the term, while his essay *The Prince* bears a wonderfully ambiguous relationship to the "mirror of princes" tradition.

Humanism is conventionally described as a literary movement that originated with Petrarch. This emphasizes the place of poetry and literature in the humanist sensibility, but does not cast much light on humanist political thinking. Taking another tack, we may begin with its hostility to Scholasticism. The humanist desire to escape syllogistic formalism and the reduction of all moral and political questions to issues in theology did not express a desire to escape rational argument, or a hankering for paganism. Machiavelli wished modern thinkers to reflect on ancient practice and to draw some very un-Christian conclusions, but he was highly unusual; when humanists turned away from Aristotle, they frequently turned to a spiritualized Platonism. This was unorthodox to the degree that Plato's leanings toward mathematical mysticism were taken up and exaggerated, but not at odds with the age-old links between Neoplatonism and Christian theology.

Deciding who is and who is not a humanist is an ungrateful task: how much enthusiasm for which aspects of classical literature must someone display, and how much dislike for syllogistic inference? Pico della Mirandola, who was uninclined to reject any source of illumination, was undeniably a humanist but forgave the medieval Schoolmen their lack of Greek and their infelicities in Latin prose. A better test is simpler. Writers who lay out their ideas in the formulaic fashion common to Aquinas and Thomistic political theorists such as Francisco de Vitoria lie on one side of the divide and are late Scholastics; essayists, utopians, and poets lie on the other side. Machiavelli is anti-Scholastic and a dubious humanist. Uncontested members of the tradition include Coluccio Salutati, Leonardi Bruni—though he refused to translate Plato's *Republic* into Latin because he thought Plato's eugenicist defense of a community of wives too disgusting to be given wide circulation—Pico della Mirandola, the author of the oration *On the Dignity of Man*, Erasmus, and Montaigne; here I begin with Christine de Pizan and emphasize Thomas More, the former almost unique as an intelligent woman taken seriously by her contemporaries, and the latter because he was both a humanist, a powerful politician, and the author of the little book that gave Utopia its name.

Christine de Pizan

Christine de Pizan's rarity value as a well-regarded woman writer in the late Middle Ages—she was born around 1363 and died sometime after 1430—hardly needs emphasis. She astonished her contemporaries by making a living by her writing at a time when almost nobody, male or female, did so. This was out of necessity—her father was a royal employee and well liked at court, but of humble origins. She married at sixteen, but her husband and father both died soon thereafter, and at the age of twenty-four she was left a widow with three children and a widowed mother to care for. Since she had friends at court but no resources of her own, writing for royal and aristocratic patrons was a possibility. Her life spanned the worst period of the Hundred Years' War between France and England; she was born as Charles V (king from 1364 to 1380) began to restore French fortunes after the Battle of Poitiers in 1356 when the English destroyed the French army and captured Charles's father, King John. But Charles died prematurely and was succeeded by his son. Known both as Charles the Well-Beloved and Charles the Mad, Charles VI, who died in 1422, was a boy of twelve at his accession and was plagued from his midtwenties by bouts of insanity. Accounts of his symptoms suggest that he was schizophrenic. The resulting dynastic infighting made France ungovernable and would have left France defenseless if the English had not themselves been racked with dissension. As it was, Charles was forced to acknowledge Henry V of England as his heir following another catastrophic defeat, at Agincourt in 1415. Christine de Pizan died just as the French began to get the upper hand in the war, inspired by Joan of Arc; her last known work was a panegyric to Joan, written before Joan's betrayal by the duke of Burgundy and execution by the English.

Christine de Pizan has become famous as the author of *The Book of the City of Ladies* and *The Book of the Three Virtues*, sometimes called *The Treasury of the City of Ladies*. We focus, not on these, but on *The Book of the Body Politic*. The more famous books are feminist manifestos, but not political in focus or purpose. They belong, as does Mary Wollstonecraft's *Vindication of the Rights of Woman* four hundred years afterward (though not her *Vindication of the Rights of Man*), to the *genre* of *la querelle des femmes*. There was a medieval literary genre that belittled women's intelligence, prudence, self-restraint, and sense of justice, and depicted women as silly, flighty, selfish, and vain. *The City of Ladies* was in the countertradition of defenses against such foolishness. It exemplifies the humanist conviction that God and Reason are on the same side: in this case on the side of the view that women can be as virtuous as men, and for the most part consists of *exempla* illustrating the virtue of women and, occasionally, the wickedness of men such as Nero.[4] No political implications are drawn. Everyone knew that women had managed estates, organized the military defense of cities, and done everything a competent man could do, just as everyone also knew that the poor and unlettered often fought more bravely and displayed more initiative in battle than their superiors and often displayed better sense in the everyday conduct of their lives—but nobody other than Plato drew the conclusion that political capacity had nothing to do with birth and sex and that neither should political authority.

The Book of the Body Politic was written around 1407. It was an advice book to the then dauphin, Louis of Guyenne; it is, as it says, a book concerning the whole body politic, prince, nobility, and "the universal people," but not only is the section devoted to the prince twice as long as that devoted to the nobility and three times as long as that devoted to the ordinary people, most of the advice to the ordinary people concerns their duties to the prince. The dauphin died eight years later, five years before his father. The book was one of a flurry of works, including reflections on the changeability of human fortune, a biography of Charles V, the later *Lamentation on the Troubles of France*—urging the duc de Berry to prevent the horrors of civil war from overwhelming France—and *The Book of Peace*, addressed to the dauphin in the year before he died. There is no way of knowing what priority Christine attached to her works. She was writing for patrons, among whom the dauphin was a virtual prisoner of the duke of Burgundy at the time she wrote *The Book of Peace*. *The Book of the Body Politic* is short and slight, but not uninteresting. The imagery of the body politic went back into antiquity—Plato used it at length in the *Republic*—but it was not much employed in formal works of moral and political advice. Commonly, the use made of it was hardly more than observing that the head as the seat of wisdom gave direction to the whole body, and so a wise king could give direction to the whole community.

In Plato the imagery had done some contentious work; Plato's tripartite division of the soul and its virtues placed temperance in the belly and assigned it as the one virtue needed by the laboring classes; the chief characteristic of democracy was, on that view, greed.[5] Pizan made a use of the metaphor that was interestingly friendlier to the common people: the ruler is the head, the knights and nobles are the active element, the chest, arms, and hands, so to speak—and the common people are the belly, legs, and feet, devoted to creating the means of subsistence.[6] The inadvisability of pressing the metaphor very far is suggested by the fact that the clergy are placed with the common people, although one might expect them to be located somewhere above the waist, and in fact they sometimes seem to be associated with the head in providing wisdom. The third part of the book is an exhortation to the "three estates" of the French cities and Paris particularly to cooperate and preserve unity; here the clergy are the

first of the estates "high noble and worthy of honour among the others,"
as the fount of good learning and piety.[7]

Any work that combines the Platonic formula of distributing the
virtues around the body politic with the formulae of the mirror of
princes will be concerned with the education of the prince. Christine
was presenting the text to the dauphin, who was eleven years old at the
time, so she begins with the education of a ruler's son before turning to
the way the son should behave once grown up. The advice is not complicated: the prince should entrust his son to a good scholar, but to a
virtuous man before a merely wise one. The wisdom the youth should
learn is classical, and the virtues he should acquire are the usual combination of Christian and Ciceronian (or Stoic) virtues. None of that is
surprising; it may seem more surprising that Christine treats classical,
mainly Roman and republican, examples as so straightforwardly relevant
to the conduct of a Christian prince, and treats Roman expectations for
consuls, dictators, generals, and senators as guides for fifteenth-century
Frenchmen. This is because she draws so heavily on a book of *exempla* by
Valerius Maximus—the *Facta et dicta memorabilia*—that was widely used in
the moral education of the upper classes. The importance of the cardinal
virtues—justice, courage, temperance, and prudence—might seem obvious; good stories about those who flourished by possessing them make
the point without belaboring it. She may have thought that as a woman
she had need of their borrowed authority.[8] *Exempla* could reinforce more
disconcerting morals, as they did in Machiavelli's *Prince* and *Discourses*.

There are perhaps four things to say about a short book that is both
highly readable and intellectually undemanding. First, it has a human
touch that many such works lack. Christine insists that the prince's
teacher be sober, cleanly dressed, and not given to talking nonsense, but
reminds him that the prince must be allowed to play children's games
and must be given treats. He is not to be fed only grammar and logic. A
second feature is how ferociously critical she is of the decayed state of the
church in her time. It is no surprise that the prince is told to guide his
conduct by the light of Christian virtue; and no surprise that he is told
to look to the good of the whole people and not only to his own. Everyone relied on the distinction between the prince who pursued the good

of his people and the prince who cared only for his own interests as the dividing line between the legitimate monarch and the illegitimate tyrant. The advice to choose wise councillors, levy moderate taxes, and be brave in battle and merciful in peacetime could be expected in any work of this sort. But the ferocity of her attack on the misconduct of clergy and bishops who have shamed themselves and their religion by turning their churches into something closer to stables than temples has the ring of real anger.[9] "They are truly devils and the infernal abyss, for as the mouth of Hell may never be filled nor satisfied no matter how much it receives or takes, neither can their desires be satisfied or filled since they have such great greed in them for money and luxuries, for which they do great evil to the people!" She was writing in the twenty-ninth year of the Great Schism, and her anger is not inexplicable.

A third unusual feature of the book is its sympathy with the common people. There is a strong sense that their lives matter, and their well-being should be the main concern of the ruling elite. "Of all the estates, they are the most necessary, those who are the cultivators of the earth which feed and nourish the human creature, without whom the earth would end in little time."[10] However, the section in which she discusses their political role is brief; it amounts to little more than an admonition to the members of the three estates—clergy, merchants, and artisans—to make their contribution to the well-being of the polity with due seriousness and deference to those set in authority. Her sympathy with their lot does not extend to thinking that ordinary folk should play a political role; given her origins, Christine is surprisingly insistent on the incapacity of ordinary people to govern themselves: they simply cannot do it, and Aristotle was right to say that one-man rule was best. Her account of the obedience the common people owe their rulers draws exclusively on the standard scriptural accounts of the nature and origins of political authority: the powers that be are ordained of God, and paying (moderate) taxes without complaint is the way to render unto Caesar the things that are Ceasar's.

The fourth feature of the book, conversely, is how un-Christian is her discussion of the virtues and obligations of the knightly class. Christine relies entirely on pagan and classical, largely Roman and republican, examples in urging appropriate behavior. They should obtain honor only by deserving it, and they should deserve it by displaying courage, perseverance, and an indifference to the financial payoff of victory, as the heroes of the Roman Republic did. Modern readers may eventually find the stream of stories lifted from Valerius wearying, but they are not without interest, and they were in any event part of the standard repertoire of didactic literature. Her ready acceptance of the savagery of Roman behavior in battle seems at odds with her pleas for peace in other works and her reflections a decade later on the sufferings of the women whose husbands had been killed or captured at Agincourt. And the cheerfulness with which she endorses Valerius's praise of the trickery and deception practiced by Roman heroes seems equally at odds with her insistence that honesty and keeping faith are indispensable virtues without which no honor can be gained. It would be wrong to think that *The Book of the Body Politic* was simply cobbled together, however. The tensions demonstrate the difficulty of writing readably and persuasively in several different genres at once. The Christian scriptures celebrate humility above prowess in war, pagan philosophers looked for self-sufficiency, but the Hundred Years' War still had many years to run before the English were expelled from everywhere but Calais.

Later Humanists: Pico's Oration

Pico della Mirandola died too young to write a mature work. He was born in 1463 and died in 1494. The oration is a very young man's work; Pico was twenty-four when he wrote it as part of his offer to prove nine hundred theses on every topic in logic, metaphysics, theology, physics, and natural history before the College of Cardinals. He was not an upstart show-off but an aristocrat who renounced his share of the family duchy to pursue a life of learning. He believed in eclecticism—that the truth could be elicited by bringing together all possible intellectual, spiritual, and religious traditions—and his range was breathtaking. We do not flinch at an enthusiasm for Plato and the Neoplatonists, but his belief in Hermes Trismegistus—a supposed Egyptian magus—may raise eyebrows, as might his faith (not uncommon at that day) in Chaldean theology and Jewish medieval kabbalistic learning. He was, nonetheless, a devout Christian; his interest in the kabbalah did not reflect respect for Judaism but the desire to refute "the stony-hearted Hebrews" out of their own works.

On the Dignity of Man was representative neither of Pico's oeuvre nor of humanist thinking generally, but it strikingly expresses some intellectual and stylistic commitments of humanism. What excites the enthusiasm of modern readers are the few paragraphs in which God tells Man to go and make of himself the highest and most intelligent thing that he can; it was the source of Walter Pater's notorious injunction that we should endeavor to "burn with a hard, gem-like flame." The idea that the task of humanity was self-creation verged on the heretical: neither Christianity nor classical thought had much room for the idea. Classical thought was too committed to the idea that everything had a fixed nature and that perfection was a matter of fulfilling it; Christianity was too committed to the idea of original sin. Pico was in fact condemned for heresy, but not because of these enthusiasms. It was for thirteen claims ranging over the nature of transubstantiation, eternal punishment, and whether Christ had really been present during the descent into hell. He defended himself energetically, but it is hard not to sympathize with his accusers.

The image Pico drew on was older than Plato and appears as a creation story in Plato's dialogue *Protagoras*: God gave all the other animals specific means of survival, such as wings, beaks, claws, armored scales, great speed. Human beings had none of these and had to rely on intelligence to flourish. More importantly, they had to invent political communities and practice justice.[11] The thought that humans needed to live in political communities just because they were not equipped with the same means of individual survival as animals was periodically rearticulated. Pico was not a romantic before his time; he did not think of self-perfection as a historical enterprise as the romantics did in the eighteenth and nineteenth centuries, and he did not see human perfection as something to be promoted politically. He was too caught up in the magical wisdom of the ancients and exotic mystics to see self-creation as something to be achieved only in the far future. The sense in which Pico is a "precursor" of later political utopians is that he inspired many thinkers who read him with pleasure. One of them was Sir Thomas More, the author of *Utopia*, who in 1510 translated the *Life* of Pico written by his nephew Francisco.

Orthodox readers in his own day—Pico was forbidden to engage in a public disputation over his nine hundred theses, and the *Oration* was published only in 1496, two years after his death—would have been startled by the claim that theology could bring us to the direct vision of the divine. It is usually thought to be a blessing of the afterlife. Pico held that we can make ourselves cherubim, one rank below the seraphim, but close enough to God to contemplate him. The political implications are obscure, and never explored by Pico; we might expect a Platonist to look to philosopher-kings, but a Christian Platonist is equally likely to turn away from politics and ask no more than space for a community of scholars intent on attaining the mystic vision of God as he truly is. This is not Montaigne's explicitly antipolitical defense of the quiet life. Montaigne did not expect the vision of blessedness to appear if we could keep perfectly still; he sought peace and disengagement for their own sake. Pico did. That attaining the blessed vision might require a strenuous engagement with Chaldean theology, the Hebrew kabbalah, and the theological speculations of Arab Neoplatonists did not unnerve Pico—those were his real interests.

Erasmus

Erasmus defines the humanist temper and the full humanist range, literary, political, and philosophical. He was born in 1469, the illegitimate son of a future priest and a physician's daughter. A native of the Netherlands, he got his classical training at the school in Deventer that produced Nicholas of Cusa and Thomas à Kempis. Without parents or money, he could not attend university and pursued his studies in a monastery. He had no spiritual vocation, but the contemplative life attracted him, and he knew that patience and self-control never hurt scholarship. Technically, he remained in monastic orders all his life, but he hankered after the wider world, and when he attached himself as a secretary to the bishop of Cambrai in 1492, he began a career in which the search for patrons bulked large. One of his main contributions to political thinking, *The Education of a Christian Prince*, which is always printed alongside a *Panegyric* for Archduke Philip of Austria, was part of a long campaign to advance himself economically. The *Panegyric* was written in 1504 and addressed to the father of the future emperor Charles V; it was therefore an apt companion for the instruction addressed to his sixteen-year-old son. Their financial motivation does not discredit either. To modern readers, the habit of laying on flattery with a trowel is unpersuasive; to early modern writers and readers, it was a literary trope with a certain ironical twist—the author told the dedicatee that he was virtuous, wise, brave, and a patron of learning, but presented him with a work that urged him to distinguish true praise from mere flattery and laid out an account of the virtuous prince that no one has ever lived up to.

The interest of *The Education of a Christian Prince* will become more obvious when we turn to Machiavelli's *Prince*. It was written three years after that work—in 1516 against 1513—and Erasmus was seeking employment, much as Machiavelli was. Erasmus played it straight, whereas Machiavelli did something with the genre that interpreters are still puzzled by. The striking feature of Erasmus's version of a mirror of princes was the insistence that peace was the highest good. Ironically, the future Charles V became a notable practitioner of war and coercive diplomacy; Erasmus subsequently made a gift of the work to Henry VIII of England, another monarch whose pacific inclinations were not obvious at the time or later. But Erasmus's defense of peace was sincere; his pacifism was deeply felt and underpinned by a great distaste for all forms of cruelty. His hatred of war was shared by his very good friend Sir Thomas More, but More was more than ready, if not positively happy, to see heretics taken out and burned at the stake; Erasmus insisted that religious differences were not a ground for quarrel of any sort, let alone for disgusting forms of execution.

The Education of a Christian Prince jolts the modern reader, not so much by its fulsome praise of Charles V as by invoking Xenophon to claim that "there is something beyond human nature, something wholly divine, in absolute rule over free and willing subjects."[12] We find the thought of absolutism on the one side and freedom and willingness on the other hard to embrace. It is in fact no different from the thought we found in Marsilius: popular consent *legitimates* government, but it does not *limit* it in the sense in which modern constitutions do. Good rulers display a divine quality that it would be absurd to restrain, but they can display it only by ruling over consenting subjects. This is not Justinian's claim that the Roman emperor held absolute legislative authority because it had been conferred on him by "the people" who had possessed it in the first place. Justinian's claim was an explanation of the pedigree of absolute authority; Erasmus gives us an account of its nature. The crucial contrast is Marsilius's: tyrants coerce the unwilling without regard to the common good, while absolute princes govern the willing in the general interest and not their own. Like Marsilius, but in a more Platonic mode, Erasmus links authority to wisdom and suggests that the good prince is a Platonic guardian, supreme not in wealth and power but in wisdom.[13]

This may be the first time since late antiquity that Plato's *Republic* makes itself felt in political theorizing. The full text had come into educated consciousness with Marsilio Ficino's translation of 1469. Erasmus thought the mark of an educated man was equal facility in Greek and Latin, which had become feasible when the Ottoman conquest of Constantinople in 1453 had driven the classical scholars and philosophers of the city to take refuge in the west, but it was still likely that an educated man would read Plato in Latin translation. Whether in Greek or in Latin translation, however, Plato's utopian scheme for a state in which kings would be philosophers and philosophers kings was now in the educational curriculum in a way it had not been. More's *Utopia*, published at the same time as *The Education of a Christian Prince*, was a jokily written but seriously intended reworking of Plato's ambitions. Like his friend, Erasmus wanted philosophically minded rulers to govern.

Erasmus imagines the prince's tutor disputing this point with "some idiot courtier," who objects that Erasmus's schemes for the education of the prince would create a philosopher and not a prince: "Do not think that it was an ill-considered thesis of Plato's, praised by the most laudable men, that the state will eventually be blessed if and when either the rulers take up philosophy or the philosophers take over the government."[14] Erasmus's gloss is important and reflects the hostility of the humanists toward the Scholastics: a philosopher is not "someone who is clever at dialectics or science" but someone who can distinguish reality and appearance, and unflinchingly cleave to the good. In fact, "being a philosopher is in practice the same as being a Christian; only the terminology is different." The insistence on the prince's ability to distinguish between appearance and reality is the great theme taken from Plato, and a main preoccupation of the educational program.

Thus, public opinion is not to be trusted, because the masses are in the grip of illusion, trussed up like the prisoners in Plato's famous cave, unable to see what is real and what is merely a shadow on the cave wall. Again, the prince is to be taught that true happiness is to be attained only by pursuing virtue; the pleasures of the flesh, the carnal amusements of sex and gluttony, are of no account compared with the unshakable happiness of the good man. This doctrine is in some respects overdetermined; the Stoic would have argued that only the virtuous man is free, since only he can spurn the temptations of the flesh and steer by the compass of his rational nature; and the Christian would have argued that the joys of the world are snares and delusions, traps set by the devil to lead us into the fiery pit and away from our heavenly destination. Erasmus knows all this; that is why the philosopher is a Christian—using different terminology.

The prince must learn early the dangers of flattery. True praise is good, for it encourages activity in the path of virtue. Flattery is a noxious drug. It gratifies the senses for a moment and undermines judgment. This thought has obvious implications for the importance of the prince's choosing his advisers wisely. Advisers who always tell him what he wants to hear and never remind him of the dangers into which he may run if he pursues a rash or thoughtless path are no use. Advisers who have an eye to their own profit and not that of their country are a danger to everyone. Although Erasmus's great friend Sir Thomas More had a sharply ironic view about the chances of the philosopher's being heeded—by this time, Plato's *Seventh Letter* was well known, and his narrow escape from death or slavery at the hands of Dionysius had become a familiar cautionary tale—Erasmus is, or appears to be, undaunted.

We once again see some familiar thoughts in novel terminology and with echoes of sources different from those encountered earlier. There are two crucial dichotomies on which everything turns. The first is the recurrent insistence on the difference between tyranny and legitimate rule. Because of what they became, we tend to think of the French and the Spanish monarchies in ways appropriate to the absolutism of Louis XIV and Louis XV, with their defenders resting on the doctrine of divine right. But whereas later defenders of absolute monarchy invoked divine right in opposition to the idea of government by consent, Erasmus adhered to the old view that the consent of the subject legitimates the ruler. Nor does he raise questions about one-man rule. He insists that the common opinion of philosophers is that monarchy is the best form of government, and does not suggest that Cicero, or Roman writers up to the time of Caesar, might not have agreed. He was not writing intellectual history; he was painting a picture. He encourages the prince's tutor to depict the tyrant in animal imagery to emphasize his full wickedness. On the one side is the picture of the legitimate ruler, full of wisdom and virtue, safe in the love of his people, and legitimated by their willing acceptance of his rule. On the other is the tyrant, a creature described as worse than the ravening bear, more dangerous than lion or poisonous snake. If the virtuous ruler partakes of the excellence of God, we know what the tyrant partakes of.

Tyrants, then, govern in their own interest and not that of the whole people, and they do not try to secure the consent of their subjects but force obedience on them as best they can. Although *The Education of a Christian Prince* is a moralistic work, it is not only that. When Erasmus urges moderation in the taxation that a prince imposes on his people, he makes the wholly practical point that a lightly taxed people will be more prosperous and provide greater resources for the government than a people who can barely keep themselves alive. He also points out, in the way familiar since Aristotle, that princes who have an eye to their own security and well-being will not render themselves objects of hatred to their subjects. Grinding them into the ground with excessive taxes inspires revolts.

Lawfulness is essential. Tyrants allow their friends to break the law, but enforce it cruelly against their enemies; a legitimate prince governs according to the law, making no exceptions save what clemency commends. What is no more present in Erasmus than in Christine de Pizan is praise of tyrannicide, and the thought that a man who kills a tyrant is a benefactor of mankind. Whatever impact Cicero had on humanism, it did not extend to his endlessly repeated praise of tyrannicide. But there is no explicit repudiation of a right of resistance, and no insistence that tyrannicide is forbidden no matter what evils the rulers may perpetrate. The reminder that rulers who alienate their subjects risk their own lives does not come with the qualification that subjects would be wicked to revolt. There is no hint of the Augustinian injunction to submit in patience to the brutalities of any system whereby a minimal peace is maintained.

The second great contrast that Erasmus insists on is between the prince who seeks peace and the prince intent on war. The most distinctive feature of the work—although we find something like it in More— is the elaborate discussion of how to pursue peace. Erasmus observes that the ancients divided the arts of statecraft into the arts of peace and the arts of war. This is an error. All of the arts of a statesman are the arts of peace, because "with them he must strive to his utmost for this end: that the devices of war may never be used."[15] The thought contains a twist we shall find again in Hobbes. Today we think of arguments against war in humanitarian terms, and there are humanitarian arguments in Erasmus. The central argument, however, is that civilization is a good in itself. A good society is prosperous and cheerful; people are not ground down by overwork, not burdened by taxation, not frightened of arbitrary and irrational laws; but what makes a society truly civilized is the level of learning it fosters; and what makes warfare so terrible is not only that it is inimical to learning—which is not the banal thought that lectures cannot be given while troops are quartered in the lecture room—but that the project of killing one's enemies is directly at odds with the project of living in a community governed by reason.

The prince needs the arts of peace. The details are familiar and classical; the prince should be generous, but not in ways that destroy the public credit, he should appoint unbribable magistrates, ensure that the law is stern but not harsh, and so, entirely plausibly, on. There are departures from the ordinary. One is Erasmus's discussion of punishments. He dislikes the whole subject, but his rule of thumb is that where there are two ways of securing compliance—more stick or more carrot—choose the gentler. Admonition and persuasion leave the chastised person a free agent, ready to act on what he now knows, whereas brutality leaves him a sullen and hostile animal. Another is when he turns to the ways in which the law can encourage work and repress idleness. Criticizing Plato's proposal to evict beggars from his republic, Erasmus observes that few people beg by preference; if old age and illness have taken a toll, the remedy is not expulsion but institutions to house the incapable. Conversely, we should not be hidebound in our view of what constitutes idleness. The inhabitants of Marseilles rightly refused to let into their town a gang of priests who wished to live in idleness by hawking relics.

By the same token, it would be right to limit the number of monasteries, since the monastic life is a kind of idleness. So is life in many universities; Erasmus had visited Cambridge and spent some years at the Sorbonne, with whose orthodox faculty he had come into conflict. Turning away from clerical idleness, he considers servants. People kept as retainers and servants merely for ostentation should be put to useful employment; that allows some sharp thoughts on soldiers: "Soldiering, too, is a very energetic kind of idleness, and much the most dangerous, since it causes the total destruction of everything worthwhile and opens up a cesspit of everything that is evil. And so, if the prince will banish from his realm all such seed-beds of crime, there will be much less for his laws to punish."[16]

The sixteenth century was not more bloody than the seventeenth, let alone the twentieth, but it was a century of continuous warfare. Dynastic alliances were formed and broken, cemented by marriage and torn apart when the marriage broke up—or the marriage was torn apart when one or other side wished to be rid of the encumbrances of the alliance. Through marital alliances the Habsburg family extended its reach to every part of Europe; Charles V's success in unifying Spain, keeping successive popes at bay, and becoming the most powerful monarch in Europe reflected his military and political talent. However, he also took care to marry Isabella of Portugal to reunite the Iberian kingdoms, and one of his last acts was to arrange the marriage of his son Philip to

Mary Tudor, queen of England. If they had produced children, a Catholic England would have become a dependency of Spain. It was thus bold of Erasmus to denounce the role of marital alliances in contemporary politics. Indeed, it was even bolder than it might seem. When he offered *The Education of a Christian Prince* to Henry VIII, Charles V had recently broken off—given his age one should say he had been got out of—an engagement to Henry VIII's sister, Mary. (Her subsequent marital career included a brief marriage to Charles's rival, Francis I of France, and a love match with the duke of Suffolk.) Erasmus's little book was written barely two years after those events reduced relations between Henry and the Habsburgs to frigid hostility.

The attack on marital alliances was nothing to the sheer ferocity of Erasmus's condemnation of war. The idea of a just war is swept aside; there may be just wars, but even if there are, we should do everything in our power not to fight them. Augustine's view that we might properly fight wars to punish nations for their wickedness is not directly controverted, but it is pointedly ignored. Christ was the Prince of Peace, and the Christian prince should do his utmost to secure a reputation as a prince of peace. Charles V's career, including as it did, the Battle of Pavia in 1525, where he captured Francis I, and the sack of Rome by imperial troops in 1527, was a wry commentary on Erasmus's hopes for the young man. Erasmus knew that he was seen as a peacemonger—he published *The Complaint of Peace* in 1512 and was part of the peace party that looked for reconciliation between the separatists of Flanders and their Spanish king. He also knew that any argument that princes should not stand on what they took to be their rights would be met with the retort that unless we are ready to stand on our rights, nobody's rights will be respected.

To this he makes the only possible response: in a world of continuous warfare, no rights are safe. A measure of give-and-take is essential; securing most of our rights through peaceful negotiation is better than trying to secure them all by war. Moreover, says Erasmus, "a prince cannot revenge himself upon his enemies without first opening hostilities against his own subjects."[17] Conscripting supplies and soldiers is painful; confining your citizens within walled cities to protect them from the enemy is scarcely better than being besieged. As to why we are so inclined to make war on each other, Erasmus offers two savage comments.

The clergy, who should be preaching peace, spend their time fomenting warfare. His condemnation was provoked by the wars in Italy that had been set off by the determination of Popes Julius II and Leo X to prevent a union of northern Italy and the Kingdom of Naples in imperial or any other hands. The Holy Roman Empire was now, effectively, the Habsburg dynastic empire; the Kingdom of Naples was in Spanish hands, and northern Italy a battleground between papal, French, and imperial (or Spanish) forces. Erasmus was unsparing in his criticism of popes and bishops who pursued worldly political interests. If Christians must fight, they should fight the Turks; but even that they ought not to be too hasty to do, seeing that there is no point in defeating the Turks if we cannot institute a Christian peace. One novelty was that Erasmus denounced, for what seems to be the first time, the hostility that stemmed from nationalism, one nation hating another for no reason beyond its otherness. "Nowadays, the Englishman generally hates the Frenchman for no better reason than that he is French. The Scot, simply because he is a Scot, hates the Englishman, the Italian hates the German, the Swabian hates the Swiss, and so on; province hates province, city hates city."[18]

When Erasmus ends by observing that people who behave like this are running into a storm with folly as their guide, he reminds us of one thing more. A feature of humanist thinking was new forms of literary expression that allowed serious arguments to be expressed in a nonserious literary form. Perhaps the most characteristic work that Erasmus wrote was his self-mocking, seriocomic tract *The Praise of Folly*. He said, probably not expecting to be believed, that he wrote it in a single week, while staying with Thomas More during 1509, recovering from illness after a journey from the Continent, and without his usual books. That is no doubt one reason why the mockery extends in the best humanist manner to citing the authority of every serious writer who had written a comic work. Its Latin title is *Encomium Moriae*, a pun uniting the Greek word for madness and his host's surname; its structure is an extended joke that keeps turning serious—it begins with Folly complaining that nobody ever makes speeches in her honor. As she says, this is very unfair, seeing how devotedly they follow her every whim, so she will make a speech in praise of herself.[19] This she does with the aid of her allies: intoxication, deep sleep, ignorance, and stupidity. This enables Erasmus to mock contemporary social, religious, and political life—while saying that since it is only Folly talking, it isn't to be taken too seriously.

No commentator has been able to decide just what he was up to. That surely would have given Erasmus pleasure. In part, he may simply have enjoyed the intellectual exercise of writing from the standpoint of sheer foolishness. It is difficult to do well; getting across a serious point in a way that requires the author to say exactly the reverse of what he intends is not easy, and Folly herself apologizes from time to time for getting carried away and speaking like a serious person. Although Erasmus was surprised at the book's popularity, getting students to emulate it was a popular pedagogical device in Tudor England, and forcing students to argue against their favorite beliefs remains a popular pedagogical device to this day. Folly becomes serious when attacking Erasmus's familiar targets, including a corrupt and spiritually bankrupt church, and she is only marginally less savage about the useless drones who lecture on logic in the universities. The peroration is a masterpiece of double meanings seriously meant; Folly takes the opportunity presented by the fact that she is only a foolish woman to set out some hair-raising theological views.[20]

The masses, she says, are trapped in the flesh, like the prisoners in Plato's allegory of the cave; they see only illusions, and they are at the mercy of the things of the flesh. Neoplatonism had inspired early Catholic theology; but appealing directly to Plato to send his readers a message about the ways in which the flesh is a prison to the spirit was unorthodox. In any event, the cause in which Erasmus wished to invoke Plato was calculated to cause offense. Using Folly as his mouthpiece allowed Erasmus to remind his readers that Christianity took a view of the world that common sense would think insane—and therefore that people who seemed insane to the world might see a deeper truth than any available to common sense. Erasmus had insurance against complaint; Saint Paul preached Christ crucified and said it was "foolishness" to the Greeks. For

Erasmus to say that Christian mysticism was insanity to the *homme moyen sensuel* was squarely in that tradition. But the argument was not wholly comfortable—either he meant that Christianity was a creed for madmen (which he did not) or that the truth of Christianity was the same truth that Plato had enunciated (which he might well have thought) and that, as he later said in *The Education of a Christian Prince*, "only the terminology is different."[21] In which case, the need for a church as well as an academy is not obvious. Certainly, a church filled with corrupt and greedy hangers-on was not needed. Erasmus never left the Catholic Church and had some quarrelsome exchanges with Luther on the subject of free will, but critics have always thought him an inspiration to Protestant as well as Catholic reformers, and for all that his patrons were absolute monarchs, he displays the modern liberal temper of mind in a very pure form.

Sir Thomas More

Erasmus's dearest friend, Thomas More, knight, lord chancellor, and Catholic martyr, perhaps went him one better with *Utopia*. More is an enigmatic figure. He was one of the cleverest men of his age, whose skill as a lawyer led him into politics and the dangerous world of the Tudor court during the reign of Henry VIII. He was Speaker of the House of Commons in the 1520s and became the most powerful of the king's ministers when he succeeded the disgraced Cardinal Wolsey as lord chancellor in 1529. It was not ambition that drove him; he combined a quick and mordant wit with a piety that almost took him into the cloister rather than the lawcourts. He was nearly ten years younger than Erasmus, born in 1474 and judicially murdered by Henry VIII in 1535, the year before Erasmus died. He was convicted of treason when he refused to swear the oath acknowledging the king's supremacy as head of the Church of England. The king, knowing how unpopular More's execution was, forbade him to make a speech on the scaffold in justification of his conduct. More obeyed to the last. "I die the King's good servant," he said, "but God's first."

What makes More an enigma is the contrast between his skepticism

about the political and social life around him—in evidence throughout
Utopia—and his readiness to accommodate himself to the brutality and
duplicity of the world of Tudor politics until he took his final stand. If
he had not died a martyr to the Catholic faith, he would have had the
reputation of a man who could justify everything his royal master did.
He may well have appreciated the irony that many years before they
fell out, he had helped Henry VIII secure the title of "Defender of the
Faith," bestowed on him by the pope in recognition of Henry's condemnation of Luther's view of the sacraments. This was in 1520 and, as usual
in controversy with Luther, provoked a furious response, to which More
wrote an anonymous reply that outdid Luther's in scatological invec-
tive. Ironically, More had at the time urged Henry to be less fulsome in
acknowledging the authority of the pope; English feelings toward the
papacy were decidedly cold: there was only one English cardinal in a college of fifty, no Englishman would ever become pope, and the English
saw no reason to have the English church governed by Italians in the
interests of the French or the Spanish.

　　Utopia is a very good read, but More's life makes it puzzling. The
word "utopia" is More's coinage. He was an excellent classical scholar
and translated several works of the Greek satirist Lucian into Latin as
a joint project with Erasmus. One of Lucian's best-known works was
a *True History*, a detailed account of events that never took place; and
one of the tall stories the friends translated was *Menippus Goes to Hell*, in
which a Cynic philosopher takes a tour of the underworld. "Utopia" read
as *outopia* means "no place," and More exploits the punning ambiguity
inherent in its similarity to *eutopia*, or "the good place." The main river
of the island of Utopia is Anydrus—waterless—and the traveler who
has returned to tell More and his Flemish friend Peter Gilles all about
the place is called Raphael Hythlodaeus—*hythlodaeus* meaning something
very like "absurd." So we have a tall story about a nonexistent island, told
by a confessedly unreliable witness. The contrast with Plato's ponderous
exposition of his plans for the ideal polity after the first book of *Republic*
could not be more marked—which suggests that part of the point of the
exercise was to write a *Republic* for a later age and provide both a defense

and an internal critique of Plato's scheme. Raphael Hythlodaeus, who admires everything about Utopia, is in effect Plato's spokesman, and the fictional "More" the defender of common sense. Both are, of course, More with the two sides of his character conducting rhetorical warfare against each other.

How far *Utopia* reveals More's political ideals is not easy to say. The simple view is as plausible as any: that More felt a great distaste for the pomp and circumstance of the rich and powerful, and anger at the misery of the poor. No sentient creature in More's England could overlook the enormous gap between the rich and powerful at one end of the social spectrum and the starving poor at the other. Much of the wealth of England at this time depended on the wool trade, and although the overall benefit to the economy was great, the impact on poor laborers who were thrown off farms converted to pasture, or found the commons enclosed for sheep runs, was severe. Tudor governments responded to unemployment by savage penalties for theft and vagrancy. Although war on the Continent took able-bodied men out of England, it was no permanent help; wars came to an end, and unemployed soldiers were more effective criminals than unemployed laborers and spread even more fear.

More's *Utopia* is certainly a running critique of the ills that beset England in the early sixteenth century. The description of the island of Utopia occupies only the second book of *Utopia*, and the first book is a long prologue notable for More's denunciation of the way that sheep have consumed men, the injustice of executing unemployed men for theft— presenting them with the choice between a quick death by strangulation or a slow death from starvation—and the wickedness of the exactions of monarchs who rob their subjects to wage predatory wars on other nations. The first book also contains a long argument over the question whether More should retire to a life of study or commit himself to public service. More was debating just that question with himself at the time. The first book's complaints are echoed in the last few pages of book 2, when Raphael Hythlodaeus makes a long speech against the tyranny of wealth and the misery of poverty—while More affects to be sitting there thinking how terrible it would be to live in a world without pomp and circumstance and aristocrats.[22] It is clear that More was genuinely attracted to the main features of Utopian society, however little chance there was of any movement toward them in his own time and country.

What are these main features? The most obvious and the root of all others is the abolition of money. The joking aspect of More's mind appears when he tells us that the Utopians employ gold for making chamber pots; they allow children to play with precious stones but expect them to grow out of such play rather rapidly. William Morris used the same imagery in *News from Nowhere* three and a half centuries later, though his variation on the chamber pot story was to establish a huge dung hill on the site of Parliament. The Utopians run a communist economy, where everyone must work for six hours a day, and every family draws on the common stock for necessities. Modern readers flinch at forced labor, but More did not. For four years, he submitted voluntarily to the monastic discipline of the Carthusians and had no qualms about disciplined hard work. The underlying logic is anyway obvious. Mankind is forced to labor; nature is a benevolent mother only to those who make use of their own natural gifts—intelligence and energy—to acquire the gifts she provides in the fertility of the soil and the availability of plants and fruits and animals for our use.

Since labor is a necessity, there is nothing to complain of in doing it under the discipline of a state. The question is whether rewards allocated under the familiar system of a monetary economy and the vagaries of the marketplace are more generous and allocated more justly and securely than under Utopian communism. Once the question is asked in those terms, the answer is inescapable. In sixteenth-century England, willing workers were thrown out of work and hanged for stealing or whipped for vagrancy; meanwhile, hordes of useless servants were maintained for display by rich men, and thrown out of employment themselves when their master died or fell on hard times. As for the rich, it was bad for their characters to be underemployed and subject to no discipline. Critics reacted to Max Weber's wonderful essay *The Protestant Ethic and the Spirit of Capitalism* by observing that many Catholics had imbibed the Protestant ethic before Protestantism arrived on the scene. More was one.

Work is a discipline; substantial equality is a dictate of justice.

Human life cannot be wholly without fear and anxiety; we all die in the end, and we are all subject to ill health and to the miseries and disappointments of everyday life. But even if all flesh is as grass, starvation is a great evil, while an austere but decent standard of living—there is good wine in Utopia—secured by work while we are strong and given gratis when we can work no longer, is enough in itself and the foundation of a life of intelligent reflection. Against that background, More's belief that the security provided by a society like Utopia is a very good bargain becomes easy to understand. Indeed, it becomes impossible to resist.

More denounced capital punishment for theft as an evil and an absurdity; the starving vagrant can hardly be expected to be deterred by it, and like Erasmus, More thought excessive harshness brutalized both criminals and noncriminals. Modern readers are unlikely to find his alternative a model of humane treatment, but by the standards of the early sixteenth century, it was mild. In Utopia thieves became slaves; they serve a lifetime sentence of hard labor, though sentences are commuted for good behavior, which provides an incentive to reform. They do not suffer brutal ill-treatment, but whereas everyone else works only as long as needed, whence More's assumption that six hours a day was enough, slaves work a long day as part of their punishment. More began a long tradition of specifying in minute detail just how life in Utopia will operate; for a debased version of the same enthusiasm (or overenthusiasm) for detail one could turn to a modern utopia, Edward Bellamy's *Looking Backward* (1883), where we find the same desire for a world without money, an emphasis on work as social duty, though a more sophisticated view of how much of it we might do, and the same incautious assumption that a wise ruler could dictate the details of everyday life to universal satisfaction.[23]

Utopian institutions are of interest as a critique of the nationalism and commercial rivalries that were beginning to dominate European politics, as they continue to do. There is almost no central government in Utopia; there is a capital, but the towns are all of the same size and layout. In the capital there is a parliament, but the only details of Utopian government that Raphael Hythlodaeus offers concern local administration. Its most obvious feature is mathematical neatness: groups of households choose leaders and these form a council that chooses a mayor for the township. There are few laws, and no lawyers; there are many intellectuals, but they study the liberal arts and think about deep matters rather than how to rob their neighbors. To the extent that any state offered a framework for Utopia it would have been Venice, but More is only half-serious about filling in the institutional gaps that Plato's *Republic* notoriously left, for the good reason that in utopias of this sort politics in the ordinary sense is a casualty of consensus, and the institutions that express and control political attachments and rivalries are absent. Venice controlled these forces rather than abolishing them by literary fiat.

Religion is described in detail. Utopians are attached to a form of theism that seems to anticipate Unitarianism; the Utopians call their God Mythras without any suggestion that this is really his name. The common elements of belief are few: there is a God, the universe is divinely ordered for the benefit of human life and the attaining of eternal happiness, and a person who conducts herself or himself with a view to salvation will lead a good and happy life on earth. Death is not to be feared, because it is the gateway to communion with God. Different beliefs flourish, and the only absolute in Utopian religious life is an absolute ban on intolerance; one of More's sharp little jokes is the narrator's tale of a Christian convert exiled for denouncing other faiths as false.[24] More's classical allegiances are visible when he says that violent attempts at converting others are put down as breaches of the peace, not as blasphemy, a category that seems unavailable in Utopia. From a man who sent heretics to the stake, this is a powerful and dangerous doctrine, though it casts a curious light on his own career. Atheists are tolerated, but not trusted; they must not proselytize in public and cannot hold public office. They are encouraged to argue with the priesthood in the hope that they may see the light rather than to give the priests useful intellectual exercise. Nonetheless, *Utopia* ends with something of a surprise; Raphael says that the one defect of Utopia was its failure to heed the Christian message but that the good news is that it has been converted to Christianity. That may be, as many commentators suggest, an affirmation of More's distinctively Christian humanism. It may, on the other hand, lead readers to wonder whether conversion will be followed by dissension and sectarianism, and whether the Utopians might not have done better to stick to Mythraism. Utopia's founder, Utopos, conquered the island with no difficulty because it was riven with religious conflict.[25]

Services are musical, the prayers are for enlightenment, and priests are highly regarded, because they are well educated and the servants of peace. More gives the priests a substantial role in the conduct of war. More was ironic where Erasmus was passionate, but the underlying thought is common to them. Utopians despise war. They also despise hunting—an aristocratic sport always praised in handbooks for princes as good training for war—because hunting, like war, is a form of butchery. Unlike most nations, the Utopians would rather secure victory by deceit and bribery than by force. A bloody victory is as bad as a bloody defeat; ideally, they subvert their opponents by bribery—which is easily done, because they have a lot of gold and silver that they do not themselves need and can use to suborn their enemies. Twentieth-century observers of the United States' travails in Vietnam sometimes thought they could have undermined the Vietcong at a vastly lower cost in both blood and money had they followed the lead of More's Utopians. More breaks with conventional views of just war by describing the Utopians as happy to wage wars of national liberation to free other people from dictatorial governments; in this they go beyond the United Nations Charter, which forbids "regime change" as a legitimate reason for making war, and perhaps display a utopian overconfidence in the ease with which one people can liberate another from its homegrown tyrants. They do not wage war to advance their self-interest beyond the demands of self-defense. One way and another, they are strikingly unlike their European contemporaries, who were about to embark on a century and a half of religious conflict and five centuries of imperialism in the Americas, Asia, and Africa.

They use their priests to minimize destruction; a priest will prevent an army from killing defeated foes, will protect the fallen, and has the authority to bring a battle to an end by declaring it ended. In time of war, priests go with the army to preserve humanity and not to pray to the almighty to massacre their enemies. The Utopians' matter-of-fact approach to conflict extends to an unwillingness to have their citizens killed in battle; their wealth allows them to hire mercenaries and to secure their loyalty by offering colossal rates of pay. They have worked out that the high death rate among their hired soldiers means they will have to pay only a small proportion of them. More imagines that the Utopians employ for preference a distant people, the Zapoletes, who are not so much unaware of the dangers they run as utterly indifferent to them; they are greedy, violent, loyal to whoever employs them but willing to kill each other without compunction, and plainly possessed of a much greater taste for excitement than the sober Utopians. The Utopians despise them, but More is not inviting the reader to wonder whether they have other employment opportunities; he is condemning warfare.

Taken seriously, these passages suggest that More's distance from the politics and religion of his own day was more than a matter of psychological reserve. How best to take *Utopia* seriously, however, is not self-evident. Utopia building is useful for something other than providing blueprints. What have come to be called "dystopian" works, such as Huxley's *Brave New World*, do not suggest that the dystopian world is immediately around the corner, or that we must take immediate and dramatic steps to prevent its arrival; they serve to sharpen our self-consciousness about the implications of what we think of as progress. *Utopia* is not a blueprint for pacifism and the abolition of social ranks, or for religious disestablishment; its comic elements not only protect More from any accusation of being a dissident and a man to be carefully watched but also protect the text itself from being treated as a statement of the politically desirable. *Utopia* has an ironic distance from reality that Plato's *Republic* does not. But it certainly serves to raise questions: do we benefit from possessing ever more wealth while others starve; must states fight for prestige; can we not tolerate religious dissenters? And so indefinitely on.

How much of what such sketches teach us is intended by their authors is a biographical mystery. Almost every work escapes its author's control in some respects, and almost any work betrays its author's intentions in both meanings of the word "betray." The one thing we should try to do is curb the urge to infer from the text to what the author "must" have intended by it. A modern reader will see in *Utopia* a cautionary tale about the way the desire for a perfect society breeds totalitarianism: the inhabitants of Utopia cannot travel without permission; premarital sexual intercourse is penalized by a lifelong prohibition on marriage for either partner; and, as More says, everyone is acutely conscious of being always under the eye of everyone else.[26] We squirm; after Orwell's *1984*, mutual surveillance means to us Big Brother. It seems much too high a price to pay, even for the peace and security on offer. We should not assume that More would share our doubts. Writing from the little room in the Tower of London where he was awaiting trial and execution, he did not complain of his loss of liberty but expressed gratitude for the simplification of his existence. This was no doubt a gallant attempt to comfort his family; he had an enviably happy marriage and was greatly loved by his children. It also reflected the hankering after a life free of earthly concerns that an admirer of Plato should have felt.

Montaigne

Erasmus and More appeal to modern readers because of their skepticism. The sixteenth-century humanist who epitomizes the use of skepticism for moral and political purposes was Montaigne. This is paradoxical, because his *essais* touch only indirectly on political organization or the management of everyday affairs; they are investigations, "assays," of the self, attempts to investigate the human psyche from the evidence of the one person whom Montaigne knew best—that is, himself. Nor are they confessional like Augustine's *Confessions*. Montaigne was interested neither in confessing his weaknesses nor in praising God for his mercy in redeeming him from them. Like Augustine, Montaigne thought that man was a mystery to himself, but there is none of Augustine's deep anguish at that fact, rather an acceptance that patience, self-control, and caution in taking anything for granted are essential for self-understanding.

The political bearing and inspiration of this Stoic, skeptical introspective concern are direct, however. In translations other than English translations, his essays are described as "moral and political," as they are. Montaigne was born in 1533, and took part in the French civil wars of the midcentury, so his discussions of courage, betrayal, the dangers of negotiation, and much else have the voice of experience.[27] These were wars of religion exacerbated by conflicts in royal and aristocratic families, and by the underlying struggle between a centralizing monarchy and an aristocracy whose power and prestige was local or regional. Montaigne came from a noble family, studied law, and was a counselor in the Bordeaux *parlement*, but found public affairs distasteful. Selling his position in the *parlement* gave him an income, but leisure made him miserable. Although his *essais* are not a record of unhappiness, they were provoked by it. The injunctions on which happiness depended were Stoic in their concern that the world should not too much touch us, Christian in their moral basis, and modern in their fascination with the individual as an individual.

Politics is more to be feared for its dangers than enjoyed for its opportunities, rulers are essential, and monarchy is the best form of rule; but wise men eschew the search for military glory and try to build good public morals on the most tolerant possible version of Christianity. As to the rest, the greatest goods are friendship, a quiet mind, and the study of those things that philosophy and religion can teach us. One should resist the temptation to credit a writer with the invention of anything, but it is hard to resist the temptation to credit Montaigne with discovering both the modern sense of individuality and the modern concept of private life. Indeed, his essays, avowedly about the one subject he really knew, namely himself, can plausibly be said to be the first modern autobiography, that is, an autobiography in the modern sense of the term.

And here we begin to see the emergence of a new conflict between the private and the public: not the traditional tension between self-interest and public spirit, or the Christian tension between the concerns of the here and now and those of the hereafter, or the Platonic tension between the search for Truth and doing our duty to our fellows, but the distinctively modern conflict between the pleasures of intimate relationships, domestic happiness, the quiet contentment of living our own lives in our own way, and the pleasures—equally real but utterly different—of public life. The door opens to a new reading of the tension between man and citizen.

CHAPTER 10

The Reformation

The Reformation

L IKE "THE RENAISSANCE," "THE Reformation" is a loose term, but
inescapable except at the price of appalling circumlocution. Neither
geographically, nor temporally, nor doctrinally does the idea of a single,
definable Reformation (or Renaissance, for that matter) bear scrutiny,
but the fact remains that before 1500 there was no institutionalized
confessional divide among western European Christians, and after 1550
there were several. The political consequences were enormous. Most of
the doctrines of leading Protestant thinkers had first been articulated by
Jan Hus and John Wyclif a century earlier; Luther drew heavily on the
fiercest and most alarming ideas of Saint Augustine; and a return to the
purity of the early church was widely demanded. But theological originality is not our topic. The impact of the new theology on the legitimation of political authority is. "How are we to govern ourselves?" takes
on a new urgency when rulers and ruled are at odds over their religious
allegiances.

Dramatic change in church governance might have occurred a century earlier during and after the Great Schism. It did not; the Reformation occurred not in the fifteenth century but in the early sixteenth.
It broke out when and where it did because the *political* hostility to the

papacy long felt by the rulers of western Europe, whose financial needs made the wealth of the church an irresistible target for cash-strapped monarchs fighting costly wars, found ideological backing in a widespread moral, spiritual, and theological hostility to the papacy. The *confessional* divide was an artifact of, and instrumental in accelerating, the long process by which churches became *national* churches. The inability of the papacy to preserve the unity of Christendom owed more to the political alliances the papacy had made to preserve its position in Italy than to any Europe-wide movement of opinion against the church as such. Neither the complaint against the worldliness of the papacy nor the wish for a more conciliar, or congregationalist, or in a broad sense democratic, form of church organization was novel. The decisive factor was the readiness of secular authorities to take control of the religious life of their own states.

The most spectacular example was English. Henry VIII broke with Rome because he wanted a male heir. He may have been convinced that his marriage to his sister-in-law Catherine of Aragon produced one daughter and several miscarriages because it violated the church's prohibition on marriage between near-relatives; then again, he may not. He was certainly pious, and took Mass five times a day when he was not hunting. The pope could not grant Henry an annulment; his predecessor had granted a dispensation to allow Henry's marriage to his dead brother's widow in the first place, and an annulment would have required him to condemn his predecessor's decision. The more decisive reason was the papacy's political weakness; Catherine was the aunt of Charles V, the Holy Roman Emperor, and the pope was virtually Charles's prisoner after Charles's sack of Rome in 1527. Henry VIII took the bold step of declaring himself head of the Church of England, and amenable bishops gave him his annulment. Henry, as distinct from his son Edward VI, was not attracted to Protestantism, whether in its Lutheran or its Calvinist form. After their acrimonious exchanges of 1520, the king was unlikely to take Luther as a spiritual mentor.[1] Until 1547 the Church of England was doctrinally and liturgically unchanged; the change, an enormous one, was that the king was the spiritual head of the church, and the church in England a creature of English law. The two swords had been put into the hands of one person.

Protestantism and Antinomianism

Because liberal democracy first took root in Protestant countries, there is a temptation to think that there is a natural affinity between the "congre-gationalist" style of governance of many Protestant churches and liberal democratic politics. The connection is not very close. Britain and the Netherlands became Protestant constitutional monarchies, while Denmark and Sweden became Protestant absolute monarchies; France passed through civil war and emerged as a Catholic absolute monarchy. Venice remained a Catholic republic. Spain was for a time almost a theocracy. How this happened is a matter for political and social historians, but the facts suggest that there is no very direct connection between the religious and political ideas of the reformers. The focus here is on the novelties and tensions in the political ideas of a few leading Protestant thinkers, with a brief glance at the ideas of the extremists. The immediate difficulty we face in talking about the *political* impact of Reformation thinkers is simple. Protestantism initially involved a turning away from institutions of all kinds. Once the role of priestly intercession in securing our salvation is denied, the idea of an institutional church is threatened; political institutions in their turn seem likely to be treated in the arm's-length fashion of Augustine's *City of God*. The state has greater institutional legitimacy than the church, since we need law and order in a way we do not need anyone to get between ourselves and the Bible and its author. That seems all we can say. But much more was said, and we must explore it.

The impetus for the late fifteenth-century attacks on prevailing institutions was not theological. The destruction of the monasteries in England and elsewhere was a consequence not of Protestantism but of princely ambitions encountering a shortage of cash; Catholic monarchs also raided church property. By the mid-seventeenth century only Italy and Spain had made no inroads into church property. Henry VIII's dissolution of the monasteries in the 1530s coincided with his decision to break with Rome and institute himself as head of the English church and was particularly violent and comprehensive, but the dissolution itself was the final episode in a prolonged budgetary crisis that had set Henry and the papacy at odds since 1515, and was not in essence different from Philip IV's assault on the fiscal privileges of the church two centuries before. What induced Henry to take the extraordinary step of making himself head of the church in England was the need to secure his divorce from Catherine of Aragon. Absent that, it is not clear that church reform would have taken the course it did in England.

The term "Protestant" itself emerged relatively late. The emperor Charles V called a meeting of the princes of the Holy Roman Empire— the Diet of Speyer of 1529—to reverse the existing policy that the local faith was a matter for local decision, and to bring the dissident principalities back into the Catholic fold. The rulers he was trying to discipline protested his decrees and took the label *protestant*. They had initially called themselves evangelicals: they based themselves on the gospels and held that the individual's conscience and the vernacular Bible were sufficient for Christian practice. This veneration of the vernacular Bible was almost the most important feature of the Reformation. The consequences for politics, science, and literature, as well as for religion narrowly conceived, were enormous. It put a premium on literacy, close reading, and thinking for oneself whose long-term effects we are living with.

The view that the Christian faith could be found in "the scriptures alone" undermined the importance of the church as a corporation. It is obvious enough that *extra ecclesia nulla salvatio* is not a Protestant doctrine; Protestantism is centrifugal rather than centripetal. The purest version of the Protestant conception of a church was articulated long after Luther, but is implicit in his first, most extreme views on the subject. Locke's *Letter Concerning Toleration* of 1698 distinguished church and commonwealth in the simplest fashion: The state is a nonvoluntary organization with the right to coerce men's behavior for the sake of the earthly well-being of a society only; a church is a voluntary society of individuals united for common and public worship of God.[2] The church comes into contact with the state only in the same way as nonreligious entities: its property will be regulated in the same way as secular property, and its rituals cannot require criminal acts. A state that tolerates all religious beliefs that are not subversive of good order, and that confines its activities to the protection of earthly security, property, and good order, need never come into conflict with a church. As to the authority that each institution wields, dissent from the (just) dictates of the state must be met with physical penalties; dissent from a church's articles of faith can be met only with separation, with no other penalties than those implicit in the separation itself.[3]

Locke felt no anxiety about the probable result: sects will multiply, and the distinction between a church and a sect will become vanishingly small. Such insouciance about the multiplication of sects was not widely shared. The Constitution of the United States explicitly rules out a federally established church, but the New England colonies persecuted dissenters from the majority faith, and Connecticut had an established church until 1818. Radical anti-establishmentarianism of the kind Locke articulated was rarely accepted by governments before the end of the eighteenth century. Put simply, Protestantism is vulnerable to antinomianism, the view that Christians have no need of law, whether the law of the state, conventional morality, or any other, for love of one another is the whole law.[4] Once governments have seen outbreaks of antinomian enthusiasm, they try to corral enthusiasm in socially manageable forms. The vulnerability of Protestantism to antinomianism stems from the thought that obedience to externally imposed law cannot secure salvation. Luther, following Saint Paul, insisted that salvation depends on God's grace and nothing else; neither indulgences nor penances nor outward performances will prevail.[5]

Inner certainty is evidence of salvation; but it may be delusive. It may be a manifestation of pride, or simple error. Nonetheless, many thinkers convinced of their own election have thought their salvation assured, irrespective of how far they obeyed the laws their earthly rulers have laid down, how far they followed or flouted the rules of conventional morality, indeed, no matter how they lived. At the end of this track lies pure antinomianism, where the elect feel so wholly saved that they preach indulgence in the sins of the flesh as a demonstration of their saved condition. Luther expressed that attitude when he wrote, though only in a private letter to Philipp Melanchthon, that we should sin bravely, confident in our redemption. As on other occasions, he later recoiled from what he had encouraged. Very small amounts of the behavior that antinomianism justifies (or even a handful of people preaching its acceptability) unsettle the respectable and unnerve the political authorities. When political authorities become unsettled, they seek order, and Protestant communities have been as ready as their Catholic counterparts to enforce order by whatever means seemed effective and no worse than the disease they were to cure.

The vulnerability of different societies to outbreaks of antinomian enthusiasm varied greatly. Societies where order was already fragile saw earlier and more extreme upsurges of religious and political radicalism: Germany suffered earlier and more strikingly, and England only mildly more than a century later during the English Civil War. A closely associated phenomenon was millenarianism; antinomianism and millenarianism are not the same entity but lead to the same conclusion: if the Second Coming is imminent, submission to local rulers seems pointless. Why entire societies are seized with a conviction that the end is nigh is mysterious, but once they are, the consequences can be appalling. The mass suicides and the like of our own day had many precursors in medieval history and later. The people to whom chiliastic myths appeal may damage other people, but they have throughout history suffered dreadful reprisals from the forces of law and order. All this occurred in full measure during the Peasants' War of the mid-1520s, when Thomas Müntzer and others launched an abortive attempt to radically democratize politics and equalize wealth, and again in a flare-up a dozen years later when Anabaptists under the leadership of John of Leiden took control of the city of Münster for several months; they were put down with extreme savagery by combined Catholic and Protestant forces. To see why these millenarian outbreaks not only ended in disaster and repression but provoked Luther to strikingly violent outbursts of indignation against all who would challenge law in any of its manifestations, we must turn to Luther's career and political ideas.

Luther: Life and Times; Theological Premises

Unsurprisingly, Luther has been written about at enormous length. The bare facts of his life nevertheless remain mysterious, not least because legends accreted around him long before his death. He contributed to the mythmaking, not because he was a fabulist but because he had a vivid imagination. A powerful sense of how things *must* have been when he was a young man led him to give different and inconsistent accounts of his early life. Most importantly, he gave conflicting accounts of his decision to embark on the monastic life, what he thought of that life at the time, what he thought of Rome on his first visit, and what made him take his famous stand on the ninety-five theses nailed to the Wittenberg church door. As with Augustine's *Confessions*, the detached observer is appalled and enthralled by the psychological spectacle. Fortunately, this does not make it impossible to give a rather brisk account of his political ideas. Luther's passions were theological and spiritual; his political ideas were less central, and detachable both from the events that provoked him to offer them to the public and from his theological commitments. Their style is unmistakably his, their content less so.

Luther was born in Eisleben, in Saxony, in 1483 and died in the same town in 1546. His father was a miner, and a man of extreme shortness of temper, who beat his son for any reason and none. Although Luther's aide and disciple Philipp Melanchthon describes Luther's mother as pious, modest, and prayerful, she seems to have been as violent as her husband, and one of Luther's several accounts of his decision to enter a monastery was that he did it to escape the cruelty of his parents. It is easy to see how such parents might have created the man whose career was marked by outbursts of uncontrollable fury against his friends as much as against his enemies. School was no respite; it was equally brutal. His secondary schooling took place at Magdeburg and Eisenach; at the age of eighteen he entered the University of Erfurt; his father intended him to be a lawyer. In 1505, however, he entered the Augustinian monastery of Erfurt. His own account of his reasons we have seen; an alternative explanation, which refers to the death of a friend and a narrow escape from death by lightning, appears to be mythmaking. The most likely explanation is that Luther suffered a spiritual crisis in his early twenties and thought the discipline of the monastic life would give coherence to his life and personality.

A dozen years later, on October 31, 1517, Luther posted on the door of the castle church at Wittenberg his ninety-five theses. They denounced an ecclesiastical scandal, the sale of indulgences to raise money for the construction of the new and magnificent St. Peter's. The theses were declared heretical in virtue of their (wholly unoriginal) insistence that no earthly power, not even that of the pope, can absolve us from our sins. This is the only conclusion one can draw from the Augustinian doctrine of salvation by grace alone. The doctrine had been watered down, and the sale of indulgences was one consequence. Indulgences were somewhere between a mere blessing and a certificate entitling one to remission of one's sins, sold to raise money for church purposes. They were believed, or half believed, to purchase a reduction of the time to be spent in purgatory postmortem. They were more importantly a form of church taxation and are morally dubious in much the same way as present-day state lotteries. The date of the posting of the theses conventionally marks the beginning of the Protestant Reformation, and the last Sunday in October is celebrated as Reformation Day. This was not a young man's outrage. Luther was thirty-four years old and well established; he was ordained priest in 1507, and steadily went through the steps for his doctorate in theology at the University of Wittenberg, where he became a professor of theology in 1511. He became district vicar of his order in 1515.

He was heavily overworked. Meeting the spiritual obligations of the order, keeping up with his intellectual work, and doing enough for three men as a monastic middle manager was too much. He was emotionally ill equipped to handle the strain; he suffered sudden collapses of energy, for which he compensated with bouts of overwork, or in the case of failures in his devotions, with bouts of self-mortification. His lectures were animated by the conviction of mankind's utter sinfulness and estrangement from God. They were at odds with the optimistic naturalism and

Aristotelianism of Aquinas's theology, and even more with the human-ism of Erasmus. Nevertheless, Luther had no need to turn against the church, any more than Augustine had seen such a need. The fact that our wills are irremediably sinful, that God has destined some to be saved and some to be damned, that God's reasons for doing so are inscrutable, and that there is nothing we can do about it does not imply that the church should be dissolved. A community of mutually concerned believers who keep each other up to the mark serves a useful purpose, even if it cannot guarantee salvation.

The external provocations of Luther's stand were clear; under Julius II and Leo X the papacy launched an avalanche of indulgences, to finance their wars on the one hand and the building of St. Peter's on the other. Luther's local archbishop, the archbishop of Brandenburg, was embroiled in the process. He was corrupt on his own account: enemies were trying to have him deposed, so he was paying bribes to an agent in Rome and recouping the cost by buying multiple benefices to receive their income, thereby committing the sin of simony. For absolution from this sin, he paid Julius II and Leo X for the necessary indulgences. Someone with a much less fastidious conscience than Luther's might have drawn the line at that. The effect was out of all proportion to the cause. Nailing theses to a church door (it is not clear that Luther actually did it) and offering to defend them was not a revolutionary gesture. Lecturers in universities often posted theses and offered to defend them against all comers, as Pico della Mirandola had tried to do with his nine hundred theses. It was a way for a lecturer to make his name. What turned the event into the beginning of a religious, social, and political revolution was the fact that Luther had a secular protector who could ensure that Luther would not suffer the fate of Jan Hus, who had been summoned to the Council of Constance a century earlier with a promise of safe-conduct, and had then been burned as a heretic.

Many German princes were, as often, at odds with their emperor, and Luther's prince, Frederick the Wise, elector of Saxony, was in no mood to defer to the seventeen-year-old emperor Charles V. Other political factors worked in Luther's favor. Germany was on edge, and the authorities hesitated to stir up unrest by taking a severe line. One source of anxiety was the lesser nobility, sometimes called "the German knights," a social group that in other countries would have counted as minor gentry. They were suffering economic hardship as their military skills became obsolete; they felt oppressed by the princes of the church and the emerging patricians of the major towns and were natural allies of Luther, whose ideas they invoked when they broke into open revolt in 1522. Behind them were the "peasants" of the impending Peasants' War. "Peasants" is misleading. The unrest was urban as much as rural, and the leaders were articulate artisans. Some Marxist historians, though not Engels, who wrote a short history of the Peasants' War in his youth, see them as the first bourgeois revolutionaries. It is more plausible to see them as typical of social groups squeezed by economic change, who are socially or geographically uprooted. Engels was right when he said that the Lutherans were a nascent bourgeoisie; they were self-controlled, far-sighted, and careful, but the participants in the revolts that broke out between 1475 and 1525 were anything but; they were antinomian, utopian, and millenarian. Luther was a useful ally to Frederick the Wise; curbing him offered no benefits and might provoke trouble.

Luther's greatest weapon was the recently invented Gutenberg printing press with movable type. The Reformation was not "the Gutenberg revolution" but it was certainly a Gutenberg revolution.[6] Pamphlets, letters, manifestos, and denunciations could be produced in multiple copies at a hitherto impossible speed and disseminated far and wide. In six years 1,300 editions of various Lutheran pamphlets made their way across Europe. Luther had always advocated the translation of the Bible into the German vernacular, and its dissemination to all who could read it or have it read to them; the printing press made this practicable. There was nothing original about wanting to make the gospels available in the common language of ordinary people; Wyclif had urged it more than a hundred years earlier; his translation of the Bible became the basis of the King James Bible. Now vernacular Bibles could be disseminated cheaply on a scale that defeated attempts to prevent it. The use of print for propaganda purposes was a greater novelty; and both Luther's followers and his foes employed it to the best of their ability. Luther is the first writer we have thus far encountered who wrote for a mass audience, with every chance of reaching it.

The ninety-five theses marked a halfway point in the evolution of Luther's ideas and the origins of Protestant political thinking. After suffering agonies over the prospect of arbitrary salvation and damnation for several years, he was struck by the idea of justification by faith in 1513; once he had absorbed its implications, his later theological ideas and their political implications needed only to be brought into the light. The doctrine of justification by faith alone, not by works, and emphatically not by the purchase of indulgences, does not imply that ordinary sinful men can save themselves by willed belief. Faith is given by God, and our role in acquiring it is strictly a matter of opening ourselves to it *if* God should give it to us.[7] We can choose to stand where the lightning may strike; but only God can launch the lightning. To make ourselves receptive to God, we must reflect on the sacrifice made by Christ. This drove Luther's insistence on the priority of the New Testament over the Old. Nor was this the quietist mysticism of Meister Eckhart or Thomas à Kempis; they may have paved the way for an acceptance of Luther's views, but fierce though he was in denouncing excessive confidence in reason—"that pert prostitute"—he urged strenuous engagement, not quiet waiting. Moreover, to be "justified" was to be no less a sinner—as a strange novel, James Hogg's *Private Memoirs and Confessions of a Justified Sinner*, reminds us. The danger in emphasizing faith, as distinct from the grace by which faith is given to us, is that it encourages individuals to rely on their own conviction of salvation as a proof that they are saved. That done, sinning boldly becomes attractive, and antinomianism lurks. One response was that of the more severe Calvinists, to emphasize that the conviction itself might be a delusion and a mark of pride. Grace was truly inscrutable.

Political Theory

After the ninety-five theses, it was only a matter of time before the church tried to discipline Luther. He pressed ahead regardless. In 1520 fourteen

of the theses were declared heretical, and a papal bull, *Exsurge Domine*—
"Rise Up O Lord"—formally excommunicated him. Luther responded
by making a public bonfire of the papal bull and a number of other
documents, including volumes of canon law. In fact, he retaliated before
his enemies struck; some six months before his excommunication, he
published *An Address to the Christian Nobility of Germany*, a work that tells us
almost everything about Luther's conception of church–state relations.

He had by this time come to the view that the sacrament of ordination, like all but four of the sacraments of the Catholic Church, was
irrelevant to a Christian's ability to relate to Christ; the doctrine of
"the priesthood of all believers" was the positive face of this denial. We
acquire through baptism a relationship to Christ that gives us the ability to assist others in finding their way to him, and a duty so to assist.
Priests are those who have a particular vocation to do this. The church is
the congregation of the faithful, and more important as a church invisible than as a church visible. This is interestingly cruder than Augustine's
similar thought; for him, the city of God was the city of the saved, and
wholly invisible. The church was not the city of God, since the church
was an association that gathered together the saved and the damned, and
it was not for us to know which was which. An actual church nonetheless
played a role in human life of some value even to those who might turn
out to be damned.

The scything attack of *An Address* left little standing. For instance, the
idea that there were distinct estates of the realm, the clergy constituting
the spiritual estates and everyone else the secular estates, was declared
incoherent; in a Christian community, *everyone* belongs to the spiritual
estate. By the same token, the legal code embodied in canon law was a
chimera; the church was not a body politic that could exercise jurisdiction over some parts of a person's life while the state exercised jurisdiction over the rest, and canon law was not law. There was a good deal of
yearning for the simplicity of the primitive church, and Luther was as
careless as the church fathers about the separation of church and state.
Godly rulers had to provide for the everyday needs of the practitioners
of the faith; this implied a state-sponsored church or some other form of
official sponsorship of religious practice. Next year, Luther attacked the

monastic life; locking monks away breached the duty to evangelize, the emphasis on monastic devotions rested on the false belief in justification by works, and clerical celibacy was absurd. A decade later he drew the implications for his own life by marrying, very happily, and begetting six children.

The question is whether this provides any foundation for secular politics. The casualness of Luther's assumption that godly rulers would attend to the needs of the community of the faithful was not surprising, since there had been more than a millennium of professedly godly rulers claiming to do that. But Luther's negative views raise large questions in an acute form. The most obvious concerns the criteria for judging whether a ruler is a godly ruler; this takes us straight back to Pope Gelasius and the doctrine of the two swords. Luther held that there was only one sword and that the earthly ruler wielded it. What he was less consistently of one mind about was the consequential question whether any person or institution had the right to decide that a given ruler was so ungodly that he might lawfully be resisted. Resistance to unjust rulers was a persistent and difficult problem for Luther. In general, he defended the traditional doctrine of passive obedience. This allowed passive *disobedience* in the last resort, but it never justified rebellion; if it came to the point where the ruler commands us to do what is manifestly in contradiction of what Christ commanded, the ruler's command must be refused, but not violently resisted. Luther read Saint Paul in the orthodox fashion; the powers that be are ordained of God, even the bad and the brutal; the Christian's role is to suffer the consequences of disobedience, not to overthrow the local ruler. Rebellion even against a bad and un-Christian ruler is (with interesting exceptions) a rebellion against God as well.

An Address was an appeal to the princes and the emperor-elect; Charles V had been elected but not yet crowned in 1520. In that year, Luther had no expectation of a world in which the German states would have different confessional allegiances, nor any inkling of what would happen when Charles V remained a staunch Catholic and waged war on his Protestant subjects. For all his astuteness, Luther was blind to the alliances that had saved his own skin. *An Address* appealed for the reformation of the church by the secular authorities. It lamented the failure of the Hohenstaufen emperors to bring the papacy to heel in the twelfth and thirteenth centuries, though Luther agreed that Frederick Barbarossa and Frederick II had overreached themselves and had suffered divine chastisement for their arrogance. *An Address*'s technique, narrowly speaking, is polemic ad hoc rather than innovative political theorizing, but the results are radical. Luther observed that the papacy hid behind three lines of defense: that the secular power has no power over the church, although the church morally superintends the secular power; that the church alone is the interpreter of scripture; and that only a pope can summon a council and give it authority. The first line of defense is laid waste by Luther's insistence on the priesthood of all believers. Once the unique standing of the church is gone, then "benefit of clergy," the clergy's exemption from many of the usual legal restraints and duties, goes with it, and we have the simple view that in a community of Christians there is a division of labor but no division of authority. The second line of defense is plainly inconsistent with the thought that every man is to read the Bible for himself.

In spite of appearances, this does not mean that there is to be no church. Luther was radical in thought and conservative in temperament. He would happily have seen the pope forced to beg for his living in the highways and byways, and St. Peter's taken down and replaced by a simple country church. Nonetheless, when he offers twenty-seven proposals for things that the emperor or a council should do to reform the church, he expounds a vision of a church with a dozen cardinals, a tiny curia, and little infrastructure; he does not sweep away the entire apparatus. He does not even propose to abolish all monastic institutions, contenting himself with the admirably sensible advice that nobody should pledge himself to the celibate life before the age of thirty.

The church's third line of defense, the insistence that only a pope can call a council, is given an equally rough handling. This, says Luther, is the same thing as insisting that the pope is an earthly potentate, but unlike all others, one who is answerable to nobody. This was hardly a startling accusation, since popes had long claimed to govern by divine right. Luther's point is cleverer than that; the pope is his own confessor, judge of the faith, and the only judge of the rightness of his actions. Other rulers, however absolute, answer to God and their consciences, but the pope has absolved himself of that obligation. The point is simple and well taken. It is in fact two points, as emerges when Luther embarks on his twenty-seven propositions. The first is that any institution needs the means of its own reform, and both the history of the church and the exigencies of the case suggest councils as the only reliable means; the same history suggests that councils need the assistance of the secular authorities to succeed. The second is that it is preposterous for the papacy to hide behind its spiritual role to cover up the reality of its actions, namely, the extraction of funds from impoverished German parishes for ostentatious enterprises in Italy such as building St. Peter's. The church needs either complete decentralization, so that every priest is responsible to his own congregation, or devolution of authority to archbishops, so that hierarchy is minimized and people with the interests of their local church at heart can serve its needs.[8]

On Secular Authority

Luther followed up *An Address* some three years later with his only work expressly devoted to the question of the nature and extent of secular authority. It is not obvious why he wrote it; there was no immediate external provocation of the kind that explains his outbursts against "the murdering hordes of peasants" or his assaults on the "Romish pontiff." This may explain why it is markedly less polemical than most of his writing. Its lack of polemics is a matter of degree: Luther begins by observing that his *Address* had been intended to tell the German ruling elite its positive duty: what it should do. It had been a complete failure; the German princes were no better Christians and no more competent rulers than they had ever been. Now it was time to tell them what not to do, but doubtless that would have as little effect as anything else he wrote.[9] Heavy irony was one of Luther's stylistic trademarks, employed here in double measures.

Still, the line of thought Luther pursued makes eminently good sense, and one can see from the beginning both where the argument will lead and where it will run into difficulties. Luther starts from the radical claim that almost everyone has made a mistake about obedience. Princes think they are entitled to rule as they choose, and the plain man thinks he must obey them no matter what they command. The plain man's mistakes are more forgivable than his rulers' errors, since they are merely mistakes; the rulers' errors are grounded in hypocrisy. What Luther thought was clear: the local rulers of Germany justify their commands as "required by the emperor," as though absolute obedience was always due to the emperor. They do not mean it. Were the emperor to try to take possession of their land or occupy a castle or two, they would resist and make an end of the doctrine of absolute obedience. They also claim that their subjects owe them absolute obedience because they are the transmission belt between the authority of the emperor and the duties of the subject; but invoking the emperor and his authority is just an excuse for overtaxing their wretched subjects and subjecting them to the tyranny of the church. They get away with it because the common people believe that they must do whatever they are told by their rulers, and misunderstand both the gospels and their Christian duty.[10]

Luther does not doubt the need for secular authority; its emblem is the sword. The sword must be employed on behalf of earthly justice, but it is the executioner's sword rather than the judge's robes that is the true symbol of earthly authority. Saint Paul's words serve their usual purpose: the powers that be are ordained of God, to be a terror to the evildoer. Luther is fiercer than most; the sword is rightly employed not only by the agents of the law but by soldiers. Christians are not only to be obedient but to serve as enforcers. The rule that murderers are to be slain is coeval with Adam, was known to Cain, and reconfirmed by God after the flood. It is divinely commanded, and we must obey. Luther knew that recourse to the sword was thought by many radicals to be forbidden by Christ's injunction "resist not evil." How, then, can it be permissible to wield the sword to put down evil?[11]

Luther did not answer the conundrum head-on, but blunted the conflict by distinguishing first between Christians and non-Christians and then between the spiritual and secular law. True Christians, who are much scarcer than the presence of so many baptized people might suggest, have no need of secular law or the secular sword. They follow the paths of justice for righteousness' sake. This includes suffering evil *done to them alone* unresistingly, acting in obedience to the commandment to resist not evil. The unrighteous do what the law requires because they are coerced: "they need the law to teach, compel and urge them to act rightly."[12] However, we are all tempted to be unrighteous; so the law is rightly imposed on all. Really good men do not need it, but they are very few, and it would be absurd to prescribe for the many in the light of what is attainable only by the few. May Christians take part in making and enforcing the law, then? Certainly, says Luther. If there is a shortage of hangmen, court officers, judges, or police, a Christian who can do these jobs must offer his services. There would be mere chaos and bloodshed in the absence of law and its enforcement; the Christian owes it to his fellows to play his part in government and law enforcement with a good conscience. We should not look out for ourselves but serve others: "you satisfy the demands of God's kingdom and the world's at one and the same time, outwardly and inwardly; you both suffer evil and injustice and yet punish them; you do not resist evil and yet you do resist it."[13] As a piece of logic it is less than perfect, but it serves very well; a good man takes up the sword for the sake of others. It might be said that a society wholly composed of true Christians would be disabled even so, since the claim that we should take up the sword to protect other people is not wholly persuasive if those others are committed to nonresistance. That may be dismissed as a quibble, because in a society of true Christians, the occasion for nonresistance would never present itself, because nobody would offer violence to anyone else, and if the society were attacked from the outside, self-defense to teach the ungodly a lesson is permitted.

Luther is less eager to argue that government backed by brute force is essential if order is to be kept than to argue two further things: first, there is no place for coercion in matters of faith, and, second, we have no business following ungodly rulers even though we may not engage in rebellion against them. The view that there is no role for coercion in the spiritual life is defended on several grounds, but mostly with the division of labor argument of *An Address*, and the theology of *The Freedom of a Chris-*

tian. Within the one community, secular law and order is maintained by providing simple external incentives—such as the desire not to be executed—which restrain the unrighteous and remind the righteous of the existence of sin and its punishment. The spiritual law, and Luther is not comfortable with the idea that it is law at all, works in the heart by faith; it is God's business whether we are obedient to his law, and God (alone) sees into our hearts.

The secular authorities have no business trying to make us believe anything in particular; all they can exact is hypocritical expressions of what we do or more probably do not believe. This is close to the view that Hobbes later expressed, which suggests that it is not in itself a defense of toleration. Locke's argument that toleration requires a state to allow people to worship as they choose, publicly, and in the company of fellow believers, needs more than the observation that secular power can secure only an outward conformity. The state may want only an outward conformity; Hobbes considered it enough. Like Luther, Hobbes thought governments wasted their time trying to see into the hearts of their subjects; but he also thought that, for the sake of peace, governments must regulate what people publicly affirmed on contentious issues, and dictate the forms of public worship. For Hobbes's purposes, outward conformity sufficed, because the object was to stop dissension that would inevitably lead to violence, not to hinder thought. In the early 1520s Luther was unafraid of dissension, because he thought religious argument could be conducted without violence; so he swept straight past Hobbes's stopping point. In 1523 he still held that heresy was not to be repressed by force. "Here God's Word must strive; if that does not accomplish the end, it will remain unaccomplished through secular power, though it fill the world with blood."[14] The larger importance of Luther's argument is that here he holds diametrically un-Augustinian views. Augustine stood firm on *compelle intrare*—we should go into the highways and byways and compel them to come in, that is, to join the true church. Luther ordinarily followed Augustine; here he did not.

An Address was directed to Christian princes, but the Christian prince will be, as Luther says, "a very rare bird." What he will do, and how he will be animated, is not difficult to describe. His life will be one of service and of love, not an insistence on his power and authority. His people will not be his people as if they were his property to do with as he pleases, but his to serve. Such a ruler would, says Luther, not be begrudged his dances and his hunts and his games by God or his subjects; in any case, he would be too busy to have much time for diversion, since the welfare of his subjects would demand all his time and attention. Given the rarity of such birds, Luther turns to the awkward topic of our duty to obey the wicked. Where they do what is right, we must follow them for the sake of the right; where they do wrong, we must refuse to assist them. If they require us to deliver up a copy of Luther's New Testament that we have in the house, we must refuse; if they come into our house and seize it, we must not resist.[15] By the same token, rulers must not follow wicked superiors into wicked courses, but must not resist when those superiors behave badly toward them. It is an awkward resting place.

Luther's role in German politics thereafter was considerable, but mostly not in ways that impact on the history of political thinking. Luther's tirades against the "murdering hordes of peasants" do not amount to a theoretical explanation of why religious radicalism must not be pushed to an extreme. Rather, he believed from the outset that the peasant wars sprang from the disobedient lower classes hoping to profit from unrest; he may also have been troubled by the fact that an essentially anarchic movement claimed to have been inspired by him. "Let whoever can, stab, smite, slay. If you die in doing it, good for you! . . . If anyone thinks this too harsh, let him remember that rebellion is intolerable and that the destruction of the world is to be expected every hour."[16] Subsequently, in "An Open Letter on the Harsh Book against the Peasants," he did something to lessen the offense he had given by emphasizing that it was only active and obdurate rebels he had written against; but he promptly went on to insist that the tract against the peasants had been entirely right, and that whether the ruler of the state was Christian, Jew, Turk, or pagan made no difference. The secular sword was to be wielded to preserve order, and it was everyone's duty to aid its wielder.[17] He was evenhanded in his denunciations; his "Open Letter" ends with the story of a German noble attempting to rape the pregnant widow of Thomas Müntzer, and although he was ferociously critical of Müntzer, Luther relishes the thought of the would-be rapist burning in hell for all eternity. Although his rhetoric is violent in the extreme, his hatred of physical violence and his fear of disorder were genuine; argument was one thing, fighting another. Religious dissension was a sign of vitality, but permissible only if we could argue without fighting. Tongues might wag, but the fist must remain unclenched. Many of his works make no great contribution to political thinking, among them his denunciations of the Jews; they do not even illuminate the lamentable history of anti-Semitism, other than to demonstrate that a change of confessional allegiance did not improve Christian attitudes toward the Jews, while his views on usury showed only that theological inventiveness does not guarantee economic insight.

The Theory of Resistance

The one point on which Luther changed his mind significantly and influentially was on nonresistance. His use of the orthodox Pauline doctrine was initially at the extreme end of the spectrum; passive disobedience is all we are permitted. Indeed, we are not only permitted but obliged to engage in passive disobedience, since otherwise we would be aiding the unrighteous in their wickedness, and this was as unjust as resisting them. Luther's twentieth-century critics have complained that he undermined the possibility of a liberal Germany by so emphasizing the absolute wickedness of rebellion; a less passive attitude toward the powers that be would have helped prevent the rise of Hitler and assured a more spirited resistance to his rule. Given the enormous number of other explanations for German subservience to authority and the lack of resistance to the Nazi regime, a decent skepticism vis-à-vis Luther's responsibility for the horrors of the twentieth century is in order. Nonetheless, attending to the situation of sixteenth-century Germany alone, we might think that Luther's adherence to Augustine's views about nonresistance was ill judged by the late 1520s.

It became apparent in 1529–30 that adherence to a literal reading of Luther's doctrine of nonresistance might require the Protestant princes to face their Catholic enemies with their hands tied behind their backs. Charles V never reconciled himself to a Germany divided between Catholics and Evangelicals, but until the end of the decade of the 1520s he was embroiled elsewhere and could not devote himself to enforcing doctrinal and political unity. When it became clear that he proposed to return all of Germany to the Catholic Church, by brute force if need be, Luther's protector, the elector John of Saxony, asked Luther whether resistance to the emperor was lawful. Other Evangelicals had argued that it was; and Luther was not a believer in nonviolence. He had argued that good Christians should fight for their prince against foreign opponents and rebels, even if their prince was a Turk. But Charles V was not a foreign prince, even if he had until this moment been more concerned with his Spanish possessions and his French rivals in Italy than with Germany. Luther and his allies were hampered by several factors. Having declared the church to be only a congregation of the faithful, they had no institutional forum that could formally declare a ruler a tyrant and depose him. This was the effect of giving away one of Gelasius's two swords; if nobody held the spiritual sword, nobody could declare a king deposed *ratione peccati*. The Protestants were also hampered by their contempt for the traditions of natural and canon law, which provided ample jurisprudential arguments for the claim that Charles had become a tyrant and forfeited his authority. It was equally impossible for them to go back to Cicero's defense of tyrannicide, although Philipp Melanchthon wrote a commentary on Cicero's *De officiis* and held ideas about resistance to tyrants much more in line with traditional constitutionalist thinking than Luther's.

The emperor's opponents certainly could not renounce self-defense. Various views were canvassed. The most persuasive was that if the emperor attacked his Evangelical subjects, he was violating the law, and they would be upholding it in resisting him. This constitutionalist position had a good pedigree and is very like Locke's subsequent justification of revolution as the act of a people defending its constitution against a tyrannical ruler. There were many ways of reaching that result, and it is evidence of the depth of Luther's discomfort with any loosening of the bonds of obedience that the one he preferred relied so heavily on the claim—implausible as it might seem—that the *positive law* of the empire required the princes to resist notorious injustice. A modern reader might have difficulty seeing how this could save the day, since an emperor might hold himself to be *legibus solutus*, above the law and able to override positive law when it seemed good to him. Nor does it sit easily with the modern mind to combine the thought that earthly monarchs have been given absolute authority by God with the thought that it can be constitutionally limited. These were tensions that the late medieval mind had resources for handling. A properly constituted secular authority shared God's absolute authority, even if its constitution meant that the authority of the earthly ruler operated within stated limits. The constitution in its entirety bound prince and subject alike *jure divino*. One might resist unlawful authority in the name of lawful authority.

Once the door to a theory of resistance had been opened by the thought that imperial authority in general required disobedience to a particular holder of imperial authority, Luther could employ arguments that had a long history and would be much employed in future. Thus, a ruler who uses unjust force has ceased to be a ruler and is in the position of a private person who is attacking us; nobody doubts that a private person can be resisted on grounds of self-defense, and a ruler who has, morally speaking, abdicated by violating his trust is a private person. This is where the hoary example of the lawfulness of a private citizen killing the consul whom he finds in bed with his wife belongs. Mostly, Luther accepted the constitutionalist claim that if the emperor was the aggressor, he was in rebellion against the lawful order and might lawfully be resisted. What he was terrified of, and others to varying degrees were less fearful of, was any doctrine that gave a right of resistance to individual subjects. This is where comparisons with Locke and later constitutionalists collapse; the Lockean right of resistance inheres in "the people," who must use their best judgment about when the time for resistance has arrived; but Locke ignores the question of who is entitled to speak for the people. In rebelling on good grounds, each of us represents all of us.[18]

Luther confined the right to resist to "inferior magistrates," to those who ordinarily had authority under the law to make decisions with the force of law; in this context, that meant the princes of the empire. Most thinkers after Luther similarly confined the right to resist a ruler to a recognized body, if not to the "inferior magistrates" that the constitution of the Holy Roman Empire suggested, then to a body such as the Estates General in France, or the governing councils of Swiss city republics such as Zurich or Geneva. Nonetheless, however cautious Luther's response, and however driven by the needs of the moment, it inspired both an ideological change and a change of tone. A movement toward a more overtly constitutionalist view of politics took place, within which a much more nuanced view of authority and resistance to authority became possible. The Catholic view continued to be that the pope was an absolute monarch, holding the authority of the Roman emperor described in Justinian's *Digest*; but a countercurrent even within the church relied on the old legal tag *nemo dat quod non habet*—nobody can give what he has not himself possessed—"the people" could not give the right to exercise unresisted power to anyone, because they had never had such a right in the first place.

Even if all authority was held on terms, the avoidance of chaos required that any discussion of the question whether there had been a breach of those terms must be confined to the right body under the right conditions—perhaps a council of the church, perhaps the Estates General. In the German context, the issue was simpler. The electors of the emperor might well think they had elected the emperor on terms; if those terms were violated, the election was invalidated. The emperor Wenceslaus was deposed by the electors in 1400 on just those grounds; they elected him to keep the peace and preserve the unity of the empire, and he had failed hopelessly to do what he was pledged to do.

Luther died in 1546. He died when Protestantism most needed a political theory to sustain it as a church militant, and his death coincided with a counterattack on Protestantism that nearly erased it in its German heartlands. From 1543 Charles V had been assembling forces to confront the so-called Schmalkaldic League of Protestant German states; in 1546 he provoked them to armed conflict and in April 1547 crushed them at the Battle of Mühlberg. Their leaders, the electors John of Saxony and Philip of Hesse, were captured and kept in prison for the next five years. In 1548 Charles outlawed Lutheranism throughout the empire, sowing the seeds of the Thirty Years' War, which ravaged Germany in the next century. Five years later the Reformation was under threat in England, where Charles's daughter-in-law, the Catholic Queen Mary secured her place in history as "Bloody Mary" by approving the death by fire of over three hundred of her Protestant subjects. Before that, the French had assisted Catholic Scots to turn back the Protestant tide, and in France itself, Francis I abandoned his temporizing policies in favor of persecution in the late 1530s, and the persecution was intensified under his successor, Henry II. By the end of the 1550s, France was in the throes of religious civil war. If Mary Tudor had not been succeeded by her younger sister Elizabeth in 1558, no major European state would have been safe for the reformed churches. Switzerland was a different matter. It experienced much violence, but both Zurich and Geneva, self-governing cities with extensive rural hinterlands, were solidly if not securely Protestant, and they generated much of what we have come to think of as Protestant political thinking.

Jean Calvin

Protestants under attack could not fold their hands and await martyrdom, but their attachment to a Pauline theory of authority was a handicap in articulating a right of resistance. No more than their Catholic opponents and predecessors did they find it easy to convert their account of the distinction between spiritual and secular authority into an argument for the legitimacy of resistance. It was easy to argue, as Luther had, that the church as such wielded no coercive authority; but that gave the secular authorities in Catholic states a free hand in putting down their Protestant enemies. Passive disobedience would not secure the Protestant future from determined rulers who did not mind how many heretics they sent to the stake. It is often said that Calvin went further than Luther in providing a theory of resistance that would meet the exigencies of the situation. This contains some but not the whole truth. Calvin was a second-generation Protestant. He was born in 1509, by which time Luther was suffering agonies of doubt in Wittenberg. Like Luther, he was

intended for the law by his father, but on the death of his father he abandoned the law for the life of a scholar. His opinions made France dangerous, and he went first to Basel, then in 1536 to Geneva, and after a period
of exile, back to Geneva in 1541, where he remained for the last twenty-
three years of his life. Geneva was a republic ruled by a city council, and
that provided a context in which Calvin could reach beyond Luther.

Calvin has been praised as a political thinker, but his political views
occupy only the last section of his *Institutes of the Christian Religion*; and this
suggests the limited place of politics in his wider concerns. Calvin was no
more eager than Luther to open the door to popular uprisings. Unlike
Luther, he was actively involved in legislating for a city republic. Like
Luther, he starts his discussion of the two governments that mankind
is under by insisting that the freedom of the Christian is not a license
to dispense with all laws and remodel all institutions; civil government
is instituted by God and demands the allegiance of Christians. More
straightforwardly than Luther, he insists that the first obligation of civil
government is the duty to "foster and protect the external worship of
God, defend pure doctrine and the good condition of the Church."[19] This
accommodates the fact that churches are institutions; and it articulates
what Luther took for granted, that the local state must look after the
local church. The central point is Luther's: a Christian may not ignore
the demands of secular government. If the kingdom of God were already
on earth, there would be no need of civil government; but here below we
are, as Augustine said, *pellegrini*, pilgrims on a journey toward that ultimate
destination; while we are here, we need civil government for our peace and
tranquillity; but we also need it to lead us toward righteousness.

Calvin's discussion of the two kingdoms to which we owe allegiance
does not imply the separation of church and state. Nor did Calvin have
in mind the easygoing approach of ancient Rome in welcoming the gods
of its defeated subjects into the city. The church must have its mode
of worship fixed by the state, individuals must be compelled to attend
services, and the pastors of the church must judge the citizens' morals.
Calvin was living in Geneva, and safe from the Catholic reaction, so he
was fighting enemies on his radical, antinomian flank, not Catholics:
there was to be no turning the world upside down, and no retreat into a

hermetic existence. Orthodoxy in matters of faith was to be preserved. Notoriously, he had Michael Servetus burned as a heretic at the gates of Geneva because Servetus denied the doctrine of the Trinity. Nonetheless, Calvin was politically innovative in linking the concerns of an early modern constitutional lawyer with those of a theorist of the polis.

He imagined a political community that not only exhibited the top-down legislative and coercive capacity that constitutes the essence of the state in all modern analyses but also conferred authority on a recognized body of intermediate magistrates. His inspiration seems to have been the Spartan constitution, in a form modified by what Ulrich Zwingli had achieved in Zurich during his brief and tumultuous rule. Zwingli was more important to political practice because of his posthumous influence on the England of Elizabeth I than for his achievements in Zurich, but Zurich displayed the political possibilities of reformation theology beyond anything Luther had seen. Born in 1484, Zwingli was a devout Catholic until 1518; but when he became a pastor in Zurich, he experienced a conversion to Luther's view that the Gospels were all-sufficient. Until his death he epitomized the church militant. He led reform in Zurich and united in his own hands the governance of both church and state. He was literally an iconoclast: the physical purification of churches was the order of the day; paintings and organs were evicted from the local churches, though Zwingli was an accomplished musician and an accomplished Greek scholar who corresponded with Erasmus. In 1529 he and Luther conducted an inconclusive disputation over the Eucharist, with Zwingli taking the radical view that the sacrament was a commemoration of the Crucifixion and that no transformation of the bread into the body of Christ took place; Luther believed in consubstantiation. Zwingli's downfall was the result of the energy that had taken him so far; he urged the expulsion of Catholicism from the other Swiss cantons, if necessary by force. This was taken as a declaration of war by Zurich's neighbors. The result was war in 1531 and Zwingli's death in battle.

His impact on Protestant theology and political practice was considerable. Like Luther, he unloosed radical forces to his "left" that he could not easily control. Unlike Luther, he was unflinching in his belief that the church must employ the coercive force of the state to maintain doctrinal and political unity. He had no problem accepting *compelle intrare*. In Zurich he unhesitatingly persecuted Anabaptists. The fundamental tenet of Anabaptism was the wrongness of infant baptism: absent a full understanding of the purpose of the rite by the person baptized, baptism must be ineffacious. Debating the Anabaptists was an ungrateful business, because there is no scriptural warrant for infant baptism, and Zwingli fell back on physical coercion. He had the leaders of the Zurich Anabaptists drowned, relishing the unkind joke implicit in the manner of their death. This uncompromising understanding of the unity of church and state was transmitted to Elizabeth's England by Zwingli's follower Heinrich Bullinger; the death toll among Catholics in England was the highest in Europe.

Violence aside, the Protestant understanding of authority had been transformed in ways that came naturally to anyone with classical republican models in mind. Zwingli imagined classical republican government revived within a religiously purified city. Classical republics never contemplated the idea that the secular magistrate would ignore the religious practices of his people, and Zwingli's vision of a devout republic did not embrace the separation of church and state. It did allow everyone to think of orderly and constitutional ways to avert tyranny. That allowed the emergence of the view for which Calvin is famous, that it was the business of a middle layer of constituted authorities to ensure that the government did not become tyrannical. This opened new possibilities. For, if the authority of even a king was held conditionally, nobody was *legibus solutus*, and "inferior magistrates" could provide a mechanism for pronouncing that a ruler had gone too far, had become a tyrant, and was de jure no longer the ruler.

The point was this. To rely on the thought that a ruler who acts outside the bounds of his office was simply a private person and might be treated like any other private person was all very well when applied to the example of the adulterous consul. The majesty of rulers was the majesty of the office; committing adultery was not part of the office. The difficulty is obvious. A policy of religious persecution is ultra vires, if it is so, not because it is a sin committed in a private capacity. It is an assault on the people, not on an individual; or to put the matter the other way around, if individuals treated policies they deplored as private offenses in the way the ancient example imagines, anyone might think himself entitled to assassinate just about any ruler whatever. And although Calvin provides an account of legitimate resistance, he consistently repeated Augustine's and Luther's message that we must put up with bad rulers in accordance with the Pauline injunction.

Calvin set all this out in a tripartite discussion of civil government: the nature and purpose of law, the role of magistrates, and the duties of the people. However magistrates may be chosen, they are accountable to God; they must always bear in mind that they will be required to render an account of their conduct in the hereafter and should conduct themselves accordingly. He gives a very slight account of the virtues of different forms of government, but sufficient for his purpose: which is to insist that even if mixed governments are best, since kingship may become tyranny and democracy turn seditious and the balance the Spartans struck is attractive, it is not the business of private men to debate forms of government but to live peaceably under the regime it has pleased God to institute for them.

So the argument proceeds almost until the very end. Whenever the private citizen asks whether it is really necessary to put up with whatever our rulers inflict on us, the reply is that we must. The consolations for following this advice are few beyond the assurance that God uses wicked men as his unwitting tools for ends beyond their imagining. Then Calvin changes gear. Having insisted yet again, "Even if the punishment of unbridled tyranny is the Lord's vengeance, we are not to imagine that it is we ourselves who have been called upon to inflict it. All that has been assigned to us is to obey and suffer," he goes on to say, "Here as always, I am speaking about private persons." If magistrates have been appointed to restrain the willfulness of kings, as were the ephors of Sparta, the demarchs of Athens, and as "perhaps" the three estates are when they assemble as the Estates General, they are not merely permitted to restrain tyrants but would commit a grave sin if they omitted to do so.[20] In the Calvinist moral and political universe, little is permitted that is not also required, and this is not one of those cases. It was left to later Calvinists to unite the constitutional theory of resistance to which

Calvin had opened the door with the contractualism that implied that "private persons" could decide that a ruler had violated his trust and had lost his authority. When they did, they created the modern, liberal theory of revolution. To reach that point, one necessity was the conviction that "most men," as Locke put it, were too slow to rebel rather than too quick. That thought never occurred to Luther or Calvin; the evidence of the times was against it.

The Radicals

A reason for the fear of chaos alluded to throughout this chapter was the presence of what one might call the extreme wing of Protestantism, namely Anabaptism. A detailed account of the political ideas of the Anabaptists in all their variety is impossible in this short compass, and perhaps impossible *tout court*; the most notable characteristic of Anabaptism *after* the Peasants' War of 1524–26, and the Münster uprising of 1534 when Anabaptists were embroiled in violent insurrection, is that it became a pacifist and apolitical creed. Even in the few decades when Anabaptists had been ready to fight, they would do so only on their own terms and for their own reasons. They were the targets of Luther's and Calvin's denunciation of Christians who will not serve the state. When they were willing to fight, they fought to the death, usually their own.

The interest of their views is twofold. First, it is clear that what provoked the Peasants' War was economic distress. It was not a political revolution, but an insurrection provoked by economic distress. Whose economic distress mattered most is hard to say, since Germany had become a kaleidoscope of states and statelets with a great diversity of local political arrangements, and economic tensions existed between town and country, within towns, and between peasants and their landlords. Peasants wanting relief from oppressive landlords certainly provided the bulk of those who fought, and were killed in very large numbers. It was said that 300,000 rebels had taken part and that, by the time the imperial armies had suppressed the rebellion, 100,000 had been killed. The religious demands of the rebels caused as much offense as their economic demands, in particular, their demand for a reduction of tithes and a say in the choice of their own pastors. Second, it was Luther who much against his will gave the Peasants' War its character. Without a Lutheran Reformation, it is very likely that there would have been an insurrection in 1524–26; peasant revolts had been a feature of German life for a century. But the tensions between the Catholic and Evangelical princes of the empire suggested that some princes might side with the rebels, and undermine the unity of the empire. Because the religious demands of the rebels were Lutheran, he was widely thought to have instigated the revolt. That partly explains the ferocity of his attack on the rebels, just as Luther's contempt for the Anabaptists underlay the ferocity of Thomas Müntzer's attacks on Luther.

Müntzer was contemptuous of conventional politics, but his views had profound political implications. The chief characteristic of the radical reformers—as distinct from the "magistral" reformers, Luther, Zwingli, and Calvin—was their reliance on the spiritual sense of the community as the basis of authority. In such unsettled times, this was not likely to yield unanimity, but to the extent that the radical Protestants had any view of political authority, it was a theory of popular sovereignty. The authority of the godly prince was drawn from the community, not from divine institution; Müntzer held an uninhibitedly ascending theory of authority. Like Luther, Müntzer began by hoping that godly princes would reform the church; unlike Luther, he believed that he was living in the "last days" and that the reform of the church was not only a Reformation but the prefiguring of an apocalyptic transformation. Once millenarianism was added to the rejection of the sacraments, the ingredients for upheaval were in place.

Initially, Müntzer's radicalism did not imply violent insurrection. His followers' violence took the form of popular iconoclasm: direct action to smash statues and destroy stained glass, shouting down unpopular ministers, and instituting a very austere Lord's Supper in place of the traditional Mass. Müntzer was operating in the dark, but the political authorities saw where violence, even when ostensibly directed only against buildings and objects, might lead, and they tried to expel the religious extremists. The Anabaptists abandoned the churches and met in private houses, which gave the authorities further grounds for suspicion, and also allowed increasingly extreme views, economic and political as well as religious, to gain ground among the Anabaptists. Müntzer and his followers claimed that the violence to which they eventually resorted was more than justified self-defense, but they can hardly have expected anything other than the repression they encountered.

Events unrolled too fast and chaotically to allow any of the protagonists to develop a coherent vision of what the godly community's political arrangements should be. To the extent that they did so in the months after the military destruction of the peasants' insurrection in May 1525, they focused on the need to institute a simple republican constitution. It was politically radical in that the nobility was denied a hereditary right to govern, and economically radical in that a nobility with no political role had no right to impose taxes. It did not propose the equalization of property; the old church would be expropriated, but no lay person's property would be touched. The claim that the radicals were hell-bent on communism, free love, and the end of all authority came from the hysterical imagining of their opponents, or deliberately mendacious propaganda. Nonetheless, they were utopians and millenarians, believing that the communities they would institute prefigured the Second Coming and the end of days. After the defeat, the radicals did two things; they agreed on their common beliefs in the so-called Schleitheim Articles, and they divided on tactics.

They agreed that their kingdom was not of this world and that the true Christian must separate himself from the world. Müntzer's hopes for the establishment of more or less anarchic godly communities were given up in the face of reality, and the Schleitheim Articles provided some minimal guidelines for the organization of a church that could survive repression. Their fears were well founded: it was made a capital offense throughout the empire to preach or practice adult baptism—the central element in Anabaptism. The wing led by Michael Sattler, who drew up the Schleitheim Articles, espoused radical pacifism, exhorting their followers to refuse military service and political office and to live as strangers to the political and judicial arrangements of the society in which they found themselves. This was not what governments looking for conscripts for their armed forces would tolerate. Sattler's views look like a recipe for head-on conflict with the authorities, but by setting out the possibility of living a spiritual life in secret, they offered the prospect that Anabaptists might secure their existence as a saving remnant with no prospect of converting others. A family might transmit the faith generation by generation to its descendants, but scarcely anyone else.

The other wing, following Balthasar Hubmaier, turned back to the Lutheran theory of authority but continued to subscribe to the quietism that Luther eventually rejected. Its members agreed that Anabaptists could hold office and wield the sword, since godly rulers needed assistance and it was right to give it. Where the ruler was ungodly, they must simply endure. Taking up arms against an appointed ruler was at one with taking up arms against God. Hubmaier's position provided the basis of a peace treaty with the authorities; its appeal to Anabaptists was that they could live openly *if* they could find a prince who would tolerate them. The drawback, as many devout and harmless people discovered in the next two centuries, was that princes were prone to change their religious allegiances, and tolerant fathers were prone to leave fanatical sons who gave their dissenting subjects the choice between death and exile.

The famous epilogue to the radicalism of the 1520s was the short-lived reign of terror that John of Leiden and Bernhard Knipperdolling instituted in Münster in 1534–35. To hang these events on Anabaptism is wholly unfair, but the enemies of the Anabaptists succeeded in doing so. What happened in Münster has been much examined. During the 1950s the madness that seized the city was thought by sociologists to provide deep insights into the making of revolutions in the twentieth century.[21] Half a century later, it seems to belong more firmly to a category sui generis of events such as the mass suicide at Jonestown in Guiana, where an apocalyptic sect followed its leader's commands to the point of killing themselves and their children with a soft drink laced with cyanide. Münster was an imperial city in Westphalia, ruled by a prince-bishop with whom the inhabitants got on badly. It turned Lutheran in the early 1530s, at much the same time that a group of itinerant messianic preachers who had been expelled from Strassburg and then from the Netherlands were looking for converts.

In January 1534 Bernhard Knipperdolling went over to these Mel-chiorite missionaries, and with Jan Matthys and Jan Bockelson—John of Leiden—set out to turn Münster into their vision of the New Jeru-salem. The Catholic prince-bishop besieged the city, assisted by Philip of Hesse, who was a Lutheran but who could recognize anarchy when he saw it. Within the besieged city, mayhem ruled; Matthys got him-self killed by leading a sortie against the besiegers in response to what he took to be the direct tactical instructions of God; John of Leiden took over and eventually proclaimed himself king. Here for once, the stories about polygamy and communism became true; John took two dozen wives, arrayed himself in fine robes, and played out an Old Tes-tament drama as the population gradually starved to death under the siege. Astonishingly, the defenders held out to the bitter end; they drove back the besieging forces in August 1534, and although local uprisings elsewhere failed to take the pressure off them, it was only in June 1535 that the city fell. Even then, it fell to betrayal. The inhabitants were massacred, men, women, and children alike; Knipperdolling and John of Leiden were tortured to death, and the authorities hunted down every-one who could be suspected of complicity in the uprising. The events had a sobering effect on the purveyors of apocalyptic visions that lasted a long time—though the man who began the whole business, Melchior Hoffman, survived it all. He had been thrown in jail in Strassburg, and remained there until he died a decade later.

CHAPTER 11

Machiavelli

Life and Times; the Political Context

MACHIAVELLI WAS BORN IN 1469 and died in 1527. His father was a notary, which tells us little more than that Machiavelli's father was literate, since there were more notaries in Renaissance Italy than available legal work required. A notary of low social standing might earn most of his living as a farmer or artisan. An upper-class notary would probably employ his legal skills in the affairs of his friends and allies, and perhaps in the political arena. One thing it tells us is that he had the humanist education that was a prelude to an education in law; it provided a training in eloquent and persuasive writing and in making suitable speeches to a court or a committee that Cicero, and the Sophists before him, had identified as crucial for the politician and the lawyer.

Little is known about Machiavelli's life before 1498, when he became second chancellor of the Florentine Republic that had been established after the overthrow of Savonarola. This was a "civil service" post. As in classical Athens, political office in the Florentine Republic was held on a brief tenure, and officeholders were either elected or chosen by lot. Without a permanent skilled bureaucracy, Florence would have been ungovernable; Machiavelli was part of that bureaucracy. A month later he was appointed secretary to the Ten of War, the committee that supervised foreign relations and military preparedness. He spent much of the next fourteen years on diplomatic missions to the papal court, to the court of Louis XII in France, and to the court of Emperor Maximilian. Because Florence was friendly to France, it took delicate maneuvering to retain the friendship of the French without incurring the hostility of the empire—to hunt with the Valois without being hounded by the Habsburgs.

In the course of these missions, Machiavelli spent a lot of time with Cesare Borgia in the Romagna and with Pope Julius II, the most war-like of Renaissance popes, whose financial exactions were one of the provocations of Luther's campaign of church reform. The stories that give piquancy to Machiavelli's advice in *The Prince* and the *Discourses on Livy* are often prefigured in his lively correspondence with his masters in Florence. One of Machiavelli's less remembered but important achievements as secretary of the Ten of War was the institution of a Florentine militia recruited from the *contado*, the countryside around Florence. He was hostile to mercenary troops, who, as he pointed out, would desert to the enemy for higher pay if the enemy could offer it, or else subvert the government of their employers. It was an innovation to treat the *contadini* as fit material for warfare; the right to bear arms had been confined to the *cittadini*, the citizen body of Florence itself. Florence's forces were no more of a match for the armies of France or the empire than those of any other Italian state of the day, but Machiavelli's reforms provided an effective militia for local hostilities. The army he created brought the interminable war with Pisa to a successful conclusion.

Machiavelli was not a great figure in the Florentine Republic, but he was well-known, and he took pleasure in doing an impossible job well. He also took pleasure in the fact that his intellect, wit, and erudition made him welcome in upper-class circles from which his origins would otherwise have excluded him. His career, but not these friendships, came to an end in 1512 when Florence's delicate balancing act between papacy, France, and empire proved impossible to sustain, and the republic surrendered to the forces of Ferdinand, the king of Spain, dedicatee of Erasmus's *Panegyric* and predecessor of the emperor Charles V. The Medici were installed as de facto hereditary dukes—though the title was not conferred for another thirty years, and republican forms were initially preserved. Machiavelli was immediately dismissed; it is not clear why, since many colleagues kept their posts, but he was closely associated with Piero Soderini, the foremost spirit of the republic, and Machiavelli's leading role in missions that would ordinarily have been entrusted to aristocrats rather than to bureaucrats reflected Soderini's confidence in him. Six months later an abortive plot to assassinate the new rulers was uncovered, and Machiavelli's name was found on a scrap of paper belonging to a conspirator. Arrested on suspicion, he was tortured and jailed, but his innocence was obvious, and he was released a few weeks later.

For the rest of his life, he lived on his farm at Percussina, seven miles from the city, writing and dreaming of a return to public life. Although he was married and had six children, he pined for the excitement of politics. Attempts to find employment with the Medici in Florence or Rome came to nothing, but he secured some writing commissions, and by the time he died was sufficiently in everyone's good graces to be buried in Santa Croce. Nonetheless, only his treatise on the creation and training of a militia, the *Arte della guerra*, was published in his lifetime. *The Prince* was written at breakneck speed in the last six months of 1513, after his release from prison, but published only in 1532. It was the first work to be put on the *Index auctorum et librorum prohibitorum* when that instrument of compulsory intellectual hygiene for adherents of the Catholic faith was created in 1559 by the pope and made permanent in 1564 by the Council of Trent; it was not removed from the Index until the twentieth century and was for many years thought to be so subversive that anyone wishing to read it for purposes of refutation had to ask permission of the pope. Permission was usually refused.

In this enforced retirement, Machiavelli remained a member of the group that met in the gardens of the Rucellai family palazzo in Florence. The *Discourses* was probably written at the request of Cosimo Rucellai, to whom it is dedicated. Like Cicero, Machiavelli thought writing a poor second best to playing an active part in politics; his famous account of the way he would settle down to write by dressing in his state robes and retiring to his study to commune with the immortal dead has a melancholy air. "For four hours I experience no boredom, I forget all my troubles and my fear of poverty, and death holds no more terrors for me."[1] It makes a great difference to what he wrote and how we should read it that Machiavelli was writing practically oriented books. They had to appeal to their dedicatee—*The Prince* was a failed job application—but they bore on one crucial question: how Florence and similar city-states could be governed. Machiavelli's answer was that everything depended on the circumstances. If it were possible to reinstate the Roman Republic, it should be done; if, as seems probable, it is not, we can only hope that a true master of the skills that enable a man to gain power and keep it will arise and establish order. This is not very distant from Bartolus's argument that tyranny may be a necessity in extreme conditions.

The Unplaceability of Machiavelli

Machiavelli has always been an elusive thinker because he was much more (and less) than a "political theorist." This is not because he longed to be active in politics; Cicero is far from unplaceable. It is because he had an astonishing impact on how Europe talked and wrote about politics after his death. Whether he made any impact on the way European politicians acted, as distinct from providing them with a target to criticize for their own hypocritical ends, is unanswerable. Frederick the Great, tongue in cheek, suggested that any ruler who was about to launch an unprovoked attack on his neighbors should first attack Machiavelli. Machiavelli's impact on political rhetoric is undeniable. "Hobbesian" is a term of art familiar to political theorists and political scientists; "Machiavellian" needs no explanation. Whereas "Hobbesian" or "Platonic" carry few pejorative overtones, "Machiavellian" is not a neutral term. The "murderous Machiavel" was a stock figure in Elizabethan drama; and high-minded denunciations of Machiavellianism are to this day part of the standard repertoire of duplicitous politicians who have never read a sentence of his work. On one occasion, President Eisenhower denounced what he took to be Machiavelli's doctrine that "the end justifies the means" without explaining just what might justify the means other than the end.

The popular image of Machiavelli as the "teacher of evil," who praised deceit and violence for their own sake is not the whole truth; most commentators think it is no part of the truth, and few scholars think it is much of the truth. Machiavelli outraged opinion because he took pains to insist that political success demands morally obnoxious acts from anyone seriously engaged in politics. This was not news; it was the lesson the Athenians taught the inhabitants of Melos. It was, however, denied by Stoicism, which was committed to the doctrine that there could be no ultimate conflict between justice and expediency, between the *honestum* and the *utile*.[2] Common sense and everyday political practice in Renaissance Italy suggested that whatever might be true once we take our fate in the hereafter into account, virtue and effectiveness were all too visibly at odds here and now. Our rulers are moved by "reason of state," which is to say the need minimally to "keep the show on the road," and where possible to maximize the state's capacity to enforce order internally and to compete effectively on the international stage. Nonetheless, the readiness to say that political success demanded an unflinching willingness to violate every moral precept appropriate to private life as sharply as Machiavelli did was novel in Christian Europe. Even more unnerving was his seeming uninterest in seeking a justification beyond political success; combating the thought that Romulus's murder of his twin, Remus, was an evil act, he admits that homicide is ordinarily a bad thing and goes on to say that once a city is founded, the freedom to commit such homicides should be denied our rulers. As to Romulus, the result justified the action. Still, "if the means accuse, the end must excuse" is not exactly a moral justification.[3]

Machiavelli's insistence on the tension between the demands of morality and the demands of political practice is more than plausible, but it is unnerving because he left that tension so visibly unresolved. What he intended his readers to feel about it is obscure. It is possible that Machiavelli suffered no more anguish about the tension between the demands of morality and the demands of *raison d'état* than did the Athenians threatening the Melians with massacre, and that he was concerned only to remind his readers of what they knew in their hearts: turning the other cheek may gain the kingdom of heaven but is likely to lose an earthly kingdom. He certainly thought that his fellow Florentines were much too willing to think they were under the peculiar protection of God, and were therefore lackadaisical about their political and military affairs. A sharp reminder of the conflict between Christian virtue and political common sense was what they needed, if not what they wanted.

More than most thinkers, Machiavelli suffers if taken too much out of context. The works we read today—*The Prince* and *Discourses on Livy*— were written to help their author realize his ambition to play a role in Florentine politics, preferably under a republic, but failing that, in any regime that would employ him. Unattractive though the advice offered in *The Prince* may be, Machiavelli's advice to a "new prince" who must stamp his authority on a republic that had prized its liberty had an obvious relevance to the restored Medici family, reinserted by a foreign army in the city that had expelled them eighteen years before.[4] The *Discourses* was written when the Medici were again unpopular, and although Machiavelli died before the short-lived restoration of the republic in 1527–30, a treatise on how the Roman Republic had gained and kept its liberty had obvious resonance. The question whether a state that has once been corrupted can regain its liberty, which preoccupies both works, has an obvious relevance both to the republics of 1494 and 1498 and to the republic of 1527–30. Most of Machiavelli's other works were written to order; *Mandragola*, his louche little play on the theme of foolish husbands, ingenious adulterers, and corrupt friars, was commissioned by Francesco Guicciardini when he was governing Modena on behalf of Leo X; Guicciardini had been Machiavelli's superior in Florence, and managed the transition to a new employer more successfully than he, though not without some personal risk. The *History of Florence* was commissioned by Leo X, the first Medici pope. Leo died before it was finished, and it was presented five years later to Clement VII, the second Medici pope, though published only in 1531. To see how Machiavelli may have expected his work to be read, we need some sense both of the constitutional arrangements and the practical politics of

Florence, Florentine relations with the papacy and with the Habsburg and Valois dynasties, the empire and France.

Florence

Florence was constitutionally a popular republic; but for most of the previous century it had been ruled de facto by the Medici family. This situation was not uncommon, but the contrast of republican institutions and more or less covert princely rule was particularly striking in Renaissance Florence. Florence was also a regional power, and its emphasis on *libertas* for citizens of Florence was not reflected in the treatment of the subordinate cities that it controlled. Florentine ideology was at odds with Florentine practice. The ideology held that *liberty* was so vital to the citizens of Florence that they would sooner die than be ruled by a tyrant; practice suggested that as long as the Medici did not *claim* to rule by hereditary right and were good managers, they would be accepted as the rulers of Florence. This is not very different from modern liberal democracies, where professional politicians beget professional politicians, or acquire them as sons- and daughters-in-law, much as law and medicine run in families. Many medieval theorists would have seen the tension between populist theory and monarchical practice as a small matter. As we have seen, the conventional wisdom was that the *regimen regale* was the best of all regimes so long as the "king"—who might be a duke or a count—governed justly, and in the common interest, not his own self-interest. The danger of a *regimen regale* was that it could degenerate into simple tyranny; but constitutional government by one temperate, wise, brave, and just man was best if it could be had. Devout republicans feared that one-man—or one-family—rule would inevitably become simple tyranny; less devout republicans thought that so long as they did not empty the state treasury or murder their rivals without recourse to law it was not truly tyranny. *Some*, but only a minority, of the citizens of Florence thought after the event that Lorenzo Magnifico had been a tyrant because he had paid himself out of the state coffers for the services he rendered the city; others might well have thought that he had neglected the family's banking business to devote himself to the greater glory of Florence and earned his pay.

During periods of acute stress, such as that of Machiavelli's employment in the chancellery, discussion turned more intensely to classical thinking about republican institutions, and during Machiavelli's lifetime with more sophistication than before. Florence was where political stress could have been expected to produce intelligent and original thought about politics. It was the center of Renaissance intellectual life. Along with Milan, Venice, and the Papal States, it was one of the dominant powers in northern and central Italy; to the south, the Kingdom of Naples was fought over by the French and Spanish crowns. Florence was a great trading state, linked to the trade routes and commercial fairs of northern Europe, and prospering on a luxury trade in textiles in particular. It was the first banking center in Europe, and the Medici had prospered by being exceptionally skilled merchants and bankers. Its prominence now made Florence vulnerable, too powerful to be ignored, too weak to act as it chose.

The Florentine constitution was a classical city-state constitution. It had been instituted in 1293 after a revolt against the incumbent nobility. The aim was to ensure that neither the nobility nor the urban poor could hold unchecked power. The city was ruled by the *signoria*, a committee of eight "priors" chaired by the *gonfaloniere* of justice. It met together with two other committees—the committee of "twelve good men" and the committee of the sixteen *gonfalonieri* of the city's sixteen districts. Legislation was considered, but not initiated, by two other councils, the Council of the People and the Council of the Commune, whose members, three hundred and two hundred, respectively, were chosen by the *signoria*; under the Medici, they were replaced by the Seventy and the Hundred. These bodies rotated membership at very frequent intervals—two to six months—and the main committees of the republic were selected by lot. The names of eligible persons were placed in bags and the names of those who were to serve were drawn out. It was common for many names to be disqualified because the persons named were in arrears with their taxes or otherwise ineligible; this gave a lot of power to the scrutinizing committee that pronounced on eligibility to be considered and to serve. In a city of perhaps eighty thousand inhabitants in Machiavelli's day, some three thousand citizens each year were called on to perform a governmental function. It is easy to imagine that the unambitious who wished to attend to their families' affairs would hope to avoid public office if someone competent would take their place, while the ambitious would think it intolerable to be reduced to guessing whether their allies would be drawn from the bags. Upper-class families spent much time and energy ensuring that their allies were in the right place to protect their interests.

Such a complex and intrinsically slow-moving system was doomed to be overturned or subverted. For a long time it was subverted in ways that kept up appearances. In the sixty years before the republic of 1494, the Medici family did not hold prominent public offices. Yet nobody doubted that they ruled Florence. Their ascent to power was far from untroubled. Cosimo de' Medici narrowly escaped death at the hands of the rival Albizzi family in 1433, when he was exiled for ten years and fined an enormous sum. The Albizzi instantly alienated their own supporters, and in 1434 Cosimo returned in triumph. He then ensured that the major bodies in the government were filled with his supporters. He achieved this partly within the constitution and partly without; an emergency council was assembled to reinstate him and remove his opponents, but he brought enough armed men to the meeting to secure his own safety and to ensure that the assembled citizens knew their duty. The Medici governed Florence within republican forms by controlling the personnel of government and ensuring that their friends were in control. The family suffered from hereditary uricemia, the disease underlying gout, and were short-lived, so their rule was never wholly secure. Because they died young, they inherited power young, and the success of any particular Medici ruler depended on temperament and innate capacity more than experience.

The two greatest Medici were Cosimo, who managed the affairs of Florence from 1434 to 1464, and Lorenzo the Magnificent, who took the reins in 1469 and died in 1492. Savonarola's Republic of Virtue came about partly because Lorenzo's successor, Piero di Lorenzo, was incompetent, but mostly for reasons outside anyone's control. In 1494

Lodovico Sforza of Milan persuaded the French king, Charles VIII, to revive his claim to the Kingdom of Naples. To everyone's surprise, Charles took up the idea and headed into Italy. Florence had for fifty years played off the papacy, the empire, and France against each other to preserve its freedom of movement. Now, the game was up. The price of avoiding a full-scale invasion and the sack of Florence was allowing the French armies free passage down the west coast of Italy and accepting French occupation of the main cities en route. Piero became the scapegoat for this disaster and was sent packing.

From 1494 to 1498, the government was in the hands of the partisans of Girolamo Savonarola, an ascetic and visionary Dominican friar, but he could achieve no more than Piero in foreign affairs, and his campaign against ecclesiastical corruption drew the hostility of the papacy. Florence had always been friendly to the papacy; if Florence resiled from its allegiance, it was vulnerable to the depredations of warlords like Cesare Borgia operating from the Papal States. The city was also vulnerable to the threat of papal interdict, which the city would lie under if Savonarola was excommunicated. By withdrawing the church's protection from the persons and property of the citizens of Florence, the papacy could threaten the city's trade throughout Europe; the goods of the excommunicated were fair game. Papal pressure and Florentine discontent resulted in Savonarola's removal from office, followed by his torture and execution for heresy. The end of the affair was the establishment of the reconstituted republic of 1498, of which Machiavelli was the servant.

Its chief novelty was the creation of the Grand Council, in imitation of that in Venice. The motive was the wish to keep a tight rein on the *grandi* or *nobili* who might be tempted to seize power for themselves; it was also a last flicker of the Florentine urge to return to what were conceived of as the most ancient institutions of the city. The rules of membership resulted in a council far larger than anyone anticipated, and over the next fourteen years attempts were made to make this unwieldy body less useless when quick decisions were needed. Whether the republic could have survived its constitutional infirmities, given reasonable luck, is anyone's guess. It did not have reasonable luck; Italy was in a state of continual upheaval; French, Spanish, German, and Swiss armies fought sporadic wars across the country, and the Italian cities and princely states made and broke alliances in a futile attempt to gain advantage from the chaos. The papacy under Alexander VI and Julius II was well to the fore in this, and its fate was typical; they were strikingly successful in cementing the papacy's control of the Papal States, but fifteen years after the fall of the Florentine Republic, Rome was sacked by mutinous imperial armies, against the wishes of their commander in chief, Emperor Charles V. The humiliation of the Medici pope Clement VII provoked the expulsion of the Medici from Florence in the summer of 1527. The republic that followed lasted only until the final restoration of the Medici three years later and Florence's transformation into a grand duchy.

The Prince

Machiavelli wrote *The Prince* following the failure of his beloved republic. What it is about is not hard to understand. The subject matter is one on which Machiavelli had often reflected during his career, as he watched Cesare Borgia imposing himself on cities whose government he had subverted, and as he contemplated the French conquest of Milan and the subsequent failure of the French to hang on to what they had taken. Machiavelli's topic is carefully specified: how a "new prince" is to take power and maintain himself in power. Nonetheless, although the topic is narrowly specified—Lorenzo de' Medici, to whom the book is dedicated, was preeminently a new prince to whose conduct chapter 5 of *The Prince* ("The Way to Govern Cities or Dominions That, Previous to Being Occupied, Lived under Their Own Laws") was all too glaringly relevant—the staying power of *The Prince* comes from its sweeping statements about human nature, the role of chance, or *fortuna*, in political life, and, above all, its insistence on the need for a clear-sighted appreciation of how men really *are* as distinct from the moralizing claptrap about how they *ought* to be that had brought so many princes and their states to ruin.

What made *The Prince* so timely emerges in the "Exhortation to Liberate Italy from the Barbarians," with which the book concludes. Lorenzo was the nephew of Pope Leo X; with the Medicis in power at

Rome and in Florence, the way was open for the two most substantial powers in central Italy to pursue an ambitious military policy: "There is no one in whom Italy can now place any hope except your illustrious family which (because it is successful and talented, and favoured by God and the Church of which it is now head) can take the lead in saving her."[5]

The Prince divides in two; the first eleven chapters consider different sorts of principalities and the way to acquire and hold them; fourteen of the remaining fifteen form a parodic mirror of princes, covering a variety of topics familiar in the literature from Cicero and Seneca down to not yet written works like Castiglione's The Courtier: military prowess, honesty, mercy, generosity, the avoidance of contempt and hatred. It ends with an exhortation to the Medici princes to unify Italy and evict the "barbarians"—the foreign forces that had rampaged through Italy since 1494, and would continue to do so for another three decades. Italian writers in the nineteenth century hailed Machiavelli as the prophet of the risorgimento, but the description of the transalpine invaders as barbarians was common enough, even on the part of popes and dukes who had rashly invited them in to promote some local quarrel. It is an anachronism to see Machiavelli as a nineteenth-century Italian nationalist, rather than someone inspired by the glories of ancient Rome.

Machiavelli begins The Prince by telling Lorenzo that he has reflected both on his own experience and on ancient history to provide genuinely new advice. That in itself represented a double change in thinking, first in departing from the Florentine desire to revert to the past—which is a trait that perhaps reappears in the Discourses—and second in using ancient history not as a moral guide as in collections of exempla but as a quarry for examples of successful practice. The Prince then runs straight into serious business, beginning with laying out its subject matter: newly acquired principalities and their retention. The single paragraph that constitutes the entire opening chapter buries a wealth of recent history when it separates out hereditary states from states that are not, states that are completely new to a family from those annexed to a state that has long been ruled by the same family, states that were formerly republics from states that were principalities, and—a wide-ranging gesture that took in both the astonishing luck of Cesare Borgia and the reinsertion of the Medici with the assistance of Spanish troops—those "acquired either with the arms of others or with one's own, either through luck or favour or else through ability."[6]

Hereditary principalities are of no interest; they present no challenge to the political skills of the prince. Long habits of obedience give the incumbent an advantage over rivals; anyone who loses a state of which he is the hereditary ruler deserves to do so, though Machiavelli well knew that misfortune makes the inhabitants of any state turn against their rulers, hereditary or not. The crucial discussion begins with chapter 3, as he first turns to the way to keep control of "mixed" principalities, by which he means states that the prince has conquered with the aim of annexing them to his present state, explains why some states remain quiet when conquered while others do not, and embarks on the contrast between states acquired by the prince's own ability and those acquired with help from others.[7] The chaos of recent events dominates the discussion, but the Roman treatment of Greece during the conquest of the early second century BCE is adduced to emphasize the point he makes several times, that the French had bungled the acquisition of power in Italy when they first captured Milan and were then driven out.

The argument is simple: an annexed state will be hard to hold if its people are culturally very different from the conqueror's own state. The French would inevitably have a harder time securing their power in Milan than in, say, Burgundy, where the inhabitants lived much as in the rest of France and spoke more or less the same language as other Frenchmen. It is, however, not impossible to retain power under such conditions; the Romans were strikingly effective in keeping a grip on conquered kingdoms. The underlying difficulty is the same in all new acquisitions: it is not hard to acquire a state, because human beings are quick to be discontented, ready to blame their present rulers for their miseries, and happy to see the back of them. Having done so, they will discover that the new rulers are no improvement on their predecessors, and very likely worse, because the costs of conquest fall heavily on the conquered population. In that case, they will, if they can, rebel against their new masters.

What is to be done? Two things: first, ensure that there are no partisans of the deposed ruler to cause trouble; second, go and live in the conquered territories. Machiavelli did not by this literally mean that Louis XII should have gone in person to live in Milan, as the instances of Turkish and Roman conquest make clear. The thought is rather that he should have installed an administration of his own that could see what was going on and nip trouble in the bud. The French could have kept hold of Milan by establishing colonies, as the Romans would have done, or by installing their own administrators throughout the region, as the Turks do. "Colonies" in this context means settlements of soldiers who are rewarded with farms rather than colonization in the imperialist sense of the next several centuries. Doing neither, they were evicted. What startles modern readers is the calmness with which Machiavelli observes, "Wanting to annex territory is indeed very natural and normal, and when capable men undertake it, they are always praised, or at least not criticised. But if men who are not capable of achieving it are bent on undertaking it at all costs, this is a blunder that deserves censure."[8] This is the voice of Greek and Roman imperialism, adjusted to the world of the Renaissance. He argues that colonies of the Roman kind are better than an army of occupation because it is cheaper to establish colonies that can support themselves than to quarter soldiers on the country; moreover, because soldiers need so many resources, paying for them arouses great irritation. The republic that Machiavelli served ground to a standstill because incessant warfare required decisions on taxation to pay for it that could not be arrived at within the unwieldy constitution; it is easy to see how much feeling hides behind these calm observations on military budgets.

The Machiavelli who was a scandal to European morality emerges in passing. As between soldiers and colonists, he says, colonists cause less anger because the only people injured are those whose land is seized for the benefit of the colonists. Since they will be few and scattered about the countryside, they do not pose a formidable problem. He then produces the underlying principle that governs the discussion: "It should be observed here that men should either be caressed or crushed; because they can avenge slight injuries, but not those that are very severe. Hence any injury done to a man must be such that there is no need to fear his revenge."[9] To a modern eye the assumption that the small farmers and other inhabitants in the countryside can safely be discounted because they are unorganized and unable to defend themselves against the evils visited upon them by the invaders is repulsive. Machiavelli accepts the assumptions of the Romans when they took over the territory of their neighbors; no Roman worried for long about the violation of their neighbors' human rights.

On the way to offering advice to princes who have taken over a republic that may not be glad to receive them, Machiavelli offers a nice vignette of the way in which a country that is used to being governed as a despotism will be easy to retain even by the not very skilled. His example is the empire of Alexander the Great. Alexander had no sooner conquered his empire than he died, sighing for new worlds to conquer, but because the subjects of Darius, king of Persia, were used to being governed in a centralized state, Alexander's heirs did not need to take extraordinary measures to preserve their power. He might have observed that Athens in contrast tried to recover its freedom and was defeated by the highly competent Antipater. In fact, he draws a contrast with the Roman experience in Gaul, where innumerable small, independent tribes had been used to liberty and did not take kindly to rule by outsiders. He expected the same would soon happen in France. Perhaps presciently in view of the wars that were to plague France in the second half of the sixteenth century, he observes that not only were Brittany and Burgundy recent enough acquisitions to remember their independence of the French crown, but the aristocracy in general was very local in its attachments and ready to revolt against a monarchy based in Paris if provoked. They are easy enough to manage if their existing way of life is not disturbed, but unlikely to acquiesce in any tighter control than that.[10]

A long tradition of genuine self-government poses problems for a new prince. In republics, "there is greater vitality, more hatred, and a stronger desire for revenge; they do not forget, indeed cannot forget, their lost liberties." That being so, there are three pieces of advice worth hewing to: a ruler should be prepared to live in the conquered state; he should utterly destroy all the old institutions; or he should leave as many as possible intact, so as to govern with the least irritation to old sentiments. Machiavelli draws his morals from the Romans and the Spartans: "The Spartans held Athens and Thebes by establishing oligarchies there; yet they eventually lost control of them. In order to hold Capua, Carthage and Numantia, the Romans destroyed them; and consequently never lost them." Initially, the Romans tried to emulate the Spartans in exercising only a loose suzerainty over Greece, but eventually had to destroy the Greek kingdoms to avoid incessant revolts. Polybius's picture of the Romans seducing their conquered subjects by offering them participation in the Roman state and its way of life is not directly contradicted, but where Polybius asked, "How did Rome acquire an empire whose peoples came to feel loyal to Rome?" Machiavelli poses a tougher question, "How does one ensure that a conquest will 'take'?" His answer boils down to the familiar binary opposition: kill or caress. Either show a respect for their institutions by governing behind the shield they provide and veil your authority; or stamp on opposition, exile or kill the previous elite, and make it clear that those who are not for you are as good as dead.

Although the first eleven chapters of *The Prince* constitute a unity, they are internally structured in an interesting fashion. Machiavelli was fascinated by the contrast between those who were astute and effective operators in the political world, and deserved congratulation, and those who were installed in power by the efforts of others or by simple good luck. *Fortuna*, or chance, is one of the most hotly debated of Machiavelli's terms, and we shall return to it. The role of chance in politics is obvious; and it is impossible not to feel that some political actors have had more than their share of good luck and others more than their share of bad. To observe that some people are thrust to prominence by chance is to say nothing startling. This understates Machiavelli's interest in the subject. Florence was superstitious almost as a matter of policy. An extravagant example soon after Machiavelli's death was that in 1527 the newly revived republic elected Christ as its king; more generally, the Florentines were unusually ready to believe that prayer and self-mortification would attract divine favor. Conversely, they seemed unable to deal with Cesare Borgia just because it seemed that fortune, along with his father, Pope Alexander VI, was on his side. Machiavelli was deeply hostile to anything that undermined the Florentines' ability to analyze the balance of forces they confronted.

He draws a crucial contrast between those who rely on their own political capacity—*virtù*—and those who rely on others or on luck. Plainly the first are less vulnerable to fortune's turning against them or to their allies' leaving them in the lurch. Cesare Borgia is a puzzle for this simple dichotomy, as we shall see. Those who display outstanding virtue and are therefore less dependent on fortune are the heroes one would expect, though the presence of Moses alongside Theseus, Cyrus, and Romulus may raise eyebrows, as Machiavelli admits. Machiavelli lets himself be distracted by his four heroes into a reflection on the fate of Savonarola that produces one of his best aphorisms. In the middle of his reflections on those who acquired a principality through their own arms, he says, "all armed prophets succeed, whereas unarmed ones fail." The figure of the armed prophet is a trope of twentieth-century political analysis. Machiavelli says, "If Moses, Cyrus, Theseus and Romulus had been unarmed, the new order which each of them established would not have been obeyed for very long. This is what happened in our own times to Fra' Girolamo Savonarola, who perished together with his new order as soon as the masses began to lose faith in him; and he lacked the means of keeping the support of those who had believed in him, as well as of making those who had never had any faith in him believe."[11] Behind Savonarola were innumerable prophetic figures who had frightened the authorities of their day but whose followers, with the exception of the militarily effective Hussites of Bohemia, lacked the capacity to overthrow their ungodly rulers.

The intellectual interest of these thoughts lies below the surface. Machiavelli had a strong sense that although there was much to be said in politics for a sudden, bold stroke, human beings were also creatures of habit, both good and bad, which argued for taking things slowly. The Florentines' ingratitude toward rulers who were devoted to the republic, but meeting with undeserved misfortune, was a long ingrained bad habit. Good habits need to be inculcated. The aid of religion was not to be scorned, nor its efficacy overestimated. Habits of obedience should be instilled by a mixture of fear and favor and backed up by whatever moral and spiritual resources came to hand; force mattered because once everyone could see that opposition was fatal, they would obey, and their beliefs would come into line with the habit of obedience. The *fact* of obedience would soon turn into a belief that they *ought* to obey. Most writers have tended to palliate the familiar fact that conquered populations come to subject themselves voluntarily in this fashion; Machiavelli did not. Force creates acceptance, reluctant at first, but willing in due course. Not to know this is to throw away the chance of success. The thought that if belief sustains authority, authority can reinforce the beliefs that then sustain it, is true enough; but it lacks the sharp edge that Machiavelli gives the observation. The fact that unarmed prophets invariably fail means that we may believe as firmly as we like that God is on our side, but it will do us no good if physical force is not on our side as well.

The Puzzle of Cesare Borgia

Ceasare Borgia is a major figure both in *The Prince* and in the *Discourses*. He presents a problem for Machiavelli. Was he, or was he not, unduly reliant on luck? Was he a skillful practitioner of the arts that new princes should possess and brought down in the end by pure bad luck; or was his success due only to luck, and was he brought down by a failure to take the measures he should have taken to ensure that bad luck could not destroy him? Of course, admirers of Machiavelli's cynical style can relish his discussion of Cesare Borgia's rise to power simply as a literary tour de force. Cesare, the brother of Lucrezia the famous poisoner,[12] was the son of the future Borgia pope Alexander VI. He was made a cardinal in his teens, but when Alexander became pope, the possibility beckoned of advancement in the secular realm. He renounced his cardinal's hat and was appointed captain general of the papal armies. Alexander's intention was to bring the Papal States firmly under the papacy's control, to enhance his son's prestige and power, and beyond that to unify the Italian states under his leadership.

This was what Machiavelli urged on Leo X and Lorenzo de' Medici in the final chapter of *The Prince*, and the policy itself was not one he deplored. What he deplored was the fact that the papacy was too weak to implement it, but too powerful to allow any other state to do so.[13] Alexander dismissed the so-called papal vicars, the agents who administered the Papal States, and left Cesare to secure the Romagna, which he did with astonishing energy and success. What would have happened if events had favored him is hard to say, but Alexander was pope for only half a dozen years (1497–1503), and Cesare himself was at death's door with malaria at the very moment his father died. He could not influence the papal succession, and his attempts to get on good terms with Julius II, who loathed the Borgias, got nowhere. Cesare fled to Naples, but was arrested, exiled, and imprisoned in Spain; he was killed in battle soon after being released in 1507. The question his career posed for Machiavelli was whether there was anything more that Cesare could have done to secure his position. Machiavelli inclines toward the view that there was not; perhaps, but only perhaps, a more prudent or long-sighted man might have thought ahead to the election of a new pope after the death of Alexander, but Machiavelli cannot find it in himself to complain.

Because of the way Machiavelli tells the story, Cesare Borgia comes across as an almost operatic villain; more seriously, he is presented as someone whose wickednesses were directed intelligently and efficiently to the end of making himself master of the Romagna. He was not gratuitously but tactically cruel. One piece of villainy that Machiavelli reports admiringly was Borgia's plot to ensure that the Orsini gave him and his father no trouble. Having persuaded the leading members of the clan that he was genuinely interested in reconciliation, he got them to a conference at Senigallia, seized them, and over the next four weeks had them strangled. Machiavelli treats the behavior of the Orsini and their friends as shockingly naïve; modern readers are likely to think that Borgia's behavior is repulsive, but it could be said on his side that the men he murdered were no strangers to the acquisition of power by murdering friends and relatives, let alone to disposing of sworn enemies.[14]

Borgia's most impressive coup de théâtre was the killing of the unfortunate Messer Remirro de Orco, an event that Machiavelli commented on admiringly in his dispatches and discusses in *The Prince*. The tale and the moral are simple. The Romagna was part of the papal patrimony, but had fallen into the hands of assorted small-time rulers who would today be called kleptocrats, whose only aim was to extract whatever they could from their wretched subjects. Borgia saw that any government that could keep the peace would be accepted, if it provided justice according to law and avoided outright banditry. The first step was to secure the peace. For this purpose, he installed Remirro de Orco, to whom he gave full power to suppress dissent and restore order. His chosen agent was effective, but his methods aroused resentment. Borgia took two steps to ensure that the resentment did not reach back to himself. The first was to establish a regular court, to which lawyers could take grievances. The second was to have Remirro de Orco arrested, "cut in two pieces," and placed in the main square at Cesena the day after Christmas together with an executioner's block and a knife. "This terrible spectacle left the people both satisfied and amazed."[15]

Understanding Machiavelli's project, which was not that of shocking the sensibilities of later ages, but reflecting on the difficulties of instituting political order, whether princely or republican, allows us to move onto terrain where a great deal of ink has been spilled. Machiavelli rounds off the discussion of the establishment of new principalities with a brief chapter on "ecclesiastical principalities." There is something unnerving about Machiavelli's account of the peculiarities of the Papal States. They are "sustained by ancient religious institutions, which have been sufficiently strong to maintain their rulers in office however they live and act. Only they have states and do not defend them, and subjects whom they do not trouble to govern. . . ."[16] That is to say, under successive popes the Papal States fell into the hands of the warring families who monopolized the College of Cardinals, and everything went to rack and ruin. "And their subjects, though not properly governed, do not worry about it; they cannot get rid of these rulers, nor even think about doing so. Only these principalities, then, are secure and successful."[17] To rub in the insult, Machiavelli then observes that since these states are governed by a higher power, there is nothing he can say about them.

Of course, there is, because he goes on to say that the model of a successful ruler is Alexander VI, Cesare's father. By guile and brute force, and the agency of his son, Alexander reestablished the papacy as a secular power to reckon with; this, thought Machiavelli, left his successor Julius II in a strong position to make the church the arbiter of the fate of Italy. Machiavelli was wrong; the monarchies of France and Spain were in a different league from the Italian states in their ability to assemble armies and keep them in the field for long campaigns. Julius II also suffered from Machiavelli's real vice, which was not a taste for wickedness for its own sake, but the belief that a deft operator could outsmart all his enemies all the time.

The second part of *The Prince* then turns into an ironic commentary on the traditional mirror of princes. Machiavelli's obsession was with military effectiveness on the one hand and the ability to form absolutely clear policy on the other. The doctrine that only the armed prophet succeeds is reinforced by reflecting on the failure of the Sforza family to keep itself in power by paying sufficient attention to military matters. "A ruler should have no other objective and no other concern, nor occupy himself with anything else except war and its methods and practices, for this pertains only to those who rule."[18] The injunction spills over into a departure from the usual advice to princes; handbooks for princes praised humane learning and taught the prince to interest himself in the social graces. Machiavelli says the only recreation the prince might usefully take up is hunting because it is a good way of learning how to read the lay of the land, and this is a valuable skill in a general. Humane letters are neither here nor there except for the acquisition of genuine historical knowledge; history provides a storehouse of great achievements to imitate, and a gallery of great men to emulate.

As to princely virtue, princes, says Machiavelli, are blamed only for shortcomings that bring about the destruction of the state. It is good to be loyal, generous, kindly, and the like, just as it is bad to be mean, lascivious, frivolous, and an unbeliever. All the same, the prince should not give much heed to his personal characteristics, save insofar as they lead him astray in matters of policy. This is a dig at Cicero's *De officiis*, though worse is to come. It may seem also to be a rejection of Aristotle's injunction that the ruler should practice self-control in the areas of sex and money. In fact, this is a topic on which Aristotle and Machiavelli are at one: concerned with the political consequences of unchastity, not unchastity as such. Seducing upper-class women creates enmities that undermine the ruler's position. It is worth remembering, however, how far Machiavelli shares the orthodox Christian pessimism about human nature. He is closer to Augustine than to Pico della Mirandola and his conviction that we might make ourselves cherubim. It is not obvious that his grim view of human nature is Christian in origin, but he believes in a version of original sin: "all men are by nature bad and will do all the evil they can." They must be disciplined by good laws, and if law has broken down, then by any means possible. Machiavelli did not have a surprising moral theory; he had a surprising readiness to confront head-on the fact that politics requires the willingness to get your hands dirty.

Then comes the advice that has so upset Machiavelli's readers, when Machiavelli analyzes the prince's *virtù*. The Machiavellian concept of *virtù* has been analyzed to death. That it does not mean "virtue" in the sense of the Christian virtues is obvious; what it does mean, less obvious. Usually, it means ability or almost any quality that makes for political success. These are reflections not on virtuous princes, as one would find in any number of pious writers, but on the qualities that make for effectiveness. *The Prince* is a reflection on the *virtù* of one man, the prince; the *Discourses* is a reflection on the *virtù* of a whole people—the Romans in particular, but also the Swiss and other citizens of successful states. The citizens of Athens and Sparta displayed *virtù*, though their obsession with confining the citizenship to the natives of their cities prevented them from achieving the glory that Rome did. Whether *virtù* is the same property in a prince and a whole people is much debated, but a plausible view is that it is formally the same property, but different in content. It is always defined in terms of the qualities that bring political success, and political success is closely linked to the achievement of glory. Whether it is the Roman people or the hoped-for savior of Italian independence in the early 1500s, political success is the goal; the polity to be established and maintained is not the same, but the enterprise is. Because the Roman people had to create and maintain a free government and did so *collectively*, the qualities they required were different from those a new prince needs. To take an obvious instance, Machiavelli never had a high opinion of the ordinary man's courage in the abstract.[19] Without good leadership and good training, the ordinary man is cowardly and incompetent, though with good leadership and training, he can display great courage and endurance. The prince, on the other hand, is ex hypothesi bold, ambitious, and ready to get himself killed in the attempt to seize power.

The sharpest contrast occurs with virtues such as honesty and loyalty. The people cannot act as an effective collectivity unless everyone treats everyone else with a high degree of honesty and mutual loyalty; these must be proper character traits and not easily turned on and turned off pragmatically. The new prince, in contrast, must be ready to change his colors at a moment's notice. He cannot afford to be so honest that he does not know how to deceive his rivals and murder them when he has the chance. Even those who are generally honest must be ready to be brutal. Machiavelli describes Hannibal's extreme cruelty, his *terribilità*, as part of his *virtù*. Given that most of us dislike behaving brutally or dishonestly, we might wonder whether political success is worth having at this price; indeed, we might wonder what constitutes political success in the first place. Can it really be defined in terms of wading in blood to a tyrant's throne?

Machiavelli leaves the reader to make up his own mind, but some of what he thinks is obvious enough, and the rest must be conjectural. The reward for successfully constructing a republic is freedom; citizens can live a civil life, a *vivere civile*, and enjoy their possessions and their liberties in peace. They will not be victimized by the rich, or invaded by foreigners, or ill treated without recourse to the law. It is possible that this is not wholly different from the ordinary person's rewards for a prince's success in securing and holding a principality. Sheldon Wolin's elegant description of Machiavelli as dealing in "an economy of violence"[20] catches the point nicely; the successful prince may get into power by unpleasant means, may maintain himself in power by unpleasant means, and may be a person whose moral character we do not care for. But he diminishes the amount of random, unpredictable, pointless violence and cruelty that we have to suffer. The prince's political reward is power. The attractions of power are not something Machiavelli troubles to analyze; true to his classical masters, he assumes that we want to exercise power and want not to have it exercised over us.

The thought that violence and treachery are a currency that politicians employ intelligently to avert their excessive and uncontrolled use catches something of Machiavelli's aims. However, his ultimate goal is one the modern world is less happy to avow as he does, other than in sporting contexts. This is the attainment of glory. If one asks why anyone would seek power in the way Machiavelli takes for granted—it is a question Machiavelli asks only in the context of observing that the unpredictability of fortune might make one wonder whether it is worth trying—the answer is that men seek glory. They want to leave a great name. Here there is a real difference in the achievements of a prince and a republic. In a principality glory is obtained by the prince; this is one reason why the romantic idea that the Renaissance saw the state as a work of art is not an inappropriate metaphor for the work of the prince. But the ordinary people are passive; they are the raw material of princely glory. In a republic the people themselves are the heroes and the achievers of glory. If *virtù* is the quality that achieves glory, it is thus both the same and different in the prince and the people; it is the same in being essentially instrumental, that is, the qualities that make for success and enable the possessors of these qualities to achieve glory through that success, and different inasmuch as different sorts of people under very different circumstances achieve glory in principalities and republics. Nor is it merely a matter of success; some highly successful rulers were mere tyrants. Agathocles, the tyrant of Syracuse, illuminates Machiavelli's view. He not only held power for a long period but drove the Carthaginians out of Sicily. But he had been freely elected by the citizens of Syracuse, and then made himself a tyrant, holding by force and treachery what he had been freely given. Needless cruelty and treachery are unforgivable.

Having laid the ground with his discussion of warfare and his scorn for the attainments of the courtier, Machiavelli launches into the characteristics of the successful prince. The most famous moment in the discussion comes in chapter 18, ominously entitled "How Rulers Should Keep Their Promises." The reader has by now been told that the prince should not *be* generous, though he should try to *appear* so, and has been reminded that it is better to be feared than to be loved—since people do not much mind revolting against the good-natured, but think twice about rebelling against the lethally severe—so it comes as no surprise that Machiavelli's advice is to keep faith only as and when it serves our ends. Honesty is a virtue and men are rightly praised for it, but a prince who is honest when he should not be makes himself a prey to his enemies. It is in this context that Machiavelli turns Cicero's advice on its head.

Lions and Foxes and Political Ethics

For Cicero the fact that even animals obey law in a certain sense—they are endowed by nature with habits useful to their survival—does not blur the distinction between man and beast. Men must obey a specifically human law; it teaches rational beings how to act for the common good. Human courage is not the lion's savagery; human intelligence is not the fox's cunning. To which Machiavelli replies, "Since a ruler, then, must know how to act like a beast, he should imitate both the fox and the lion, for the lion is liable to be trapped, whereas the fox cannot ward off wolves. One needs, then, to be a fox to recognise traps and a lion to frighten away wolves." Once more, the ruthless Alexander VI is praised for his duplicity: he "was concerned only with deceiving men; and he always found them gullible."[21]

One question must occur to the reader who reads Machiavelli in a friendly spirit. Setting aside the wickedness of rulers who follow his advice, can anyone act with quite the amoral verve and flair that Machiavelli advocates? Machiavelli takes the question seriously; but he circles around it, first asking how rulers can avoid being despised—mostly by being ferocious in repressing rivals and opponents—and then what they must do to gain a reputation. The discussion once more displays Machiavelli's taste for the spectacular; his hero is Ferdinand of Aragon, who united the Iberian Peninsula, drove out the Moors from their last strongholds, and, by a mixture of guile and military skill, first seized the Kingdom of Naples from its previous ruler with French assistance and then turned around and evicted the French. But Machiavelli admits that we cannot always be on top of events; often we have to cobble together a strategy in circumstances we would not have chosen. Then caution is better than rashness. The concession seems to be wrung from him. The sole point on which Machiavelli and the advice books coincide is the need to avoid flatterers. Like generations of political scientists after him, Machiavelli observes that princes have a hard time obtaining impartial advice, because people will tell them whatever they think the prince wants to hear. The remedy is to appoint to one's service people who are described in terms that sound very like a description of the former secretary of the Ten of War.

The Prince ends with a double peroration. The true peroration is, of course, the exhortation to liberate Italy from the barbarians. The pre-peroration is the engaging chapter on the role of fortune in human affairs. Short though *The Prince* is, one could be forgiven for thinking after a quick reading that being a Machiavellian hero is an exhausting and unprofitable activity; when there is peace, we must be active in making preparations for war; we should befriend the ordinary people, but not be too familiar with them, lest we become despised; we must watch out for our enemies and strike before they do, but we must not attend too carefully to the dangers of assassination, because only the incompetent or the oppressive run much risk. Steering a delicate path between an excess of caution and an overdose of rashness promises to be hard work, too.

Is the task hopeless? Machiavelli observes that it is a common view that "the affairs of the world are so much ruled by fortune and by God that the ability of men cannot control them." It is a view by which he is tempted, especially in view of the chaos that has gripped Italy for the previous two decades. Nonetheless, he refuses to agree that human freedom is of no account, and is "disposed to hold that fortune is the arbiter of half our actions, but that it lets us control roughly the other half."[22] It is interestingly unclear just what Machiavelli thinks. He sometimes suggests that all fortune amounts to is forces that we are commonly bad at controlling: "I compare fortune to one of those dangerous rivers that, when they become enraged flood the plains, destroy trees and buildings, move earth from one place and deposit it in another. . . . But this does not mean that when the river is not in flood, men are unable to take precautions, by means of dykes and dams, so that when it rises next time, it will either not overflow its banks, or if it does, its force will not be so uncontrolled or damaging."[23] That suggests the usual Machiavellian moral: men are chronically idle about taking precautions while things are going well. They are lulled into thinking that all will be well, because things are going well at present, and then something happens that they might have prevented but that they have foolishly taken no trouble to prevent. And as a result they are destroyed.

At other times fortune is represented as a real force for good or evil, even if it is not *wholly* outside our control even then. How well we do in a risky political enterprise is very much a matter of whether our style, temperament, characteristic mode of operation suits the conditions; sometimes the schemes of a cautious man will come adrift because the situation demands boldness, and sometimes the cautious man will succeed where the bold one does not. If—but it is very much the if of *per impossibile*—"it were possible to change one's character to suit the times and circumstances, one would always be successful."[24] Machiavelli then embarks on a set-piece on the character of Julius II. The Florentines found him entirely impossible to deal with; they could not deal with his rages, they could not predict his plans, and he himself may not quite have known what he was going to do next. But he was a bold military leader and during a very brief pontificate strikingly successful.

That, says Machiavelli, was because he was bold and impetuous, and the times suited him. Had he lived when a more cautious policy was required, he would have been undone because he could not possibly have acted otherwise than he did. All the same, says Machiavelli, in terms that cause our eyebrows to lift, "it is better to be impetuous than cautious, because fortune is a woman, and if you wish to control her, it is necessary to treat her roughly. And it is clear that she is more inclined to yield to men who are impetuous than to those who are calculating. Since fortune is a woman, she is always well disposed towards young men, because they are less cautious and more aggressive, and treat her more boldly."[25] How much more than a rhetorical flourish this may be, it is impossible to say. Machiavelli never suggested that he held distinctively un-Christian views; on the other hand, he never said anything to suggest deep piety. Since he cared a great deal about his literary skills, it might have been no more than decoration to make a point of some seriousness; on the other hand, it may have been something deeper than lip service to the idea that fate is an active force in the world, bringing us to good and evil on a whim. Polybius, after all, thought a lot about the reality of *tyche*, or fate, chance, fortune.

From *The Prince* to the *Discourses*

The Prince ends with an exhortation to Leo X to unite Italy and render the Medici forever glorious by expelling the barbarians from Italian soil. Machiavelli's hope is for Italy to recover its ancient Roman glory, and this theme connects *The Prince* and the *Discourses*. The *Discourses* purports to be, and often really is, a commentary on Livy's *History of Rome*. It is broken into three books, of which the first is a sustained discussion of the principles underlying the creation and sustaining of a successful republic; the second focuses on the expansion of Rome, and the third on the importance of great leaders in the life of the Roman Republic. Writers on Machiavelli have some difficulty deciding whether it is astonishing that the *Discourses* is very different from *The Prince*, or whether it is the similarities in the two works that are really astonishing. Part of the answer is that the principles of statecraft that underlie both works are very much the same. Examples of useful ruthlessness often appear briefly in *The Prince* and are discussed at length in the *Discourses*; Cesare Borgia's exploits reinforce the lessons of the Romans; Julius II's impetuousness is praised; and the view of human nature in *The Prince* underpins his complaint in the *Discourses* that even men of the vilest character do not know how to be thoroughgoing in their wickedness and flinch just when they ought to go to extremes.[26]

Although the principles of statecraft and the underlying view of human nature are the same, the occasion and the purpose of the discussion are very different. Republics are not principalities—here thought of as states ruled as if they are the personal possession of a prince—and the focus of the *Discourses* is the creation of a self-sustaining constitutional order in a republic. The model is Polybius. Machiavelli held many views that readers of Polybius would find familiar, and he confronted the same puzzle about Rome's success in reforming its constitutional arrangements by trial and error. The body politic is rightly thought of as like the human body. It is usually essential to be born healthy, since just as a sickly child may, with luck and care, survive a long time, but never do much, so an ill-constructed state will never amount to much on the world stage. But Rome interests Machiavelli in the sixteenth century as it had Polybius and Cicero long before, because it violates that maxim. It went through several constitutional upheavals in its early years when it threw out its kings and adopted a republican constitution, and again when the secession of the plebs forced the ruling elite to open public offices to the lower classes. If it is harder to rebuild one's boat in midocean than to make it watertight before leaving shore, the Romans show that some people have the talent, energy, and good luck to get away with rebuilding on the voyage.

Writers on Machiavelli have debated at length what he thought he was claiming for himself when he claimed that in writing the *Discourses* he was traveling "a new route."[27] He says that he is using historical evidence properly, a thing that "the proud indolence" of these Christian states prevents Italian rulers from doing. It is not clear who these indolent princes are, nor what he thinks distinguishes his use of history from that of previous writers. To the extent that he commits himself to any principle more profound than a contempt for anyone who confuses analysis with moralizing, he echoes Thucydides. Human nature is the same at all times and places, so whatever has happened in the past can be emulated if worth emulating or avoided if it should be avoided. He comments on the absurdity of contemporary aristocrats and rich men who dig up antique statues and have modern copies made of them, but who do not see how much more valuable it would be to understand the actions and ideas of great political and military leaders of the ancient world and learn how to copy them. Indeed, his great complaint appears to be that the majority of those who read history "take pleasure in the variety of events which history relates, without ever thinking of imitating the noble actions, deeming that not only difficult but impossible, as though heaven, the sun, the elements, and men had changed their motions and power, and were different from what they were in ancient times."[28] Machiavelli is not a writer who excites the desire to carp, but his reliance on the uniformity of human nature to underpin what one might describe as the method of "look, analyze, copy" seems on its face to consort badly with his recognition that circumstances change and that we had better change with them. The one thing for which we ought not to reproach him is a failure to appreciate that the cultural, religious, and social *milieu* of the ancient world was too unlike that of Renaissance Italy for "look, analyze, copy" to work. Social thinkers in the nineteenth century ascribed many of the disasters of the French Revolution to the sheer impossibility that eighteenth-century Parisians should be like Romans of the third century BCE. It is not obvious that the complaint has the same force in an Italian city-state three centuries earlier.

Machiavelli's detachment from conventional moralizing has tempted commentators to think that the novelty is that Machiavelli set out to practice what later ages would recognize as political science, an inductively based comparative inquiry into what methods work where, when, and how. This is wholly implausible. Apart from Machiavelli's toleration of internal contradiction, as when he says at one point that Rome was poor and at another that Rome was rich, there is nothing to suggest he had such a conception of science. It would have been surprising if he had, since it would have antedated the scientific self-consciousness of natural scientists themselves by two centuries. Other commentators have made much of his seeming endorsement of the cyclical theory of history that appears in Plato's *Republic* and was borrowed for his own purposes by Polybius.

The *Discourses* is certainly Polybian at the level of style and intellectual concerns, even though Polybius was reflecting on events in his own lifetime whereas Machiavelli is commenting on Livy's account of the foundation and growth of the early republic. Polybius's historical style, and the pleasure he takes in men's securing their ends by deft acts of deceit is very like Machiavelli's; nonetheless, the so-called cyclical theory of history is neither a theory nor very cyclical. What it offers Machiavelli is reinforcement for his conviction that the wheel of fate turns unpredictably. Princes of sufficient flair and republics with good laws allied to good arms can master necessity for a time, but the historical judgment to which Machiavelli is most attached is that success breeds failure, because in the end the imperial republic is corrupted by wealth. And like Polybius, Machiavelli leaves the reader unsure whether chance, *tyche*, or *fortuna* is an active force in history.

Machiavelli does what he does in *The Prince*, which is offer prudential maxims illustrated and defended by appeal to historical events. Machiavelli's reputation as a "teacher of evil" rested on *The Prince*, but his insistence that when the means accuse, the end must excuse is every bit as prominent in the *Discourses*, which is indeed where the aphorism comes from. Machiavelli adopts what would be an uncompromisingly republican standpoint, except that it is *either* republics *or* kingdoms that men are praised for founding; what is indefensible is the institution of a tyranny. How far that conflicts with *The Prince* is an open question; there Machiavelli seems almost to take the view that Hobbes later made famous, that tyranny is but "monarchy misliked." It seems that he thought it perfectly proper to adopt dictatorial methods in emergency as the Romans did, but perfectly intolerable to establish an enduring tyranny. That, after all, is the moral of his defense of Romulus's actions in slaying Remus; one must do whatever it takes to get a political society up and running, but the tyrant is the enemy of his people, is rightly killed by whoever can do it, and is the polar opposite of the lawful ruler. Machiavelli's views on tyranny are conventional in the classical tradition, but decidedly non-Pauline.

For all that, he is committed to the view that only autocrats can institute or restore a state. There must be a founding moment when the new order is laid down, just as there must be a similar moment if a state is rescued by being returned to its first principles in a revolutionary reconstitution. Moses, Romulus, and Theseus are the heroes of both *The Prince* and the *Discourses*. But the emphasis in the *Discourses* falls on what Machiavelli describes as *ordini*, which is not rendered absolutely faithfully as "laws"; much as Rousseau does later, when he appears to distinguish between the fundamental laws of a political system and "decrees," so Machiavelli seems to have in mind something very like the laws that define the constitutional order. It is an idea with which states with written constitutions are wholly familiar, and indeed the constitution of

Germany today is called the "Basic Law." Beginnings are very different from sustainings; the irregular, often violent, and improvised actions of the founder hero must be succeeded by the regular election of leaders according to law.

The element that is hardly touched on in *The Prince* but is very prominent in the *Discourses* is religion. The Romans are praised for taking religion both seriously and unseriously. They took religion seriously in the sense that they understood the importance of religion as social cement. It is a useful aid to public morality; it urges courage in battle; it reinforces the respect for ancestors and affection for children on which solidarity across generations depends. Christianity is on the whole ill suited for such purposes; being other-worldly, it takes people's minds off their political and military duties and makes them attend only to their own salvation. It is a milk and water religion, urging its adherents to turn the other cheek. The Romans were not known for turning the other cheek. Educated Romans did not take religion seriously as a matter of metaphysics; metaphysics was for philosophers, not for the man in the street, let alone for the legionary. A relaxed view of the truth of religion allowed the leaders of Roman society to manipulate the practices and rituals of Roman religious observance as they needed. It was wise to ensure that the auguries before battle predicted success, and a competent commander would know how to do it. However, it was also essential that common soldiers treated the auguries with respect and that anyone who insulted them was promptly executed.

Machiavelli's animus is directed at the institution of the papacy rather than at Christianity or at other nonpagan religions. Chapter 12 of the *Discourses* is entitled "The Importance of Giving Religion a Prominent Influence in a State; and How Italy Was Ruined Because She Failed in This Respect through the Influence of the Church of Rome."[29] Early Christianity could have provided the basis for social cohesion, loyalty, good morals, and public spirit; but early sixteenth-century Italy shows what happens if there is an institution in the midst of society that is both corrupt considered as a religious institution—which sickens all of what passes for religion, and makes them irreligious—and inept as a political institution—one that has lost its grip on its possessions and has invited foreign powers into Italy, to the detriment both of its own subjects and those of all the other Italian states. It is observations such as these that got Machiavelli's works onto the Index.

Three further doctrines of the *Discourses* bear examination, since they had a considerable impact on republican thought and are by no means a reworking of commonplaces. One is Machiavelli's claim that a certain amount of uproar in a republic is conducive to liberty. There seems to be no prior defense of this proposition, and it is at odds with the entire tendency of Christian thinking, with its emphasis on harmony; it is at odds also with the utopian tradition running back to Plato's *Republic* and with all previous republican thinking. It must certainly be true that all defenders of mixed constitutions rely on the common people, or whatever proportion of them they include in "the people" to stand up for their own political rights; if they did not do so, they could not fulfill their role in the system of checks and balances. All classical writers— Aristotle, Polybius, and Cicero among them—took it for granted that they would do so, and were less afraid that they might be too passive than that they would get out of hand. Machiavelli's doctrine is perfectly clear, and offered as a novelty. The secession of the plebeians forced the ruling elite to take seriously the fact that the lower classes fed the city and kept the elite clothed and housed; it encouraged the lower classes to insist on their rights and privileges in the Roman state. It therefore gave notice to those who might oppress them that they would not stand for it, and so preserved liberty.[30] Indeed, continued class conflict and the permanent tension between the upper and lower classes made Rome both powerful and free. We need not accept this rosy view of the freedom available to the Roman lower classes to see the point; it was made by Edmund Burke and many others long afterward. It was shocking to Machiavelli's contemporaries, who thought that endorsing the usefulness of uproar was, in the conditions of early sixteenth-century Italy, much like pouring oil on a raging fire; had they looked north to Reformation Germany, they might have taken an equally cool view about the virtues of disputatiousness.

A second idea that makes a reappearance in republican writers thereafter is Machiavelli's defense of the popular republic against the aristocratic republic. The argument is intricately wound in with another about the merits of a republic designed for longevity as against one designed for increase. The Roman Republic was an expansive republic, and Machiavelli admired it for that reason. Even though Venice had acquired a maritime empire in the Adriatic and beyond, and substantial territories in the terra firma, it was a republic designed for longevity. Machiavelli's passion for a state that cut a great figure on the stage of world events led him to side with Rome against Venice. The defense of a popular rather than an aristocratic republic is not really an argument about the virtues of Rome in particular, but a defense of Florentine populism against Venetian narrowness. The argument runs thus: republics are endangered by "gentlemen"—there are many synonyms, such as *nobili* or *grandi*—who are defined by Machiavelli not simply as men who are rich or wellborn but as those with the vices of feudal landowners. These vices, as in More's *Utopia*, center on their keeping large numbers of retainers who are a threat to the peace both when they are employed to further the political ambitions of their masters and when they have been dismissed from his service and know no way to make a living save banditry. It is the ability of the *grandi* and *nobili* to raise private armies and subvert the state that alarms him; on this matter he and Cicero would speak with one voice.

Venice seemed to be a puzzle because it was aristocratic but had not been ruined by the ruling aristocracy. Venice practiced *guberno stretto*, a "narrow" regime in which eligibility for office was confined to the descendants of those who had been eligible when the Great Council was "closed" in 1297, at the end of a long series of earlier reforms; it was an aristocratic republic, managed by a narrow oligarchy. Florence had adopted *guberno largo*, a "wide" regime, to keep the aristocrats in check and ensure that decisions on taxation and other important matters were made by a wider rather than a smaller body of citizens. In abolishing the Great Council on their return in 1512 and physically destroying the hall in which it met, the Medici were announcing that they would govern as de facto princes behind a republican screen, and that the screen would be an aristocratic rather than a popular republic. Machiavelli's puzzle was to explain why Venice had not been ruined by its gentlemen. His answer was that they were not gentlemen except in name. They were rich merchants whose wealth was in money and goods. As long as traders remain traders, they pose no threat to the republic. They cannot prosper by reducing their fellow citizens to servitude, and they have no interest in maintaining private armies on the landed estates that ex hypothesi they do not have. Later political sociologists agreed.

Finally, then, the fatal question and the third of Machiavelli's surprising thoughts. Like Polybius, Machiavelli thinks that success cannot endure indefinitely, and like Hume after him, he thinks the works of man are destined to decay, no matter what. Within a dozen pages of the end of the *Discourses*, Machiavelli is still insisting that if "on the decision to be taken wholly depends the safety of one's country, no attention should be paid either to justice or to injustice, to kindness or to cruelty, or to its being praiseworthy or ignominious. On the contrary, every other consideration being set aside, that alternative should be wholeheartedly adopted which will save the life and preserve the freedom of one's country."[31] Over and over, he insists that half measures always lead to ruin, that boldness often achieves what caution cannot, as though the cultivation of Roman dash and vigor will carry everything before it. Yet he also says that success is self-defeating, that no republic can last forever, that corruption will always attend the achievement of great things.

A successful republic will acquire more territory, incorporate more citizens, become prosperous. When it becomes prosperous, people will begin to turn in on themselves and think about their own wealth rather than the good of the republic. The martial virtues will decline, and taste for soft living will creep in. Mercenaries will be hired to replace citizen-soldiers. The very rich will think how they can turn their wealth into power, and so subvert the republic. The ordinary people will remain uncorrupted longer than their betters, but they, too, can be suborned and turned into willing accomplices of the men who offer them a share of the loot or an exemption from the demands of the republic. Then there will be the decline and fall that the Roman Republic went through. A strong man lives longer than an unhealthy one, but both die in the end; and so it is with states. Readers' reactions to Machiavelli depend heavily on their reactions to such banal, but important, truths about human existence. It is clear that Machiavelli thought that life was for the living and that death was its inevitable companion; and by the same token that the world of politics had its own raison d'être, which only the fainthearted or slow-footed would fail to be moved by. Those who were neither fainthearted nor slow-footed but who marched to a different drummer could always retire to a monastery and contemplate eternal verities. It does not seem that Machiavelli would have condemned them for so doing; but he had nothing to say to them.

NOTES TO BOOK ONE

CHAPTER 1: WHY HERODOTUS?

1. Aristotle, *The Politics* (1.7), p. 19.
2. Herodotus, *The Histories*, pp. 449–50.
3. Thucydides, *Peloponnesian War*, p. 107.
4. Cartledge, *Thermopylae*, passim.
5. Thucydides, *Peloponnesian War*, p. 92.
6. Ibid.
7. Ibid., p. 97.
8. Ibid., p. 295.
9. Madison, Hamilton, and Jay, *The Federalist Papers*, pp. 122, 152, 292.
10. Plato, *Apology*, in *The Last Days of Socrates*, pp. 56–57, 64–65; Xenophon, *Socrates's Defence*, in *Conversations of Socrates*, pp. 41–49.
11. Plato, *Crito*, in *The Last Days of Socrates*, pp. 94–96; Xenophon, *Conversations of Socrates*, p. 195.

CHAPTER 2: PLATO AND ANTIPOLITICS

1. Wolin, *Politics and Vision*, pp. 27ff.
2. Marx and Engels, *The Communist Manifesto*, p. 244.
3. Aristotle, *The Politics* (2.2), p. 31.
4. Ibid. (2.6), pp. 39–43.
5. Xenophon, *Conversations of Socrates*, passim.

6. The story is told in Plato's *Seventh Letter*, p. 113; Xenophon, *Conversations of Socrates*, p. 195.

7. Xenophon, *Socrates's Defence*, in *Conversations of Socrates*, pp. 47–48.

8. Aristophanes, *Clouds*, p. 23.

9. Plato, *Gorgias*, pp. 32–33.

10. Ibid., p. 76.

11. Plato, *The Republic*, p. 50.

12. Nietzsche, *On the Genealogy of Morality*, pp. 28–29.

13. For instance, Frank, *Passions within Reason*; and for other primates, Frans de Waal, *Good Natured*.

14. Huxley, *Brave New World*, pp. 35–36.

15. Hobbes, *Leviathan*, pp. 86–87.

CHAPTER 3: ARISTOTLE: POLITICS IS NOT PHILOSOPHY

1. Aristotle, *The Politics* (1.4–7, slaves; 12–13, women), pp. 12–15, 27–30.

2. Ibid. (1.12), p. 27.

3. Ibid. (1.7), p. 19.

4. Ibid. (1.2), p. 13.

5. Though some commentators think the conventional ordering of *Politics* is anyway not what Aristotle originally intended.

6. Aristotle, *Politics* (7.2), pp. 168–69.

7. Ibid. (1.2), p. 8.

8. Locke, *Second Treatise* (sections 89–90), in *Two Treatises of Government*, pp. 325–26.

9. Aristotle, *Politics* (1.5), p. 17.

10. Ibid. (7.2), p. 181.

11. Ibid. (1.4), p. 15.

12. Ibid. (7.7), p. 175.

13. Ibid. (1.10), p. 25.

14. Ibid. (4.6), p. 100.

15. Ibid. (7.10), pp. 180–81.

16. Ibid. (3.13), pp. 80–83.

17. Ibid. (3.1), p. 62.

18. Thucydides, *The Peloponnesian War*, pp. 164–72.

19. Aristotle, *Politics* (3.7), p. 71.

20. Ibid. (4.9), pp. 104–5.

21. Lipset, *Political Man*, foreword, pp. 7–10.

22. Hobbes, *Leviathan*, p. 119.

CHAPTER 4: ROMAN INSIGHTS: POLYBIUS AND CICERO

1. Seneca, *De brevitate vitae*, 5.1.
2. *De legibus*, too, is set in his country villa at Tusculum.
3. Polybius, *The Rise of the Roman Empire*, p. 342.
4. Plato, *Gorgias*, p. 140.
5. Aristotle, *The Politics* (4.6), pp. 100–101.
6. *The Ethics of Aristotle* (1.3), p. 28.
7. Polybius, *Rise of the Roman Empire* (bk. 6), pp. 302–52.
8. Aristotle, *Politics* (2.6), p. 42.
9. Ibid. (4.8–9), pp. 102–5.
10. Machiavelli, *Discourses on Livy* (1.1–6), pp. 19–38.
11. Polybius, *Rise of the Roman Empire*, p. 342.
12. Ibid., pp. 342–44.
13. Cicero, *On the Commonwealth*, p. 32.
14. Berlin, "Two Concepts of Liberty," in *Four Essays on Liberty*, for the distinction.
15. Wood, *Empire of Liberty*, p. 20.
16. Cicero, *On Duties*, pp. 142–44.
17. Ibid., p. 19.
18. Machiavelli, *The Prince*, pp. 61, 68–69.

CHAPTER 5: AUGUSTINE'S TWO CITIES

1. Romans 13:1–7.
2. Augustine, *The City of God* (21.14), p. 1072.
3. Brown, *Augustine of Hippo*, p. 39.
4. Ibid., pp. 151ff.
5. Herrin, *The Formation of Christendom*.
6. Dewey, *A Common Faith*, in *Later Works*, 9:3–20 ("Religion versus the Religious").
7. Lane Fox, *Pagans and Christians*, emphasizes the point throughout.
8. Brown, *Augustine of Hippo*, pp. 35ff.
9. Augustine, *Confessions* (5.5–10), pp. 76–85.
10. Ibid. (1.10), p. 9.
11. Ibid. (7.9–13), pp. 121–26.
12. By Peter Brown, quoted in the introduction to *City of God*, p. xiv.
13. Augustine, *City of God* (5.24), pp. 231–32.
14. Lane Fox, *Pagans and Christians*, pp. 37ff.
15. Cicero, *On the Commonwealth*, pp. 59–60.
16. Augustine, *City of God* (1.9), pp. 13ff.

17. Augustine, *Confessions* (2.9–17), pp. 28–34.
18. Augustine, *City of God* (14.26), pp. 628–29.
19. Ibid. (5.17), p. 217.
20. Augustine, *Confessions* (1.7), p. 9.
21. Hobbes, *Leviathan*, chaps. 30 et seq.
22. Augustine, *City of God* (5.26), p. 235.
23. Ibid.
24. Ibid. (14.23–24), pp. 623–27.
25. Ibid. (1.19–20), pp. 29–33.
26. Ibid.
27. Ibid. (2.21), p. 80.
28. Ibid. (19.21), pp. 950–52.
29. Ibid. (4.15), p. 161.
30. Ibid. (19.6), p. 928.
31. Ibid. (19.16), pp. 944–45.
32. Ibid. (19.6), pp. 926–28.

PREFACE TO PART II

1. Hume, "The Independency of Parliament," in *Political Essays*, p. 24.
2. Russell, *Autobiography*, pp. 333–35.
3. Augustine, *City of God* (5.17), p. 218.

CHAPTER 6: BETWEEN AUGUSTINE AND AQUINAS

1. Most famously articulated in Ullman, *A History of Political Thought in the Middle Ages*, pp. 12ff.
2. As always, Romans 13 is the key text.
3. Augustine, *City of God* (19.17), pp. 945–46.
4. Ibid.
5. Ibid. (1.17–20), pp. 26–33.
6. Lane Fox, *Pagans and Christians*, pp. 418–27.
7. See John of Salisbury, *Policraticus*, below, pp. 219–23.
8. The Declaration of Right, February 1689.
9. Locke, *Second Treatise* (sec. 242), in *Two Treatises of Government*, p. 427.
10. Matthew 16:19.
11. Augustine, *City of God* (5.23), p. 235.
12. Matthew 22:21.
13. Aristotle, *Ethics* (5.7), p. 158.

14. *History of Sir Charles Napier's Administration of the Province of Scinde*, p. 35.

15. I Timothy 6:10.

16. Locke, *First Treatise* (sec. 42), in *Two Treatises of Government*, p. 170; Hume, *Enquiries concerning Human Understanding and concerning the Principles of Morals*, pp. 186–87.

17. Garnsey, *Thinking about Property*, pp. 217–18.

18. Gibbon, *Decline and Fall of the Roman Empire*, 6:16.

19. Ibn Khaldun, *The Muqadimmah*.

20. Burns, ed., *Cambridge History of Medieval Political Thought*, pp. 605–6.

21. Quoted ibid., pp. 288–89.

22. Haskins, *The Renaissance of the Twelfth Century*.

23. E.g., John of Salisbury, *Policraticus* (8.17), pp. 190ff.

24. Fortescue, *On the Laws and Governance of England*, p. xxxii.

25. John of Salisbury, *Policraticus* (4.1), pp. 27–30.

26. Ibid. (8.19–20), pp. 210–13.

27. Ibid. (4.1), pp. 27–30.

CHAPTER 7: AQUINAS AND SYNTHESIS

1. Aquinas, *Political Writings*, pp. xviii–xxii.

2. *Aquinas on Politics and Ethics*, p. xvi.

3. Ibid., p. xix. The phrase comes from *Commentary on the Sentences of Peter Lombard*, II.

4. Aquinas, *Political Writings*, pp. xxiv–xxv.

5. Brian Tierney, *The Crisis of Church and State*, pp. 139–49.

6. Ibid., pp. 139–41; Ernst Kantorowicz, *Frederick the Second*.

7. Aristotle, *Politics* (1.4–7), pp. 16–19.

8. Aquinas, *Political Writings*, p. 207.

9. Ibid., pp. 5–6, 43–44.

10. Ibid., p. 9.

11. Ibid., pp. 4–6 et seq.

12. Ibid., p. 54.

13. Ibid., p. 3, quoting *City of God* (19.15), pp. 942–43.

14. Ibid., pp. 83ff.

15. Ibid., pp. 91–92.

16. Ibid., pp. 96–97, 126ff.

17. Ibid., pp. 220–34.

18. Ibid., p. 127.

19. Ibid., p. 208.

20. Ibid., pp. 216–17.

21. Locke, *First Treatise* (sec. 42), in *Two Treatises of Government*, p. 170.
22. Aquinas, *Political Writings*, p. 207.
23. Ibid., p. 240.
24. Ibid., p. 241.
25. Ibid., p. 244.
26. Ibid., pp. 277–78.
27. Ibid., p. 271.
28. Ibid., p. 270.
29. Ibid., pp. 267–69.
30. Ibid., pp. 276–77.
31. Ibid., p. 273.
32. Ibid., pp. 233ff.

CHAPTER 8: THE FOURTEENTH-CENTURY INTERREGNUM

1. Marsilius of Padua, *Defensor pacis*, pp. 72–73.
2. *The Inferno of Dante*, canto 3, line 60.
3. Tierney, *The Crisis of Church and State*, pp. 185–86.
4. Ibid., p. 187.
5. But Antony Black describes it as a "masterpiece" in *Political Thought in Europe*, p. 60.
6. Dante, *Monarchy* (1.4), pp. 8–9.
7. Ibid. (1.3), p. 7.
8. Ibid. (2.9), pp. 53–58.
9. Ibid. (3.10), pp. 80–81.
10. Ibid. (3.8), p. 75.
11. Marsilius of Padua, *Defensor pacis* (1.1.3), pp. 4–5.
12. Ibid. (1.2.1), p. 8.
13. Ibid. (1.13.3), p. 51.
14. Dahl, *A Preface to Democratic Theory*, pp. 63ff.
15. Marsilius of Padua, *Defensor pacis* (2.3.2ff.), pp. 109ff.
16. William of Ockham, *A Short Discourse on the Tyrannical Government*.
17. Nicholas of Cusa, *The Catholic Concordance*.

CHAPTER 9: HUMANISM

1. Baron, *In Search of Florentine Civic Humanism*; Grafton in Burns and Goldie, eds., *Cambridge History of Political Thought, 1450–1700*, pp. 15ff.
2. Machiavelli, "Exhortation," in *The Prince*, pp. 87–91.

3. E.g., Erasmus, *The Education of a Christian Prince*, below, pp. 302–6.

4. Christine de Pizan, *The City of Ladies*, pp. 1–2, 237–40.

5. Plato, *The Republic* (bk. 8), pp. 266ff.

6. Christine de Pizan, *The Book of the Body Politic* (3.1), p. 90.

7. Ibid. (3.4), p. 95.

8. Ibid. (1.1), p. 4.

9. Ibid. (1.7), pp. 12–14.

10. Ibid. (3.10), p. 107.

11. Plato, *Gorgias, Menexenus, Protagoras*, pp. 156–57.

12. Erasmus, *Education of a Christian Prince*, p. 1.

13. Ibid., p. 2.

14. Ibid., p. 15.

15. Ibid., p. 65.

16. Ibid., p. 83.

17. Ibid., p. 107.

18. Ibid., pp. 107–8.

19. Erasmus, *The Praise of Folly*, p. 8.

20. Ibid., pp 80–87.

21. Erasmus, *Education*, p. 15.

22. More, *Utopia*, pp. 106–7.

23. Edward Bellamy, *Looking Backward*, pp. 66ff.

24. More, *Utopia*, p. 94.

25. Ibid.

26. Ibid., pp. 79–81.

27. Michel de Montaigne, *Complete Essays*.

CHAPTER 10: THE REFORMATION

1. See above, p. 312, for Henry's defense of the sacraments against Luther.

2. Locke, *Letter concerning Toleration*, in *Selected Political Writings*, pp. 129–32.

3. Ibid., p. 135.

4. Romans 13:8.

5. Luther, "Freedom of a Christian," in *Selected Political Writings*, pp. 27ff.

6. John Man, *The Gutenberg Revolution*; Marshall McLuhan, *The Gutenberg Galaxy*.

7. Luther, "Freedom of a Christian," pp. 29–30.

8. Luther, "To the Christian Nobility," in *Selected Political Writings*, pp. 39–49.

9. *Luther and Calvin on Secular Authority*, p. 5.

10. Ibid.

11. Ibid., p. 4.

12. Ibid., p. 9.

13. Ibid., p. 15.

14. Luther, *Selected Political Writings*, p. 30.

15. Ibid., p. 29.

16. Ibid., p. 88.

17. Ibid., pp. 97–98.

18. Locke, *Second Treatise* (paragraphs 241–42), in *Two Treatises of Government*, p. 427.

19. *Luther and Calvin on Secular Authority*, p. 49.

20. Ibid., p. 82.

21. Norman Cohn, *The Pursuit of the Millennium*.

CHAPTER II: MACHIAVELLI

1. Machiavelli, letter to Francesco Vettori, December 10, 1513, in *The Prince*, p. 93.

2. Burns and Goldie, eds., *Cambridge History of Political Thought, 1450–1700*, pp. 55–56.

3. Machiavelli, *Discourses on Livy* (1.9), pp. 138–39.

4. Machiavelli, "Dedicatory Letter," in *The Prince*, pp. 3–4.

5. Machiavelli, *The Prince*, p. 88.

6. Ibid., p. 5.

7. Ibid., pp. 6–14.

8. Ibid., p. 13.

9. Ibid., p. 9.

10. Comparing ibid., pp. 8 and 16.

11. Ibid., p. 21.

12. Who makes a cameo appearance in Max Beerbohm's wonderful spoof "'Savonarola' Brown" in *Seven Men*.

13. Machiavelli, *Discourses* (1.12), p. 152.

14. Machiavelli, *The Prince*, p. 25.

15. Ibid., p. 26.

16. Ibid., pp. 39–40.

17. Ibid., p. 40.

18. Ibid., pp. 51–52.

19. Machiavelli, *Discourses* (1.57), pp. 258ff.

20. Wolin, *Politics and Vision*, pp. 197–99.

21. Machiavelli, *The Prince*, pp. 61–62.

22. Ibid., pp. 84–85.

23. Ibid., p. 85.

24. Ibid., p. 86.
25. Ibid., p. 87.
26. Machiavelli, *Discourses* (1.27), pp. 185–86.
27. Ibid., introduction, pp. 103–5.
28. Ibid., p. 105.
29. Ibid., pp. 149–53.
30. Ibid. (1.4), pp. 118–20.
31. Ibid. (3.41), p. 528.